Harden's

London
Restaurants

2008

"Gastronomes' bible" Evening Standard

Reviews of over 1800 restaurants

Restaurant reviews online
The latest restaurant news
Updated restaurant information
Online restaurant bookings
& share your restaurant views

www.hardens.com

© **Harden's Limited 2007**

ISBN 978-1-873721-78-0

British Library Cataloguing-in-Publication data:
a catalogue record for this book is available from
the British Library.

Printed in Italy by Legoprint

Research assistants: Marc McDermott, Elizabeth Koslov,
Brian Cameron

Harden's Limited
14 Buckingham Street
London WC2N 6DF

Would restaurateurs (and PRs) please address
communications to 'Editorial' at the above address,
or ideally by email to: editorial@hardens.com

The contents of this book are believed correct at
the time of printing. Nevertheless, the publisher
can accept no responsibility for errors or changes in
or omissions from the details given.

CONTENTS

RATINGS & PRICES

Ratings

Our rating system is unlike those found in other guides (most of which tell you nothing more helpful than that expensive restaurants are, as a general rule, better than cheap ones).

What we do is to compare each restaurant's performance – as judged by the average ratings awarded by reporters in the survey – with other restaurants in the same price-bracket.

This approach has the advantage that it helps you find – whatever your budget for any particular meal – where you will get the best 'bang for your buck'.

The following qualities are assessed:

F	—	Food
S	—	Service
A	—	Ambience

The rating indicates that, ***in comparison with other restaurants in the same price-bracket***, performance is…

❶	—	Exceptional
❷	—	Very good
❸	—	Good
④	—	Average
⑤	—	Poor

Prices

The price shown for each restaurant is the cost for one (1) person of an average three-course dinner with half a bottle of house wine and coffee, any cover charge, service and VAT. Lunch is often cheaper. With BYO restaurants, we have assumed that two people share a £5 bottle of off-licence wine.

Telephone number – all numbers should be prefixed with '020' if dialling from outside the London area.

Map reference – shown immediately after the telephone number.

Rated on Editors' visit – indicates ratings have been determined by the Editors personally, based on their visit, rather than derived from the survey.

Website – the first entry in the small print (after any note about Editors' visit)

Last orders time – listed after the website (if applicable); Sunday may be up to 90 minutes earlier.

Opening hours – unless otherwise stated, restaurants are open for lunch and dinner seven days a week.

Credit and debit cards – unless otherwise stated, Mastercard, Visa, Amex and Maestro are accepted.

Dress – where appropriate, the management's preferences concerning patrons' dress are given.

Special menus – if we know of a particularly good value set menu we note this (e.g. "set weekday L"), together with its formula price (FP) calculated exactly as in 'Prices' above. Details change, so always check ahead.

HOW THIS GUIDE IS WRITTEN

Survey

This guide is based on our 17th annual survey of what Londoners think of their restaurants; it is by far the largest annual survey of its type. Since 1998, we have also surveyed restaurant-goers across the rest of the UK. The out-of-town results are published in our national 'Restaurant Guide' (formerly called 'UK Restaurants') published in association with Rémy Martin Fine Champagne Cognac. This year the total number of reporters in our combined London/UK survey, conducted mainly online, exceeded 8,000, and, between them, they contributed almost 100,000 individual reports.

How we determine the ratings

In most cases, ratings are arrived at statistically. This essentially involves 'ranking' the average rating each restaurant achieves in the survey – for each of food, service and ambience – against the average ratings of the other establishments which fall in the same price-bracket. A few restaurants – usually those which have opened after the survey began – are rated by ourselves, as editors, personally. To emphasise the personal (non-democratic) basis of such assessments, we include a small-print note – "Rated on Editors' visit".

How we write the reviews

The tenor of each review is broadly determined by the ratings of the establishment concerned (which we derive as described above). We also pay some regard to the proportion of positive nominations (such as for 'favourite restaurant') compared to negative nominations (such as for 'most overpriced'). To explain why a restaurant has been rated as it has, we extract snippets from survey comments ("enclosed in double quotes"). A short review cannot possibly reflect all the nuances from, sometimes, several hundred reports, and what we try to do is to illustrate the key themes which emerge.

Editors' visits

We have – anonymously and at our own expense – visited almost all the restaurants listed in this book. As noted above, in the case of a few restaurants which open in the months before the guide goes to press, we use these experiences not only to inform our review but also as the basis of the ratings awarded. More generally, however, our personal views about any particular restaurant are irrelevant: the reviews we write (and ratings the guide awards) reflect our best analysis of the survey responses.

Richard Harden   **Peter Harden**

SURVEY MOST MENTIONED

These are the restaurants which were most frequently mentioned by reporters. (Last year's position is given in brackets.) An asterisk* indicates the first appearance in the list of a recently-opened restaurant.

1	J Sheekey (1)
2	Chez Bruce (4)
3	The Wolseley (5)
4	Bleeding Heart (6)
5	Hakkasan (2)
6	Gordon Ramsay (3)
7	The Ivy (7)
8	Oxo Tower (11)
9	La Poule au Pot (9)
10	Andrew Edmunds (10)

11	Le Gavroche (12)
12	Pétrus (24)
13	Arbutus*
14	Gordon Ramsay at Claridge's (8)
15	Le Caprice (21)
16	Galvin Bistrot de Luxe (22)
17	Nobu (13)
18	La Trompette (16)
19	Yauatcha (19)
20	Locanda Locatelli (20)

21	maze (14)
22	Zuma (15)
23	The Cinnamon Club (17)
24	Scott's*
25	Tom Aikens (18)
26	The Square (22)
27	The Anchor & Hope (28)
28	Amaya (27)
29	Moro (32)
30=	The Don (36)

30=	Savoy Grill (-)
32=	L'Atelier de Joel Robuchon*
32=	The River Café (30)
32=	Bentley's (40)
35	St Alban*
36=	Racine (29)
36=	St John (36)
38	Coq d'Argent (-)
39	Blue Elephant (33)
40	Roussillon (-)

SURVEY NOMINATIONS

Ranked by the number of reporters' votes.

Top gastronomic experience

1   Gordon Ramsay (1)
2   Chez Bruce (2)
3   Le Gavroche (3)
4   Pétrus (6)
5   Tom Aikens (5)
6   L'Atelier de Joel Robuchon*
7   maze (7)
8   Gordon Ramsay at Claridge's (4)
9   La Trompette (8)
10   Locanda Locatelli (-)

Favourite

1   Chez Bruce (1)
2   The Wolseley (4)
3   J Sheekey (3)
4   The Ivy (2)
5   Le Caprice (5)
6   La Trompette (6)
7   Moro (9=)
8   Gordon Ramsay (7)
9   Galvin Bistrot de Luxe (-)
10   Andrew Edmunds (-)

Best for business

1   The Wolseley (3)
2   Bleeding Heart (1)
3   The Don (3)
4   Coq d'Argent (6)
5   1 Lombard Street (2)
6   The Square (5)
7   Savoy Grill (7)
8   Smiths (Top Floor) (-)
9=   The Ivy (10)
9=   Rhodes 24 (8)

Best for romance

1   La Poule au Pot (1)
2   Andrew Edmunds (2)
3   Bleeding Heart (3)
4   Chez Bruce (4)
5   Le Caprice (6)
6   Café du Marché (8)
7   Oxo Tower (9=)
8   The Ivy (5)
9   Clos Maggiore (9=)
10   Blue Elephant (-)

Best breakfast/brunch

1 The Wolseley (1)
2 Giraffe (2)
3 Smiths (Ground Foor) (4)
4 Carluccio's Caffè (3)
5 Simpsons-in-the-Strand (5)
6 Balans (7)
7 Le Pain Quotidien (-)
8 Pâtisserie Valerie (5=)
9 Tapa Room (-)
10 Electric Brasserie (8=)

Best bar/pub food

1 The Anchor & Hope (1)
2 The Eagle (2)
3 The Anglesea Arms (3)
4 The Havelock Tavern (-)
5= The Engineer (5)
5= The Gun (6)
7 Thos Cubitt*
8 St John's (7)
9= The Pig's Ear (-)
9= Churchill Arms (8=)

Most disappointing cooking

1 Oxo Tower (1)
2 The Ivy (2)
3 Gordon Ramsay at Claridge's (5)
4 The Wolseley (3)
5 Tom Aikens (4)
6 Locanda Locatelli (8=)
7 St Alban*
8= Savoy Grill (-)
8= Bluebird Brasserie (7)
10 Cipriani (6)

Most overpriced restaurant

1 Oxo Tower (1)
2 Nobu (7)
3 Cipriani (2)
4 Gordon Ramsay at Claridge's (9)
5 Sketch (Gallery) (3)
6 The River Café (6)
7 Hakkasan (5)
8 The Ivy (4)
9 Gordon Ramsay (10)
10 Le Pont de la Tour (-)

SURVEY HIGHEST RATINGS

FOOD	SERVICE

£70+

FOOD	SERVICE
1 Gordon Ramsay	1 Gordon Ramsay
2 Aubergine	2 Pétrus
3 Pétrus	3 Le Gavroche
4 Le Gavroche	4 Aubergine
5 One-O-One	5 The Square

£55-£69

FOOD	SERVICE
1 Chez Bruce	1 Chez Bruce
2 Zuma	2 Foliage
3 The Ledbury	3 The Ledbury
4 Rasoi Vineet Bhatia	4 The Goring Hotel
5 Foliage	5 Roussillon

£45-£54

FOOD	SERVICE
1 La Trompette	1 Oslo Court
2 Morgan M	2 Lundum's
3 Roka	3 La Trompette
4 The Painted Heron	4 Odin's
5 Amaya	5 Racine

£35-£44

FOOD	SERVICE
1 Sukho Thai Cuisine	1 Edokko
2 Tsunami	2 Lamberts
3 Inside	3 Sotheby's Café
4 Edokko	4 Upstairs Bar
5 Lamberts	5 Caraffini

£34 or less

FOOD	SERVICE
1 Golden Hind	1 Uli
2 Lahore Kebab House	2 Golden Hind
3 Kastoori	3 Flat White
4 Hot Stuff	4 Babur Brasserie
5 Flat White	5 Emiles

AMBIENCE

1 The Ritz
2 The Lanesborough
3 Blake's
4 Pétrus
5 Hakkasan

1 Les Trois Garçons
2 Landmark
3 La Porte des Indes
4 Clos Maggiore
5 Rules

1 Archipelago
2 Crazy Bear
3 La Poule au Pot
4 The Wallace
5 L'Aventure

1 Upstairs Bar
2 Ffiona's
3 Holly Bush
4 Café du Marché
5 Annie's

1 Andrew Edmunds
2 Bar Italia
3 Gordon's Wine Bar
4 Troubadour
5 LMNT

OVERALL

1 Pétrus
2 Gordon Ramsay
3 Le Gavroche
4 Aubergine
5 The Ritz

1 Chez Bruce
2 Foliage
3 The Ledbury
4 J Sheekey
5 Atelier/Joel Robuchon

1 La Trompette
2 L'Aventure
3 Barrafina
4 Oslo Court
5 Archipelago

1 Upstairs Bar
2 Edokko
3 Lamberts
4 Sukho Thai Cuisine
5 Café du Marché

1 Flat White
2 Babur Brasserie
3 Golden Hind
4 Emile's
5 Andrew Edmunds

SURVEY BEST BY CUISINE

These are the restaurants which received the best average food ratings (excluding establishments with a small or notably local following).

Where the most common types of cuisine are concerned, we present the results in two price-brackets. For less common cuisines, we list the top three, regardless of price.

For further information about restaurants which are particularly notable for their food, see the cuisine lists starting on page 246. These indicate, using an asterisk*, restaurants which offer exceptional or very good food.

British, Modern

£45 and over		Under £45	
1	Chez Bruce	1	Inside
2	The Glasshouse	2	Lamberts
3	Notting Hill Brasserie	3	Emile's
4	Lindsay House	4	Ottolenghi
5	Le Caprice	5	The Anglesea Arms

French

£45 and over		Under £45	
1	Gordon Ramsay	1	Comptoir Gascon
2	Aubergine	2	Galvon Bistrot de Luxe
3	Pétrus	3	Magdalen
4	La Trompette	4	Le Cercle
5	Le Gavroche	5	The Food Room

Italian/Mediterranean

£45 and over		Under £45	
1	Assaggi	1	Pizza Metro
2	Quirinale	2	Latium
3	Zafferano	3	Sarracino
4	Locanda Locatelli	4	Salt Yard
5	Theo Randall	5	Il Bordello

Indian

£45 and over		Under £45	
1	Rasoi Vineet Bhatia	1	Lahore Kebab House
2	The Painted Heron	2	Kastoori
3	Amaya	3	Hot Stuff
4	The Cinnamon Club	4	New Tayyabs
5	Benares	5	Mirch Masala

Chinese

£45 and over
1. Yauatcha
2. Hunan
3. Ken Lo's Memories
4. Hakkasan
5. Kai Mayfair

Under £45
1. Mandarin Kitchen
2. Royal China
3. Four Seasons
4. Good Earth
5. Singapore Garden

Japanese

£45 and over
1. Zuma
2. Roka
3. Umu
4. Nobu
5. Nobu Berkeley

Under £45
1. Tsunami
2. Edoko
3. Café Japan
4. Pham Sushi
5. Chisou

British, Traditional
1. Fuzzy's Grub
2. The Anchor & Hope
3. St John Bread & Wine

Vegetarian
1. Mildred's
2. Food for Thought
3. The Gate

Burgers, etc
1. Lucky Seven
2. Haché
3. Gourmet Burger Kitch.

Pizza
1. Pizza Metro
2. Il Bordello
3. Oliveto

Fish & Chips
1. Golden Hind
2. Nautilus
3. Fish Club

Thai
1. Sukho Thai Cuisine
2. Amaranth
3. Patara

Fusion
1. Tsunami
2. Nobu
3. Ubon

Fish & Seafood
1. One-O-One
2. J Sheekey
3. Mandarin Kitchen

Greek
1. The Real Greek
2. Daphne
3. Costa's Grill

Spanish
1. Barrafina
2. Moro
3. Fino

Turkish
1. Kazan
2. Haz
3. Ev

Lebanese
1. Ranoush
2. Maroush
3. Noura

TOP SPECIAL DEALS

The following menus allow you to eat in the restaurants concerned at a significant discount when compared to their evening à la carte prices.

The prices used are calculated in accordance with our usual formula (i.e. three courses with house wine, coffee and tip).

Special menus are by their nature susceptible to change – please check that they are still available.

Weekday lunch

£60+	Gordon Ramsay
£50+	The Capital Restaurant
	Connaught (Angela Hartnett)
	Le Gavroche
	The Greenhouse
	Pied à Terre
	The Ritz
	Savoy Grill
£45+	Brunello
	L'Oranger
£40+	Dorchester Grill
	Foliage
	Gordon Ramsay at Claridge's
	The Ledbury
	Odette's
	Rasoi Vineet Bhatia
	Theo Randall
	Tom Aikens
£35+	Aubergine
	L'Escargot (Picasso Room)
	5 Cavendish Square
	Giardinetto
	Kensington Place
	The Conservatory
	La Noisette
	Roussillon
£30+	Babylon
	L'Etranger
	Ikeda
	Oxo Tower (Brass')
	Papillon
	Pappagallo
	La Poule au Pot
	Royal China Club
	Le Suquet
	Tamarind
	Timo
	La Trouvaille
£25+	Baltic
	Bradley's
	Café du Jardin
	Cantina del Ponte
	Chez Kristof
	Ebury Wine Bar
	Enoteca Turi
	Esenza
	Fish Hook
	The Forge
	Frantoio
	Galvin Bistrot de Luxe
	Gastro
	Greig's
	High Road Brasserie
	Kew Grill
	L-Restaurant & Bar
	Lobster Pot
	Momo
	Mon Plaisir
	Moti Mahal
	Potemkin
	Princess Garden
	Saki Bar & Food Emporium
	Sam's Brasserie
	San Lorenzo Fuoriporta
	Sargasso Sea
	La Saveur
	Shanghai Blues
	The Spread Eagle
	Vino Rosso
	Vivat Bacchus
	Wild Honey
£20+	La Cage Imaginaire
	Le Chardon
	Chez Patrick
	China Tang
	Chisou
	Le Deuxième
	Il Falconiere
	The Fire Stables
	Franklins
	Garbo's
	Grumbles
	The Haven
	Lime
	The Lock Dining Bar
	Lou Pescadou
	La Mancha
	Mediterraneo
	Ooze
	The Quality Chop House
	Quilon
	Scarlet Dot
	Soho Spice
	Thai Elephant
	Thai on the River
	Tsunami
£15+	Daphne
	Durbar

The East Hill
The Horseshoe
kare kare
Khan's of Kensington
Lemonia
Lowiczanka
Memsaheb on Thames
Monty's
Newton's
La Petite Auberge
Le Querce
Shikara
Shimo
Soho Japan
Ten Ten Tei
Tentazioni
3 Monkeys
Yum Yum

£10+ Fish in a Tie
Galicia
Goya
Kolossi Grill
Malabar Junction
Moroccan Tagine
Ragam
Sakonis

£5+ Centrepoint Sushi
Daquise
Jashan

Pre/post theatre (and early evening)

£50+ Lindsay House
Savoy Grill

£45+ Brunello

£35+ The Cinnamon Club
La Noisette

£30+ Beotys
Hush
Papillon
Quaglino's
La Trouvaille

£25+ Bradley's
The Forge
Frederick's
Octave
Orso

San Lorenzo
Fuoriporta
Shanghai Blues

£20+ Mela
Soho Spice

£15+ Chiang Mai
Mon Plaisir

Sunday lunch

£50+ Dorchester Grill

£45+ Brunello
Savoy Grill

£30+ Papillon

£25+ Bradley's
The Little Square
Sargasso Sea

£20+ Duke of Cambridge
The Mason's Arms
Quilon

£15+ Lowiczanka

THE RESTAURANT SCENE

A record year

This year, we record 158 new openings (see page 20): about 16% higher than last year (136), and 11% more than the former record figure of 142, recorded two years ago.

At 89, closures (see p 21) are notably higher than the mid-60s figures recorded in each of the two preceding years. History suggests that, once established, a rising trend in closures will last at least two years. The coming year may, therefore, see restaurants closing on quite a scale (possibly exceeding the record number of 113, noted four years ago).

Ramsay rule coming to an end?

Since Gordon Ramsay really began empire-building – with the lacklustre Claridge's opening (2001) – there have been concerns about the potential pitfalls of his rapid expansion.

But the ongoing pre-eminence of his flagship, *Gordon Ramsay*, has disarmed any serious worries. Every year, for example, he has pulled off a hat trick in our survey: not only leading the poll for 'top gastronomic experience', but also achieving both the highest food rating, and the highest overall rating (combining Food, Service and Ambience).

Until now, that is: this year, he only walked away with the first of those three 'trophies'.

Some good news for Ramsay is that the new highest overall rating was achieved by one of his own group. The bad news is that many people think of *Pétrus* as Marcus Wareing's restaurant. And, on many other fronts, the survey sounds a warning note for the F-word chef. His newest London restaurant, *La Noisette*, has quickly emerged as a Kitchen Nightmare. The first of his new gastropubs (*The Narrow*) is thought fair enough, but would pass without comment if it were not for his backing. Culinary standards at *Claridge's* have markedly dipped. And perhaps most significantly, regular restaurant-goers are losing interest: despite the Ramsay media barrage, his top three restaurants (other than *Pétrus*) have slipped down the most-mentioned list (p 9).

Failing some major re-direction of Gordon's energies back to London, and restaurants – and away from America, TV studios and pubs – this is beginning to look like the end of an era.

Who might seize the crown?

Gordon Ramsay's strongest rivals in the survey were Marcus Wareing at *Pétrus*, and William Drabble at *Aubergine* – both of whose food-ratings came within 1/100 of a point of *Gordon Ramsay*. And then there's the amazing *Chez Bruce*, which actually outscored all the above (but whose aims, at around half the price, are rather different). But perhaps it's new openings that most threaten Ramsay's position. This autumn will see the London début not only of the world's most Michelin-starred chef, Alain Ducasse, but also the arrival in town of Claude Bosi. The latter, when based in Ludlow, regularly achieved one of the UK's highest food ratings, occasionally even beating… yes, you guessed it.

Market trends

London's restaurant scene is entering a new era, perhaps not of maturity, but at least a sort of early middle age. The following seem to us the trends of the moment:

● Having been a concept restaurants were keen to distance themselves from in the '90s, traditional British cooking is now trendy. Once the preserve of a few old-timers (such as *Rules*), the cuisine was 're-discovered' in 1994 by *St John* (which seemed positively eccentric when it opened). Since then, it has largely being nurtured in the ever-growing gastropub sector. Now, it is breaking out from the boozers, to all market levels except temples of *haute cuisine* – examples include *Canteen, Great Queen Street, Magdalen* and *Scott's*.

● 'Green' considerations are beginning to tell. This is most obvious in establishments dedicated to local sourcing (such as *Konstam at the Prince Albert* and *Acorn House*), and is another factor contributing to the more general popularity of indigenous cuisine noted above.

● The grazing/tapas trend – which seemed to have faltered – now seems stronger than ever, being, for example, the preferred style of two of the biggest successes of the year (*L'Atelier de Joel Robuchon* and *Barrafina*), and also of the press critics' favourite of recent times, *La Petite Maison*. London's best fish restaurant, *One-O-One*, is relaunching with grazing options as this guide goes to press.

● Japanese cuisine continues to establish itself as a mainstream option. This year we recorded more Japanese openings than Indian ones.

● Resurgent Mayfair is becoming established as the prime location for restaurants with 'destination' pretensions – a pre-eminence likely to be confirmed by such autumn openings as *Alain Ducasse at the Dorchester* and *Hibiscus*. Bayswater and Marylebone are also making strong headway.

● London is shifting eastwards. Until recently 'E' and 'EC' openings were a relative rarity. This year, however, saw more easterly openings than at all other compass points bar west.

Every year, we select what seem to us to be the ten most significant openings of the preceding 12 months. This year, our selection is as follows:

Acorn House   Great Queen Street
L'Atelier de Joel Robuchon   Magdalen
Bacchus   La Petite Maison
Barrafina   Rhodes W1 Restaurant
Dinings   Scott's

Prices

The average price of dinner for one at establishments listed in the guide is £38.78. Prices have on average risen by 3.0% in the past 12 months – for all practical purposes at the same rate as retail prices. In dearer (£50+) place generally, prices are up just 1.9%, but the 20 most expensive places of all (£80+) have succeeded in inflating their prices by 4.4%.

OPENINGS AND CLOSURES

Ortega
Pacific Oriental
Le Pain Quotidien *various*
Pearl Liang
La Petite Maison
The Phoenix *SW1*
Piccolino *W1*
Prima
The Prince Arthur
The Queen's Arms
Le Querce
Rajasthan, *Houndsditch*
Raviolo
Rhodes W1 Restaurant
Ristorante Semplice
Rocket *EC2*
The Roebuck
Rooburoo
The Rosendale
Rossopomodoro *W11*
Rotisserie *N20, NW6*
St Alban
St Germain
Sake No Hana
Salaam Namaste
Salade
Santa Maria del Sur
La Saveur
Seabass *W2*

Seaport
Shimo
Sitaaray
Skylon
Snazz Sichuan
So
Square Pie Co *WC1*
Stanza
The Stonhouse
Suka
Suzie Wong
Texture
Three Crowns
Tiffinbites
Tom's Place
Trenta
Tsar
2 Amici
2 Veneti
Vino Rosso
Vivezza
Wahaca
The Wallace
The Warrington
Wild Honey
Wood Street
Yumenoki
Zaffrani
Zaytouna

Abbey *EC1*
Armadillo
Astor Bar & Grill
Babes 'n' Burgers
Balham Kitchen & Bar
Barcelona Tapas *Bell Ln E1*
Base *SW3*
Bank *Aldwych*
Ben's Thai (see The Warrington)
Berkeley Square Cafe
Blue Kangaroo
Bluebird Club
Café Bagatelle
Café Fish
Calabash
Canyon
Chelsea Kitchen
Christophers in the City
Circus
Les Coulisses

Cristini *Seymour Pl W2*
CVO Firevault
Deya
Dine
Eddalino
Entrecôte Café de Paris
Est, Est, Est
L'Estaminet
Exotika
Fairuz *W2*
Fina Estampa
Fiore
1492
Gabrielle's
Ghillies *SW18*
Ginger
Glas
Globe
Gravy
Harlem *SW9*

Closures (cont'd)

The Han of Nazz
Harry Ramsden's *W1*
Hosteria del Pesce
The Ifield
Just Gladwin's
Just the Bridge
Lightship
Lillo e Franco
Little Earth Café
Luigi's
Maison Blanc Vite
Manzi's
Mawar
Matilda's
Mocotó
Mr Jerk
Nathalie
Neal Street
Noto *EC4*
Origin
The Painted Heron *SE11*
The Penthouse
The People's Palace
La Perla *SW6*
Pescador Too

Le Petit Train
Pizzeria Castello *SE1*
Rocco
Sabai Sabai
Sabras
Sarkhels
Satu
Savarona
The Sea Cow *SW6*
Siam Central
La Spighetta
Spoon+
Sri Siam City
Sri Siam Soho
Stratfords
Teca
Ultimate Burger *N10*
Tugga
W'sens
Winkles
Wizzy
Xich-lo
Zim Zum
Zinc

EATING IN LONDON FAQs

How should I use this guide?

This guide can be used in many ways. You will often wish to use it to answer practical queries. These tend to be geographical – where can we eat near…? To answer such questions, the Maps (from page 301) and Area Overviews (from page 265) are the place to start. The latter tell you all the key facts about the restaurants – perhaps dozens – in a particular area in the space of a couple of pages.

But what if you'd like to be more adventurous and seek out new places purely for interest's sake or for a truly special occasion? That's the main point of this brief section – to give you a handy overview of London's dining scene, and also some thoughts as to how you can use the guide to lead you to eating experiences you might not otherwise have found (or perhaps even contemplated).

What makes London special?

London is not Paris, Rome or Madrid, which are mainly of note for their French, Italian and Spanish restaurants respectively. Although there is some sign of a resurgence of interest in a cuisine which may be said to be genuinely British, it is still fair to say that British cuisine is still generally perceived to have lost its way over 200 years ago.

Like New York, London's real strength has always been its cosmopolitanism. Perhaps for the first time, though, the city has now reached the stage where it can really be said to offer a good range of restaurants offering all of the world's major cuisines (and many minor ones too).

The greatest weakness nowadays is probably in the cuisines of China. The greatest strength is as a centre – arguably the leading centre worldwide – of Indian restaurants. 'Indian' cooking is now available at every price-level, in every part of town, in eating-places of every style and level of grandeur, and with a vast range of different regional influences.

Which is London's best restaurant?

Gordon Ramsay is the biggest name in UK gastronomy, and his Royal Hospital Road flagship remains one of London's best restaurants. In terms of overall experience, however, it lost out in this year's survey to its stablemate *Pétrus,* and in culinary terms it is almost equalled by both *Pétrus* and *Aubergine.* For a grand, old-fashioned dinner, *Le Gavroche* – London's original grand stand-alone French restaurant – remains hard to beat. The survey found the very best food of all at *Chez Bruce* – a grand 'local' restaurant whose stellar standards belie its distant Wandsworth location.

For further 'best' restaurant suggestions, consult the double-page spread on pp 10 and 11.

What's 'in' at the moment?

The all-purpose answer to that question in recent times has been the famous *Ivy*, but it is no longer the must-have table it once was. Some lower-profile names – such as at *Ivy* stablemates *Le Caprice* and *J Sheekey* – are more sought-after by those in the know. The larger and more obvious *Wolseley* also makes a good all-purpose fashionable destination (especially for business). The new *St Alban* seems to have something of an instant thespian/media following, but nothing much broader. Also new, *L'Atelier de Joel Robuchon* combines high chic with good and interesting Gallic cooking.

Mayfair has very much re-established itself as a key see-and-be-seen destination of late, thanks to such arrivals as the trashy-but-fun *Cipriani*, and the re-launch of the all-purpose success-story of the moment, *Scott's*. Mid-2007 opening *La Petite Maison* looks set to capture those of a Côte d'Azur sensibility (and, ideally, the yacht to go with it). At the younger, more fashion-driven end of the Mayfair market, Mourad Mazouz's *Sketch* and *Momo* retain quite a following.

For younger City and international types, *Nobu*-imitator *Zuma* has become, and remains, the destination of choice – even in preference to the two West End *Nobu*s. Other oriental restaurants with a fashionable following include *Roka*, *Hakkasan* and *Yauatacha*.

I'm not fussed about 'scenes' – where can I get a good meal at reasonable cost?

The best tip of all, if you have the choice, is to lunch, rather than dine. If you do that, you can experience some of London's very grandest restaurants – for example, *Le Gavroche* – for less than many lesser restaurants charge for dinner. See the list of suggestions on page 16.

One of the greatest successes of recent times has been *Arbutus* – right in the heart of Soho – which has always put offering value right at the heart of the package offered. Its recent offshoot *Wild Honey* offers a broadly similar approach, but in a more comfortable Mayfair setting. *Galvin Bistro de Luxe* and *Racine* are in some ways similar, but their prices are pitched a notch higher.

At the top end of the middle market, the restaurant portfolio assembled by Nigel Platts-Martin has an unparalleled reputation. The stellar *Chez Bruce* is the one people tend to talk about, but *The Glasshouse*, *The Ledbury* and *La Trompette* are all very impressive too. Another top value suggestion, down south London way, is *Lambert's*.

The names above, however, are just the beginning. Look through the Area Overviews beginning on page 265. These should quickly enable you to find value – wherever in town you're looking and whatever your budget – for any particular occasion.

And for the best of British tradition?

There are few long-established British restaurants of any note. Of these the most recommendable are *Rules* and – only if money is no object – *Wilton's*. Most people will probably find the former more fun. For a very British meal, the clubby St James's restaurant *Green's* is also well worth considering.

Most of the grand hotel dining rooms nowadays are not of particular interest. The grandest of the traditional experiences – albeit in a style which owes as much to France as it does to Britain – is to be had at the *Ritz*, where the cooking seems, after decades in the doldrums, to be on the mend. The overall experience in the room usually hailed as London's prettiest is certainly memorable. For a truly British experience, the outstanding hotel is the *Goring*.

The City preserves some extraordinary olde-worlde places such as *Sweetings* and *Simpson's Tavern*. Ancient taverns worth seeking out on grounds of charm alone include the *Grenadier*, the *Trafalgar Tavern*, the *Windsor Castle* and *Ye Olde Cheshire Cheese*.

The Smithfield restaurant *St John* has for many years pioneered a rebirth of English cooking. For some reason this 'new-traditional'-style of *St John* cooking (or, usually a slightly less offal-rich version of it) seems to have become largely the province of gastropubs – most obviously the *Anchor & Hope* – but a few pure restaurants, such as *Magdalen* and *Great Queen Street* have recently picked up the baton.

The new eco-restaurants – such as *Acorn House* and *Konstam at the Prince Albert* – which particularly prize locality of supply also, of necessity, explore some dishes from the truly English canon in a way that has not been the fashion for some decades, as do the diner-style *Canteens*.

Isn't London supposed to be a top place for curry?

As noted above, London is arguably the world's leading Indian restaurant city. At the top end, names such as *Rasoi Vineet Bhatia*, and then the likes of *Amaya*, *The Cinnamon Club*, *Tamarind*, *Vama* and *Zaika* are pushing back the frontiers.

If you want to eat the best-value food you will ever find in London, however, you need to avoid the obvious postcodes (in which all of the fashionable Indian mentioned above are located).

Two of the most accessible of the quality budget subcontinentals are the East End duo – which are strictly speaking Pakistani not Indian – *New Tayyabs* and the *Lahore Kebab House*. There are many brilliant options, many very reasonably priced: look for the asterisked restaurants in the Indian and Pakistani lists starting on pages 261 and 263 respectively.

What are gastropubs?

Many pubs have re-invented themselves as informal restaurants in recent times. *The Eagle* was the original (1991). For the top ten current names see p11, but the trend shows no sign of running out of steam and the flow of good new openings continues. Generally, the pub tradition of ordering at the bar is kept, but some of the grander establishments offer full table service and have really become restaurants in all but name.

Can't we just grab a bowl of pasta?

Especially in the more affluent parts of town, Italian restaurants have traditionally been a default stand-by choice. The market being well provided with standard trattorias, the emphasis in recent years has been expansion at both the cheaper end of the market – pizzerias remain enormously popular – and the gourmet end. In recent years, some excellent high-level Italians have emerged – see the list on page 14.

What about the exotic East?

London has traditionally had quite a reasonable number of good traditional Chinese (usually Cantonese) restaurants. Most of the best places are not in fact in Chinatown, and the most notable concentration of mid-range restaurants is in Bayswater (where top names include *Royal China*, *Four Seasons* and *Mandarin Kitchen*). Recently Alan Yau has brought a lot of buzz to the fashionable Chinese restaurant sector, with *Hakkasan* and *Yauatcha*. Szechuan cuisine is in vogue at the moment, thanks to the opening of *Bar Shu* and *Snazz Szechuan*.

Until quite recently, London was very backwards in Japanese cuisine, but this is really no longer the case. We went through a period when every fashionable opening seemed to be Japanese, and such mega-successful openings as *Nobu*, *Nobu Berkeley, Zuma, Roka* and *Umu* have now definitively addressed the deficiency. Alan Yau's forthcoming opening *Sake no Hana* looks set to make waves at the 'purist' end of the market.

You said diverse: what about other cuisines?

A major hit of recent times has been the cuisines of North Africa and the Eastern Mediterranean. These cuisines lend themselves well to good budget experiences. London was traditionally notably deficient in Mexican (and Latin American) restaurants, but this has been something of a buzz area in the last few years, with openings such as *Crazy Homies, Green & Red Bar & Cantina, Mestizo* and *Taqueria*.

DIRECTORY

Comments in "double quotation-marks" were made by reporters.

Establishments which we judge to be particularly notable have their NAME IN CAPITALS.

A Cena TW1   £42   ❷❷❷
418 Richmond Rd   8288 0108   1–4A
*Just over Richmond Bridge, this "very friendly" modern Italian,
in St Margarets, is one of the brightest sparks in the area, offering
a "simple" menu and an "interesting wine list". / 10.30 pm; closed
Mon L & Sun D; booking: max 6, Fri & Sat.*

The Abbeville SW4   £31   ④❸❷
67-69 Abbeville Rd   8675 2201   10–2D
*Even if the food is only "average", this "welcoming" Clapham hang-
out has a big local fan club, thanks to its "totally unpretentious and
informal" atmosphere. / www.theabbeville.com; 10.30 pm.*

Abeno WC1   £34   ❸❸④
47 Museum St   7405 3211   2–1C
*Staff "squirting on sauces" as they prepare your okonomiyaki
("half omelette/half pancake") makes for a "fun" experience at this
slightly "boring"-looking Japanese, near the British Museum.
/ www.abeno.co.uk; 10 pm.*

Abeno Too WC2   £31   ❷❷❸
17-18 Great Newport St   7379 1160   4–3B
*"Having the food cooked in front of you adds to the fun", at this
"homely" Japanese, whose "cheap" and "interesting" Osaka-style
omelettes make an ideal Theatreland snack. / 11 pm; no booking.*

The Abingdon W8   £43   ❸❷❷
54 Abingdon Rd   7937 3339   5–2A
*This "upscale gastropub" is probably the most "reliable", "friendly"
and "buzzing" spot for "a good bite" near Kensington High Street,
and the "booths in the back are great" (if you can get one).
/ www.theabingdonrestaurant.com; 11 pm, Mon 10.30 pm.*

About Thyme SW1   £39   ④❸④
82 Wilton Rd   7821 7504   2–4B
*Fans applaud the "imaginative mix of Spanish and French food"
on offer at this "friendly" Pimlico bistro; critics, though, say it's still
"not worth the money". / www.aboutthyme.co.uk; 11 pm.*

Abu Zaad W12   £17   ❷❸❷
29 Uxbridge Rd   8749 5107   7–1C
*"Gorgeous", charcoal-grilled kebabs are the highlight of the "great-
value" fare at this family-run Syrian café, near Shepherd's Bush
Market; no booze. / www.abuzaad.co.uk; 11 pm.*

The Academy W11   £32   ❸④❷
57 Princedale Rd   7221 0248   6–2A
*"Tastier-than-usual" gastropub fare wins a keen (but entirely local)
following for this "pleasant" and "relaxed" Holland Park boozer.
/ www.academybar.com; 10.30 pm, Sun 9 pm; no Amex.*

L'Accento Italiano W2   £39   ❸④④
16 Garway Rd   7243 2201   6–1B
*A well-established Bayswater Italian, generally – but not invariably –
tipped as a "good local". / 11 pm; closed Sun.*

Acorn House WC1 NEW   £40   ❸❸❸
69 Swinton St   7812 1842   8–3D
A "worthy" (low-carbon) King's Cross newcomer, which impressses
many reporters with its "fresh", "seasonal" and "locally-sourced"
dishes, and – given that this is a training-restaurant – by the
standard of service too; a Hackney offshoot opens in late-2007.
/ www.acornhouserestaurant.com; 10 pm.

Adam Street WC2   £64   ❸❸❷
9 Adam St   7379 8000   4–4D
In the surprisingly thin area near the Strand, this attractive,
subterranean club dining room makes "a great place for a business
lunch" (with an "interesting wine list"); join, and you can save
yourself the £10/head guest fee! / www.adamstreet.co.uk; L only (open for
D to members only), closed Sat L & Sun.

Adams Café W12   £25   ❸❷❷
77 Askew Rd   8743 0572   7–1B
"The owners are like old friends", to regulars at this "bright and
friendly" Shepherd's Bush BYO caff; by day it's a greasy spoon,
but by night it offers "generous" tagines, cous-cous and the like.
/ 11 pm; closed Sun.

Addendum
Apex City Of London Hotel EC3   £53   ❸❷④
1 Seething Ln   7977 9500   9–3D
"Very much a place for suits" – chef Tom Illic's "well-executed"
cuisine generally pleases reporters at this "slick", year-old dining
room, near Tower Bridge. / www.apexhotels.co.uk; 9.45 pm; closed
Sat & Sun.

Addie's Thai Café SW5   £26   ❷❷❸
121 Earl's Court Rd   7259 2620   5–2A
Handily-located (by Earl's Court tube), this "cheap, cheerful and
reliable" oriental caff is "a regular haunt for locals".
/ www.addiesthaicafe.co.uk; 11 pm; closed Sat L & Sun L.

Admiral Codrington SW3   £42   ④④❸
17 Mossop St   7581 0005   5–2C
Especially "when the retractable roof is raised", the dining room
of this "smart" Chelsea pub makes a "light" and "lovely" venue;
the cooking, however – always "fairly standard" – had more off-
days this year. / 11 pm.

The Admiralty
Somerset House WC2   £45   ⑤④⑤
Strand   7845 4646   2–2D
These lofty but small chambers in the heart of London's
greatest public palazzo do have their fans (especially as an
"impressive" lunch location); there are many critics, though,
who just find it an "odd" place ("like a railway waiting room"),
with "uninspired" food and "haphazard" service.
/ www.theadmiraltyrestaurant.com; 10.15 pm; closed Sun D.

Afghan Kitchen N1   £18   ❷④④
35 Islington Grn   7359 8019   8–3D
"Cheap", "tasty" and "interesting" nosh (if from a "limited" menu)
wins praise for this tiny Islington pit stop; service, though, is "pretty
poor", and the "cramped" setting "more IKEA than Kabul". / 11 pm;
closed Mon & Sun; no credit cards.

Aglio e Olio SW10 £30 ❷❸④
194 Fulham Rd 7351 0070 5–3B
*"Simple Italian dishes, swiftly prepared and rapidly served" make
this "loud" and "cramped" spot "the ultimate in cheap and
cheerful" eating... by Chelsea standards, anyway. / 11.30 pm.*

Agni W6 £26 ❷❶④
160 King St 8846 9191 7–2C
*It's "not on the nicest part of King Street" and a bit "cramped" and
"basic", but this Hammersmith two-year-old is "a wonderful find" –
it offers "fresh and exciting" cooking ("a spin on Indian street
food") and "impeccable" service. / www.agnirestaurant.com; 11 pm;
Mon-Thu D only, Fri-Sun open L & D.*

Al Duca SW1 £41 ❸❸❸
4-5 Duke of York St 7839 3090 3–3D
*"Dependable", "sound", "reliable" – these are the adjectives
reporters typically apply to this "staple" St James's Italian, where
prices are "very gentle, by the standards of the area".
/ www.alduca-restaurant.co.uk; 11 pm; closed Sun.*

Al Forno £28 ④❷❷
349 Upper Richmond Rd, SW15 8878 7522 10–2A
2a King's Rd, SW19 8540 5710 10–2B
*"For a party, or dining out with friends", some reporters tip these
west London Italians, praising their "energetic" staff, "fun"
ambience and "delicious" pizza; critics, though, can find them
"tired". / SW15 11 pm; SW19 11.30 pm.*

Al Hamra W1 £45 ④④④
31-33 Shepherd Mkt 7493 1954 3–4B
*"On a summer day, you can't beat sitting outside and grazing
on mezze", says fans of this veteran Shepherd Market Lebanese;
reports are variable, though, and service can be "sloppy".
/ www.alhamra.co.uk; 11.30 pm.*

Al Sultan W1 £38 ❷❷⑤
51-52 Hertford St 7408 1155 3–4B
*"Amazing mezze" steal the show at this "usually very good"
Shepherd Market Lebanese; arguably, though, its low-key premises
could use a "face lift". / www.alsultan.co.uk; 11 pm.*

Al-Waha W2 £32 ❸❸④
75 Westbourne Grove 7229 0806 6–1B
*"Authentic" food, and "endearing" service make this Bayswater
Lebanese an "excellent neighbourhood stand-by".
/ www.alwaharestaurant.com; 11.30 pm; no Amex.*

Alain Ducasse
Dorchester W1 NEW £100
53 Park Ln 7629 8888 3–3A
*International superstar-chef Alain Ducasse is finally set to open
a London outpost in late-2007; his New York venture (at the Essex
House Hotel) was never the success which might have been
expected – let's hope he's learned from the experience...
/ www.thedorchester.com.*

Alastair Little W1 £57 ❸❷⑤
49 Frith St 7734 5183 4–2A
*"They keep it simple, and to good effect", say fans of this "stark"
Soho fixture named after – but no longer associated with –
the famed chef; it's not without detractors, though, who dismiss
it as a "sterile" place that's "trading on its reputation". /* 11.30 pm;
closed Sat L & Sun.

Alba EC1 £43 ❸❷④
107 Whitecross St 7588 1798 9–1B
*"Super" Piedmontese cuisine and a "wonderful" North Italian wine
list have long been the draws to this "reasonably-priced" veteran,
in a "dingy street near the Barbican"; off-nights, though, are not
unknown. /* www.albarestaurant.com; 11 pm; closed Sat & Sun.

Albannach WC2 £48 ⑤④④
66 Trafalgar Sq 7930 0066 2–3C
*Overlooking a "pumping" bar, this mezzanine-restaurant has its
work cut out as a dinner-destination; it doesn't help, though,
that the Scottish cuisine is often "underwhelming".
/* www.albannach.co.uk; 10 pm; closed Sun; set always available £31 (FP).

The Albion N1 NEW £36 ❸⑤❸
10 Thornhill Rd 7607 7450 8–3D
*"Another gastropub to add to Islington's plethora"; this newly
trendified old inn – with its "very pretty garden" –
is "much improved" on most accounts; critics, though, say the food
is "OK, but not more", and find service wanting.
/* www.the-albion.co.uk; 10 pm.

Ali Baba NW1 £20 ❷❸⑤
32 Ivor Pl 7723 5805 2–1A
*"Remarkably like a typical family restaurant in Egypt", this front-
room-style operation – "dominated by a large TV set" – is located
behind a Marylebone take-away, and serves "cheap" food that's
"simple but tasteful"; BYO. /* midnight; no credit cards.

Alisan HA9 NEW £29 ❶❷④
The Junction, Engineers Way, Wembley 8903 3888 1–1A
*"Outstanding" dim sum (from an ex-Yauatcha chef) wins praise for
this "futuristic" but "soulless" Cantonese newcomer beside the new
Wembley Stadium; "the other food is good, but not world-beating".
/* www.alisan.co.uk; Mon-Thu 11 pm, Fri & Sat 11.30 pm, Sun 10.30 pm.

All Star Lanes £34 ④④❷
Victoria Hs, Bloomsbury Pl, WC1 7025 2676 2–1D
Whiteley's, 151 Queensway, W2 7313 8360 6–1C NEW
Old Truman Brewery, 3 Dray Walk, E1 awaiting tel 9–1D NEW
*"A really fun night out" (even if "the food isn't the main attraction")
can be had at these "classy"-looking, "diner-style" bowling alleys,
in Bloomsbury and Bayswater (and, soon, the East End).
/* www.allstarlanes.co.uk; WC1 10.30 pm, Fri & Sat midnight, Sun 9 pm.

Alloro W1 £49 ❷❷❸
19-20 Dover St 7495 4768 3–3C
*"A good all-rounder, especially for a business lunch" –
this "very slick" and "spacious" Mayfair Italian serves
up "fantastic" food (and a "huge" wine list) to a largely besuited
clientele. /* 10.30 pm; closed Sat L & Sun.

Alma SW18 £36 ❸❸❷
499 Old York Rd   8870 2537   10–2B
"A good buzzy atmosphere" has long been the mainstay of this Wandsworth pub; its "better-than-average grub" seems to be holding up well under new management. / www.thealma.co.uk; 10.30 pm, Sun 9 pm.

The Almeida N1 £41 ④④④
30 Almeida St   7354 4777   8–2D
"Uninspiring, dull and impersonal" – this "well-spaced" Gallic venture, in Islington, has gradually conformed to the classic pattern of 'Conran' ineptitude; perhaps – under the new 'D&D London' banner – the proprietors will be able to put it back to rights. / www.almeida-restaurant.co.uk; 11 pm.

Alounak £26 ❸⑤❸
10 Russell Gdns, W14   7603 1130   7–1D
44 Westbourne Grove, W2   7229 0416   6–1B
"BYO keeps costs down", at this "lively" Olympia Persian (with a spin-off in Bayswater); it serves "delicious" bread, and "good" mezze and kebabs, but service can be "sloppy". / 11.30 pm; no Amex.

Amano Café SE1 £29 ❸❸❸
Victor Wharf, Clink St   7234 0000   9–3C
"Interesting wraps", "great soups", "delicious smoothies" and other "healthy" snacks "never fail to please" fans of this Borough Market café. / www.amanocafe.com; 10.30 pm; no Amex.

Amaranth SW18 £22 ❷❸④
346 Garratt Ln   8871 3466   10–2B
"Book ahead", if you want to enjoy the "great-value" eating at this "basic" but mega-popular BYO Thai in Earlsfield; ratings slipped a notch this year, though, as a result of gripes about "brusque" service and a "lack of ambience". / 10.30 pm; D only, closed Sun; no Amex.

Amato W1 £26 ❸❷❸
14 Old Compton St   7734 5733   4–2A
A "delightfully buzzy" Soho café that's a "favourite" with some reporters, thanks to its "sinfully delicious" pastries and "great" coffee. / www.amato.co.uk; Mon-Sat 10 pm, Sun 8 pm; no booking.

Amaya SW1 £54 ❶❸❷
Halkin Arc, 19 Motcomb St   7823 1166   5–1D
This sleek and "classy" Belgravia subcontinental wins many rave reviews for its innovative "grazing" formula (which incorporates "light" and "exciting" dishes from an open grill); service, though, can sometimes come "with attitude". / www.amaya.biz; 11 pm.

Ambassador EC1 £35 ❸❷④
55 Exmouth Mkt   7837 0009   9–1A
A "bare" and "no-nonsense" Clerkenwell yearling, where the staff are "amiable", and the food is usually "varied" and "imaginative". / www.theambassadorcafe.co.uk; 10.15 pm; closed Sun D.

Amerigo Vespucci E14 £40 ❸❷❸
25 Cabot Sq   7513 0288   11–1C
"A refreshing change, in corporate Canary Wharf" – this "classic" old-style Italian, lost among the skyscrapers, is a "charming" destination (by local standards), and its outside tables have a "great position overlooking the water". / www.amerigovespucci.co.uk; 11.30 pm; closed Sat L & Sun.

Amici SW17 £34 ④④❷
35 Bellevue Rd   8672 5888   10–2C
*Some reporters say this large and "buzzy" Italian yearling
on Wandsworth Common is "much better than its predecessor"
(Pomino, RIP); supporters praise its "comfort-food-type cooking",
but others say it's "not always reliable". / www.amiciitalian.co.uk;
10.30 pm.*

Anarkali W6 £28 ❸❷④
303-305 King St   8748 6911   7–2B
*For some locals, this Hammersmith Indian of decades' standing
is an "all-time-favourite in an unstable world", thanks to its "great
food and friendly service". / www.anarkalirestaurant.co.uk; midnight.*

The Anchor & Hope SE1 £35 ❶❷❷
36 The Cut   7928 9898   9–4A
*"You have to camp out for days for a table", at this "chaotic", no-
bookings legend near Waterloo; again the survey's No. 1 gastropub,
it has won a huge reputation for its "amazing" and "gutsy" British
fare. / 10.30 pm; closed Mon L & Sun D; no Amex; no booking.*

ANDREW EDMUNDS W1 £34 ❸❶❶
46 Lexington St   7437 5708   3–2D
*It may be small and "cramped", but this "eternally popular" Soho
townhouse – with its "quirky", "snug" and "Bohemian" charm –
remains many a Londoner's "No. 1 choice for romance"; its "lovely"
staff serve up "simple", "straight-up" food, plus an "exceptional-
value" wine list. / 10.30 pm; no Amex; booking: max 6.*

Angelus W2 NEW £40
4 Bathurst St   7402 0083   6–2D
*Opening soon after this guide goes to press, this Bayswater pub-
conversion is the first solo project by Thierry Tomasin – previously
head sommelier at Le Gavroche and maître d' at Aubergine;
it should be one to watch; price given is our guesstimate.*

The Anglesea Arms W6 £38 ❶④❷
35 Wingate Rd   8749 1291   7–1B
*Near the top of London's "gastropub premier league" –
this "brilliant" boozer, near Ravenscourt Park, serves up "incredibly
flavourful" cooking at very "reasonable prices" in a "relaxed"
(if "cramped") setting; service – traditionally "slow" – "has got
better" under a new owner. / Tue-Sat 10.30 pm, Sun & Mon 10 pm;
no Amex; no booking.*

The Anglesea Arms SW7 £31 ④④❷
15 Sellwood Ter   7373 7960   5–2B
*This "very popular" traditional South Kensington boozer has
a lovely terrace, which is "jammed on a warm summer night";
the "straightforward" scoff is incidental. / www.angleseaarms.com;
10 pm.*

Anglo Asian Tandoori N16 £24 ❸❶❸
60-62 Stoke Newington Church St   7254 3633   1–1C
*"It's been around for yonks", but this "Stoke Newington staple"
is still "always a winner", thanks to its "reliable" food and its
"smiling" staff ("who deliver a plethora of freebies").
/ www.angloasian.co.uk; 11.45 pm.*

Annex 3 W1 £44 ④④❸
6 Little Portland St   7631 0700   2–1B
Despite "totally OTT" décor, this 'maximalist' yearling,
near Broadcasting House, has totally failed to make any waves with
reporters – the backers "should stick to their City places" (Trois
Garçons and Loungelover, a bar). / www.annex3.co.uk; midnight; D only,
closed Sun.

Annie's £35 ④❷❶
162 Thames Rd, W4   8994 9080   1–3A
36-38 White Hart Ln, SW13   8878 2020   10–1A
"Mismatched furniture and heavy drapes" help create
a "very romantic", "front-room" feeling at these "friendly"
neighbourhood spots (in Strand on the Green and Mortlake); their
"generous", "comfort" food helps make them a "favourite weekend
brunch haunt". / W4 10 pm, SW13 11 pm.

Antipasto & Pasta SW11 £30 ❸❸❸
511 Battersea Park Rd   7223 9765   10–1C
A consistently satisfactory Battersea Italian, of most note for its
50%-off-food offer (selected days). / 11.30 pm; need 4+ to book.

Aperitivo W1 £33 ❸❷❷
41 Beak St   7287 2057   3–2D
A "sociable" Soho spot, whose "Italian tapas"-style cuisine strikes
many reporters as a "brilliant" and "interesting" concept, even if
realisation can be up-and-down. / 11 pm; closed Sun.

Apostrophe £13 ❸❸❷
16 Regent St, SW1   7930 9922   3–3D
10 Grosvenor St, W1   7499 6511   3–2B **NEW**
20/20 Opt' Store, 216 Tott' Ct Rd, W1   7436 6688   2–1C
23 Barrett St, W1   7355 1001   3–1A
40-41 Great Castle St, W1   7637 5700   3–1C
215 Strand, WC2   7427 9890   4–2D
42 Gt Eastern St, EC2   7739 8412   9–1D
3-5 St Bride St, EC4   7353 3704   9–2A
A "bright and fresh" French café/bakery chain, whose "delicious
pastries, sandwiches and tartes" (plus "excellent coffee") win
universal acclaim. / www.apostropheuk.com; L & afternoon tea only, Barrett
St 8pm; no Amex; no booking.

Aquasia
Conrad International SW10 £52 ⑤⑤④
Chelsea Harbour   7823 3000   5–4B
Only for a "superb" breakfast can this hotel dining room – with its
"great setting" overlooking Chelsea Harbour – be recommended;
its more general cuisine tends to "bland", and the ambience can
be "morgue-like". / www.conradhotels.com; 10.30 pm; closed Sun D.

Arancia SE16 £28 ❷❷❷
52 Southwark Park Rd   7394 1751   11–2A
"Still going strong" – after a decade in business, this "delightful
find", in deepest Bermondsey, continues to offer "simple" but
"well prepared" Italian dishes, in a homely setting. / 11 pm; closed
Mon & Sun.

The Arbiter SW6 NEW £27 ❸❸❸
308-310 North End Rd   7385 8001   7–2D
A new "Danish-influenced" Fulham gastropub – successor to Meum
Cor (RIP) – which wins praise for its "quality" cuisine (including
a "cracking" smörgåsbord) and "smiling" service.
/ www.arbiter-pubs.co.uk; 10 pm; closed Mon L.

ARBUTUS W1 £44 ❷❷❸
63-64 Frith St   7734 4545   4–2A
"Gastronomic finesse, but without a fine-dining price-tag",
has made a smash foodie hit of this "spectacular" Soho yearling,
where "unfussy" (but "intriguing") dishes are complemented
by "exceptional-quality" wines (available by the carafe); the setting,
though, strikes some reporters as rather "cramped" or "canteen-
like". / www.arbutusrestaurant.co.uk; 10.30 pm.

Archduke Wine Bar SE1 £37 ❺❸④
Concert Hall Approach, South Bank   7928 9370   2–3D
The spirit of South Bank renewal has so far missed this "bustling"
old wine bar, in railway arches near the Festival Hall – it feels quite
"inviting", but its dated cuisine can be "distinctly underwhelming".
/ 11 pm; closed Sat L & Sun.

The Arches NW6 £36 ④❷❷
7 Fairhazel Gdns   7624 1867   8–2A
"One of the best lists in London, especially at the price" makes this
"quirky" Swiss Cottage bar "a wine lover's dream"; no one actually
mentions the food. / 10.30 pm; no Amex.

Archipelago W1 £49 ❸❶❶
110 Whitfield St   7383 3346   2–1B
"Like a cross between a harem and a junk shop", this "ultra-quirky"
venue in the shadow of the Telecom Tower makes "a great place
for a date", and its "fascinating" and "exotic" menu "turns out
better than you'd expect". / www.archipelago-restaurant.co.uk; 10.30 pm;
closed Sat L & Sun.

The Ark W8 £44 ④❸❷
122 Palace Gardens Ter   7229 4024   6–2B
This odd shed, off Notting Hill Gate, has its own "very cosy" charm;
it has seen "years of changing régimes" – "the current Italian one
offers consistent quality", but even fans can find it "over-pricey".
/ www.ark-restaurant.com; 11 pm; closed Mon L & Sun.

Ark Fish E18 £33 ❷❸⑤
142 Hermon Hill   8989 5345   1–1D
"Very good seafood" wins a big thumbs-up for this "upmarket fish
'n' chip restaurant", in South Woodford; it gets "frantic" and
"noisy", though, and "they don't take bookings, so you have
to queue". / www.arkfishrestaurant.co.uk; Tue-Thu 9.45 pm, Fri & Sat
10.15 pm, Sun 8.45 pm; closed Mon; no Amex.

Arkansas Café E1 £28 ❷④④
107b Commercial Spitalfields Mkt   7377 6999   9–1D
"You don't go here for the variable service or the junk-shop décor",
but the "first-class" burgers (and other BBQ dishes) at Bubba's
"eccentric" Spitalfields Market gaff have many admirers. / L only,
closed Sat; no Amex.

Artigiano NW3 £44 ❸❷❸
12a Belsize Ter   7794 4288   8–2A
*A Belsize Park "favourite", which seems to be re-establishing its
reputation for "high-quality" Italian food and "friendly" service.*
/ www.etruscarestaurant.com; 10.30 pm; closed Mon L; set dinner £29 (FP).

L'Artista NW11 £26 ❸❸❸
917 Finchley Rd   8731 7501   1–1B
*"Heaving till late", this "noisy" pizzeria remains a linchpin
of Golder's Green life – "the food is average", says an Italian
reporter, but "at least it's authentic". / 11.30 pm.*

L'Artiste Musclé W1 £34 ④④❶
1 Shepherd Mkt   7493 6150   3–4B
*The "spitting image of a slightly shabby Parisian bistro" –
this Shepherd Market fixture may serve "basic" fare, but it has
a wonderfully "convivial" atmosphere. / 11 pm.*

Arturo W2 £41 ④❷④
23 Connaught St   7706 3388   6–1D
*After a couple of years in business, this "elegant" Bayswater Italian
"seems to be slipping"; its "incredibly cheap" lunch menu, however,
is well worth knowing about. / www.arturorestaurant.co.uk; 10 pm.*

Asadal WC1 £50 ❸④⑤
227 High Holborn   7430 9006   2–1D
*"Interesting" BBQ dishes win praise for this "authentic" Korean
yearling, which has a "dungeon"-like setting, beneath Holborn tube;
prices are "steep", though, and some reporters find it a "let-down".
/ www.asadal.co.uk; 11 pm.*

Asia de Cuba
St Martin's Lane Hotel WC2 £66 ❸④❷
45 St Martin's Ln   7300 5588   4–4C
*It may be "full of itself" – and charge "shocking" prices – but this
"eccentric" style-scene, on the fringe of Covent Garden, still offers
"a fun night out"; on the food front, its "far-out" fusion sharing
plates are "surprisingly OK" (and "great for group dining").
/ www.morganshotelgroup.com; midnight, Thu-Sat 12.30 am, Sun10.30 pm.*

Ask! Pizza £25 ④④❸
Branches throughout London
*"Cheerful" branches in attractive locations are the main plus-point
of this popular pizza multiple; the food seems increasingly "mass-
produced", though, with fewer reporters now seeing this as a peer
to PizzaExpress or Strada. / www.askcentral.co.uk; 11 pm; some booking
restrictions apply.*

ASSAGGI W2 £59 ❶❶❸
39 Chepstow Pl   7792 5501   6–1B
*"For great produce, simply and beautifully cooked, Nino Sassu
is the man"; his food yet again won this unlikely venture –
a Spartan room over a Bayswater pub – the survey's vote
as London's top Italian; "passionate" staff play a "theatrical"
supporting rôle. / 11 pm; closed Sun; no Amex.*

Les Associés N8 £32 ❸❷❸
172 Park Rd   8348 8944   1–1C
*You feel "like you're eating in someone's front room", when you visit
this "authentically French" Crouch End fixture, which offers cooking
that's "good, by local restaurant standards". / www.lesassocies.co.uk;
10 pm; Tue-Sat D only, closed Mon & Sun D.*

Atami SW1 NEW £50 ❸❸④
37 Monck St 7222 2218 2–4C
*This large and would-be "stylish" Japanese operation has been
a "welcome addition" to Westminster's (lacklustre) restaurant
scene; its cuisine is "interesting", if perhaps rather "overpriced".*
/ www.atami-restaurant.com; 10.30 pm; closed Sun D.

L'ATELIER DE JOEL ROBUCHON WC2 £70 ❶❷❷
13-15 West St 7010 8600 4–2B
*Who cares if it's "outrageously pricey"? – this "exquisite" Parisian
import has been an "awesome" addition to London, offering
a "bite-size" cuisine that's "so good it should be illegal";
the "beautiful", "dark" and "sophisticated" ground floor is usually
tipped over the "more conventional" dining room upstairs.*
/ 10.30 pm.

The Atlas SW6 £34 ❷④❷
16 Seagrave Rd 7385 9129 5–3A
*"Fresh and flavoursome" Mediterranean cooking has made quite
a name for this "cosy" gastropub near Earl's Court 2; such is its
popularity, though, that "it can get uncomfortably crowded".*
/ www.theatlaspub.co.uk; 10.30 pm; no Amex; no booking.

Atma NW3 NEW £34 ❷❷❸
106c Finchley Rd 7431 9487 8–2A
*"Interesting" dishes – especially from south India – are winning
a strong local following for this "reasonably-priced" Belsize Park
newcomer; service is "warm" and "attentive" too. / 11.30 pm.*

Atrium SW1 £40 ⑤⑤④
4 Millbank 7233 0032 2–4C
*"Proof that politicos have no taste!" – this "airy" venue, at the foot
of the Westminster media centre, remains of most note for its
"sloppy" service, and its often "dismal" cuisine.*
/ www.atriumrestaurant.com; 9.30 pm; closed Sat & Sun.

Aubaine £41 ④⑤❸
4 Heddon St, W1 7440 2510 3–2C NEW
260-262 Brompton Rd, SW3 7052 0100 5–2C
*"Delicious-looking customers" outshine the "boring" menu and
"appalling" service at this "fashionably-located" Brompton Cross
bakery-cum-bistro; it now has an offshoot just off Regent Street.*
/ SW3 10.30 pm – W1 11 pm; W1 closed Sun.

AUBERGINE SW10 £88 ❶❷❸
11 Park Wk 7352 3449 5–3B
*Though he works "in the shadow of Ramsay" (who kicked off his
own solo career at this Chelsea dining room), William Drabble's
"divine" cuisine was – to within a thousandth of a point – rated the
equal of his predecessor's this year; "they sure know how
to charge" for it, of course (but there's an "exceptional"-value lunch
menu). / www.auberginerestaurant.co.uk; 11 pm; closed Sat L & Sun;
set weekday L £38 (FP).*

Aurora W1 £38 ❸❷❶
49 Lexington St 7494 0514 3–2D
*A "chilled" vibe and "friendly" service help make this Soho "gem"
a "really intimate" West End haven ("particularly in summer,
thanks to its courtyard"); its "tasty" food "won't break the bank"
either. / 10.30 pm; closed Sun.*

Aurora
Great Eastern Hotel EC2 £62 ❸❸❷
40 Liverpool St 7618 7000 9–2D
"Perfect for power lunches"; having thrown off the Conran yoke,
this "grand" and "ornate" City chamber wins acclaim for its
"good food, knowledgable staff, and excellent wine list"; it's still
"pricey" though, and at quieter times can seem "cavernous".
/ www.aurora-restaurant.co.uk; 10 pm; closed Sat & Sun; booking: max 8.

Automat W1 £42 ❸❹❸
33 Dover St 7499 3033 3–3C
An "upscale" American diner that's a fashionable destination for
Mayfair types; Stateside, though, you'd be unlucky to find service
as "slow" or "surly" as it can be here. / www.automat-london.com;
11 pm; closed Sun D.

L'Aventure NW8 £50 ❷❶❶
3 Blenheim Ter 7624 6232 8–3A
Catherine is a "wonderful hostess", and helps create
a "very French" and "romantic" atmosphere at this "tucked-away"
St John's Wood favourite, which has a "brilliant summer terrace";
the Gallic menu is "not adventurous", but it "really works". / 11 pm;
closed Sat L & Sun.

The Avenue SW1 £55 ❹❹❹
7-9 St James's St 7321 2111 3–4D
With its "unimaginative" food and "airport departure lounge"
styling, this "cavernous", '90s-style mega-brasserie, in St James's,
is really only popular for business nowadays; perhaps new owners
D&D London (fka Conran Restaurants) will be able to sort it out.
/ www.egami.co.uk; midnight; closed Sun.

The Aviary SW20 £34 ❹❹❸
193 Worple Rd 8947 2212 10–2A
For "decent cooking in a culinary dessert" many locals recommend
this Raynes Park spot; critics don't doubt it "means well", but fear
it "doesn't come up to scratch". / www.theaviary.co.uk; 11 pm;
closed Mon.

Awana SW3 £46 ❷❸❸
85 Sloane Ave 7584 8880 5–2C
"Seriously good" Malaysian cooking (not least, "amazing satay")
is winning greater acclaim for this smart Chelsea yearling;
it's "at the top end of its price scale", though, so "frequent online
offers are worth seeking out". / www.awana.co.uk; 11.30 pm.

Axis WC2 £62 ❹❸❹
1 Aldwych 7300 0300 2–2D
This "very '90s" basement, on the fringe of Covent Garden,
was "modern and exciting when it opened", but nowadays seems
increasingly "sterile" (and "a bit pricey" too); it's still popular for
business, though, and handy pre-theatre. / www.onealdwych.com;
10.45 pm, Sat 11.30 pm; closed Sat L & Sun.

Aziz SW6 £29 ❷❸❸
24-32 Vanston Pl 7386 0086 5–4A
"A big hit for breakfast and for coffee" – this deli attached to a
"fun" Fulham Moroccan (formula price £36) attracts more reports
than its parent, and is "deservedly popular" with the "local hordes",
especially on a sunny day (when you can sit out). / www.delaziz.co.uk;
10.30 pm.

Azou W6 £27 ❸⓿❸
375 King St 8563 7266 7–2B
A "friendly", family-run North African café in Hammersmith;
fans say it's "fantastic" – with "good-value" tagines and so on –
and even less-enthusiastic reporters consider it "a handy stand-by".
/ www.azou.co.uk; 11 pm; closed Sat L & Sun L.

Babes 'n' Burgers W11
275 Portobello Rd
"Organic burgers freshly made in front of you" were the highlight
at this "downmarket"-feeling Notting Hill caff; news of its closure
reached us just as this guide was going to press.

Babur Brasserie SE23 £32 ⓿⓿❷
119 Brockley Rise 8291 2400 1–4D
This "haute" Indian "transcends" its "unlikely" Honor Oak Park
location, and is "really worth a detour"; it offers "exceptional" food
("regularly showcasing the cuisines of different regions") and
"utterly attentive" service, in a "classy" modern setting.
/ www.babur.info; 11.30 pm.

Babylon
Kensington Roof Gardens W8 £61 ④④❷
99 Kensington High St 7368 3993 5–1A
"Come on a sunny day if possible", to "revel in the view" – and to
walk in the "captivating" garden (1.5 acres) – at Richard Branson's
"fabulously-located" rooftop dining room; the food, though, is "dull",
and notably "overpriced". / www.virgin.com/roofgardens; 11 pm; closed
Sun D; set weekday L £34 (FP).

Bacchus N1 NEW £60 ❸❸④
177 Hoxton St 7613 0477 1–2C
"Go, if you're adventurous" to this Hoxton pub-conversion; the thrill
has nothing to do with the "dodgy" location, but rather with Nuno
Mendes's "conceptual and cutting-edge" cuisine (in the "molecular"
style of El Bulli) – it's "not always successful", but it is always
"interesting". / midnight; closed Sat L & Sun.

Back to Basics W1 £42 ⓿❸④
21a Foley St 7436 2181 2–1B
"Small, cramped, noisy and quite splendid" – this Fitzrovia bistro
offers an "amazing choice" of "really fresh fish" (and seafood)
at "superb" prices. / www.backtobasics.uk.com; 10.30 pm; closed Sun.

Baker & Spice £35 ❷④④
54-56 Elizabeth St, SW1 7730 3033 2–4A
47 Denyer St, SW3 7589 4734 5–2D
75 Salusbury Rd, NW6 7604 3636 1–2B
20 Clifton Rd, W9 7266 1122 8–4A NEW
A small café/bakery chain, known for its "sublime breads" and
"amazing pastries"; even by the standards of its chichi locations,
though, it's "shockingly expensive", and service "isn't great" either.
/ www.bakerandspice.com; 7 pm, Sun 5 pm; closed D; no Amex; no bookings.

Balans £34 ⑤④❸
34 Old Compton St, W1　7439 3309　4–2A
60 Old Compton St, W1　7439 2183　4–3A
239 Old Brompton Rd, SW5　7244 8838　5–3A
214 Chiswick High Rd, W4　8742 1435　7–2A
187 Kensington High St, W8　7376 0115　5–1A
The "buzzy, young atmosphere" is all there is to shout about nowadays, at these "mostly gay" diners – the food "just gets worse and worse"; people of all persuasions, though, find them "good for a quick brunch". / www.balans.co.uk; varies from midnight to 6 am, 34 Old Compton St 24 hrs; some booking restrictions apply.

Baltic SE1 £45 ❸❸❷
74 Blackfriars Rd　7928 1111　9–4A
A "sin-inducing bar" (with "a fantastic selection of home-made vodkas") drives the "perennially buzzy" vibe at this "fun" and "cavernous" space, by Southwark tube; its "modern Eastern European" cooking is on the "interesting" side of "OK". / www.balticrestaurant.co.uk; 10 pm; set weekday L £25 (FP).

Bam-Bou W1 £41 ❸❸❶
1 Percy St　7323 9130　2–1C
"Beautiful, colonial Franco/Vietnamese décor" and "fabulous" cocktails contribute to a "seductive" ambience at this "buzzing" Fitzrovia townhouse; the oriental fare is usually "delicious" too, but service can be "erratic", and critics find bills excessive. / www.bam-bou.co.uk; 11 pm; closed Sat L & Sun; booking: max 6.

The Banana Leaf Canteen SW11 £26 ❸❷❸
75-79 Battersea Rise　7228 2828　10–2C
"For a quick meal near Clapham Junction", this "crowded" canteen – "with long shared tables" – offers "cheap" and "tasty" food in a "buzzy" ("loud") setting. / 11 pm; need 6+ to book.

Bangkok SW7 £31 ❸❷④
9 Bute St　7584 8529　5–2B
"I've been a patron for 35 years", says a typical fan of "London's original Thai", in South Kensington; it looks "tired" nowadays, but its "slightly Anglicised" food is realised to a "consistently good" standard. / 10.45 pm; closed Sun; no Amex.

Bank Westminster
St James Court Hotel SW1 £48 ④④④
45 Buckingham Gate　7379 9797　2–4B
Complaints of "assembly-line" cooking, and "dilatory" service suggest this large bar/brasserie near Buckingham Palace (now bereft of its Aldwych sibling) is losing its way, but it still makes a handy business option in a thin area. / www.bankrestaurants.com; 10.30 pm; closed Sat L & Sun; set dinner £31 (FP).

Bankside £30 ⑤⑤④
32 Southwark Bridge Rd, SE1　7633 0011　9–4B
1 Angel Ct, Throgmorton St, EC2　0845 226 0011　9–2C
At best, these "well-priced" modern brasseries make "good stand-bys", and a "useful option for large groups wanting to eat cheaply"; critics, though, say they are "disappointing, even for the price" – "I'd have preferred McDonalds". / www.banksiderestaurants.co.uk; SE1 10.30 pm, EC2 10 pm; SE1 closed Fri-Mon, EC2 closed Sat & Sun.

Banners N8 £32 ❸❷❶
21 Park Rd 8348 2930 1–1C
Brunch here may be "a bit of a local cliché", but Crouch End's "perennial" favourite "still rocks" – the "buzzy" vibe is the highpoint, but the "comfort food with a twist" is certainly "very solid". / 11.30 pm, Fri midnight; no Amex.

The Bar & Grill EC1 £44 ❸❸❷
2-3 West Smithfield 0870 4422 541 9–2A
"Very good burgers" are the star attraction at this smart but tightly-packed Smithfield outfit; it's "nothing special" overall, but – for "work do's" and the like – it's a consistent stand-by. / www.blackhouserestaurants.com; 10 pm; closed Sat L & Sun.

Bar Bourse EC4 £50 ④④④
67 Queen St 7248 2200 9–3C
It's "pricey", but this basement bar/restaurant near Mansion House remains a useful business rendezvous in these parts. / www.barbourse.co.uk; L only, closed Sat & Sun.

Bar Capitale £30 ❸④④
The Concourse, 1 Poultry, EC2 7248 3117 9–2C
Bucklersbury Hs, 14 Walbrook, EC4 7236 2030 9–3C
Busy Italian pit stops which fuel the City's long-hours culture with "excellent breakfasts", "fresh sandwiches" and "very good pizza". / www.mithrasbars.co.uk; 10 pm; closed Sat & Sun.

Bar du Musée SE10 £38 ④④❸
17 Nelson Rd 8858 4710 1–3D
With its "large and lively" dining area, and "calm" tables on an elegant rear terrace, this Greenwich bar/restaurant could be quite a destination... so it's a shame it's so terribly unreliable. / 10 pm; no Amex.

Bar Estrela SW8 £25 ❸❷❷
111-115 South Lambeth Rd 7793 1051 10–1D
As you "sip your ice-cold Sagres" and "watch Benfica on the blaring TV" you can "imagine you're in Lisbon" at this "brilliant" Vauxhall café – a "real neighbourhood scene", offering "filling" food at "great-value prices". / midnight.

Bar Italia W1 £18 ④❷❶
22 Frith St 7437 4520 4–2A
"First choice for a shot of espresso", with some "great people-watching" on the side – this "fantastic" 24/7 veteran remains a linchpin of Soho life: "it's always fab, but especially late-night". / open 24 hours, Sun 3 am; no booking.

Bar Shu W1 £38 ❷④❸
28 Frith St 7287 6688 4–3A
"A must for any fan of Sichuan cooking" – this much-acclaimed Soho yearling continues to make waves with its "fiery" and "strikingly different" cuisine. / www.bar-shu.co.uk; 11.30 pm.

Barcelona Tapas £28 ④⑤❸
481 Lordship Ln, SE22 8693 5111 1–4D
1 Beaufort Hs, St Botolph St, EC3 7377 5111 9–2D
24 Lime St, EC3 7929 2389 9–2D
13 Well Ct, EC4 7329 5111 9–2B
A once-celebrated tapas mini-chain; it's generally rated at the "OK-stand-by" level nowadays. / www.barcelona-tapas.com; 10.30 pm, Sat 11.30 pm; all City branches closed Sat & Sun.

Barnes Grill SW13 £37 ④④④
2-3 Rock's Ln   8878 4488   10–1A
Prices are "high" ("hardly a surprise for an AWT venture") at this "rather suburban" grill-restaurant, and its "simple" food is "OK, but nothing special"; take "dark glasses" so as best to appreciate the "bizarre" décor. / 10.30 pm; closed Mon L.

The Barnsbury N1 £38 ❸❸❸
209-211 Liverpool Rd   7607 5519   8–2D
This "relaxing" Islington boozer is a "top dog in an area well-served by gastropubs" (and benefits in particular from "a charming courtyard"); it's getting "too popular", though, and "not quite as good as it used to be". / www.thebarnsbury.co.uk; 10 pm.

Barrafina W1 NEW £49 ❶❶❷
54 Frith St   7813 8016   4–2A
"Tapas the way they should be" – "as good as Barcelona" – have instantly made the Hart brothers' "slick and cool" new 27-seater, in the heart of Soho, a raging success (even if it is "a tad pricey"); "arrive early, or you'll have to queue". / www.barrafina.co.uk; 11 pm; closed Sun; no booking.

Basilico £30 ❷❸④
690 Fulham Rd, SW6   0800 028 3531   10–1B
26 Penton St, N1   0800 093 4224   8–3D
515 Finchley Rd, NW3   0800 316 2656   1–1B
175 Lavender Hill, SW11   0800 389 9770   10–2C
178 Upper Richmond Rd, SW14   0800 096 8202   10–2B
"Quality thin-base crusts, piled high with interesting toppings" – plus "speedy delivery" – inspire many votes for this popular chain as supplier of "the best take-away pizza by miles". / www.basilico.co.uk; 11pm; no Amex; no booking.

Bayee Village SW19 £30 ❸❷❸
24 High St   8947 3533   1–4A
This "comfortable" Chinese, in the heart of Wimbledon Village, has had a "very serious face-lift" in recent times; the jury is out as to whether it's "moved up a class", or is now "overpriced". / www.bayee.com; 10.45 pm, Fri & Sat 11.15 pm.

Beach Blanket Babylon £65 ⑤⑤❶
45 Ledbury Rd, W11   7229 2907   6–1B
19-23 Bethnal Green Rd, E1   awaiting tel   1–2D NEW
"You don't go for the food or service" ("appalling"), but "great cocktails" and a "beautiful" Gothic interior can still make this (once groundbreaking) Notting Hill hang-out a "very romantic" destination; an offshoot is to open in Shoreditch around the publication date of this guide. / 11.30 pm.

Beauberry House
Belair Park SE21 £46 ④④④
Gallery Rd, Dulwich Village   8299 9788   1–4C
The terrace at this "fabulously-located" operation, overlooking Belair Park, is "good for a leisurely lunch", or a "romantic" one; reports on its other aspects, though – from its "French/Japanese" cuisine to its "contemporary" interior – are very mixed. / www.beauberryhouse.co.uk; 10.30 pm; closed Mon & Sun D; no Amex.

Bedford & Strand WC2 £37 ⑤❷❸
1a Bedford St 7836 3033 4–4D
The "distinctly average" bistro fare is "totally secondary" to the
"very interesting wine" on offer at this "lively" basement bar,
just off the Strand; "despite being barely sign-posted, it's packed,
so they're doing something right". / www.bedford-strand.com; 11 pm;
closed Sun; set always available £24 (FP).

Bedlington Café W4 £22 ❸❸④
24 Fauconberg Rd 8994 1965 7–2A
"The food has slipped a bit" over the years, but this "greasy caff"-
turned-Thai, in deepest Chiswick, still mainly attracts praise as an
"excellent", "cheap 'n' cheerful" option; licensed or you can BYO.
/ 10 pm; closed Sun L; no credit cards.

Beirut Express £22 ❸❸④
65 Old Brompton Rd, SW7 7591 0123 5–2B [NEW]
112-114 Edgware Rd, W2 7724 2700 6–1D
"You get a lot for the money" – "excellent juices" and "very fresh"
kebabs and salads – at these "busy" and "fun" Lebanese cafés;
the new South Kensington branch is already "doing very good
business". / W2 2am, SW7 midnight; W2 no credit cards.

Beiteddine SW1 £42 ❸❷⑤
8 Harriet St 7235 3969 5–1D
A "solid" and "reliable" Lebanese of long standing; so far, at least,
the ever-greater glossiness of neighbouring Sloane Street has
resolutely refused to rub off. / midnight.

Belgo £35 ④④④
50 Earlham St, WC2 7813 2233 4–2C
72 Chalk Farm Rd, NW1 7267 0718 8–2B
Fans insist you get "the best beer and mussels in London", at these
"crowded", "neo-Industrial" Belgian beer halls, in Covent Garden
and Camden Town; for dissenters, though, the food's just "distinctly
average", and "overpriced" too. / www.belgo-restaurants.com; 11.30 pm,
Mon-Thu 11 pm, Sun 10 pm.

Bellamy's W1 £60 ❸❸❷
18-18a Bruton Pl 7491 2727 3–2B
"Hidden-away in a very pleasant mews", Gavin Rankin's "posh"
Mayfair brasserie is a "gem"; it offers "solid" ("if not creative") fare
and "polite" service, in a "classically elegant" setting. / 10.15 pm;
closed Sat L & Sun; set dinner £32 (FP).

Belvedere W8 £50 ❸❶❶
Holland Pk, off Abbotsbury Rd 7602 1238 7–1D
This landmark in the very heart of Holland Park offers
"the complete package" – not just a "beautiful" location, but also
"gorgeous" Art Deco styling, "attentive" service and "well-cooked"
("straight-down-the-middle") cuisine; summer Sunday lunches are
a particular highlight. / www.belvedererestaurant.co.uk; 10 pm; closed
Sun D; set dinner £29 (FP).

Benares W1 £63 ❷❸❸
12 Berkeley Hs, Berkeley Sq 7629 8886 3–3B
Thanks to his "fabulous, subtle and exotic" modern Indian cuisine,
Atul Kochar's "ultra-modern" (if "slightly cold") Mayfair venture has
earned many accolades; service can be "erratic", though,
and prices sometimes seem "horrendous".
/ www.benaresrestaurant.com; 10.30 pm; closed Sat L.

Bengal Clipper SE1 £34 ❷❷❷
Shad Thames   7357 9001   9–4D
This "well-spaced" South Bank Indian has "impeccable" service, and offers a "delicious" and "slightly different" menu, often to the "relaxed sound of a live pianist". / www.bengalclipper.co.uk; 11.30 pm.

Benihana £53 ❹❸❹
37 Sackville St, W1   7494 2525   3–3D
77 King's Rd, SW3   7376 7799   5–3D
100 Avenue Rd, NW3   7586 9508   8–2A
"Watching the chefs prepare your food with gusto" is a "fun" experience (especially for kids), say fans of this international teppan-yaki chain; critics, though, find the ambience "like a party at McDonalds", and say: "you can only pay so much to watch a man catch a prawn in his hat!" / www.benihana.co.uk; 10.30 pm.

Benja W1 NEW £39 ❷❷❸
17 Beak Street   7287 0555   3–2D
Just off Regent Street, a "cramped" but lavishly-decorated Thai newcomer, praised by all early-days reporters for its "nice food and good service". / 10.45 pm; closed Sun.

The Bentley Hotel SW7 £78 ❹❸❹
27-33 Harrington Gdns   7244 5555   5–2B
After Andrew Turner's departure from the 1880 restaurant at this "elaborate" South Kensington hotel, "it all went downhill"; the management seems to be aware of this, and a total re-jig of the dining facilities – including shifting the main room to the ground floor – is mooted for some point in late-2007. / www.thebentley-hotel.com; 10 pm; D only, closed Mon & Sun; booking: max 8.

Bentley's W1 £58 ❸❸❸
11-15 Swallow St   7734 4756   3–3D
Richard Corrigan's "elegant" transformation of this WW1-era dowager, just off Piccadilly, again wins torrents of praise for its "classic" seafood; the "fun" downstairs oyster bar outscores the "more formal" restaurant upstairs, though, and there have been growing gripes about "average" food and "amateurish" service. / www.bentleysoysterbarandgrill.co.uk; midnight; booking: max 12.

Benugo
BFI Southbank SE1 NEW £34 ❷❸❷
Belvedere Rd   7401 9000   2–3D
"Perfect for a pre-movie date"; this stylish new South Bank arts-venue café – which has "no menu similarities to the eponymous sandwich chain" – offers "straightforward" and "well-priced" brasserie fare in a "really relaxing" setting. / www.benugo.com; 11 pm.

Benugo £12 ❷❸❸
14 Curzon St, W1   7629 6246   3–4B
23-25 Gt Portland St, W1   7631 5052   3–1C
V&A Museum, Cromwell Rd, SW7   7581 2159   5–2C
BFI Southbank, Belvedere Rd, SE1   7401 9000   2–3D
116 St John St, EC1   7253 3499   9–1A
82 City Rd, EC1   7253 1295   9–1C
"In the domain of fast(-ish) food sandwich chains, Benugo still stands above the crowd", say fans of this small but growing multiple; it offers a "great range" of sandwiches and snacks, plus "brilliant coffee". / www.benugo.com; 9.30 pm; W1 & EC1 branches closed Sat & Sun; W1 & EC1 branches, no credit cards.

Beotys WC2 £47 ④❸④
79 St Martin's Ln   7836 8768   4–3B
For such a prominently-situated restaurant, the Frangos family's age-old Theatreland stalwart inspires remarkably little feedback; with its dated Franco/Greek fare and club-like décor, it still has its fans, though, especially for business. / 11.30 pm; closed Sun; set pre theatre £31 (FP).

Bermondsey Kitchen SE1 £36 ❸④❸
194 Bermondsey St   7407 5719   9–4D
"Interesting" food comes in "generous portions", at this bright and "enjoyable" local hang-out; standards, though, can be "inconsistent". / www.bermondseykitchen.co.uk; 10.30 pm; closed Sun D.

Bertorelli's £38 ⑤⑤④
11-13 Frith St, W1   7494 3491   4–2A
19-23 Charlotte St, W1   7636 4174   2–1C
37 St Martin's Ln, WC2   7836 5837   4–4C **NEW**
44a Floral St, WC2   7836 3969   4–2D
15 Mincing Ln, EC3   7283 3028   9–3D
1 Plough Pl, EC4   7842 0510   9–2A
A (largely) West End Italian chain, seen by some reporters as a "fairly safe" stand-by; critics, though, say its "execrable" food and "appalling" service make it "a complete sham". / www.santeonline.co.uk; 9.30 pm-11 pm; WC2 & Charlotte St closed Sun, EC3 & EC4 closed Sat & Sun.

Best Mangal W14 £24 ❷❷④
104 North End Rd   7610 1050   7–2D
"Great properly char-grilled meat" is the highlight at this small and "efficient" Turkish outfit, near West Kensington tube. / midnight; no Amex.

Bevis Marks EC3 £47 ❸❶❸
4 Heneage Ln   7283 2220   9–2D
"Still the best kosher restaurant in London" – this "unique" ("lean-to") annex, joined to an ancient City synagogue, offers very "decent" cuisine in a "calming" and "sophisticated" setting. / www.bevismarkstherestaurant.com; 8 pm; closed Fri D, Sat & Sun.

Beyoglu NW3 £24 ❸❷④
72 Belsize Ln   7435 7733   8–2A
"A warm welcome" and "tasty, reasonably-priced" nosh win consistent praise for this "cheerful" Belsize Park Turkish local. / www.beyogulu.co.uk; 11 pm; no Amex.

Bibendum SW3 £67 ④❸❷
81 Fulham Rd   7581 5817   5–2C
"The most splendid setting, especially on a sunny lunchtime" – plus "one of the best wine lists in town" – makes the airy first-floor dining room of this "heart-of-Chelsea" landmark a firm favourite for many reporters; the food is "nothing exceptional" though, and "very expensive" for what it is. / www.bibendum.co.uk; Mon-Fri 11 pm, Sat 11.30 pm, Sun 10.30 pm; booking: max 12.

Bibendum Oyster Bar SW3 £38 ❸❸❸
Michelin Hs, Fulham Rd   7589 1480   5–2C
"Great shellfish platters" and "excellent chablis" are the sort of epicurean delights that commend this "civilised" fixture to well-heeled Chelsea types, for whom it remains "a good stand-by for a quick lunch or dinner". / www.bibendum.co.uk; 10.30 pm.

Big Easy SW3 £45 ④④❸
332-334 King's Rd   7352 4071   5–3C
This "really American" and "loud" Chelsea "crabshack" is "still packed" with fans of its "steak 'n' seafood combos" (and of its "fun and lively bands"); a crash in the ratings, though, confirms it's "gone downhill" of late. / www.bigeasy.uk.com; 11.30 pm, Fri & Sat 12.30 am.

Bincho Yakitori
Oxo Tower SE1 NEW £31 ❷❷❷
2nd Floor, Barge House St   7803 0858   9–3A
Adjoining Tamesa@Oxo, this second-floor South Bank yakitori (Japanese skewer) parlour opened in mid-2007; a visit here offers a rare combination of interesting food, friendly service and a view – and all at reasonable prices! / Rated on Editors' visit; www.bincho.co.uk; 11.30 pm.

Bistro 1 £20 ④❷❸
27 Frith St, W1   7734 6204   4–3A
75 Beak St, W1   7287 1840   3–2D
33 Southampton St, WC2   7379 7585   4–3D
"The food's not Cordon Bleu", but "it's amazing to find somewhere as cheap and as good" as this "serviceable" Mediterranean chain, whose "staff are so friendly, you can't help but love them!" / www.bistro1.co.uk; 11.30 pm.

Bistro Aix N8 £40 ❸❸❷
54 Topsfield Pde, Tottenham Ln   8340 6346   8–1C
It's "a triumph", say north London fans of this "lovely" little Crouch End spot, which serves "consistent" bistro fare (not least "excellent, home-made bread"). / www.bistroaix.co.uk; 11 pm; closed Mon.

Bistrot 190
Gore Hotel SW7 £46 ④⑤④
190 Queen's Gate   7584 6601   5–1B
It's potentially "charming" and has "a fabulous location for the Albert Hall", but this South Kensington brasserie is still getting it wrong – the food "fails to impress", and service can be "so slow". / www.gorehotel.com; 11 pm.

Bistrotheque E2 £41 ④❷❷
23-27 Wadeson St   8983 7900   1–2D
A "brutal, old industrial building", in Bethnal Green, houses this "hip" 'n' "humming" joint, whose attractions include "excellent cocktails in the downstairs bar", a drag cabaret some nights, and a "great brunch"; more generally, though, the "staple" food tends to "average". / www.bistrotheque.com; 10.45 pm; closed weekday L.

Black & Blue £41 ❸❸④
90-92 Wigmore St, W1   7486 1912   3–1A
105 Gloucester Rd, SW7   7244 7666   5–2B
215-217 Kensington Church St, W8   7727 0004   6–2B
205-207 Haverstock Hill, NW3   7443 7744   8–2A
1-2 Rochester Walk, SE1   7357 9922   9–4C
"A good place for serious carnivores" – this "better-than-average chain" offers "flavour-packed burgers" and "delicious" steaks in "understated" surroundings. / www.blackandblue.biz; 11 pm, Fri & Sat 11.30 pm; SW7, W1 & NW3 10.30 pm; no booking.

Blah! Blah! Blah! W12   £25   ❸❸❸
78 Goldhawk Rd   8746 1337   7–1C
This long-established BYO veggie, near Goldhawk Road tube, seems "less Bohemian" and more "grown-up" since a recent facelift; fans say the food is "always creative", but it's not as highly rated as once it was. / www.gonumber.com/2524; 10.30 pm; closed Sun; no credit cards.

Blakes
Blakes Hotel SW7   £101   ④④❶
33 Roland Gdns   7370 6701   5–2B
"For a dinner with romantic promise", fans find this datedly-glamorous South Kensington basement "unbeatable"; the object of your affections better be worth it, though – the food can be "dire", and prices are "unbelievably high". / www.blakeshotel.uk.com; 10.45 pm.

Blandford Street W1   £42   ④④④
5-7 Blandford St   7486 9696   2–1A
After six years in business, this Marylebone venture still only inspires a modest volume of feedback; fans do praise its "interesting" food, but reports overall are mixed, and it's as a business haunt that the place is most tipped. / www.blandford-street.co.uk; 10.30 pm; closed Sat L & Sun.

BLEEDING HEART EC1   £46   ❷❷❷
Bleeding Heart Yd, Greville St   7242 8238   9–2A
It's "bleedin' hard to find", but this "top-class" Holborn "gem" is as mega-popular for business entertaining as it is for "intimate dîners-à-deux"; "top-notch" Gallic food (and a "head-spinning" wine list) are served in an "unusually cosy" (and historic) setting. / www.bleedingheart.co.uk; 10 pm; closed Sat & Sun.

Blue Elephant SW6   £51   ❸❸❶
3-6 Fulham Broadway   7385 6595   5–4A
"Pagodas, bridges, streams, fish and foliage" create a "magical" and "truly stunning" vista at this "jungle-oasis", in deepest Fulham; critics have always found the place "a bit of a theme-park", though, and the once-excellent Thai food has seemed more "incidental" in recent years. / www.blueelephant.com; midnight, Sun 10.30 pm; closed Sat L (except Stamford Bridge match days).

Blue Jade SW1   £29   ❸❶❸
44 Hugh St   7828 0321   2–4B
"It doesn't spring many surprises", but this "staple" Thai, in a Pimlico back street, is "a handy stand-by in a culinary desert", and offers a "warm" welcome. / 11 pm; closed Sat L & Sun.

Blue Lagoon   £32   ④❸❸
23 Haymarket, SW1   7930 7800   4–4A
284 Kensington High St, W14   7603 1231   7–1D
An "OK but unexciting" Thai duo – the better-known branch by far is the one which is convenient for a bite pre/post-Kensington Odeon. / www.blue-lagoon.co.uk; 11.30 pm.

The Blue Pumpkin SW17   £32   ④❸④
16-18 Ritherdon Rd   8767 2660   10–2C
"Extremely reasonable prices" boost the appeal of this "friendly" Tooting bistro (but it can get "noisy"). / www.bluepumpkin.co.uk; 10 pm.

Bluebird SW3 £56 ④❸❷
350 King's Rd 7559 1000 5–3C
*The re-named Conran empire (D&D London) relaunched this huge
Chelsea hangar in mid-2007; pre-revamp, the survey had found
"remarkably indifferent" standards – in the early days of the new
régime, the straightforward British menu was of high quality,
but prices were lofty too.* / Rated on Editors' visit;
www.bluebird-restaurant.co.uk; 10.30 pm.

Bluebird Café SW3 £42 ⑤⑤④
350 King's Rd 7559 1000 5–3C
*Judging by the "terrible" food and the "remarkably disinterested"
service, this Chelsea café would seem to rely solely on the
attractions of its "fantastic" location (and nice outside tables).*
/ *www.bluebird-restaurant.co.uk; 10 pm, Sun 6 pm; no booking.*

Blueprint Café
Design Museum SE1 £48 ④④❸
28 Shad Thames, Butler's Wharf 7378 7031 9–4D
*A "fantastic" first-floor location, overlooking Tower Bridge, is the
special attraction of this D&D London (fka Conran) operation,
on the South Bank; some reporters think the food is "imaginative"
too, but others find it merely "adequate".* / *www.blueprintcafe.co.uk;
10.45 pm; set brunch £30 (FP).*

Bodean's £32 ④④❸
10 Poland St, W1 7287 7575 3–1D
Fulham Broadway, SW6 7610 0440 5–4A
169 Clapham High St, SW4 7622 4248 10–2D
*"If you like Americana", these "authentic" BBQs – with their "wall-
to-wall US sport on TV", and "huge" portions of ribs and "burnt
ends" – are the "real thang"; or, to put it another way, they're
"lard-arse heaven", and "not worth going out of your way for".*
/ *www.bodeansbbq.com; 11 pm.*

La Bodeguita del Medio W8 NEW £38 ④④❸
47 Kensington Ct 7938 4147 5–1A
*A new bar/restaurant in an alleyway off Kensington High Street;
its "credible" Cuban atmosphere and "excellent" cocktails rather
outshine the basic tapas on offer, but at least prices are "fair".*
/ Rated on Editors' visit; *www.bdelmlondon.com; 11 pm.*

Bohème Kitchen & Bar W1 £39 ④④❸
19 Old Compton St 7734 5656 4–2A
*It's the "very buzzy" vibe that stands out at this "trendy" Soho
bar/bistro, next to Café Bohème; the food is "only OK".*
/ *www.bohemekitchen.co.uk; midnight, Sun 10.30 pm.*

Boiled Egg & Soldiers SW11 £22 ❸④④
63 Northcote Rd 7223 4894 10–2C
*The "posh fry-ups" at this "manic" café have legendary status,
down Nappy Valley way, as "a great hangover cure" ("if you can
fight your way past the baby buggies", that is); service, though,
is sometimes "terrible".* / 6.30 pm, Sun 4 pm; L & afternoon tea only;
no Mastercard or Amex; no booking.

Boisdale SW1 £52 ④❸❶

13-15 Eccleston St 7730 6922 2–4B

The "completely non-PC" charms of this perennially "buzzing" Belgravia bar/restaurant (decked out "Scottish hunting lodge" style) win many fans – "serious steaks" are a lead attraction, as is the "wonderful range of whiskies" (plus jazz at the weekends); critics, though, find it "overpriced". / www.boisdale.co.uk; 11.15 pm; closed Sat L & Sun.

Boisdale of Bishopsgate EC2 £48 ④④④

202 Bishopsgate, Swedeland Ct 7283 1763 9–2D

An "extensive" wine list helps make this City offshoot of the Belgravia bar/restaurant a good place for a boozy business lunch; the Scottish-themed food "could be more imaginative", though, and service can be "woeful". / www.boisdale.co.uk; 9.30 pm; closed Sat & Sun.

Bombay Bicycle Club £34 ❸❸❸

128 Holland Park Ave, W11 7727 7335 6–2A
3a Downshire Hill, NW3 7435 3544 8–2A
95 Nightingale Ln, SW12 8673 6217 10–2C

It's the "light and airy" Wandsworth original of this "classy" Indian chain which inspires most feedback (and enthusiasm) – even if the cuisine is "more mainstream" than it used to be, this is "still a popular choice". / www.thebombaybicycleclub.co.uk; 11 pm; D only ex NW3, Sun open L & D.

Bombay Brasserie SW7 £50 ❷❷❷

Courtfield Close, Gloucester Rd 7370 4040 5–2B

Some reporters say it's "tired", but – for its many devotees – this "posh" Indian "old-favourite", by Gloucester Road tube, is still "a total winner", with "tasty" food and a "loud" and "jolly" atmosphere (especially in the conservatory); "the Sunday buffet is a must". / www.bombaybrasserielondon.com; 11.30 pm.

Bombay Palace W2 £38 ❶❷④

50 Connaught St 7723 8855 6–1D

It has a "nondescript" setting north of Hyde Park, but this low-profile Indian (part of an international chain) is "one of London's best-kept secrets" – the "extraordinarily good" food "has few rivals in town", and service is extremely "pleasant and professional". / www.bombay-palace.co.uk; 11.30 pm.

Bonds
Threadneedles Hotel EC2 £52 ④❸❸

5 Threadneedle St 7657 8088 9–2C

This "spacious" and "sophisticated" former banking hall is often hailed as "one of the better City business lunch options"; in recent times, it's been a "very expensive" destination where "nothing stands out", but a new chef aims to raise its game. / 10 pm; closed Sat & Sun; set always available £28 (FP).

Il Bordello E1 £39 ❷❶❷

75-81 Wapping High St 7481 9950 11–1A

"Supersize me!", say fans of the "pizzas-like-bicycle-wheels", and other "hearty" fare, offered by this "ever-popular" Wapping Italian; you may have to sit "elbow-to-elbow" with other guests, but service is "outstanding". / 11 pm; closed Sat L.

La Bouchée SW7 £42 ❷❸❶

56 Old Brompton Rd   7589 1929   5–2B
*Offering "splendid" food at "good-value" prices, this "dark" and
"characterful" South Kensington bistro has a candlelit interior which
manages to "feel just like Paris"; "don't go if you're claustrophobic",
though.* / www.boudinblanc.co.uk; 11 pm.

Le Bouchon Bordelais SW11 £44 ④④❸

5-9 Battersea Rise   7738 0307   10–2C
*"Superb Chateaubriand" is the menu highlight at this veteran
Battersea bistro; despite Michel Roux's involvement, though,
feedback is very uneven, and some visits here are "a let-down".*
/ 11 pm.

Boudin Blanc W1 £47 ❸❸❷

5 Trebeck St   7499 3292   3–4B
*This "cosy", rustic-style bistro – "tucked-away" in Shepherd Market
– is a "jewel", and "always busy"; service, though, can sometimes
be "a bit too authentically French".* / www.boudinblanc.co.uk; 11 pm.

Boulevard WC2 £37 ④④❸

40 Wellington St   7240 2992   4–3D
*On most accounts, this "unpromising-looking" brasserie is "worth
knowing about" for a "cheap and cheerful" meal in Covent Garden
(and, for a lighter bite, there's a handy adjoining deli too); there are
critics, though, who just find it "pointless".*
/ www.boulevardbrasserie.co.uk; midnight.

Boulevard Bar & Dining Room W1 £39 ❸④❸

55-59 Old Compton St   7287 0770   4–3A
*This year-old offshoot of the well-established Covent Garden
brasserie has yet to take Soho by storm, but is a "good-value"
stand-by, and makes "a great place to chill for a weekend brunch".*
/ www.boulevardsoho.com; midnight; booking essential; set dinner £19 (FP).

Bowler Bar & Grill SW3 〖NEW〗 £39 ❸❷❸

2a Pond Pl   7589 5876   5–2C
*As judged by the vast number of former occupants (most recently
Iniga, RIP), this Chelsea basement is one of the trickiest sites
in town; our early-days visit to its friendly new steakhouse formula,
inspired some hope that the jinx might finally be shaken off!* / Rated
on Editors' visit; www.bowlerbarandgrill.co.uk; midnight, Sat 1 am; closed
Mon L & Sat L.

Boxwood Café
The Berkeley SW1 £57 ④❸❸

Wilton Pl   7235 1010   5–1D
*A "rather up-and-down" Ramsay experience, in a Belgravia
basement – as this guide went to press, it emerged that it may
close, at least temporarily, in early 2008.* / www.gordonramsay.com;
11 pm; booking: max 8.

The Brackenbury W6 £38 ❸❸❸

129-131 Brackenbury Rd   8748 0107   7–1C
*This "textbook local" – in a quiet Hammersmith back street –
is strongly tipped for its "intimate" style, its "inventive" cooking,
and its "nice outside tables for the summer"; this year, however,
it has sometimes seemed "uninspired".* / 11 pm; closed Sun D.

Bradley's NW3 £43 ❸❷④
25 Winchester Rd 7722 3457 8–2A
A Swiss Cottage local which fans say is "recovering from a few dips in recent years"; at its best, it offers "lovely" food in a "sophisticated" (if sometimes rather quiet) setting. / 11 pm; closed Mon & Sun D; set weekday L £27 (FP).

Brady's SW18 £25 ❷❸❸
513 Old York Rd 8877 9599 10–2B
"Old-fashioned fish 'n' chips are done beautifully" (or you can opt for fish "grilled, with a salad"), at the Brady family's "simple" and "unchanging" Wandsworth "chippy-cum-restaurant". / 10.30 pm; closed Mon L & Sun; no Amex; no booking.

La Brasserie SW3 £43 ④④❸
272 Brompton Rd 7581 3089 5–2C
"The food is secondary to the ambience", at this "very French" hang-out, by Brompton Cross, where "the crowd makes for great people-watching"; it's as a weekend brunch spot that it really comes into its own. / www.labrasserielondon.co.uk; 11 pm; no booking, Sat L & Sun L.

Brasserie Pierre EC2 NEW £40 ④❷❸
33 Broadgate Circle 7628 1592 9–2D
Recently relaunched under unchanged (French) ownership, this City bar/brasserie (formerly called Les Coulisses) can make a "convenient" location for a quick "fill-up"; for anything more ambitious though, the level of je-ne-sais-quoi doesn't justify the prices. / Rated on Editors' visit; www.brasseriepierre.com; 8.30 pm; closed Sat & Sun.

Brasserie Roux
Sofitel St James SW1 £50 ❸❸❸
8 Pall Mall 7968 2900 2–3C
"Easily accessible", near Trafalgar Square, this "comfortable" brasserie offers "quality cooking at reasonable prices", in a "spacious" setting; "very good pre-theatre", it also makes an "excellent venue for business lunches". / www.sofitelhotelstjames.com; 11.30 pm.

Brasserie St Quentin SW3 £43 ④❸❸
243 Brompton Rd 7589 8005 5–2C
It doesn't help that it lies "in the shadow of Racine" (a near-neighbour), but there's still a sense of drift in reports on this "civilised" Knightsbridge veteran; for many (more mature) reporters, though, it remains a "reliable" stand-by (especially for the "good-value set lunch"). / www.brasseriestquentin.co.uk; 10.30 pm.

Bread & Roses SW4 £25 ④④❸
68 Clapham Manor St 7498 1779 10–1D
A "fantastic beer garden" (and, for parents, a "child-friendly" approach) makes this "Clapham stand-by" a destination that's "especially good for Sunday lunch in warm weather"; "shame about the food", though. / 11 pm, Fri & Sat midnight; no Amex; no booking.

Brew Wharf SE1 £38 ❸④④
Brew Wharf Yd, 1 Stoney St 7378 6601 9–4C
A beerhall-brasserie, interestingly housed in railway arches on the South Bank; it can be "noisy", and service "can be indifferent", but the simple food is "usually good". / www.brewwharf.com; 9.30 pm.

Brian Turner
Millennium Hotel W1   £63   ⑤④⑤
44 Grosvenor Sq   7596 3444   3–2A
Brian should stick to his TV shows, if the current "awful"
performance of this Mayfair dining room is anything to go by –
the food is "nothing special", and the setting is "dull" and "clinical".
/ 10.30 pm; closed Sat L & Sun.

Brick Lane Beigel Bake E1   £5   ❷④⑤
159 Brick Ln   7729 0616   1–2D
"The best beigels in town" – "they're so cheap and so good" –
guarantee queues into the wee hours at this "dingy" 24/7 East End
institution. / no last orders (open 24 hours); no credit cards; no booking.

The Bridge SW13   £37   ❸④④
204 Castelnau   8563 9811   7–2C
A "good gastropub", to the south of Hammersmith Bridge;
it generally pleases the locals, not least with its "great garden".
/ midnight.

Brilliant UB2   £32   ❷④④
72-76 Western Rd   8574 1928   1–3A
"Excellent Indian cooking" maintains the reputation of this large
Punjabi veteran, in deepest Southall. / www.brilliantrestaurant.com;
11.30 pm, Fri & Sat midnight; closed Mon, Sat L & Sun L; booking:
weekends only.

Brinkley's SW10   £42   ④④❷
47 Hollywood Rd   7351 1683   5–3B
"Awesome wine value" helps draw "a good Chelsea crowd"
("no tourists!") to John Brinkley's "ever-popular restaurant and wine
bar"; well, it can't be the food… / www.brinkleys.com; 11 pm; closed
weekday L.

Britannia W8   £38   ④④❸
1 Allen St   7937 6905   5–1A
"All very well, but do we really need another gastropub like this?" –
though handily-located (just off Kensington High Street), the year-
old reincarnation of this attractive pub "must try harder".
/ www.britanniakensington.co.uk; 11 pm.

La Brocca NW6   £30   ④❸❷
273 West End Ln   7433 1989   1–1B
An "always-packed" West Hampstead basement, long a "friendly"
fixture, offering "reasonably-priced" pizza and pasta; even some
locals, though, feel the food is "distinctly average".
/ www.labrocca.co.uk; Sun-Thu 11 pm, Fri & Sat 11.30 pm; booking: max 8.

Brompton Quarter Café SW3 NEW   £48   ⑤⑤④
223-225 Brompton Rd   7225 2107   5–2C
It does have fans – especially for breakfast or brunch – but this
"cleverly"-designed Knightsbridge café "hasn't got its act together",
and some reporters dismiss it as "ghastly and overpriced".
/ www.bromptonquartercafe.com; 10.30 pm.

The Brown Dog SW13 NEW   £35   ❸④❸
28 Cross St   8392 2200   10–1A
This cute backstreet pub – "in Barnes's 'Little Chelsea'" –
has undergone "an atmospheric renovation"; its food
is "imaginative, and of some quality", but service doesn't always
measure up. / 10 pm.

(The Grill)
Brown's Hotel W1 £68 ④❷④
Albemarle St 7493 6020 3–3C
With its "quiet and spacious" setting and its "traditional British" menu, this "club-like" Mayfair dining room is perfect "for great aunts and important business deals"; the atmosphere "lacks sparkle", though, as does the food. / www.roccofortehotels.com; 10.30 pm; no booking at weekends.

Browns £36 ⑤⑤④
47 Maddox St, W1 7491 4565 3–2C
82-84 St Martin's Ln, WC2 7497 5050 4–3B
Islington Grn, N1 7226 2555 8–3D
Butler's Wharf, SE1 7378 1700 9–4D
Hertsmere Rd, E14 7987 9777 11–1C
8 Old Jewry, EC2 7606 6677 9–2C
This English bar/brasserie chain does have its fans, but the food tends to "dull", and it's sometimes just "pure and utter rubbish". / www.browns-restaurants.com; 10 pm-11 pm; WC2 Wed-Sat midnight; EC2 closed Sat & Sun; W1 L only.

Brula TW1 £38 ❷0❷
43 Crown Rd 8892 0602 1–4A
A "cosy interior" – "like someone's front room" – and "polite" and "attentive" staff set the scene at this "charming St Margarets bistro", where "straightforward" Gallic fare comes at "good-value" prices. / www.brula.co.uk; 10.30 pm.

Brumus
Haymarket Hotel SW1 NEW £52 ④❷⑤
1 Suffolk Pl, Haymarket 7470 4000 2–2C
A new, upmarket Italian dining room – part of a trendy (Firmdale) hotel – in the heart of the touristy West End; the food is OK, but prices are so high, and the ambience so lacking, it's hard to see why anyone would bother. / Rated on Editors' visit; www.brumus.com; 11 pm.

Brunello
Baglioni Hotel SW7 £75 ④❸❸
60 Hyde Park Gate 7368 5700 5–1B
It's the "really decadent" ambience (and, perhaps, the wine list) which makes this Kensington design-hotel dining room of note – the Italian cooking is "good, but in no way as good as the price level suggests". / www.baglionihotellondon.com; 10.45 pm; set pre theatre £48 (FP).

Buchan's SW11 £40 ❸❸❷
62-64 Battersea Bridge Rd 7228 0888 5–4C
"Almost like a club"; this long-established Scottish-themed wine bar in Battersea remains – for its 'members' – a "reliable" stand-by, even if the cooking can be "hit-and-miss". / www.buchansrestaurant.co.uk; 10.45 pm.

The Builder's Arms SW3 £34 ❸④❷
13 Britten St 7349 9040 5–2C
"A good atmosphere, time and time again" underpins the popularity of this Chelsea backstreet gastro-boozer; the food is "nothing earth-shattering", but of "consistent quality". / www.geronimo-inns.co.uk; 10 pm, Sun 6pm; no Amex; no booking.

The Bull N6   **£44**   ④❸④
13 North Hill   0845 456 5033   1–1C
*"Ridiculous" prices feature in far too much of the feedback on this
year-old Highgate gastropub – a shame, as more upbeat reports
suggest it's potentially a "genuinely great" all-rounder.*
/ www.inthebull.biz; 10.30 pm; closed Mon L.

Bumpkin W11 NEW   **£46**   ④④❸
209 Westbourne Park Rd   7243 9818   6–1B
*It's quickly won a "huge following", but this "rustic" Notting Hill
pub-conversion (ground floor brasserie/first-floor restaurant) divides
opinion – to fans, it's a "groovy" hang-out offering "good", "staple"
British fare, but critics just find it "pretentious" and
"way overpriced". / www.bumpkinuk.com; midnight, Sun 10.30 pm.*

Buona Sera   **£30**   ④❸❷
289a King's Rd, SW3   7352 8827   5–3C
22 Northcote Rd, SW11   7228 9925   10–2C
*With its "unique" double-decker seating, the "fun" Chelsea branch
of this Italian duo is very different from the "buzzy" Clapham
original ("a brilliant spot for young families"); both offer "decent"
and "cheap" pizza and pasta (though standards are "not quite
what they were"). / midnight; SW3 closed Mon.*

Busaba Eathai   **£27**   ❷❸❷
106-110 Wardour St, W1   7255 8686   3–2D
8-13 Bird St, W1   7518 8080   3–1A
22 Store St, WC1   7299 7900   2–1C
*"Much better than Wagamama" – Alan Yau's "inviting",
communal-seating cafés offer a "fantastic-value" formula
of "cheap" and "punchy" Thai dishes, served in a "classy", dark-
wood setting; the Soho branch is "always crowded (expect
to queue)". / 11 pm, Fri & Sat 11.30 pm, Sun 10 pm; W1 no booking;
WC1 need 12+ to book .*

Bush Bar & Grill W12   **£35**   ⑤④④
45a Goldhawk Rd   8746 2111   7–1C
*"Stuck down an alley off a scruffy bit of road", this "barn-like"
Shepherd's Bush hang-out is arguably the "best of a bad bunch
locally"; it offers "excellent cocktails" (which fuel "the Beeb scene
at the bar"), but the food is "lazy". / www.bushbar.co.uk; 11 pm; closed
Sun D.*

Bush Garden Café W12   **£14**   ❸④❷
59 Goldhawk Rd   8743 6372   7–1C
*A "dream" of a café, by Goldhawk Road tube, offering "great"
(largely organic) snacks, a "laid-back" ambience and a "lovely"
garden ("especially with kids"); service, though, can be "painfully
slow". / 6 pm; L only.*

Butcher & Grill SW11   **£39**   ④④⑤
39 Parkgate Rd   7924 3999   5–4C
*This "cold" Battersea yearling (a mix of brasserie and butcher's
shop) seems to draw inspiration from the Harvey Nics empire
where its backers first met – perhaps it's no coincidence that,
just like most HN properties (such as Oxo Tower), it too often
seems "overpriced" or "disappointing". / www.thebutcherandgrill.com;
11 pm; closed Sun D.*

Butcher's Hook SW6 £36 ❸❸❸
477 Fulham Rd 7385 4654 5–4A
Fans of this Fulham gastropub near Stamford Bridge hail it as a "superb all-rounder", with "interesting", "seasonal" food and "friendly" staff; others, though, "having read good reviews, found it generally disappointing". / www.thebutchershook.co.uk; 10.30 pm; no Amex.

Butlers Wharf Chop House SE1 £52 ④④④
36e Shad Thames 7403 3403 9–4D
One of the weaker D&D (fka Conran) operations – this plainly-furnished South Bank river-sider – with its "Manuel-ish" service and its "pretty average" food – too often seems "overpriced"; the view of Tower Bridge, though, is "amazing". / www.chophouse.co.uk; 10 pm.

La Buvette TW9 £37 ❸❸❷
6 Church Walk 8940 6264 1–4A
This "friendly French bistro", by a churchyard, makes a "quiet retreat from the bustle of Richmond High Street"; it's an offshoot of Brula, and most reporters reckon it a "delightful" destination (especially when you can sit outside). / www.brula.co.uk; 10.30 pm.

C Garden SW3 NEW £44 ❸⓪❸
119 Sydney St 7352 2718 5–3C
"The garden is unbeatable in summer", say fans of this "friendly" new Italian (on the venerable Chelsea site that was long Dan's, RIP); there's the odd "dreadful" report, but we had an enjoyable meal here, and most of the (few) initial reports are upbeat. / www.cgarden.co.uk; 11 pm; closed Sun D.

C&R Cafe W1 £27 ❷④④
3-4 Rupert Ct 7434 1128 4–3A
"In a bit of town not exactly short on good, quick Asian eats", this "basic" diner – in a Chinatown alley – "stands out" for its "tastes straight from Malaysia" (at "cheap" prices). / 11 pm.

The Cabin SW6 £38 ❸❷❷
125 Dawes Rd 7385 8936 10–1B
"Amazing burgers" and "great steaks" win local raves for this "cheap and cheerful" yearling, in deepest Fulham. / www.thecabinbarandgrill.co.uk; 10.30 pm; D only, ex Sun open L & D.

Cactus Blue SW3 £37 ⑤⑤④
86 Fulham Rd 7823 7858 5–2C
"What a waste of a good margarita!"; this Chelsea Tex/Mex scores well as a "buzzing, funky bar" – as a restaurant, however, "it's disappointing from beginning to end". / www.cactusblue.co.uk; 11 pm; D only.

Café 209 SW6 £20 ❸❷⓪
209 Munster Rd 7385 3625 10–1B
Joy, the owner, is "a brilliant comedy act in her own right", and helps ensure a visit to this "buzzy" BYO Fulham Thai is "a complete laugh"; for the money, "the food is pretty good too". / 10.30 pm; D only, closed Sun, closed Dec; no credit cards.

Le Café Anglais
Whiteley's W2 NEW £40

151 Queensway   awaiting tel   6–1C

Those of us who've wondered if Rowley Leigh (until recently chef at Kensington Place) hasn't been 'coasting' for years will get the chance to find out when, in the autumn of 2007, he strikes out on his own at this ambitious Gallic newcomer in Bayswater – part of a plan to 'raise the tone' at Whiteleys; price given is our guesstimate.

Café Bohème W1 £39 ④④❷

13 Old Compton St   7734 0623   4–2A

"It won't get a Michelin star", but this "vibrant" heart-of-Soho bar/café/brasserie makes "a good place to kick off a night on the town". / www.cafeboheme.co.uk; 2.45 am, Sun 11.30 pm; booking: max 7.

Café des Amis du Vin WC2 £42 ④❸❸

11-14 Hanover Pl   7379 3444   4–2D

"Ideally located for the ROH", this Covent Garden old-timer is a natural pre- or post-show; the main dining room is "overpriced", though – those in the know head for the "cosy" (and cramped) basement bar, with its "unparalleled cheese" and "amazing wine". / www.cafedesamis.co.uk; 11.30 pm; closed Sun.

Café du Jardin WC2 £42 ④④④

28 Wellington St   7836 8769   4–3D

"As a pre-theatre venue", this "brilliantly-located" Covent Garden corner veteran is a "dependable" and fair-value stand-by; at other times, it becomes more apparent that it's "nothing exciting". / www.lecafedujardin.com; midnight; set weekday L £26 (FP).

Café du Marché EC1 £42 ❷❷❶

22 Charterhouse Sq   7608 1609   9–1B

"Very Frenchly-romantic" – and also "just far enough from the Square Mile to be good for business" – this "secluded" Clerkenwell stalwart is an "excellent all-rounder", offering "top-quality" bourgeois cuisine and "discreet and friendly" service. / www.cafedumarche.co.uk; 10 pm; closed Sat L & Sun; no Amex.

Café Emm W1 £24 ④❷❷

17 Frith St   7437 0723   4–2A

For a "quick, substantial and cheap" bite, this "friendly" and "atmospheric" Soho stand-by "never disappoints". / www.cafeemm.com; 10.30 pm; no Amex; no booking after 6.30 pm.

Café España W1 £25 ❸❷❷

63 Old Compton St   7494 1271   4–3A

"A brilliant Soho atmosphere", "friendly" staff and "good-value" tapas (and other Spanish dishes) combine to make it "hard to get a table" at this "bustling" little café. / 10 pm; no Amex; no booking.

Café in the Crypt
St Martin's in the Fields WC2 £21

Duncannon St   7839 4342   2–2C

This "interesting" crypt beneath St Martin-in-the-Fields will be re-launched when the great Trafalgar Square church re-opens in late-2007; let's hope they revamp the former "school-dinners" cuisine too. / www.stmartin-in-the-fields.org; 7.30 pm, Wed-Sat 11 pm; no Amex; no booking.

Café Japan NW11   £28   ❶❷④
626 Finchley Rd   8455 6854   1–1B
"Nothing beats the sushi", at this "friendly" and "inspired"
(but "scruffy") café opposite Golder's Green station; "it is telling
that most of the menu is in Japanese, and that most of the diners
ARE Japanese". / www.cafejapan.co.uk; 10 pm; closed Mon,
Tue, & Wed L–Fri L; no Amex.

Café Laville W2   £38   ④④❷
453 Edgware Rd   7706 2620   8–4A
"Perched over the canal", and with "splendid views of Little Venice",
this small café has an "unbeatable" location "for brunch, light lunch
or afternoon tea"; food and service, though, are "average".
/ www.cafe-laville.co.uk; 11 pm; no Amex.

Café Lazeez W1   £32   ❸④❸
21 Dean St   7434 9393   4–2A
Only the Soho branch of this once notably "original" Indian chain
now survives – a shame, as most reports still say the food
is "consistently good". / www.cafelazeez.com; 11.45 pm, Fri & Sat
1.30 am.

Café Med NW8   £36   ④④④
21 Loudon Rd   7625 1222   8–3A
"What a terrace!"; it's only the al fresco dining possibilities, though,
which make this "pub-style" St John's Wood operation (now the sole
remnant of the former chain) of any note. / 11 pm; booking essential.

Café Pacifico WC2   £37   ④④❸
5 Langley St   7379 7728   4–2C
"Huge jugs of margaritas in the bar" help "pass the time" while
you wait for a table at this "loud" and "over-crowded" Covent
Garden Tex/Mex; the food "isn't that authentic", though, and the
service can be "poor". / 11.45 pm.

Café RED NW5 `NEW`   £37   ④❸❸
298 Kentish Town Rd   7482 7300   8–2C
Just north of Kentish Town tube station, this light and bright new
operation makes a pleasant all-day stand-by; on our early-days visit,
baked goods seemed the best bet. / Rated on Editors' visit; 11 pm;
no Amex.

Café Rouge   £30   ⑤⑤④
Branches throughout London
Can new owners – Gordon Ramsay's backers Blackstone – buck up
this "formulaic" French chain?; with its "industrial" fare and this
"very variable" service, it's certainly in crying need of the Kitchen
Nightmares treatment; for "a quick breakfast", though, or with
kids, it can be "just about OK". / www.caferouge.co.uk; 11 pm.

Café Spice Namaste E1   £41   ❷❷❸
16 Prescot St   7488 9242   11–1A
Cyrus Todiwala's "slightly out-of-the-way", east-City Indian
is "as different as you can imagine from the dross in nearby Brick
Lane"; its "friendly" staff deliver "outstanding" and "original"
(going-on "eccentric") dishes in a setting that's "part hippie,
part Salvation Army Hall". / www.cafespice.co.uk; 10.30 pm; closed
Sat L & Sun.

Caffè Caldesi W1 £50 ❸❸❸
118 Marylebone Ln   7935 1144   2–1A
The "imaginative, light Tuscan lunch menu" (served in the bar) gets
top billing at this Marylebone bistro-offshoot of Caldesi; at other
times, it makes a "reliable" enough destination, but can seem
a little "overpriced". / www.caldesi.com; 10.30 pm; closed Sun.

Caffè Nero £12 ❹❸❸
Branches throughout London
"Hot, strong and delicious" coffee – "the closest the chains get
to an Italian brew" – helps win these popular cafés many fans;
devotees say they "beat Starbucks hands down" (but the survey
overall puts them ahead only by a whisker). / 7 pm-11 pm,
City branches earlier; most City branches closed all or part of weekend;
no credit cards; no booking.

Caffè Vergnano £8 ❸❷❷
62 Charing Cross Rd, WC2   8922 6308   4–3B
Royal Festival Hall, SE1   7921 9339   2–3D NEW
"The best coffee" – "like black gold in a cup" – is the key selling
point of this unpretentious Theatreland coffee shop (which now has
a branch near the Festival Hall); "great strudel too".

La Cage Imaginaire NW3 £34 ❸❷❶
16 Flask Walk   7794 6674   8–1A
The "lovely" setting of this "cosy" Hampstead spot is straight out
of a picture-book; the food may be "a blast from the past", but it's
"amazingly well-priced". / 11 pm; set weekday L £20 (FP).

Caldesi W1 £52 ❸❹❹
15-17 Marylebone Ln   7935 9226   3–1A
For "solid" Tuscan fare (including "perfect pasta"), many reporters
rave about this "cosy" and "cramped" Italian veteran, near the
Wigmore Hall; "it's difficult to see why prices are so high", though,
and the "upfront" service can sometimes hit the wrong note.
/ www.caldesi.com; 11 pm; closed Sat L & Sun.

Cambio de Tercio SW5 £48 ❷❷❷
163 Old Brompton Rd   7244 8970   5–2B
For "a great take on modern Spanish food" – "made even better
by now offering smaller dishes" – it's hard to beat this "terribly
noisy" Earl's Court spot; its wine list is "better than many in Spain!"
/ 11.30 pm.

Camden Bar & Kitchen NW1 NEW £30 ❹❸❸
102 Camden High St   7485 2744   8–3C
This comfortably Bohemian newcomer, quietly located away from
the markets, comes into its own for a burger, or for brunch.
/ 10.30 pm; no Amex.

Camden Brasserie NW1 £39 ❹❹❺
9-11 Jamestown Rd   7482 2114   8–3B
"Does it have bad feng shui?" – this local institution seems ever
more "vibeless" in its 'new' modern site (to which it shifted three
years ago), and often just seems "uninspiring" nowadays.
/ www.camdenbrasserie.co.uk; 11 pm.

Camerino W1 £54 ④④⑤
16 Percy St 7637 9900 2–1C
It once showed a lot of promise, but this potentially "very pleasant" Fitzrovia Italian has "taken its eye off the ball", and its "run-of-the-mill" standards can now make it seem "way overpriced".
/ www.camerinorestaurant.com; 11 pm; closed Sat L & Sun; set always available £30 (FP).

Camino N1 NEW £45 ④❸④
3 Varnishers Yd, Regent Corner 7841 7331 8–3C
We found it utterly characterless, but some press reviewers have been kinder to this summer-2007 newcomer – an Hispanic bar/restaurant, near King's Cross station. / Rated on Editors' visit; www.barcamino.com; Mon-Wed midnight, Thu-Sat 1 am; closed Sun.

Canteen £33 ④❸❸
Royal Festival Hall, SE1 0845 686 1122 2–3D NEW
Crispin Pl, Old Spitalf'ds Mkt, E1 0845 686 1122 9–1D
The "back-to-basics" ethos of this "trendy" and "buzzing" British-retro diner, in Spitalfields, has made it a smash hit with foodie-luvvies, but its actual achievement is notably "hit-and-miss"; it now has a twin, in the spiritually-perfect setting of the revamped Festival Hall. / E1 11 pm - SE1 11 pm; not weekend L.

Cantina del Ponte SE1 £41 ⑤④④
Butler's Wharf Building, 36c Shad Thames 7403 5403 9–4D
"Great views" are the only undoubted plus at this waterfront pizzeria, near Tower Bridge, which is part of D&D London (fka Conran Restaurants); year in, year-out, its all-round performance is impressively mediocre. / www.cantina.co.uk; 11 pm; set weekday L £26 (FP).

Cantina Italia N1 £32 ❷❷❷
19 Canonbury Ln 7226 9791 8–2D
A "regular-haunt", for some locals – this Islington spot may be "noisy", but it serves "generous" pizza and pasta in "friendly" style. / www.cantinaitalia.co.uk; 11 pm, Fri & Sat 11.30 pm; D only, ex Sun open L & D; no Amex.

Cantina Vinopolis
Vinopolis SE1 £47 ④④④
1 Bank End 7940 8333 9–3C
"Nice wine... shame about food", at the South Bank's wine museum; the dining operation occupies "intriguing" and "cathedral-like" vaults, which are "intriguing" but can seem "lacking in intimacy". / www.cantinavinopolis.com; 10.30 pm; closed Sun D.

Il Cantuccio di Pulcinella SW11 £29 ④❶❸
143 St John's Hill 7924 5588 10–2C
Wandsworth locals are divided over this "very friendly" Italian – fans say it's "reliable" and sometimes "spectacular", but critics say they "won't be rushing back". / www.ilcantucciodipulcinella.co.uk; 11.30 pm; closed Tue L; no Amex.

Cape Town Fish Market W1 NEW £45
5 & 6 Argyll St awaiting tel 3–1C
South African concepts don't always shine under London's grey skies, so it will be interesting to see how this new 'restaurant, sushi bar, fish market', near the Palladium, fares; price given is our guesstimate.

THE CAPITAL RESTAURANT
CAPITAL HOTEL SW3 £82 ❷❷❸
22-24 Basil St 7591 1202 5–1D
Eric Chavot's "faultless" cuisine maintains the first-rank position
of this long-established Knightsbridge hotel dining room (where the
"fantastic" set lunch is particularly worth seeking out); the setting,
though, can seem a trifle "dull". / www.capitalhotel.co.uk; 10 pm;
set weekday L £53 (FP).

LE CAPRICE SW1 £55 ❷❶❶
Arlington Hs, Arlington St 7629 2239 3–4C
"Lower-key than the Ivy, but far classier" – this "slick" '80s
brasserie, behind the Ritz, remains an "all-time favourite" for many
reporters; "take your date here to show them you've got style,
but don't need to show off". / www.caprice-holdings.co.uk; midnight.

Caraffini SW1 £42 ❸❶❷
61-63 Lower Sloane St 7259 0235 5–2D
It's "unbeatable", say fans of this "warm and buzzy" Sloane Square
veteran, which "hits the 'classic Italian' nail right on the head";
if there is a criticism, it's that the cuisine "lacks wow-factor".
/ 11.30 pm; closed Sun.

Caramel SW1 £29 ④❷❸
77 Wilton Rd 7233 8298 2–4B
A "busy, swift and compact" Pimlico spot that gets "choc-full" for
weekend brunch; at other times, it offers quick 'n' simple bites
of "decent quality". / 11 pm; closed Mon D & Sun D.

Caravaggio EC3 £47 ④⑤④
107-112 Leadenhall St 7626 6206 9–2D
"They only get away with it because it's the City" – with its
"indifferent" food and "disappointing" service, this "open-plan"
Italian, near Leadenhall Market, often seems "way overpriced".
/ www.etruscarestaurants.com; 10 pm; closed Sat & Sun.

Caricatura W1 NEW £37 ❸❸❸
33 North Audley St 7629 7070 3–2A
This new Mayfair Italian – from the Dino's catering dynasty –
makes a handy option for a light meal; pizza is the menu
backbone, but salads and so on are also available. / Rated on Editors'
visit; 11.30 pm.

Carluccio's Caffè £28 ④④❸
Branches throughout London
Quality is still "slipping" at this hugely successful Italian deli-café
chain, whose "faux-foodie vibe" is increasingly at odds with the
often "slapdash" standards; "decent coffee", though.
/ www.carluccios.com; 11 pm; no booking weekday L.

Carnevale EC1 £34 ❸❸❸
135 Whitecross St 7250 3452 9–1B
Fans of this very small veggie near the Barbican say its "simple but
good-quality" dishes can still be "rather fabulous"; doubters,
though, put its standards somewhere round "passable" nowadays.
/ www.carnevalerestaurant.co.uk; 11 pm; closed Sat L & Sun; no Amex.

Carpaccio's SW3 £51 ⑤④❷
4 Sydney St   7352 3433   5–2C
A "very buzzy" South Kensington Italian, with something of a name
as "Euro-central"; it has its fans, but also many critics, who find the
the food "unbelievably average" and the prices "extortionate".
/ www.carpaccios.com; 11.30 pm; closed Sun.

Casale Franco N1 £39 ❸❷❸
rear of 134-137 Upper St   7226 8994   8–3D
"Oddly-located" down an Islington alleyway, this well-established
Italian is a "fun" place, with a "buzzing" atmosphere and
"top pizzas". / 11 pm; closed Mon & weekday L; need 6+ to book.

Castello SE16 £26 ❷❸④
192-196 Jamaica Rd   7064 4631   11–2A
This Bermondsey Italian was once one of two to carry the Castello
name (Pizzeria Castello, at Elephant & Castle, having now closed);
its "lovely" pizza and pasta attracts pretty consistent reports, and it
has a "handy" location too ("just two blocks from the tube").
/ 11 pm; closed Mon, Sat L & Sun.

The Castle SW11 £27 ❸④❸
115 Battersea High St   7228 8181   10–1C
"The best burgers" are a highlight of the "good choice" of dishes
on offer at this backstreet Battersea boozer; for the summer,
there's a cute garden. / 10 pm.

Cat & Mutton E8 £37 ④④④
76 Broadway Mkt   7254 5599   1–2D
A "hip and happening" gastroboozer where the "good, simple fare"
is "decent" enough, but – certainly for Hackney – comes "at high-
end prices". / www.catandmutton.co.uk; 10 pm; closed Mon L & Sun D.

Cây Tre EC1 £28 ❸④⑤
301 Old St   7729 8662   9–1B
This "cramped" and "tatty" Shoreditch canteen has a strong
reputation for its "stunning" and "cheap" Vietnamese fare;
on current feedback, the verdict is that "it was once wonderful,
and is still quite good". / www.vietnamesekitchen.co.uk; 11 pm.

Cecconi's W1 £60 ④④❷
5a Burlington Gdns   7434 1500   3–3C
Like all Nick ('Soho House') Jones's joints, it's the "atmosphere,
not the food" which is the mainstay of this "smart" Mayfair
"people-watching den"; it's at its best for a "buzzy" brunch
or lunch – at dinner, the Italian fare can seem "average and
overpriced". / www.cecconis.co.uk; midnight.

Cellar Gascon EC1 £35 ❸❸❸
59 West Smithfield Rd   7796 0600   9–2B
Club Gascon's neighbouring offshoot is likewise known for its
"excellent" tapas, but there were some surprisingly "mediocre"
dishes reported this year; its "unique and entertaining" wine list is,
however, an unfailing attraction. / www.cellargascon.com; midnight; closed
Sat & Sun.

Centrepoint Sushi WC2 £22 ❸❸❸
20-21 St Giles High St   7240 6147   4–1B
"Above a Japanese-Korean grocery store, right by Centre Point",
this "unexpected and authentic" café makes an excellent "cheap
and cheerful" choice; "good sushi" is the highlight, but other dishes
are also available. / www.cpfs.co.uk; 10.30 pm; set weekday L £7 (FP).

Le Cercle SW1 £40 **❶❷❷**
1-5 Wilbraham Pl 7901 9999 5–2D
"Truly exceptional French tapas" and "carefully chosen" wines-by-the-glass "encourage gastronomic adventure" at Club Gascon's Belgravia offshoot; the "ethereal" décor – complete with "intimate booths" – manages to make this a "most unbasement-y" basement. / www.lecercle.co.uk; 11 pm; closed Mon & Sun.

Chakalaka SW15 £35 **❸❸④**
136 Upper Richmond Rd 8789 5696 10–2B
"For homesick Saffas", this East Putney spot offers "enjoyable springbok and kudu steaks" and other "tasty South African specialities"; despite the rather "stilted" décor, the atmosphere is usually "lively" too. / www.chakalakarestaurant.com; 10.45 pm; closed weekday L; set dinner £23 (FP).

Chamberlain's EC3 £58 **❸④④**
23-25 Leadenhall Mkt 7648 8690 9–2D
"Reliable" but "shockingly expensive" – this City fish specialist is "definitely one for the expense account"; the staff – complains one reporter – combine "the worst aspects of Polish, French and English waiters"! / www.chamberlains.org; 9.30 pm; closed Sat & Sun; set dinner £34 (FP).

Chamomile NW3 £21 **❸❷❸**
45 England's Ln 7586 4580 8–2B
"From healthy muesli to an artery-bursting full English" – this "very good neighbourhood café", in Belsize Park, is "a great place for a quick bite", especially at the beginning of the day. / 6 pm; L only; no Amex.

Champor-Champor SE1 £45 **❷❷❶**
62 Weston St 7403 4600 9–4C
"Zany" décor and "exciting" Malay/fusion fare help create "an intriguing and romantic experience" at this "really unusual" and "fun" hide-away, in a Borough backstreet. / www.champor-champor.com; 10.15 pm; closed L, closed Sun; booking: max 12.

The Chancery EC4 £45 **❷❷❸**
9 Cursitor St 7831 4000 9–2A
"An out-of-the-way back alley" provides the site for this "wonderful" Clerkenwell "find" – "a perfect business lunch spot", thanks to its "very high standard of cooking", and "speedy" and "charming" service; "some art on the wall", though, "would not go amiss". / www.thechancery.co.uk; 10.30 pm; closed Sat & Sun.

The Chapel NW1 £32 **④❸❸**
48 Chapel St 7402 9220 6–1D
"Still offering good food", this "unpretentious" early-wave (1995) food-led pub, near Edgware Road tube, continues to please reporters most of the time. / 11 pm.

Chapter Two SE3 £40 **❷❷❸**
43-45 Montpelier Vale 8333 2666 1–4D
"By far the best place in Blackheath" – this "great local" (sibling to Chapter One, in Bromley) offers "well-composed" food, "consistently good" service and a "buzzy" atmosphere. / www.chaptersrestaurants.co.uk; 10.30 pm, Fri-Sat 11 pm.

Le Chardon SE22   £35   ❸❸❸
65 Lordship Ln   8299 1921   1–4D
"Quirky" premises – "a converted Victorian butcher's shop" –
create an "engaging" atmosphere at this East Dulwich fixture;
its "old school" Gallic cooking is "not sophisticated", but "tasty and
hearty". / 11 pm; set weekday L £21 (FP).

Charles Lamb N1   £29   ❸❸❷
16 Elia St   7837 5040   8–3D
This "lively" year-old boozer ("off Islington's main drag") has quickly
won a good local following with its "interesting", "Spanish-
influenced" food. / www.thecharleslambpub.co.uk; 9 pm; closed Mon L,
Tue L & Sun D; no Amex; no booking.

Charlotte's Place W5   £37   ④④④
16 St Matthew's Rd   8567 7541   1–3A
"Tucked-away in a quiet corner of Ealing" (on the Common),
this "romantic"-looking "neighbourhood" spot offers some hope
of "salvation" in a rather thin area; critics, though, say it "doesn't
quite make it on any front". / www.charlottes.co.uk; 10.30 pm; closed
weekday L & Sun D; no Amex.

The Chelsea Brasserie
Sloane Square Hotel SW1 NEW   £43   ④④⑤
7-12 Sloane Sq   7881 5999   5–2D
Some reporters were "impressed" by this Gallic newcomer,
in Sloane Square, but it has inspired sharply mixed views; critics
just find it "awful": "a waste of good real estate in an area that still
needs a high-quality, reasonably-priced brasserie".
/ www.chelsea-brasserie.co.uk; 10.30 pm.

Chelsea Bun Diner SW10   £23   ❸❸④
9a Lamont Rd   7352 3635   5–3B
"Fry-ups to die for" – hangover cures par excellence – are famously
the attraction of this World's End diner, which is always "busy"
(especially at weekends). / www.chelseabunrestaurant.co.uk; midnight,
Sun 10 pm; no Amex; no booking, Sat & Sun.

Cheyne Walk Brasserie SW3   £60   ❸④❸
50 Cheyne Walk   7376 8787   5–3C
"In an idyllic part of Old Chelsea", this "lively" restaurant in a
former pub – featuring a "fantastic" open grill – has been a real
hit; it can seem "very overpriced", though, and "service is definitely
better if you're French". / www.cheynewalkbrasserie.com; 10.30 pm; closed
Mon L & Sun D; booking essential; set always available £31 (FP).

CHEZ BRUCE SW17   £56   ❶❶❷
2 Bellevue Rd   8672 0114   10–2C
"It's a true local with no airs and graces", but Bruce Poole's
"peerless" venture, by Wandsworth Common, is again voted
Londoners' favourite, thanks to its "superlative" food (this year,
the best-rated in the capital bar none), its "unrivalled" wine and its
"awesome" service; can an expansion in early-2008 make it even
better? / www.chezbruce.co.uk; 10.30 pm; booking: max 6 at D.

Chez Gérard   £40   ⑤④④
Thistle Hotel, 101 Buck' Palace Rd, SW1   7868 6249   2–4B
31 Dover St, W1   7499 8171   3–3C
8 Charlotte St, W1   7636 4975   2–1C
119 Chancery Ln, WC2   7405 0290   2–2D
45 Opera Ter, Covent Garden, WC2   7379 0666   4–3D

Chez Gérard (Cont)

9 Belvedere Rd, SE1   7202 8470   2–3D
64 Bishopsgate, EC2   7588 1200   9–2D
14 Trinity Sq, EC3   7480 5500   9–3D
1 Watling St, EC4   7213 0540   9–2B

This "disappointing" steak-frites chain isn't a patch on what it once
was, but still has fans "for an informal business lunch"; the new
'Brasserie Chez Gérard' formula offers a different menu, and a
modicum of hope. / 10 pm-11.30 pm; City branches closed all or part
of weekend.

Chez Kristof W6   £45   ❸❸❸

111-115 Hammersmith Grove   8741 1177   7–1C

"Off the beaten track", in a Hammersmith backwater, this "stylish"
neighbourhood "favourite" draws fans from far and wide with its
"buzzy" vibe (and its large summer terrace); the Gallic cuisine
is "good, but perhaps a little expensive for what you get"
(and some tables are "a bit too cosy"). / www.chezkristof.co.uk;
11.15 pm, Sun 10 pm; set weekday L £28 (FP).

Chez Liline N4   £41   ❶❸⑤

101 Stroud Green Rd   7263 6550   8–1D

Its location is "not the most stylish", and the exterior "may not fill
you with confidence" (nor the "bleak" interior, come to that),
but this "surprising" Finsbury Park veteran is still well worth truffling
out for its "ridiculously fresh" and "excitingly-spiced" Mauritian fish
cooking. / 11 pm; closed Sun L.

Chez Lindsay TW10   £37   ❸❸❸

11 Hill Rise   8948 7473   1–4A

"Brilliant galettes" and "excellent" cider help lend an "authentic"
Breton ambience to this "pleasant" spot – a "neighbourhood
crêperie", with a "lovely location" near Richmond Bridge. / 11 pm;
no Amex.

Chez Marcelle W14   £25   ❶④④

34 Blythe Rd   7603 3241   7–1D

Marcelle is "cook, greeter, hostess, and friend", at this "anomalous"
Lebanese institution, in Olympia, which "doesn't seem to be run
on commercial grounds"; a recent revamp has left the infamously
"drab" décor more "welcoming". / 10 pm; closed Mon, Tue-Thu D only;
no credit cards.

Chez Patrick W8 NEW   £39   ④❸④

7 Stratford Rd   7937 6388   5–2A

This "bright" French fish place – "quietly-located" in Kensington –
is "much the same" as when the site was called Stratford's (RIP);
regulars debate whether Patrick (Lou Pescadou's former manager)
has improved it or not – overall, it's "pleasant all-round" (or, if you
prefer, "not particularly amazing"). / www.chezpatirickinlondon.co.uk;
11 pm; set weekday L £22 (FP).

Chi Noodle & Wine Bar EC4   £22   ❸❷❷

5 New Bridge St   7353 2409   9–2A

A "tucked-away" pan-Asian spot, near Ludgate Circus, that's
"a major cut above the Wagamamas of the world".
/ www.chinoodle.com; 10.30 pm; closed Sat & Sun.

Chiang Mai W1 — £30 ❷④④
48 Frith St   7437 7444   4–2A

A Soho veteran where the story – "spicy" north Thai cooking, "let down by the décor" – is just the same as ever. / 11 pm; closed Sun L; set pre theatre £19 (FP).

Chimes SW1 — £29 ④④④
26 Churton St   7821 7456   2–4B

"Not a bad bolt hole" – this "friendly" Pimlico stalwart offers a "cheap" and "simple" formula focussed on "filling traditional pies and cider". / www.chimes-of-pimlico.co.uk; 10.15 pm.

China Tang
Dorchester Hotel W1 — £75 ⑤④④
53 Park Ln   7629 9988   3–3A

"Are they kidding?" – HK style guru David Tang's "'30s Shanghai"-style basement "promises much", but takes a major beating from reporters for its "dull" food, "cramped" tables, "clunky" service and "scary" prices; "loved the bar", though. / 11.30 pm; set weekday L £21 (FP).

The Chinese Experience W1 — £30 ❸❷④
118-120 Shaftesbury Ave   7437 0377   4–3A

It may get "crowded", but service is "prompt" and "cheerful" at this ever more popular "contemporary"-style canteen, on the fringe of Chinatown; lunchtime dim sum can be "first-class" – evenings are "not as good". / www.chineseexperience.com; 11 pm.

Chisou W1 — £40 ❷❷❸
4 Princes St   7629 3931   3–1C

"Popularity amongst the Japanese community" attests to the "excellent" quality of the sushi and other dishes (particularly seafood) at this "elegantly utilitarian" (and "speedy") café, near Oxford Circus. / www.chisou.co.uk; 10.15 pm; closed Sun; set weekday L £21 (FP).

Chor Bizarre W1 — £42 ❷❸❷
16 Albemarle St   7629 9802   3–3C

"Eclectic" décor sets the scene for some "good food" (and at "sensible prices" too), at this "OTT" Mayfair Indian; it's never won the following it deserves – perhaps a recent refurb' will broaden its appeal. / www.chorbizarre.com; 11.30 pm; closed Sun L.

Chowki W1 — £28 ❸④④
2-3 Denman St   7439 1330   3–2D

"A good, cheap West End stand-by", near Piccadilly Circus; its "interesting" Indian cooking "isn't outstanding, like it used to be", but the place still offers overall "value for money". / www.chowki.com; 11.30 pm.

Choys SW3 — £34 ④❷④
172 King's Rd   7352 9085   5–3C

After over half a century in business, it's no surprise that this Chelsea Chinese seems a bit "dated"; the staff are "lovely", though, and the food is "reliable". / midnight.

Christopher's WC2   £54   ④④④
18 Wellington St   7240 4222   4–3D
*It occupies a "lovely" building, but Christopher Gilmour's "grand"
Covent Garden American is "a very uninspiring use of a potentially
good location", and its surf 'n' turf menu is "outrageously
overpriced"; the "tasty brunch" is the best bet.*
/ www.christophersgrill.com; 11.30 pm; booking: max 12; set dinner £31 (FP).

Chuen Cheng Ku W1   £29   ❸④④
17 Wardour St   7437 1398   4–3A
*"Watch out for the trolleys – the dim sum just keeps coming!" –
at this vast Chinatown landmark; the dishes are arguably better
elsewhere, but the experience here is "busy", "cheap", and "fun".*
/ www.chuenchengku.co.uk; 11.45 pm.

Churchill Arms W8   £17   ❷④❷
119 Kensington Church St   7792 1246   6–2B
*"An old favourite still knocking out top-quality Thai cuisine
at amazing prices" – the "pretty" ("butterfly-themed") rear annex
of this "cluttered" traditional boozer, off Notting Hill Gate,
is "so wildly popular, it's hard to book". / 10 pm; closed Sun D.*

Chutney SW18   £27   ❷❶❷
11 Alma Rd   8870 4588   10–2B
*"A real find" – this recently-revamped Indian is beginning to make
quite a name for itself down Wandsworth way, thanks to its
"very friendly" staff and its "scrumptious" cooking. / 11.30 pm;
D only.*

Chutney Mary SW10   £54   ❷❷❷
535 King's Rd   7351 3113   5–4B
*"Still going strong", this "very pleasant" contemporary Indian
on the Chelsea/Fulham border continues to please most reporters
with its "imaginative" (and "sometimes sublime") cuisine; if you get
a table in the conservatory, it can be quite "romantic" too.*
*/ www.realindianfood.com; 11.15 pm, Sun 10 pm; closed weekday L; booking:
max 12.*

Chutneys NW1   £24   ❸④④
124 Drummond St   7388 0604   8–4C
*Meals which are "always filling and scrummy" maintain the appeal
of this Little India veggie – it's "very good for what you pay"
("particularly the buffet lunches"). / 11 pm; no Amex; need 5+ to book.*

Ciao Bella WC1   £31   ❸❶❶
90 Lamb's Conduit St   7242 4119   2–1D
*There's "always a queue" for entry to this "old-fashioned"
Bloomsbury favourite – a "heaving" place, where "wonderful" staff
serve up "quick, cheap and traditional Italian scoff".*
/ www.ciaobellarestaurant.co.uk; 11.30 pm.

Cibo W14   £41   ❷❷④
3 Russell Gdns   7371 6271   7–1D
*This once-celebrated Italian in an Olympia backstreet goes largely
unnoticed nowadays; fans insist it's "still performing so well",
though, and all of the (few) reports it inspires say the cooking
is "delicious". / www.ciborestaurant.net; 11 pm; closed Sat L & Sun D.*

Cicada EC1 £39 ❷❷❸
132-136 St John St 7608 1550 9–1B
*"Trendy" for longer than is reasonable, Will Ricker's "casual",
"noisy" and "bustling" Clerkenwell bar/diner still offers "interesting"
(and sometimes "amazing") Asian-Fusion fare.*
/ www.rickerrestaurants.com; 11 pm; closed Sat L & Sun.

Cigala WC1 £42 ❹❸❸
54 Lamb's Conduit St 7405 1717 2–1D
*Opinion on this "noisy" Bloomsbury Hispanic is as mixed as ever –
fans find it "fun" and "consistently satisfying", but, for critics,
the cuisine is just "poorly prepared" and "overpriced".*
/ www.cigala.co.uk; 10.45 pm.

Cinnamon Cay SW11 £36 ❹❹❹
87 Lavender Hill 7801 0932 10–1C
*"Inventive fusion food", with "an Aussie twist", wins many fans for
this "buzzing" ("noisy") Battersea spot – sometimes, though,
it "tries so hard to be different" that it ends up just being
"average".* / www.cinnamoncay.co.uk; 10.30 pm; D only, closed Sun.

The Cinnamon Club SW1 £57 ❷❸❷
Old Westminster Library, Great Smith St 7222 2555 2–4C
*"Zingy" cuisine (with much "delicate use of spices") has made this
"elegant" Westminster restaurant – with its "interesting" setting
in a former library – one of London's foremost 'nouvelle Indians';
at lunch, it is a notably "suit-y" destination.* / www.cinnamonclub.com;
10.45 pm; closed Sun; set pre theatre £38 (FP).

Cipriani W1 £70 ⑤⑤④
25 Davies Street 7399 0500 3–2B
*"The best people-watching in town" – a mêlée of "aspiring
supermodels", "oligarchs" and "Eastern European beauties on a
mission" – draws a "vibrant" throng to this Mayfair Venetian; well,
it can't be the "dull" food, the "hilarious" prices, or the too-often-
"contemptuous" service.* / www.cipriani.com; 11.45 pm.

City Café
City Inn Westminster SW1 £38 ❹❷❸
30 John Islip St 7932 4600 2–4C
*"You'd expect it to be clinical and dull", but this "modern" hotel
brasserie is in fact a "comfortable" and "reliable" stand-by – in this
'emerging' area (near Tate Britain), it makes "a good staple for
a business meal".* / www.citycafe.co.uk; 11 pm.

City Miyama EC4 £48 ❷❸⑤
17 Godliman St 7489 1937 9–3B
*"It's not cheap, but you get what you pay for", say fans of this
"hidden-away" City Japanese, where "the best" sushi and
"welcoming" service compensate for the "drab" basement setting.*
/ 9.30 pm; closed Sat D & Sun.

The Clarence SW12 £27 ❸❸❸
90 Balham High Rd 8772 1155 10–2C
*A year-old Balham gastro-boozer, whose "chilled" style and
"good range of decent grub" win a strong-thumbs up from locals.*
/ 10 pm; no Amex.

Clarke's W8 £52 ❷❷❸
124 Kensington Church St   7221 9225   6–2B
*"Memorable" meals using "wonderful, seasonal ingredients" inspire
the usual glowing accounts of Sally Clarke's California-inspired
Kensington "classic"; even fans say you "must sit upstairs", though,
and this year has seen the emergence of a few claims that it has
"has lost its way".* / www.sallyclarke.com; 10 pm; closed Mon D & Sun;
booking: max 14.

The Clerkenwell Dining Room EC1 £48 ❸❸④
69-73 St John St   7253 9000   9–1B
*"For a swift business lunch", in particular, this low-key Farringdon
spot is a pretty safe choice – dishes are generally "well-executed",
and service is "attentive".* / 11 pm; closed Sat L & Sun.

Clifton E1 £20 ❸❷④
1 Whitechapel Rd   7377 5533   9–2D
*"A better sort of Brick Lane eatery" – this Indian fixture is one of a
handful on this famous East End street to stand out, and it makes
a decent fist of most of the items on its "vast menu".*
/ www.cliftonrestaurant.com; midnight, Sat & Sun 1am.

Clos Maggiore WC2 £55 ❸❷❶
33 King St   7379 9696   4–3C
*With its "romantic" conservatory, this "beautiful" – "magical",
even – fixture makes an unexpected "find" amidst the hurly-burly
of Covent Garden; the food is "decent" too, but "totally
overshadowed by the awesome wine list".* / www.closmaggiore.com;
10.30 pm, Sat 11 pm; closed Sat L & Sun.

The Club Bar & Dining W1 £42 ④④④
21 Warwick St   7734 1002   3–2D
*This "loud" new brasserie, off Regent Street, has attracted very
little feedback, perhaps because – in the evening – it's more like
"a bar which happens to do food"; "excellent deals at lunch",
however, may be worth checking out.* / www.theclubbaranddining.co.uk;
11 pm; closed Sat L & Sun.

Club Gascon EC1 £70 ❷❸❸
57 West Smithfield   7796 0600   9–2B
*Still "the place to go for foie gras" – it pops up time and again
in the "intriguing", "tapas-style" Gascon dishes at this foodie
Mecca, near Smithfield Market, and the wines from SW France are
"wonderful", too; "rocketing" prices, however, are a cause
of growing concern.* / www.clubgascon.com; 10 pm; closed Sat L & Sun.

Club Mangia
The Punch Tavern EC4 £20 ❷❷❷
99 Fleet St   7353 6658   9–2A
*The "chilled" approach of this "very friendly" pub is at odds with its
setting in a beautiful old City tavern; at lunch, it serves a "winning
buffet" of "home-cooked" food – there's also an evening menu –
all at "reasonable prices".* / www.punchtavern.com; 11.45 pm; closed
Sat & Sun.

Coach & Horses EC1 £35 ❸❸④
26-28 Ray St   7278 8990   9–1A
*"Good and seasonal British food" has made a name for this
Clerkenwell gastropub, behind the Guardian; one or two reporters,
though, fear it is "resting on its laurels".* / www.thecoachandhorses.com;
10 pm; closed Sat L & Sun D.

Cochonnet W9 £35 ❸④④
I Lauderdale Pde   7289 0393   I–2B
"Excellent thin pizzas" and "other simple fare" win "a good
following" locally for this "busy" and "relaxed" Maida Vale fixture.
/ www.cochonnet.co.uk; 10.30, pizza until close at midnight.

Cock Tavern EC1 £22 ❸❷⑤
Central Markets   7248 2918   9–2A
"Down under Smithfield Market", this odd no-frills basement
boozer is renowned for its "really well-cooked British fare",
in particular its "excellent breakfasts"; NB limited opening hours.
/ 5 pm; closed Sat & Sun.

Cocoon W1 £50 ④④❸
65 Regent St   7494 7600   3–3D
This "Austin Powers-style" operation, on a first-floor site near
Piccadilly Circus, is "a beautiful venue for a cocktail"; if you're
eating, the pan-Asian food isn't bad, it's just that prices are
"outrageous". / www.cocoon-restaurants.com; 11.45 pm; closed Sat L & Sun.

The Collection SW3 £60 ⑤⑤④
264 Brompton Rd   7225 1212   5–2C
Its location couldn't be more fashionable, but this trashy South
Kensington Eurofest is hard to like – it "needs a face lift" (unlike
most of its punters), and the food is "eye-wateringly expensive for
what you get". / www.the-collection.co.uk; 11.30 pm; D only, closed Sun.

La Collina NW1 £34 ❸❸❸
17 Princess Rd   7483 0192   8–3B
"Much-loved in Primrose Hill", this "cramped" yearling is –
on most reports – the "perfect local Italian"; it has a "pretty"
garden too. / 11 pm; Mon-Thu D only, Fri-Sun open L & D; no Amex.

Le Colombier SW3 £47 ❸❷❷
145 Dovehouse St   7351 1155   5–2C
"You don't have to be of a certain age, but it helps", best to enjoy
a visit to this "civilised" and "quintessentially French" bistro on a
quiet Chelsea backstreet; the "classic" fare, though, is arguably
an attraction secondary to those of the "welcoming" service and
the "superlative" terrace. / www.lecolombier-sw3.co.uk; 10.30 pm.

Como Lario SW1 £38 ④❷❷
22 Holbein Pl   7730 2954   5–2D
This "slightly dated" trattoria – with its "crowded, cheerful, happy"
style and "pretty good, standard" fare – is somewhere between
a "perennial favourite" and a "stereotypical" Chelsea Italian.
/ www.comolario.uk.com; 11.30 pm; closed Sun.

Comptoir Gascon EC1 £37 ❶❷❷
61-63 Charterhouse St   7608 0851   9–1A
"Don't take the Eurostar to Paris, take the Circle Line
to Farringdon", say fans of this "genius" spin-off from the swankier
Club Gascon; it serves "outstanding versions of French rustic
classics" and "fantastic" wine – all at "sensible" prices.
/ www.comptoirgascon.com; 10 pm; closed Mon & Sun; booking essential.

(Angela Hartnett)
The Connaught W1   £84

Carlos Pl   7592 1222   3–3B

*In late summer 2007, it was announced that the Ramsay group
and Angela Hartnett, would no longer be involved with this
legendary panelled chamber; it is set to re-open in late-2007, after
a total refurb (and enlargement). /* www.angelahartnett.com; 11 pm;
jacket; booking: max 8; set weekday L £51 (FP).

The Contented Vine SW1   £37   ④④④

17 Sussex St   7834 0044   5–3D

*"In the gastronomic desert of Pimlico", this "hit-and-miss" wine bar
is "OK… as a local stand-by on a rainy day". /* www.contentedvine.com;
10.30 pm.

Il Convivio SW1   £47   ❸0❸

143 Ebury St   7730 4099   2–4A

*This "serene" Belgravia Italian offers an impressive combination
of "good" food, an "exceptional" wine list, an "airy" setting,
and "immaculate" service; even some fans, though, feel it curiously
"lacks wow-factor". /* www.etruscarestaurants.com; 10.45 pm; closed Sun.

Coopers Arms SW3   £38   ❸④❸

87 Flood St   7376 3120   5–3C

*This "off-the-beaten-track" Chelsea pub "couldn't really be called
a gastropub", but it's an agreeable place, serving "tasty" scoff,
and "serves its purpose" well. /* Not yet; 9.30 pm.

Coq d'Argent EC3   £56   ④④❸

1 Poultry   7395 5000   9–2C

*An "unbeatable" 6th-floor location – with "lovely" terraces and
"stunning" views – is the star feature of this D&D London
(fka Conran) operation, by Bank; it's "a predictable and expensive,
if reliable, pit stop for City deal-makers". /* www.coqdargent.co.uk;
10 pm; closed Sat L.

Cork & Bottle WC2   £33   ⑤④❶

44-46 Cranbourn St   7734 7807   4–3B

*Despite its "bonkers" location – next to a sex shop, off Leicester
Square – this "secret" basement wine bar has long offered
"a marvellous escape from the West End crowds"; the dated menu
"is only a sideline" to a wine list that's "one of the best in town".
/* www.donhewitson.com; 11.30 pm; no booking after 6.30 pm.

Costa's Fish Restaurant W8   £21   ❷❷④

18 Hillgate St   7727 4310   6–2B

*On a good day, you still get "brilliant fish 'n' chips" at this venerable
Greek-run chippy, near Notting Hill Gate. /* 10 pm; closed Mon & Sun;
no credit cards.

Costa's Grill W8   £21   ④❸❸

12-14 Hillgate St   7229 3794   6–2B

*"Nothing has changed in 20 years" (more like 50, Eds), at this
Greek "gem", off Notting Hill Gate, where the food may
be "ordinary" but it's very "cheap"; there is a "glorious" courtyard
for warm weather. /* www.costasgrill.com; 10.30 pm; closed Sun (closed
3 weeks in Aug).

Cottons £37 ④⑤❸
55 Chalk Farm Rd, NW1   7485 8388   8–2B
70 Exmouth Mkt, EC1   7833 3332   9–1A
"If you fancy something different", these colourful Caribbean Rhum shacks offer "special" cocktails and a fun vibe; head for the Camden Town original, though – it's less "hit-and-miss" than its Exmouth Market spin-off. / www.cottons-restaurant.co.uk; EC1 11 pm, Fri-Sat 12.45 am; NW1 11 pm; NW1 Mon-Fri L; EC1 Sat D; EC1 no Amex; EC1 no shorts.

The Cow W2 £47 ❸④❷
89 Westbourne Park Rd   7221 0021   6–1B
"Loud, crowded and not for the faint-hearted" – Tom Conran's Bayswater boozer is a "gem" for those seeking "shellfish to die for" and "the best pint of Guinness in town"; prices are notably "above-average", though (as they are in the cosy, "bistro-style" room upstairs). / www.thecowlondon.co.uk; 10.30 pm; no Amex.

Crazy Bear W1 £46 ❷❷❶
26 Whitfield St   7631 0088   2–1C
From its "ultra-cool bar" to its "magical loos", this "funky" Fitzrovia oriental feels simply "amazing", and it's "definitely one for a date"; the Thai food is "unexpectedly good" too, making the place a real "all-round winner". / www.crazybeargroup.co.uk; 10.30 pm; closed Sat L & Sun.

Crazy Homies W2 £31 ❷⑤❷
127 Westbourne Park Rd   7727 6771   6–1B
Tom Conran's "hectic" Notting Hill hang-out is "one of the best Mexicans in London", offering "excellent" grub and "top margaritas too"; on a bad day, though, service can be the "worst ever". / 10.30 pm; closed weekday L; no Amex.

Crescent House W11 NEW £46 ❸④❸
41 Tavistock Cr   7727 9250   6–1B
Opened in mid-2007, this hidden-away Notting Hill pub-conversion boasts a chef with an impressive pedigree; we enjoyed our early-days visit to the pretty upstairs dining room, but the slow service was part of a formula that seemed unduly grand (and expensive) for the setting. / Rated on Editors' visit; www.crescenthouse.uk.com; 11 pm.

Cristini W2 £38 ❸❷❸
28 Sussex Pl   7706 7900   6–1D
A small and cute Italian, which makes a "good-value" Bayswater stand-by – the food is "always surprisingly good". / www.cristini.co.uk; 10.30 pm; closed Mon L & Sat L; no Amex.

Criterion Grill W1 £55 ⑤⑤❷
224 Piccadilly   7930 0488   3–3D
After a brief flirtation with the Frankies format, this "beautiful" neo-Byzantine chamber is now back with the sort of mainly Gallic menu with which the boss (MPW) should be right at home – sadly, however, the food is often "ghastly", and the service is "very variable" too. / 11.30 pm.

Cross Keys SW3 £43 ④④❷
1 Lawrence St   7349 9111   5–3C
For its fans, this "hidden" Chelsea watering hole is "a great all-rounder", offering "simple" food in a "cosy" setting; not all reporters, however, are convinced. / www.thexkeys.co.uk; 10.30 pm.

The Crown & Sceptre W12   £30   ❸❸❷
57 Melina Rd   8746 0060   7–1B
*"Retro" decor and "reliable pub fare" add to the appeal of this
"fun and friendly" boozer, in a Shepherd's Bush backstreet.*
/ www.fullers.co.uk; 9.45 pm.

Cru N1   £42   ④④❷
2-4 Rufus St   7729 5252   9–1D
*"In the middle of Hoxton, but not so trendy you don't dare enter" –
this attractive wine bar pleases most reporters with its "tapas-type"
cuisine.* / www.cru.uk.com; 11 pm; closed Mon.

Crussh   £11   ❷❷④
1 Curzon St, W1   7629 2554   3–3B
BBC Media Village, Wood Ln, W12   8746 7916   6–2A
27 Kensington High St, W8   7376 9786   5–1A
One Canada Sq, E14   7513 0076   11–1C
Unit 21 Jubilee Pl, E14   7519 6427   11–1C
48 Cornhill, EC3   7626 2175   9–2C
6 Farringdon St, EC4   7489 5916   9–2A
*"All the goodness you need during a day in the office" – "fabulous
smoothies", "wholesome soups" and "unusual sandwiches" – is on
offer at this health-conscious chain.* / www.crussh.com; 4.30 pm-7 pm;
some branches closed all or part of weekend; no credit cards.

The Cuckoo Club W1   £75   ⑤⑤④
99-101 Regent St, Victory Hs   7287 4300   3–3D
*You'd have to be cuckoo to seek out this Mayfair supper club for its
food ("awful") or its service ("terrible"); "watching the Eurotrash-
wannabes is interesting", though.* / www.thecuckooclub.com; 10 pm;
D only, closed Sun-Tue.

Cumberland Arms W14   £31   ❸④④
29 North End Rd   7371 6806   7–2D
*"In a notoriously bad area for places to eat", this Olympia pub
is praised by locals for its "relaxed" style, and "man-sized" portions
of "hearty" Mediterranean grub.* / www.thecumberlandarmspub.co.uk;
10.30 pm.

Curve
London Marriott West India Quay E14 £45   ④④⑤
52 Hertsmere Rd   7517 2808   11–1C
*"Shame about the atmosphere" (it's dull and corporate) at this
hotel dining room, overlooking Canary Wharf; there's a "tasty"
menu, though, majoring in "the freshest fish" – "you pick it,
and how you'd like it cooked".* / 10.30 pm.

Cyprus Mangal SW1   £24   ❶❷④
45 Warwick Way   7828 5940   2–4B
*A Pimlico pit stop, where "you walk through the kebab shop to get
to the restaurant at the back" – it serves "enormous portions"
of "explosively fresh" grills, at "unbeatable" prices.* / Sun-Thu
midnight, Fri & Sat 1 am; no Amex.

The Czechoslovak Restaurant NW6 £24   ❸❸④
74 West End Ln   7372 1193   1–1B
*"Good traditional Central European fare at very reasonable prices"
wins fans for this "old-fashioned" West Hampstead émigrés' club,
whose dining area "feels like someone's front room".*
/ www.czechoslovak-restaurant.co.uk; 10 pm; closed Mon; no credit cards.

Da Mario SW7 £35 ❸❷❸
15 Gloucester Rd   7584 9078   5–1B
A "reliable" Italian, which does "good pasta" and "great pizza";
it's handy for the Albert Hall, and "super for the kids" too.
/ www.damario.co.uk; 11.30 pm.

Dalchini SW19 £30 ❸④❸
147 Arthur Rd   8947 5966   10–2B
Reports on Mrs Sarkhel's Wimbledon Park fixture were more mixed
than usual this year; fans say its "interesting", "Hakka/Chinese/
Indian" cooking is "worth a detour" – sceptics that it's "good value,
but otherwise uninspiring". / www.dalchini.co.uk; 10.30 pm, Fri & Sat
11 pm; no Amex.

Dans le Noir EC1 £49 ⑤❶❷
29 Clerkenwell Grn   7253 1100   9–1A
"You'll probably only go once", but this gimmicky Clerkenwell
yearling – where "you eat in the dark, and the staff are blind" –
can still be "a brilliant experience"; the food, though, is somewhere
round the level of "school dinners". / www.danslenoir.com; 9.30 pm;
D only.

Daphne NW1 £29 ❸❷❷
83 Bayham St   7267 7322   8–3C
"Staff making a real effort" add to the "cosy" charm of this family-
run Greek/Cypriot stalwart, in Camden Town; the "reasonably-
priced" menu includes some "delicious" fish specials. / 11.30 pm;
closed Sun; no Amex; set weekday L £18 (FP).

Daphne's SW3 £50 ❸❸❷
110-112 Draycott Ave   7589 4257   5–2C
Fans say it's "still fabulous", but this "charming" and "romantic"
Brompton Cross Italian – once the hottest address in town –
operates more at the "solid stand-by" level nowadays
(and detractors feel it's "trading on its reputation and location").
/ www.daphnes-restaurant.co.uk; 11.30 pm; booking: max 12.

Daquise SW7 £27 ④④❸
20 Thurloe St   7589 6117   5–2C
The "cosy" interior of this "timeless" Polish "relic", by South
Kensington tube, remains "untouched by fashion" – its food is no
great shakes, but at least it's "cheap". / 11 pm; no Amex; set weekday L
£8 (FP).

The Dartmouth Arms SE23 £33 ❸❸❷
7 Dartmouth Rd   8488 3117   1–4D
"In an area gastronomy forgot", this Forest Hill gastropub makes
a "great find", with "high-quality food" and a "pleasant"
atmosphere; prices, though, are "creeping up".
/ www.thedartmoutharms.com; 12.30 am, Sun 10.30 pm.

Daylesford Organics SW1 NEW £35 ④❸❶
44B Pimlico Rd   7881 8060   5–2D
"A welcome addition to Pimlico" – this "luxuriously organic"
("is that an oxymoron?") diner/food store has instantly established
itself as a "stylish" local rendezvous for breakfast, coffee or a light
bite. / www.daylesfordorganic.com; 8 pm, Sun 5 pm.

De Cecco SW6 £35 ④④④
189 New King's Rd 7736 1145 10–1B
This "casual" Parson's Green veteran is something of a
"neighbourhood classic", and it serves "generous portions
of standard Italian food"; it's not, however, quite the buzzy
destination it once was. / www.dececcorestaurant.com; 11 pm; closed
Sun D.

Deep SW6 £50 ❷❸❸
The Boulevard, Imperial Wharf 7736 3337 5–4B
This ultra-minimalist venture suffers from a soulless setting in a
major new residential riverside development; such feedback
as there is praises its fish-based cuisine as outstanding, and fans
insist the place will "really take off when Imperial Wharf
is complete". / www.deeplondon.co.uk; 11 pm; closed Mon, Sat L & Sun D;
set always available £33 (FP).

Defune W1 £64 ❶❸⑤
34 George St 7935 8311 3–1A
Arguably, "the sushi is the best in town", at this Japanese stalwart
in Marylebone; "there's not much atmosphere", though,
and "do they have to charge quite so much?" / 11 pm; set always
available £39 (FP).

Delfina Studio Café SE1 £39 ❶❶❸
50 Bermondsey St 7357 0244 9–4D
"Wonderful", "innovative" food and "brilliant" service again win
strong acclaim for this "really cool" venture, in an "airy warehouse"
space, in Bermondsey; "shame it's open for dinner only on Fridays".
/ www.delfina.org.uk; 10 pm; L only, except Fri when open L&D, closed
Sat & Sun.

Delfino W1 £36 ❷❸④
121a Mount St 7499 1256 3–3B
"A good spot for a work lunch or a post-drinks dinner" –
this "friendly" Mayfair pizzeria is an "easy" choice in a pricey bit
of town, and usually "very busy". / www.finos.co.uk; 11 pm; closed
Sat L & Sun.

La Delizia SW3 £23 ❸④④
63-65 Chelsea Manor St 7376 4111 5–3C
This tiny spot "in a quiet backwater" looks "plain and unassuming",
but some locals still tip it for "the best pizza in Chelsea". / 10.45 pm;
no Amex.

The Depot SW14 £41 ④④❸
Tideway Yd, Mortlake High St 8878 9462 10–1A
"If you can get a window seat", you're rewarded with "a heavenly
view" of the Thames at this well-established spot by Barnes Bridge;
food and service, though, are perennially "unremarkable".
/ www.depotbrasserie.co.uk; 10.45 pm.

Le Deuxième WC2 £43 ❸❷④
65a Long Acre 7379 0033 4–2D
"Dependable" and "fairly-priced" – this "smart" Covent Garden
"stand-by" is most worth knowing about for its "good-value set
menus" (both at lunch, and pre-/post-theatre). / www.ledeuxieme.com;
midnight; set weekday L £23 (FP).

Devonshire House W4 £39
126 Devonshire Rd 8987 2626 7–2A
*This Chiswick gastropub has been a hit-and-miss affair in recent
times; as this guide goes to press, however, there are press reports
that it is set to become the third member of Gordon Ramsay's fast-
expanding pub empire. / www.thedevonshirehouse.com; 10.30 pm; closed
Mon; no Amex.*

Dexter's Grill SW17 £33 ④❸❸
20 Bellevue Rd 8767 1858 10–2C
*Recently revamped, this Wandsworth diner is known for its
"very kid-friendly" attitude and "great burgers"; standards can
be rather "limp", though. / www.tootsies.co.uk; 11 pm.*

dim T £26 ④④❸
32 Charlotte St, W1 7637 1122 2–1C
1a Hampstead Ln, N6 8340 8800 8–1B **NEW**
3 Heath St, NW3 7435 0024 8–2A
Tooley St, SE1 7403 7000 9–4C **NEW**
*As a "nice, bright places to eat", this "cheap" oriental group has its
fans (and its new South Bank branch has "great views of Tower
Bridge and the river"); the food, though, is "variable" going-on
"routine". / 11 pm, NW3 Sat 11.30 pm; NW3 no booking 7.30 pm -
9.30 pm.*

Diner £26 ❷④❷
18 Ganton St, W1 7287 8962 3–2C **NEW**
128 Curtain Rd, EC2 7729 4452 9–1D
*You get the "authentic US diner experience", at this Shoreditch
spot – now with a larger offshoot, just off Carnaby Street – which
does "excellent" burgers, "awesome" chilli fries and "great"
breakfasts. / W1 12.30 am, Sun midnight - EC2 midnight, Sun & Mon
10.30 pm.*

Dinings W1 NEW £30 ❶❷④
22 Harcourt St 7723 0666 8–4A
*"A marvel of minimalism"; ex-Nobu chef Tomonari Chiba's
"brilliant", if "tiny" and basic, Marylebone newcomer serves some
"heavenly" Japanese dishes (including notably "delicious sushi and
sashimi") at "good prices". / 10.30 pm; closed Sat L & Sun.*

Dish Dash £30 ❸④❷
9 Park Walk, SW10 7352 1330 5–3B **NEW**
11-13 Bedford Hill, SW12 8673 5555 10–2C
*This Balham north African has a good "buzz", and serves
"excellent-value" breads, dips and so on; there's now a Chelsea
branch, which is "more spacious, and perhaps better". / midnight.*

Diverso W1 £48 ④④⑤
85 Piccadilly 7491 2222 3–4C
*For a place so prominently sited, near Green Park tube,
this rustically-styled Italian attracts pitifully few reports – on the
upside, though: "you can always get a table for a last-minute
business lunch". / 11.30 pm; closed Sun L.*

Diwana Bhel-Poori House NW1   £21   ③⑤④
121-123 Drummond St   7387 5556   8–4C
*This "odd little place", in the Little India by Euston Station,
maintains a disproportionate following among reporters for its
"tasty, cheap and reliable" veggie fare (and you can BYO); service,
though, is sometimes "incredibly unhelpful". / 10.45 pm; need 10+
to book; set always available £11 (FP).*

$ EC1   £33   ④④❸
2 Exmouth Mkt   7278 0077   9–1A
*If you eat at this trendy and attractive Clerkenwell pub-conversion,
opt for the "great burgers"; arguably, though, it's best just to "stick
to the bar downstairs". / www.dollargrills.com; 11 pm, Fri & Sat 11.30 pm.*

The Don EC4   £49   ❷❷❷
20 St Swithin's Ln   7626 2606   9–3C
*"A real gem in the Square Mile"; this "slick" but "unstarchy"
business favourite – "hidden"-away near Bank – offers
"very satisfactory" Gallic cuisine and a "totally pornographic" wine
list; if you're in the mood for a "less fancy" feel, head for the
"crowded" cellar. / www.thedonrestaurant.com; 10 pm; closed Sat & Sun.*

don Fernando's TW9   £33   ❸❷❸
27f The Quadrant   8948 6447   1–4A
*By Richmond Station, this large and "very lively" family-run tapas
joint is an invariably "reliable" stand-by – "it just goes on and on".
/ www.donfernado.co.uk; 11 pm; closed Mon & Tue; no Amex; no booking.*

Don Pepe NW8   £32   ❸❷❷
99 Frampton St   7262 3834   8–4A
*This "little hide-away" – London's oldest tapas bar –
is "not something you expect to find", near Lords; it offers "the full
Spanish experience", with "a warm welcome", "good tapas",
"unbeatable prices"… "and lots of Spaniards". / 11.30 pm;
closed Sun.*

Donna Margherita SW11   £40   ❸❸④
183 Lavender Hill   7288 2660   10–2C
*"Great pizza" is the highlight of the "slightly idiosyncratic" menu
of this Battersea Italian; it's a "genuine" sort of place, invariably
tipped as a "wonderful local". / www.donna-margherita.com; 11 pm,
Sat & Sun 10.30 pm.*

Dorchester Grill
Dorchester Hotel W1   £75   ④❸④
53 Park Ln   7629 8888   3–3A
*What is going on at the Dorchester?; it's not just the "camp"
Scottish revamp that's made this (once-lovely) grand hotel dining
room such a "hideous" disaster-zone – its cuisine, once quite good,
is at best only "OK" nowadays, and it comes at "extravagant"
prices. / www.thedorchester.com; 11 pm; set Sun L £50 (FP).*

Dover Street Restaurant & Bar W1   £45   ⑤④❸
8-10 Dover St   7491 7509   3–3C
*Dancing and live music really "add to the experience" of an evening
at this classic Mayfair dine 'n' dance venue; the food, though,
is "really very uninspiring"; at lunch it's no better, but it
is ludicrously cheap. / www.doverstreet.co.uk; 2 am; closed Sat L & Sun;
no jeans or trainers.*

Dragon Castle SE17 £29 ❷❸❸
114 Walworth Rd   7277 3388   1–3C
"Incredibly welcome" in "the desert around Elephant & Castle",
this surprising yearling offers "the best dim sum south of the river",
and other "very fresh" and "distinctive" Chinese dishes, in a
"spacious" setting. / 11 pm.

The Drapers Arms N1 £39 ❸❸❷
44 Barnsbury St   7619 0348   8–3D
It got off to such a spectacular start, that some reporters bemoan
the "decline" of this elegant gastro-boozer, in a "leafy" Barnsbury
street; to be fair, though, "it ticks all the boxes" for a good local –
not least an "interesting" menu and a "lovely" garden.
/ www.thedrapersarms.co.uk; 10.30 pm; closed Sun L; booking: max 8.

Drones SW1 £48 ❹❸❹
1 Pont St   7235 9555   5–1D
The "fabulous Sunday lunch" has its fans, but MPW's quietly-
located Belgravian disappointed a fair few reporters this year –
the cooking is often "unimaginative", and the place needs
"more buzz". / www.whitestarline.org.uk; 11 pm; closed Sat L & Sun D.

The Drunken Monkey E1 £23 ❹❹❹
222 Shoreditch High St   7392 9606   9–1D
"As the night goes on, the DJ ramps up the volume", at this
Clerkenwell pub-conversion, praised by most reporters for its
"quick, cheap noodles and dim sum". / www.thedrunkenmonkey.co.uk;
11.45 pm; closed Sat L.

Duke of Cambridge SW11 £36 ❹❹❷
228 Battersea Bridge Rd   7223 5662   10–1C
It remains "a real hit with the locals", but this Battersea boozer
seems to rely heavily for custom on the undoubted charms of its
spacious and prominently-located premises. / www.geronimo-inns.co.uk;
10 pm, Sun 8 pm; no Amex; set Sun L £21 (FP).

The Duke of Cambridge N1 £39 ❸❹❸
30 St Peter's St   7359 3066   1–2C
This "all-organic" Islington gastropub is often "rammed full" –
its "yummy" food strikes some reporters as "overpriced", though,
and service can be "slow and inattentive". / www.sloeberry.co.uk;
10.30 pm.

Duke on the Green SW6 NEW £41 ❸❸❸
235 New King's Rd   7736 2777   10–1B
"A welcome addition to the Fulham scene" – this newly revamped
Parson's Green boozer has "accommodating" service, and offers
"decent", "unfussy" food. / www.dukeonthegreen.co.uk; midnight.

The Duke's Head SW15 NEW £30 ❷❸❷
8 Lower Richmond Rd   8788 2552   10–1B
"A wonderful location" by the Thames is a highpoint of this newly-
revamped landmark pub, near Putney Bridge; other plusses include
"simple, tasty food", and – for parents – an "impressively child-
friendly" attitude. / www.dukesheadputney.co.uk; 10.30 pm.

Durbar W2 £25 ❷❸❹
24 Hereford Rd   7727 1947   6–1B
After 50 years in business, this family-run Bayswater subcontinental
is still unanimously hailed as a "reliable" and "friendly" destination,
offering food that's "very fresh and clean-tasting". / 11.30 pm;
set weekday L £15 (FP).

E&O W11 £43 ❷❷❶
14 Blenheim Cr   7229 5454   6–1A
*For "smashing fusion tapas" and "cool people", it's still hard to beat
this eternally-"buzzy" Notting Hill pan-Asian – "the best branch"
of Will Ricker's mini-'chain', and a London "benchmark".
/ www.rickerrestaurants.com; 11 pm; booking: max 6.*

The Eagle EC1 £25 ❷④❷
159 Farringdon Rd   7837 1353   9–1A
*"The original gastropub, and still the best", say the many loyal fans
of this "crushed" and "loud" Clerkenwell "institution" (est 1992);
despite some "ups and downs in recent years", its "simple"
Mediterranean cooking "hasn't lost its touch". / 11 pm, Sun 5 pm;
closed Sun D; no Amex; no booking.*

Eagle Bar Diner W1 £27 ❸④❷
3-5 Rathbone Pl   7637 1418   4–1A
*"Great cocktails" fuel a "funky vibe" at this "American diner,
done London-style", just off Oxford Street; its burgers – from an
"exotic" selection – are "amazing", and the shakes are
"unmissable". / www.eaglebardiner.com; 10.45 pm, Thu-Sat midnight,
Sun 5.30 pm; closed Sun D; no Amex; need 6+ to book.*

Ealing Park Tavern W5 £37 ❷❷❷
222 South Ealing Rd   8758 1879   1–3A
*A "standard-bearer" in the ranks of "classy" gastropubs; with its
"hearty fare", "reliably good" service and "simple, Victorian, wood-
panelled interior", this South Ealing favourite is "always busy".
/ 10 pm; closed Mon L; booking: max 10.*

Earl Spencer SW18 £32 ❷❸❷
260-262 Merton Rd   8870 9244   10–2B
*"There are no duds on the menu", at this large and "lovely" pub-
conversion; its "extremely fresh and tasty" food makes it "an oasis
of gastronomy in sunny Southfields". / www.theearlspencer.co.uk; 10 pm;
no booking.*

The East Hill SW18 £35 ❸❸❷
21 Alma Rd   8874 1833   10–2B
*A "lively" pub beloved of Wandsworth locals, not least for its
"great" food served "with a smile". / www.geronimo-inns.co.uk; Mon-Wed
10 pm, Thu-Sat 10.30 pm, Sun 8.30 pm; no Amex; set weekday L £19 (FP).*

The Easton WC1 £29 ❷❷❷
22 Easton St   7278 7608   9–1A
*A "perfect gastropub", say fans of this "spacious" hang-out,
near Exmouth Market, which serves food that's almost invariably
"well-executed". / 10 pm; closed Sat L; no Amex.*

Eat £11 ❸❸⑤
Branches throughout London
*"A great place for a quick bite", acclaimed for its "fantastic soups
and pretty good sandwiches, salads, juices, and so on"; leading
competitor Pret is still ahead in the rating stakes, though.
/ www.eatcafe.co.uk; 4pm-8pm; most City branches closed all or part
of weekend; no credit cards; no booking.*

Eat & Two Veg W1 £31 ⑤④④
50 Marylebone High St   7258 8595   2–1A
*Though potentially "fun", this "gimmicky" Marylebone diner
is "a poor advertisement for vegetarianism" – for too many
reporters, its "flavourless" dishes just "don't deliver".
/ www.eatandtwoveg.com; 11 pm.*

The Ebury SW1   £43   ④④④
11 Pimlico Rd   7730 6784   5–2D
New ownership has done nothing to arrest the slide at this "trendy"
Pimlico pub-conversion, where the food is often "average",
and service "can take forever"; there's both a brasserie (sometimes
"ear-splittingly loud") and a more sedate restaurant upstairs.
/ www.theebury.co.uk; 10.30 pm.

Ebury Wine Bar SW1   £41   ④④❸
139 Ebury St   7730 5447   2–4A
"A bit more effort would go a long way", at this "old-favourite"
Belgravia bistro – it's seemed "very, very average" of late.
/ www.eburywinebar.co.uk; 10 pm; May-Aug closed Sun L; set weekday L
£26 (FP).

Eco   £29   ❸❸❸
162 Clapham High St, SW4   7978 1108   10–2D
4 Market Row, Brixton Mkt, SW9   7738 3021   10–2D
"Fab pizza" is about all that the branches of this odd duo have
in common; Clapham is a "loud, young and buzzing" scene,
whereas in Brixton you eat at "a small shop" in "the unique
surroundings of a Caribbean indoor market". / SW4 11 pm,
SW9 5 pm; SW9 L only, closed Wed & Sun; SW9 no booking.

Ed's Easy Diner   £23   ④❸❷
12 Moor St, W1   7434 4439   4–2A
Trocadero, 19 Rupert St, W1   7287 1951   3–3D
15 Gt Newport St, WC2   7836 0271   4–3B
For "classic, kitsch '50s Americana", you won't do much better
than these "fun" retro-diners, where "the burgers are fine, but the
shakes are wonderful"; the long-established Chelsea branch is now
closed. / Rupert St 10 pm, Fri & Sat midnight; Moor St 11.30 pm;
WC2 10 pm, Sun 7 pm; no Amex; no booking.

Edera W11   £48   ④❸⑤
148 Holland Park Ave   7221 6090   6–2A
On rosier reviews, this is "a classy local Italian, ideal for wealthy
Holland Parkers" – the less charitable verdict is that it's
a "pretentious" joint, charging "rip-off prices" for food that's only
"goodish". / 11 pm.

Edokko WC1   £36   ❶❶❸
50 Red Lion St   7242 3490   2–1D
It looks "unassuming", but this "very authentic" Japanese, by Gray's
Inn, elicits a hymns of praise from reporters for its "outstanding-
value" cooking (including the "exceptional" set lunch); service
is "lovely" and "efficient" too. / 11 pm; closed Sat D & Sun; no Amex.

Efes   £28   ④❸④
1) 80 Gt Titchfield St, W1   7636 1953   2–1B
2) 175-177 Gt Portland St, W1   7436 0600   2–1B
These Turkish old-timers in Marylebone are "fading… and not
just the décor"; fans, though, insist they're "still wonderful", thanks
to their characterful service and "great kebabs at very reasonable
prices". / Gt Titchfield St 11.30 pm, Gt Portland St midnight; Gt Titchfield
St closed Sun.

Eight Over Eight SW3 £45 ❷❸❷
392 King's Rd 7349 9934 5–3B
"Sleek" and "very buzzy" – this Chelsea hang-out is very like its
sibling E&O, offering a "healthy and delicious" menu of oriental
"fusion" fare to a similarly "glam" crowd. / www.rickerrestaurants.com;
11 pm; closed Sun L.

Ekachai £25 ❷❹❸
Southside Shopping Cntr, SW18 8871 3888 10–2B
9-10 The Arcade, Liverpool St, EC2 7626 1155 9–2D
"A speedy Thai for City lunching" – it's "often busy, and for good
reason", given its "cheap" and "tasty" scoff; it now has
a Wandsworth offshoot. / EC2 10.30 pm - SW18 10 pm, Fri & Sat
10.30 pm; EC2 closed Sat & Sun.

Electric Brasserie W11 £43 ❹❹❷
191 Portobello Rd 7908 9696 6–1A
There's "top people-watching" to be had at this "loud", "see-and-
be-seen" brasserie, beloved of the "Notting Hill set"; to fans,
the food is "appealing in a simple kind of way" (especially for
a burger or brunch) – to cynics, it's just "unimpressive".
/ www.the-electric.co.uk; 10.45 pm.

Elena's L'Etoile W1 £51 ❸❷❷
30 Charlotte St 7636 7189 2–1C
Elena Salvoni – octogenarian doyenne of maîtresses d' – oversees
the "stalwart professional service" at this "timeless" Fitzrovia
"favourite"; its "old-world charm" and "old-school French" food
provide "a solid foundation for a lost afternoon".
/ www.elenasletoile.co.uk; 10.30 pm; closed Sat L & Sun.

Elephant Royale
Locke's Wharf E14 £39 ❹❸❷
Westferry Rd 7987 7999 11–2C
"Great riverside views" are the special feature of this "kitsch"-
looking Thai at the tip of the Isle of Dogs; unsurprisingly, the food
is "not particularly cheap". / www.elephantroyale.com; Mon-Thu
10.30 pm, Fri & Sat 11 pm, Sun 10 pm.

11 Abingdon Road W8 £40 ❹❹❺
11-13 Abingdon Rd 7937 0120 5–1A
Some reporters feel it made quite "a promising start", but this
"understated" Kensington yearling isn't cutting it – the food
is "uneven", service can be "slow" and the ambience is "dull".
/ www.abingdonroad.co.uk; 10.45 pm.

Elistano SW3 £42 ❹❹❹
25-27 Elystan St 7584 5248 5–2C
It's still "noisy", "crowded" and a bit of a "scene", but this Chelsea
Italian has "gone downhill" in recent years; service is "cursory",
and prices are "steep, for what you get". / 10.30 pm.

The Elk in the Woods N1 £38 ❹❹❷
39 Camden Pas 7226 3535 8–3D
An "edgy", "dark" and "very quirky" Islington hang-out that's
"a nice mix of bar and restaurant"; it's popular for "light meals",
like breakfast – for more substantial fare, it can seem "a bit basic".
/ www.the-elk-in-the-woods.co.uk; 10.30 pm; no Amex.

Emile's SW15 £31 ❷❷❷
96-98 Felsham Rd   8789 3323   10–2B
This Putney backstreet "gem" has been on cracking form of late, with "delicious" food and a "really great little wine list", all at notably "reasonable" prices; part of its charm used to be "old-fashioned" approach – let's hope a recent minimalist revamp doesn't wreck it! / www.emilesrestaurant.co.uk; 11 pm; D only, closed Sun; no Amex.

Emni N1 NEW £29 ❸❸④
353 Upper St   7226 1166   8–3D
"Better than your average high street Indian" –
this "accommodating" (and handily-sited) newcomer is a "welcome addition" to Islington. / www.emnirestaurant.com; 11 pm, Fri midnight.

The Empress of India E9 NEW £41 ④④④
130 Lauriston Rd   8533 5123   1–2D
"More restaurant than pub" – this newly-converted boozer has "opened to much excitement" down Victoria Park way; fans praise its "imaginative" fare, but there are critics (with whom we side) who find it "quite disappointing". / www.theempressofindia.com; 10 pm.

The Engineer NW1 £42 ❸④❷
65 Gloucester Ave   7722 0950   8–3B
Crammed with "effortlessly-cool locals", this "bubbly" Primrose Hill "stalwart" serves "good" gastro-grub in an "erratic but friendly" style; "booking is essential for the garden". / www.the-engineer.com; 11 pm; no Amex.

Enoteca Turi SW15 £46 ❷❶❸
28 Putney High St   8785 4449   10–2B
It may seem "unpretentious", but this family-run Putney Italian can be quite a "memorable" destination; the "enormous" wine list is a major plus, but the "rustic" cooking is "bursting with flavour" too, and service "really goes the extra mile". / www.enotecaturi.com; 11 pm; closed Sun; set weekday L £29 (FP).

The Enterprise SW3 £42 ❸❷❷
35 Walton St   7584 3148   5–2C
The bar scene can be "like a grown-up meat-market", but that only adds to the "fun" and "very buzzy" atmosphere at this "welcoming" and (surprisingly) "unpretentious" Chelsea hang-out; the food's "not bad" either. / www.theenterprise.com; 10.30 pm; no booking, except weekday L.

Epicurean Lounge EC1 £34 ❸④④
10 Clerkenwell Grn   7490 5577   9–1A
You eat on "uncomfy benches", at this offbeat outfit in Clerkenwell; it offers "interesting" pizza-based meals (plus tasty Hispanic dishes and kebabs), but – despite a palpable feeling that they're "trying hard" – results are "erratic". / www.epicureanlounge.com; 11 pm; closed Sun; set always available £22 (FP).

Eriki £37 ❶❶❸
4-6 Northways Pde, Finchley Rd, NW3   7722 0606   8–2A
122 Boundary Rd, NW8   7372 2255   8–3A NEW
"An unusual menu" is "cooked to perfection", at this "friendly" Indian that's "quite glam... for Finchley Road"; together with its new St John's Wood offshoot, it's winning an impressive following. / NW3 & NW8 10.45 pm; NW3 Sat L - NW8 Sun, Mon L.

Esarn Kheaw W12   £25   ❶❸④
314 Uxbridge Rd   8743 8930   7–1B
*"I thought it was a myth that it was London's best Thai... after four
months in Thailand, I can say it really is the best and
most authentic in town..." – one reporter says it all regarding this
"unspectacular"-looking stalwart in "deepest Shepherd's Bush".
/ www.esarnkheaw.co.uk; 11 pm; closed Sat L & Sun L.*

L'Escargot W1   £48   ❷❷❷
48 Greek St   7437 2679   4–2A
*It's perhaps a bit "forgotten" these days, but MPW's "classy" Soho
"classic" still serves up a brilliant all-round experience –
the "traditional" setting is "spacious" and "comfortable", service
is "helpful without being intrusive", and the Gallic cuisine
is "consistently good" and "inventive". / www.whitestarline.org.uk;
11.30 pm; closed Sat L & Sun.*

L'Escargot (Picasso Room) W1   £62   ❷❶❷
48 Greek St   7437 2679   4–2A
*Above the main brasserie, this "lovely" room offers a "luxurious"
combination of "sophisticated" cuisine, "great" wine and
"wonderful" service. / www.whitestarline.org.uk; 11.30 pm; closed Mon,
Sat L & Sun; set weekday L £39 (FP).*

Esenza W11   £46   ❸❷④
210 Kensington Park Rd   7792 1066   6–1A
*This "friendly" Notting Hill Italian attracts surprisingly little
feedback; for sceptics, the food is merely "not bad", but supporters
insist it's "really good value". / www.esenza.co.uk; 11.30 pm;
set weekday L £28 (FP).*

L'Etranger SW7   £60   ❸❸❸
36 Gloucester Rd   7584 1118   5–1B
*The wine cellar is "magnificent" – and fans still praise "excellent"
food – at this Japanese/French establishment, near Kensington
Gardens; it's "gone downhill", though, and doubters find the staff
"stuck-up", and prices "ridiculous". / www.circagroupltd.co.uk; 11 pm;
closed Sat L; set weekday L £30 (FP).*

Ev Restaurant, Bar & Deli SE1   £29   ❸❸❷
97-99 Isabella St   7620 6191   9–4A
*Under railway arches near Southwark tube, the flagship of the Tas
group is a "low-key" but "buzzy" sort of place, offering "good-
value" Turkish fare; "delightful" terrace too. / www.tasrestaurant.com;
11.30 pm.*

Everest Inn SE3   £26   ❸❷④
39 Tranquil Vale   8852 7872   1–4D
*There is the odd negative report, but this "sweet" Nepalese
yearling, in Blackheath, still mostly wins rave reviews for its "fresh"
and "delicious" curries, and its "staff who couldn't be nicer".
/ www.everestinn.co.uk; 11.30 pm, Fri & Sat midnight.*

Eyre Brothers EC2   £47   ❸❸❸
70 Leonard St   7613 5346   9–1D
*This "funky" Shoreditch Iberian is typically tipped as a
"very reliable" choice – "under-rated" even – and it has quite
a business following; there's a small gang of refusniks, though,
who say it's just all-round "dreary". / www.eyrebrothers.co.uk; 10.30 pm;
closed Sat L & Sun.*

Fairuz W1 £41 ❷❸④
3 Blandford St 7486 8108 2–1A
Now bereft of its Bayswater sibling, this "friendly" Marylebone Lebanese is still of note for its "fresh" and "worthwhile" cuisine. / www.fairuz.uk.com; 11.30 pm.

Fakhreldine W1 £48 ❸❸④
85 Piccadilly 7493 3424 3–4C
"Wonderful views over Green Park" and "consistently good food" are the most evident attractions of this stylish Mayfair Lebanese; it's "a little expensive", though, and – when not full – can feel rather "hotel-like". / www.fakhreldine.co.uk; midnight.

Il Falconiere SW7 £37 ❸❷④
84 Old Brompton Rd 7589 2401 5–2B
"Don't be put off by the plain décor" – go for the £10 set lunch and you get "exceptional value" food and "keen" service at this veteran South Kensington trattoria. / www.ilfalconiere.co.uk; 11 pm; closed Sun; set weekday L £22 (FP).

La Famiglia SW10 £42 ❸❷❷
7 Langton St 7351 0761 5–3B
"Very friendly and casual staff" (who are "very nice with children") and "cooking like mama used to make" maintain a devoted fan club for this "stalwart" World's End Italian; "go on a warm night and sit in the garden". / www.lafamiglia.co.uk; 11.45 pm.

The Farm SW6 £39 ❷❸❷
18 Farm Ln 7381 3331 5–3A
New owners have made this stylish Fulham spot the "great local gastropub" that – on launch – it never was; now it's a "cosy" and "relaxing" place (with a "light" and "restaurant-like" dining room) serving "super" food at "reasonable" prices. / www.thefarmfulham.co.uk; 11 pm.

El Faro E14 £34 ❶❷❸
3 Turnberry Quay 7987 5511 11–2C
It may be "stuck in the middle of nowhere", but "brilliant-quality" dishes (plus "impressive" wine) make it "worth the trek" to this ace new waterside tapas bar/restaurant, near Crossharbour DLR. / www.el-faro.co.uk; 11 pm.

The Fat Badger W10 NEW £37 ④④❸
310 Portobello Rd 8969 4500 6–1A
"It's worth the trek up the Portobello Road", say fans of the "traditional-with-a-twist" grub at this new North Kensington local; critics, though, just dismiss it as an "Identikit joint" serving "distinctly average" food in a "fashionably distressed" setting. / www.thefatbadger.com; sun 9 pm; no Amex.

Fat Boy's £27 ❸❸❸
33 Haven Grn, W5 8998 5868 1–2A
431-433 Richmond Rd, TW1 8892 7657 1–4A
68 High St, TW8 8569 8481 1–3A
10a-10b Edensor Rd, W4 8994 8089 10–1A
"Smiley service" and "pretty cheap" prices are the cornerstones of the ongoing popularity of these "generally OK" west London Thais; the Richmond branch has "a great garden". / 11 pm.

Faulkner's E8   £28   ❷❸⑤
424-426 Kingsland Rd   7254 6152   1–1D
"You don't get much sophistication" – just "wonderful, no-nonsense fish 'n' chips" – at this long-running "slice of the East End" (in Dalston), still often hailed as the "best chippy in London". / 10 pm; need 8+ to book.

Feng Sushi   £29   ❸④❸
26 Elizabeth St, SW1   7730 0033   2–4A
218 Fulham Rd, SW10   7795 1900   5–3B
101 Notting Hill Gate, W11   7727 1123   6–2B
21 Kensington Church St, W8   7937 7927   5–1A
1 Adelaide St, NW3   7483 2929   8–2B
13 Stoney St, SE1   7407 8744   9–4C
Royal Festival Hall, SE1   7261 0001   2–3D **NEW**
"More than adequate" sushi and other fare make this attractive café/take-way chain a useful "cheap and cheerful" option. / www.fengsushi.co.uk; 11 pm, Sun-Wed 10 pm, SE1 Thu-Sat 10.30 pm; SE1 closed Sun; no Amex.

The Fentiman Arms SW8   £34   ④④❷
64 Fentiman Rd   7793 9796   10–1D
"Time for a bit of competition in SW8!" – this Kennington gastro-boozer takes flak for being "hit-and-miss" and "hideously overpriced", but still gets "unbelievably busy". / www.geronimo-inns.co.uk; 10 pm, Fri-Sat 10.30 pm, Sun 9 pm; no Amex.

Ferrari's SW17   £29   ④④④
225 Balham High Rd   8682 3553   10–2C
It can seem "formulaic", but this large, "lively" and somewhat suburban Balham Italian does deliver the "occasional surprise" on the food front. / www.ferrarisrestaurants.co.uk; 11 pm.

Ffiona's W8   £42   ❸①①
51 Kensington Church St   7937 4152   5–1A
"Ffiona is on hand to offer tips and advice", at her "friendly", "front room-style", candlelit bistro, in Kensington; even though the food can be "hit-and-miss", fans say the overall experience is a "joy". / www.ffionas.com; 11 pm; D only, closed Mon.

Fifteen Restaurant N1   £81   ⑤⑤④
15 Westland Pl   7251 1515   9–1C
There are reporters who "go cynical" to Jamie Oliver's charitable Hoxton project but still "leave happy"; for many, though, it's just "a disaster" – a "depressed" basement with "indifferent" service, charging "shocking" prices for food that's "at best average". / www.fifteenrestaurant.com; 9.30 pm; booking: max 6; set always available £43 (FP).

Fifteen Trattoria N1   £54   ④④④
15 Westland Pl   7251 1515   9–1C
"The best cooked breakfast in town" (with "everything organic, and done to a turn") is the highlight of Jamie's (somewhat) less expensive ground-floor operation; otherwise, "the prices and the reputation seem unjustified". / www.fifteenrestaurant.com; 10 pm; booking: max 12.

The Fifth Floor Café
Harvey Nichols SW1   **£42**   ⑤④④
109-125 Knightsbridge   7823 1839   5–1D
*"Poor ingredients, badly cooked... but how many ladies come here
for the food anyway?" – that's the question at the "buzzy" but
"ridiculously expensive" café, over the Knightsbridge department
store. / www.harveynichols.com; 10.30 pm, Sun 6 pm; closed Sun D;
no booking at L; set dinner £27 (FP).*

The Fifth Floor Restaurant
Harvey Nichols SW1   **£56**   ④④④
109-125 Knightsbridge   7235 5250   5–1D
*"Someone needs to inject a bit of pizzazz" into this "tired" and
"sterile" chamber, above the Knightsbridge department store;
it's "nowhere near as fashionable as it once was".
/ www.harveynichols.com; 11.30 pm; closed Sun D.*

Fig N1   **£39**   ❷⓿❷
169 Hemingford Rd   7609 3009   8–3D
*"Tucked-away in a small terraced house, in the back streets
of Barnsbury", this "welcoming bolt-hole" makes a good "romantic
hide-away", with "very personal" service and "adventurous" food.
/ www.fig-restaurant.co.uk; 10 pm; closed Mon, Tue-Sat D only, closed Sun D;
no Amex.*

La Figa E14   **£33**   ❸❷❷
45 Narrow St   7790 0077   11–1B
*"Unbeatable pizzas" and other "realistically priced", "traditional"
dishes come in "massive" portions, at this "always-busy" Docklands
favourite – "a great all-rounder". / 10.30 pm.*

Fine Burger Company   **£28**   ❸④④
50 James St, W1   7224 1890   3–1A
256 Muswell Hill Broadway, N10   8815 9292   8–1C
330 Upper St, N1   7359 3026   8–3D
O2 Centre, Finchley Rd, NW3   7433 0700   8–2A
37 Bedford Hill, SW12   8772 0266   10–2C
*They may be "atmosphere-free" zones, but these kitchen-style
operations win a big thumbs-up for their "genuine home-made
American patties", "tasty buns" and "wonderful shakes";
fans insist they "outstrip GBK", but the ratings put them
a respectable second. / www.fineburger.co.uk; 11 pm.*

Fino W1   **£50**   ⓿❷❸
33 Charlotte St   7813 8010   2–1C
*The "stunning" tapas at the Hart brothers's "slick" (and "pricey")
Fitzrovian are an "eye-opener", and it is again tipped by some
reporters as "London's best Spanish restaurant"; the "simple but
stylish" basement setting is invariably "buzzing".
/ www.finorestaurant.com; 10.30 pm; closed Sat L & Sun; booking: max 12.*

Fire & Stone WC2   **£30**   ④④❸
31-32 Maiden Ln   0845 330 0139   4–3D
*For many fans, the "daunting" array of "bizarre toppings" on offer
at this "large and buzzy" Covent Garden venture "makes pizza
interesting again"; service can slip, though, and critics feel that
"some of the concoctions should never have left the drawing
board". / www.coventgardenrestaurants.com; 11 pm.*

The Fire Stables SW19 £38 ④⑤❸
27-29 Church Rd   8946 3197   10–2B
"Noisy, unpretentious and fun" – this Wimbledon bar ("don't waste time with the restaurant") has been an asset to a thin area in recent years; some reports suggest it's "lost its way", though, and "small portions" are a recurrent complaint. / 10.30 pm; booking: max 8, Sat & Sun; set weekday L £24 (FP).

Firezza £28 ❷❸⑤
12 All Saints Rd, W11   7221 0020   6–1B
48 Chiswick High Rd, W4   8994 9494   7–2B
276 St Paul's Rd, N1   7359 7400   8–2D
40 Lavender Hill, SW11   7223 5535   10–1C
205 Garrett Ln, SW18   8870 7070   10–2B
The "best take-away pizzas in London" – sold by the quarter or half metre, with "perfect crusts, and generous toppings" – are to be found at this "awesome" small chain; seating, where available, tends to be "school-canteen"-style. / www.firezza.com; 11 pm; no Amex.

First Floor W11 £39 ⑤❸❶
186 Portobello Rd   7243 0072   6–1A
This "OTT" room – "at the centre of Portobello Market" – is "magical" (in a shabby-chic sort of way); if only the the same could be said for the "really disappointing" food... / www.firstfloorportobello.co.uk; 11 pm; closed Mon & Sun D.

Fish Central EC1 £23 ❷❸④
149 Central St   7253 0229   9–1B
"A line of taxi-drivers queueing for eat-in and take away" attests to the "top-quality fish 'n chips" – plus "a range of tempting alternatives" – on offer at this modern Clerkenwell chippy. / www.fishcentral.co.uk; 10.30 pm; closed Sun.

Fish Club SW11 £29 ❶❷④
189 St John's Hill   7978 7115   10–2C
"The chippy goes upmarket, but stays true to its roots", say fans of this "incredibly welcoming", "no-frills" Battersea two-year-old, which serves up "fabulous" fish (including some "alternative options"), with "fantastic chips" and "very good mushy peas"; (option to BYO at £2.50 corkage). / www.thefishclub.com; 10 pm; closed Mon.

Fish Hook W4 £46 ❷❸④
6-8 Elliott Rd   8742 0766   7–2A
Michael Nadra's "brilliantly-prepared" fish ("ordered in full or half portions") "maintains the high standards set by the South African predecessor" on this Chiswick site; it's still "way too cramped, though". / www.fishhook.co.uk; 10.30 pm; set weekday L £27 (FP).

Fish in a Tie SW11 £21 ④❸❷
105 Falcon Rd   7924 1913   10–1C
"It's difficult to eat as cheaply and as well" as at this "cramped", "chaotic" and "buzzing" bistro, behind Clapham Junction; the fare "may not be gourmet, but there's lots of it". / 11.45 pm; no Amex; set weekday L £13 (FP).

Fish Shop EC1 £40 ❸❸④
360-362 St John's St   7837 1199   8–3D
This "basic" and "slightly out-of-the-way" Islington spot offers "simple" fish dishes to "consistently good" standards; late-evening diners: "beware the post-Sadler's Wells rush". / www.thefishshop.net; 11 pm, Sun 8 pm; closed Mon.

fish! SE1 £39 ④④④
Cathedral St 7407 3803 9–4C
A "handy" location, by Borough Market, may explain why this ultra-
"minimalist" glass "shed" can get "overly-crowded"; it offers
a "simple" and "unadulterated" fish formula, but can seem
"pricey" for what it is. / www.fishrestaurantsltd.com; 10.30 pm.

Fishmarket
Great Eastern Hotel EC2 £65 ④④④
40 Liverpool St 7618 7200 9–2D
Fans insist it does the "best oysters in town", but this smart City fish
venue suffers mixed reviews, not least concerning its "ludicrous"
prices. / www.great-eastern-hotel.co.uk; 10.15 pm; closed Sat & Sun.

Fishworks £39 ❸④④
89 Marylebone High St, W1 7935 9796 2–1A
212 Fulham Rd, SW10 7823 3033 5–3B **NEW**
177 New King's Rd, SW6 7384 1009 10–1B **NEW**
188 Westbourne Grove, W11 7229 3366 6–1B **NEW**
6 Turnham Green Ter, W4 8994 0086 7–2A
134 Upper St, N1 7354 1279 8–3D
57 Regent's Park Rd, NW1 7586 9760 8–3B
54 Northcote Rd, SW11 7228 7893 10–2C **NEW**
13/19 The Sq, Old Mkt, TW9 8948 5965 1–4A
"Sparklingly fresh fish" – "simply cooked" – still wins many fans for
this fast-growing chain of café/fishmongers; its branches are "plain"
and "jammed-in", though, and there are a fair number of reports
of "inept" service and "inflated" prices. / www.fishworks.co.uk; 10 pm;
W4 closed Sun D.

5 Cavendish Square W1 £64 ④❸❷
5 Cavendish Sq 7079 5000 3–1C
"The place to take an impressionable date, but strictly not for
minimalists" – this "OTT" venue in a vast townhouse, north
of Oxford Street, is mainly of note for its "loud décor" and
"thumping" bar; the food in the "subdued" restaurant is incidental.
/ www.no5ltd.com; 10.30 pm; closed Sat L & Sun D; set weekday L £39 (FP).

Five Hot Chillies HA0 £20 ❷❷④
875 Harrow Rd 8908 5900 1–1A
It's "worth the trek" to Sudbury, to seek out this "basic" but
"bustling" BYO canteen, which serves "real" Indian dishes
"extremely cheap". / 11.30 pm; no Amex.

Flâneur EC1 £44 ❸④❸
41 Farringdon Rd 7404 4422 9–1A
The "strange setting" – "among the shelves of an upmarket deli" –
divides views on eating at this Farringdon spot, but it is pretty clear
that it's more "fun" for breakfast or lunch than in the "quieter"
evenings; "the food is tasty… when it arrives". / www.flaneur.com;
10 pm; closed Sun D.

The Flask N6 £25 ④④❶
77 Highgate West Hill 8348 7346 1–1C
"Don't want to leave London for authentic country pub
atmosphere?" – this ancient and "lovely" Highgate coaching inn
is "perfect", even if its "good, no-fuss grub" only plays a minor rôle
in the experience. / 10pm.

Flat White W1   £9   ❷❷❸
17 Berwick St   7734 0370   3–2D
"It's all about the coffee" – "these guys are wild-eyed and intense
about it" – at this Kiwi-run café in Soho; some of the snacks,
though, are "delectable" too. / www.flat-white.co.uk; L only; no credit
cards.

Florians N8   £36   ④❸④
4 Topsfield Pde   8348 8348   1–1C
A "friendly" Crouch End veteran, serving "large portions" of Italian
nosh; fans say it's "a cut above your local pasta joint", but drifting
ratings support those who fear it's "going downhill".
/ www.floriansrestaurant-crouchend.co.uk; 11 pm; no Amex.

Floridita W1   £55   ⑤⑤❸
100 Wardour St   7314 4000   3–2D
"Vast, monolithic" Soho Cuban, where the "great music" and
"excellent cocktails" can make for a "fun" time... if you don't
choke on the prices levied for the "terrible" food (and "inattentive"
service). / www.floriditalondon.com; 2 am; D only, closed Sun.

Foliage
Mandarin Oriental SW1   £72   ❶❶❷
66 Knightsbridge   7201 3723   5–1D
This "understated" and "well-spaced" Knightsbridge dining room
is currently on top form, with its "enthusiastic" staff serving
up Chris Staines's "sublime" dishes; lunch is "unbeatable value"
too, especially if you bag a table with a park-view.
/ www.mandarinoriental.com; 10.30 pm; booking: max 6; set weekday L
£44 (FP).

Food for Thought WC2   £16   ❷④④
31 Neal St   7836 0239   4–2C
"Big bowls" of "healthy", "top-value" nosh are the mainstay of this
"old-style" veggie, which occupies a "packed" Covent Garden
basement. / 8 pm, Sun 5 pm; no credit cards; no booking.

The Food Room SW8   £39   ❶❷④
123 Queenstown Rd   7622 0555   10–1C
"The prices are a real bonus", at this "excellent neighbourhood
place", in Battersea; its "interesting" Gallic-inspired cooking
is served by "knowledgeable" staff, but the ambience "needs
lightening up". / www.thefoodroom.com; 10.30 pm; D only, closed Sun-Tue.

Footstool
St Johns SW1   £36   ⑤⑤④
St John's, Smith Sq   7222 2779   2–4C
"Should try harder" – the unchanging verdict on this Westminster
crypt; in default of much else hereabouts, though, it remains handy
(despite the "uneven" service) "for a quick working lunch" or "pre-
concert". / www.digbytrout.co.uk; L only (ex concert evenings), closed
Sat & Sun.

The Forge WC2 NEW   £43   ④❶❸
14 Garrick St   7379 1531   4–3C
"Exemplary" service features in most reports on this new occupant
of the interesting Covent Garden site that was L'Estaminet (RIP);
as at its siblings, Café du Jardin and Deuxième, however, reactions
to the cooking are muted. / midnight; set weekday L £27 (FP).

Formosa Dining Room
The Prince Alfred W9   £40   ④❸❸
5a Formosa St   7286 3287   6–1C
*For most reporters, this annex to an "impressive" Victorian pub
in Maida Vale is a "reliable" destination; at the prices, though,
some feel it "should be better". / 10.45 pm; no Amex.*

(Fountain)
Fortnum & Mason W1   £40
181 Piccadilly   7734 8040   3–3D
*This famous St James's store is undergoing a major make-over
to celebrate 300 years in business, which will enhance the range
of in-house dining options; the long-established buttery, with its own
entrance in Jermyn Street, re-opens in late-2007 – let's hope it's all-
day virtues have not been too much 'improved'!*
/ www.fortnumandmason.co.uk; 7.30 pm; closed Sun; no booking at L.

Four O Nine SW9 NEW   £42   ❷❷❷
409 Clapham Rd   7737 0722   10–1D
*"A great addition to Clapham" – at this dining room above a pub,
an ex-Chez Bruce chef offers some "good-value" cooking in "cool"
surroundings. / www.fouronine.co.uk; 10.30 pm; closed Mon L,
Tue L & Thu L.*

Four Regions TW9   £35   ❸❷❸
102-104 Kew Rd   8940 9044   1–4A
*Recently-revamped, this Richmond Chinese has a more-than-local
fan club, having provided "a reliably high standard" of cooking for
many years now. / 11.30 pm.*

The Four Seasons W2   £26   ❷⑤⑤
84 Queensway   7229 4320   6–1C
*There's "always a queue" – but it's "well worth the wait" – say fans
of this Bayswater stalwart, which "looks like any other Chinese",
but serves "the best roast duck in the world"; "it's a shame, though,
that you have to put up with such surly and inconsistent service".
/ 11 pm.*

The Fox EC2   £36   ❸❸❸
28 Paul St   7729 5708   9–1C
*A determinedly 'real' Shoreditch pub, which serves "good beers"
and a "limited but excellent menu" of gutsy traditional scoff.
/ www.thefoxpublichouse.com; 10 pm; closed Sat L & Sun D; no Amex.*

The Fox & Hounds SW11   £33   ❷❷❷
66 Latchmere Rd   7924 5483   10–1C
*"It retains a fun and casual pub atmosphere" (complete with "well-
kept beer"), but this Battersea boozer is every bit a "first-class"
gastropub, and serves "an inventive and frequently-changing
blackboard menu". / 10.30 pm; Mon-Thu D only, Fri-Sun open L & D;
no Amex.*

The Fox Reformed N16   £32   ④④❸
176 Stoke Newington Church St   7254 5975   1–1C
*This "hard-to-categorise" Stoke Newington stand-by can be quite
a "charming" venue (with a "rather pleasant" small garden);
the food, though, is "unexciting" and service can hit the wrong note.
/ www.fox-reformed.co.uk; 10.30 pm, Sat & Sun 10 pm; closed weekday L.*

Foxtrot Oscar SW3   £38

79 Royal Hospital Rd   7352 7179   5–3D

*This famously cliquey '70s-style Chelsea bistro is set for a major
relaunch in the autumn of 2007; long-time (Old Etonian) proprietor
Michael Proudlock remains the 'front' man, but backers now
include Gordon Ramsay... should be interesting.*
/ www.foxtrotoscarchelsea.com; 11 pm; closed Sun D; no Amex.

Franco's SW1   £51   ④④④

61-63 Jermyn St   7499 2211   3–3C

*The Hambro family may have "spent a fortune" on tarting up this
age-old St James's Italian, but the food is still "average", and service
can be "patchy"; critics find the prices "insane" too.*
/ www.francoslondon.com; 10.45 pm; closed Sun.

Frankie's Italian Bar & Grill   £33   ⑤⑤❸

3 Yeomans Row, SW3   7590 9999   5–2C
68 Chiswick High Rd, W4   8987 9988   7–2B
263 Putney Bridge Rd, SW15   8780 3366   10–2B

*"Lamentable" service and "terrible" food inspire scathing reports
on Franco Dettori and Marco Pierre White's posh pizza 'n' burger
chain; its "weird" ("casino-like") branches do, however, exert
a certain "glitzy" appeal. / www.frankiesitalianbarandgrill.com; 11 pm;
W4 Mon-Fri L.*

Franklins   £38   ❸④④

205-209 Kennington Ln, SE11   7793 8313   1–3C **NEW**
157 Lordship Ln, SE22   8299 9598   1–4D

*In Dulwich – and now also Kennington (on the former Painted
Heron site) – these are "brilliant" locals, say fans, offering "short
but imaginative" British menus (majoring in meat and offal);
expansion, however, seems to have been associated with a fair few
off-days of late. / www.franklinsrestaurant.com; 10.30 pm; set weekday L
£23 (FP).*

Frantoio SW10   £40   ❸❶❷

397 King's Rd   7352 4146   5–3B

*It's taken a while, but this family-run Italian at World's End
is "now firmly established in the area", thanks not least to its
"very helpful" staff and its "realistic" prices. / 11.15 pm; set weekday L
£26 (FP).*

Fratelli la Bufala NW3   £36   ④⑤⑤

45a South End Rd   7435 7814   8–2A

*"Hit-and-miss" cooking and "atrocious" service are sapping
enthusiasm for this once-promising Hampstead Italian; fans still say
it's a "more than adequate local", offering "real pizza" – critics
slam a "total sham". / 11 pm; no Amex.*

Frederick's N1   £48   ❸❷❷

106 Camden Pas   7359 2888   8–3D

*Some still say it "needs a make-over", but this "lovely" Islington
"old favourite" made something of a ratings comeback this year;
particular attractions include an "airy" and "romantic"
conservatory, and a "fairly-priced" wine list. / www.fredericks.co.uk;
11 pm; closed Sun; no Amex; set pre theatre £28 (FP).*

The Freemasons SW18   £35   ❸❷❷

2 Wandsworth Common Northside   7326 8580   10–2C

*An "ideal" gastropub, in Wandsworth – the atmosphere is "chilled",
the staff are "friendly" and the "hearty" food is "done really well".
/ www.freemasonspub.com; 10 pm.*

Freemasons Arms NW3   £38   ④④❷
32 Downshire Hill   7433 6811 8–2A
A "chilled but cosy" vibe (and "gorgeous" garden) may help explain why this Hampstead gastropub is usually "brimming with people" – foodwise, "it could do better". / www.freemasonsarms.com; 10 pm.

French House W1   £45   ④❸❸
49 Dean St   7437 2477 4–3A
A certain mystique surrounds 'The French', and its "tiny" first-floor dining room is certainly "full of Soho atmosphere"; at present, however, its "simple" and "old-fashioned" Gallic fare seems to be going through a pretty "ordinary" patch. / www.frenchhousesoho.com; 11 pm; closed Sun; booking: max 8.

Fresco W2   £15   ❷❷④
25 Westbourne Grove   7221 2355 6–1C
"Awesome juices", "fantastic falafel wraps" and "very fresh" mezze make this "good-natured" Bayswater pit stop quite a "cheap and cheerful" favourite. / 11 pm.

Friends SW10   £37   ❸❷④
6 Hollywood Rd   7376 3890 5–3B
"Delicious Roman-style pizzas" win many, er, friends for this "welcoming" and "efficient" Italian, at the far end of Chelsea; it can get pretty "noisy". / 11.20 pm, Sat & Sun 10.30 pm; closed weekday L, Sat D & Sun D; no Amex.

Frocks E9   £37   ④④④
95 Lauriston Rd   8986 3161 1–2D
This cosy bistro, near Victoria Park, was one of the first trendy-ish places in the East End; local fans say its still "never disappointing" – critics that "it used to be good, but now isn't". / www.frocks-restaurant.co.uk; 10.30 pm, Sun 9 pm; closed weekday L; no Amex.

La Fromagerie Café W1   £25   ❶❷❷
2-4 Moxon St   7935 0341 3–1A
"A magnificent cheese shop, offering delicious lunch bites and fabulous salads" (and "really imaginative breakfasts" too); "the only complaint about this Marylebone deli is that the capacity isn't larger"! / www.lafromagerie.co.uk; 7pm; L only; no booking.

The Frontline Club W2   £42   ④❸❷
13 Norfolk Pl   7479 8960 6–1D
"Diverting photographs" add interest to the "atmospheric" interior of this "classy" dining room – part of a journalists' club in a "dreary" corner of Paddington; the food is only "passable", but the wine list offers "excellent value". / www.frontlineclub.com; 10.30 pm.

Fryer's Delight WC1   £9   ④④⑤
19 Theobald's Rd   7405 4114 2–1D
A "definitely no-frills" Holborn institution, traditionally reputed as a "top place for old-fashioned fish 'n' chips"; critics, though, feel it's over-rated. / 10 pm; closed Sun; no credit cards; no booking.

Fuego Pizzeria SW8   £20   ❸❷⑤
388 Wandsworth Rd   7622 7999 10–1D
"Wandsworth Road is a better place since Fuego arrived" – this year-old pizzeria makes a very handy Lambeth stand-by. / 11 pm.

Fujiyama SW9 £20 ❷④❸
7 Vining St   7737 2369   10–2D
*"Down a dodgy-looking lane in Brixton", this "buzzing" Japanese
local serves up a good "cheap and cheerful" formula, which
includes "great sushi".* / www.fujiyama.com; midnight; no Amex.

Fung Shing WC2 £37 ❷❸⑤
15 Lisle St   7437 1539   4–3A
*The food at this once-"upmarket" Chinatown stalwart has its ups
and downs, and its décor remains badly "in need of a face lift";
the seafood cuisine is still "a cut above", though – "some dishes are
truly superb".* / www.fungshing.co.uk; 11.15 pm.

Furnace N1 £30 ❸❸❸
1 Rufus St   7613 0598   9–1D
*"Happening", "loud" and "friendly", this Hoxton hang-out serves
a "good range" of pizzas, with "interesting toppings", at "cheap"
prices.* / 11 pm; closed Sat L & Sun; no Amex.

Fuzzy's Grub £13 ❶❶❸
6 Crown Pas, SW1   7925 2791   3–4D
15 Basinghall St, Unit 1 Mason's Ave, EC2   7726 6771   9–2C **NEW**
56-57 Cornhill, EC3   7621 0555   9–2C **NEW**
10 Well Ct, EC4   7236 8400   9–2B
62 Fleet St, EC4   7583 6060   9–2A
*A "simple concept, brilliantly executed"; "sandwiches don't come
better" than the "monster" "Sunday-roasts-in-a-bap" which are
charmingly served at these "upmarket greasy spoons" –
"the queues are getting longer as word gets out".*
/ www.fuzzysgrub.com; 3 pm-4 pm; closed Sat & Sun; no credit cards;
no booking.

Gaby's WC2 £27 ❸❸⑤
30 Charing Cross Rd   7836 4233   4–3B
*"The best, most central, and cheapest place for a quick bite" in the
West End – this "simple" deli-veteran serves "superb salt beef",
"great falafels", "brilliant mezze", and so on.* / midnight; no credit
cards.

Gail's Bread £14 ❷❷❸
138 Portobello Rd, W11   7460 0766   6–1B **NEW**
64 Hampstead High St, NW3   7794 5700   8–1A
*"Sublime" bread and pastries have carved out an ardent (if still
small) fanclub for this growing bakery/café mini-chain; "everyone
loves the new one in Portobello".* / W11 8 pm - NW3 9 pm.

Galicia W10 £30 ④④❷
323 Portobello Rd   8969 3539   6–1A
*This "incredibly authentic" veteran tapas bar, in North Kensington,
still mostly delivers "tasty" and "cheap" dishes; it provoked the odd
"disappointing" report this year, though.* / 11.30 pm; closed Mon;
set weekday L £14 (FP).

Gallipoli £24 ④❸❷
102 Upper St, N1   7359 0630   8–3D
107 Upper St, N1   7226 5333   8–3D
120 Upper St, N1   7359 1578   8–3D
*"Brimming with exotic atmosphere", these "heaving" Turkish
bistros, in Islington, offer "tasty" scoff at "very cheap" prices;
"you do run the risk of being next to an office leaving party or hen
night", though.* / www.cafegallipoli.com; 11 pm, Fri & Sat midnight;
107 Upper St closed Mon.

Galvin at Windows
Park Lane London Hilton Hotel W1   £68   ❸❸❷
22 Park Ln, 28th Floor   7208 4021   3–4A
"The restaurant is now as impressive as the views", say fans of the Galvin brothers' "elegant" year-old relaunch of this 28th-floor Mayfair eyrie; given the location, though, it's perhaps no surprise that it can seem "painfully overpriced".
/ www.hilton.co.uk/londonparklane; 10.30 pm; closed Sat L & Sun D.

GALVIN BISTROT DE LUXE W1   £44   ❶❶❷
66 Baker St   7935 4007   2–1A
Chris & Jeff Galvin's "slick", year-old 'Bistrot de luxe', in Marylebone, is rapidly emerging as a modern classic – "cuisine bourgeoise" is "beautifully executed" and "professionally" served, in a "classy" and "club-like" setting. / www.galvinbistrotdeluxe.co.uk; 10.45 pm; set weekday L £28 (FP).

Ganapati SE15   £26   ❷❷❸
38 Holly Grove   7277 2928   1–4C
An "unexpected" Peckham Rye spot that's developing quite a following, thanks to its "welcoming" style and its "tasty" and "interesting" south Indian cuisine. / www.ganapatirestaurant.com; 10.45 pm; closed Mon; no Amex.

Garbo's W1   £38   ④❸④
42 Crawford St   7262 6582   2–1A
This "old-faithful" – in Greta's old Marylebone home – serves up "well-cooked" (if slightly plodding) Scandinavian fare; its smörgåsbord lunch is "always reliable and good value".
/ 10.30 pm; closed Sat L & Sun D; set weekday L £24 (FP).

The Garden Café NW1   £31   ④④❷
Inner Circle, Regent's Pk   7935 5729   8–4B
On a summer's day', this café "tucked-away in Regent's Park" provides a "lovely" outdoor setting for some "reasonable" food; service, though, can be "slow". / www.thegardencafe.co.uk; L only; no Amex.

Garrison SE1   £38   ❸❸❶
99-101 Bermondsey St   7089 9355   9–4D
A "funky" make-over of this boozer near Bermondsey Market has created a "buzzing" – if "crowded" – setting, where the "modern-style pub food" is usually "spot-on". / www.thegarrison.com; 10.30 pm.

Gastro SW4   £44   ④⑤❷
67 Venn St   7627 0222   10–2D
Fans of this "quirky" Clapham bistro still trumpet it as a "fun" and "relaxed" favourite; service is "bad" though, and the food "irritatingly inconsistent" – it wouldn't be so bad if it wasn't "blinking expensive"! / midnight; no Amex; set weekday L £26 (FP).

The Gate W6   £36   ❷❸④
51 Queen Caroline St   8748 6932   7–2C
"Blindingly good veggie fare to satisfy the most-committed carnivore" has built a big reputation for this "busy" former church hall near Hammersmith Broadway; a "great courtyard" is a particular summer boon. / www.thegate.tv; 10.45 pm; closed Sat L & Sun.

Gaucho £35 ❷❸❸
Chelsea Farmers' Mkt, Sydney St, SW3   7376 8514   5–3C
30 Old Brompton Rd, SW7   7584 8999   5–2B
*"Very good steaks" ensure these "buzzy" Argentinian joints are
regularly "full to the brim"; the shed-like SW3 branch has a great
terrace. / www.elgaucho.co.uk; SW3 6.30 pm, SW7 11.30 pm; SW3 L only,
SW7 D only; SW3 no credit cards; SW3 no booking in summer or weekends,
SW7 no bookings before 7 pm.*

Gaucho Grill £49 ❸④④
25 Swallow St, W1   7734 4040   3–3D
125 Chancery Ln, WC2   7242 7727   2–1D
89 Sloane Ave, SW3   7584 9901   5–2C
64 Heath St, NW3   7431 8222   8–1A
2 Moore London, Riverside, SE1   7407 5222   9–4D NEW
Tow Path, TW10   8948 2944   1–4A NEW
29 Westferry Circus, E14   7987 9494   11–1B
5 Finsbury Ave, Broadgate, EC2   7256 6877   9–1C
1 Bell Inn Yd, EC3   7626 5180   9–2C
*Veggies beware – there's "cow-skin everywhere!" – at this South
American chain, tipped by many reporters for "London's
best steaks"; it's a "good solid bet" for many types of event
(but, with the "superb" Argentinian wine list, particularly for
business). / www.gaucho-grill.com; 11 pm; EC3, EC2 & WC2 closed
Sat & Sun.*

LE GAVROCHE W1 £123 ❷0❷
43 Upper Brook St   7408 0881   3–2A
*"Old-school in the best possible way" – Michael Roux Jr's Mayfair
institution of 40 years' standing still offers "sensational" Gallic
cooking, "legendary" service and a "definitive" wine list; prices,
of course, are "extra-terrestrial". / www.le-gavroche.co.uk; 10.45 pm;
closed Sat L & Sun; jacket required; set weekday L £54 (FP).*

Gay Hussar W1 £39 ④❸❷
2 Greek St   7437 0973   4–2A
*A "wonderful", "timeless" and "conspiratorial" ambience still
breathes life into this "old, old, old Soho" favourite, famed for its
pinko politico-associations; its "hearty" Hungarian food – "heavy
and lacking in subtlety" – is "much as ever". / www.gayhussar.co.uk;
10.45 pm; closed Sun.*

The Gaylord E14 £22 ❷④④
141 Manchester Rd   7538 0393   2–1B
*"The location may not be the best", but this Isle of Dogs Indian
offers a surprisingly "varied" menu, which includes some
"very interesting" dishes. / www.gaylordrestaurant.com; midnight.*

Gazette SW11 NEW £31 ❸❸④
79 Riverside Plaza, Chatfield Rd   7223 0999   10–1C
*It has a "rather obscure location" (hidden away near the south end
of Wandsworth Bridge), but this all-day newcomer is "worth a visit",
thanks not least to its "good and reliable French cooking".
/ www.gazettebrasserie.co.uk; 11.30 pm.*

Geale's W8 £38 ④❸❸
2 Farmer St   7727 7528   6–2B
*This age-old chippy, near Notting Hill Gate, re-opened after
a major revamp in the summer of 2007; its new format is as
a would-be trendy fish bistro – not, in our view, an improvement
on the original. / Rated on Editors' visit; www.geales.com; 11.30 pm;
closed Mon.*

Geeta NW6 £18 ❸❷⑤
57-59 Willesden Ln 7624 1713 1–1B
*This ultra-"basic" Kilburn veteran is known for its "home-cooked"
south Indian nosh at "great" prices (and you can BYO);
most reports still say it's "fantastic value" – as last year, though,
feedback was less settled than usual. / 10.30 pm, Fri & Sat 11.30 pm;
no Amex.*

Gem N1 £21 ❷❷❸
265 Upper St 7359 0405 8–2D
*"Paradise for both veggies and carnivores" – this "very friendly"
Kurdish restaurant in Islington offers "fantastic" mezze and
"succulent" grills, at "ludicrously cheap" prices. / midnight.*

George & Vulture EC3 £39 ⑤④❶
3 Castle Ct 7626 9710 9–3C
*"You can almost imagine Pepys walking in to grab a quick bite",
at this "atmospheric" City chophouse; even after making due
historical allowances, though, its "school dinners" fare could
be "a lot better". / L only, closed Sat & Sun.*

Getti £44 ④④❸
16-17 Jermyn St, SW1 7734 7334 3–3D
42 Marylebone High St, W1 7486 3753 2–1A
*Supporters insist that these West End Italians offer "good" food
("for a chain"), even if it is rather "unexciting"; its "airy" branches
are perhaps of most interest for lunch (or pre-theatre).
/ www.getti.com; 10.45 pm.*

Giardinetto W1 £58 ❸❸⑤
39-40 Albemarle St 7493 7091 3–3C
*Pity about the "lack of ambience" at Maurizio Vilona's small
contemporary Italian, near the Ritz – his "unusual" dishes are
sometimes "outstanding", and the wine selection is "amazing".
/ www.giardinetto.co.uk; 11 pm; closed Sat L & Sun; set weekday L £37 (FP).*

Gilgamesh NW1 £55 ④⑤④
The Stables, Camden Mkt, Chalk Farm Rd 7482 5757 8–2B
*With its "wildly OTT" interior and its 800 seats, this "trendy"
Camden Town yearling is certainly "unique"; even those who find
the pan-Asian grazing dishes "delicious" though, can feel it's
"too expensive", and critics say this is a "tacky" sort of place,
with "appalling" service. / www.gilgameshbar.com; midnight, Fri & Sat
12.30 am; closed Sun D.*

Gili Gulu WC2 £21 ④⑤⑤
50-52 Monmouth St 7379 6888 4–2B
*"Not great sushi, but a cheap place to fill up"; the food at this "all-
you-can-eat" oriental buffet "can be less than impressive" but –
with careful choice – is "usually OK". / 11 pm; no Amex; no booking.*

95

Giraffe £33 ④❸④

6-8 Blandford St, W1   7935 2333   2–1A
270 Chiswick High Rd, W4   8995 2100   7–2A
7 Kensington High St, W8   7938 1221   5–1A
29-31 Essex Rd, N1   7359 5999   8–3D
46 Rosslyn Hill, NW3   7435 0343   8–2A
Royal Festival Hall, Riverside, SE1   7928 2004   2–3D
27 Battersea Rise, SW11   7223 0933   10–2C

"So long as you don't mind kids", brunch is the "top attraction"
at this "jolly" and "hectic" world-food chain – more generally,
however, drifting survey ratings support those who say it's "not as
good as it was". / www.giraffe.net; 10.45 pm; no booking at weekends;
set dinner £22 (FP).

Glaisters SW10 £34 ❸❸❷

4 Hollywood Rd   7352 0352   5–3B

This "calm" Chelsea bistro of long standing sometimes seems
rather overlooked nowadays; fans, though, love its "genuine"
approach, and say the food's "nothing amazing, but good and very
reasonably-priced". / www.glaisters.co.uk; 11 pm; set always available
£22 (FP).

The Glasshouse TW9 £52 ❶❶❸

14 Station Pde   8940 6777   1–3A

"A worthy sibling to Chez Bruce" – this "light and airy"
(if somewhat "squashed-in and noisy") "neighbourhood gem",
by Kew Gardens station, once again wins all-round raves for its
"superb" and "unfussy" cuisine and its "charming" and "efficient"
service; "excellent" wine too. / www.glasshouserestaurant.co.uk; 10.30 pm.

Golden Dragon W1 £28 ④⑤④

28-29 Gerrard St   7734 2763   4–3A

"One of the usual suspects", on Chinatown's main drag; though
an "old-style" favourite for some reporters, it's "pretty standard".
/ midnight.

Golden Hind W1 £18 ❶❶❸

73 Marylebone Ln   7486 3644   2–1A

"The best fish 'n' chips in London" – bar none – are to be had
at this "traditional" Marylebone chippy; "arrive early if you want
a table". / 10 pm; closed Sat L & Sun.

Goldfish NW3 NEW £38 ❷❸④

82 Hampstead High St   7794 6666   8–2A

A "cute", 'modern Chinese' newcomer, in the heart of Hampstead
– a "helpful" sort of place, where the cooking is sometimes "really
interesting". / 10.30 pm.

Good Earth £40 ❷❷❸

233 Brompton Rd, SW3   7584 3658   5–2C
143-145 The Broadway, NW7   8959 7011   1–1B

This "civilised" and "professional" Chinese mini-chain is (practically)
"always dependable"; "outstanding" veggie dishes attract particular
praise. / 10.45 pm.

Goodness W4 NEW £29 ④④❸

30-34 Chiswick High Rd   8987 9174   7–2B

A sense of "unrealised potential" permeates feedback on this
"child-friendly" newcomer, near Stamford Brook tube; the décor
is "groovy" and the food is "well-sourced", but the interior can feel
"cavernous", and service is sometimes "terrible".
/ www.goodness-restaurant.co.uk; 10 pm; no Amex.

Gopal's of Soho W1 £27 ❸❷④
12 Bateman St 7434 1621 4–2A
*An "excellent no-frills Indian" – one of surprisingly few such places
in the heart of the West End. / 11.30 pm.*

GORDON RAMSAY SW3 £109 ❶❶❷
68-69 Royal Hospital Rd 7352 4441 5–3D
*Mark Askew's cuisine may still be "flawless" and Jean-Claude's
service "unrivalled", but – following a rather "anaemic" revamp,
and with ever more "exorbitant" prices – Ramsay's Chelsea HQ is
now at risk of losing its customary pre-eminence; despite (for the
12th year) topping reporters' nominations as London's
'top gastronomic experience', it failed – for the first time this
decade – to achieve either the best survey rating for its food, or for
the overall experience offered. / www.gordonramsay.com; 11 pm; closed
Sat & Sun; no jeans or trainers; booking: max 8; set weekday L £61 (FP).*

GORDON RAMSAY AT CLARIDGE'S
CLARIDGE'S HOTEL W1 £87 ④❸❷
55 Brook St 7499 0099 3–2B
*"Capitalising on Ramsay's name"; this Art Deco-style Mayfair
chamber may look "impressive", but the cooking too often seems
"conservative, going-on boring" nowadays – by a growing margin,
reporters find it "nothing like as good as in Royal Hospital Road",
and "ludicrously" pricey too. / www.gordonramsay.com; 11 pm; no jeans
or trainers; booking: max 8; set weekday L £44 (FP).*

Gordon's Wine Bar WC2 £22 ⑤❸❶
47 Villiers St 7930 1408 4–4D
*"It's got to be Gordon's!"; nothing to do with the "overpriced" food,
though – "it's the ambience" of this "secret", "dark" and "dingy"
cellar, near Embankment tube, which makes it a sure-fire "winner"
(and, for the summer, there's a huge terrace).
/ www.gordonswinebar.com; 11 pm; no booking.*

The Goring Hotel SW1 £68 ❸❶❷
15 Beeston Pl 7396 9000 2–4B
*"Dignified, discreet and quintessentially English" – the "grown-up"
dining room of this "charming", family-owned hotel, near Victoria,
is a "virtually flawless oasis" of "old-fashioned" values; its food
is "absolutely reliable" (and includes, of course, the "best civilised
breakfast"). / www.goringhotel.co.uk; 10 pm; closed Sat L; booking: max 12.*

Gourmet Burger Kitchen £20 ❷④④
15 Frith St, W1 7494 9533 3–2A
13-14 Maiden Ln, WC2 7240 9617 4–4D
163-165 Earl's Court Rd, SW5 7373 3184 5–2A
49 Fulham Broadway, SW6 7381 4242 5–4A
107 Old Brompton Rd, SW7 7581 8942 5–2B
160 Portobello Rd, W11 7243 6597 6–1B
50 Westbourne Grove, W2 7243 4344 6–1B
131 Chiswick High Rd, W4 8995 4548 7–2A
200 Haverstock Hill, NW3 7443 5335 8–2A
44 Northcote Rd, SW11 7228 3309 10–2C
333 Putney Bridge Rd, SW15 8789 1199 10–2B
84 Clapham High St, SW4 7627 5367 10–2D
Condor Hs, St Paul's Churchyard, EC4 7248 9199 9–2B

Gourmet Burger Kitchen (Cont)

*These ubiquitous "fuel stops" are widely acclaimed for
"the best burgers in town" (and "by a mile"); it's important to note
that it's the food, though, that makes this the survey's most talked-
about chain – the atmosphere's "very average", and service can
be "painfully slow". / www.gbkinfo.com; 10.45 pm; no Amex; no booking.*

Gourmet Pizza Company   £28   ❸④❸

7-9 Swallow St, W1   7734 5182   3–3D
Gabriels Wharf, 56 Upper Ground, SE1   7928 3188   9–3A
18 Mackenzie Walk, E14   7345 9192   11–1C

*"Great pizza" with "interesting toppings" wins praise for this small
chain; its SE1 branch – with its "lovely" outside tables – is arguably
"the best of the cheap eateries that now line the South Bank".
/ www.gourmetpizzacompany.co.uk; W1 10 pm, Sat & Sun 11.30 pm;
E14 10 pm, Sat & Sun 11 pm; SE1 10.45 pm; E14 closed Sat & Sun;
W1, need 8+ to book, SE1 need 7+ to book.*

Gow's EC2   £44   ❸④④

81-82 Old Broad St   7920 9645   9–2C

*"Fine for business, but nothing exciting" – this "traditional" City
"haunt" offers "a super range of fresh fish daily"; for "great value",
seek out the set-price dinner menu. / www.ballsbrothers.co.uk; 9.30 pm;
closed Sat & Sun; booking: max 10; set dinner £29 (FP).*

The Gowlett SE15   £26   ❸❷❸

62 Gowlett Rd   7635 7048   1–4C

*"Pizzas cooked thin and crispy" – plus "plenty of good beer" –
win strong local approval for this "excellent" Peckham boozer.
/ www.thegowlett.com; 10.30 pm.*

Goya   £33   ④❸❸

2 Ecclestone Pl, SW1   7730 4299   2–4B
34 Lupus St, SW1   7976 5309   2–4C

*The food at these "reliable" and "relaxed" Spanish joints
is "nothing special", but they have their uses –
the "unatmospheric" Victoria branch is a "handy stand-by" near
the coach station, and its sibling is "somewhere in Pimlico that's
actually nice!" / www.goyarestaurant.co.uk; 11.30 pm; set weekday L
£13 (FP).*

Grafton House SW4   £45   ❸❸❸

13-19 Old Town   7498 5559   10–2D

*For a "chilled" brunch, this trendy Clapham yearling makes "a great
destination"; the food at other times is "good", too, but the setting
"can lack atmosphere". / www.graftonhouseuk.com; 10.30 pm; D only,
ex Sun L only; booking essential.*

Gran Paradiso SW1   £41   ❸❸❸

52 Wilton Rd   7828 5818   2–4B

*"An oasis in the Pimlico desert" – this old-fashioned Italian is never
going to set the world alight, but has a loyal (generally older)
following, thanks to its "consistent" cooking and "family-run" style.
/ 10.45 pm; closed Sat L & Sun.*

The Grapes E14   £40   ❷❸❶

76 Narrow St   7987 4396   11–1B

*"A great little find in the East End" – this ancient Thameside pub
serves "cracking fish" (and "the best Sunday roasts"); you can eat
in the bar, but the main menu is served in the "smarter" and
"cosier" upstairs room, which has "great views". / 11 pm; closed
Sun D.*

Grazing EC3 NEW   £15   ❷❸④
19-21 Great Tower St   7283 2932   9–3D
*A new City snackery, offering "fantastic breakfasts" – and, at lunch,
"quality roast-meat sarnies, carved while-u-wait" – to eat in and
take away. / www.grazingfood.com; L only; no credit cards.*

Great Eastern Dining Room EC2   £40   ❷❷❷
54 Gt Eastern St   7613 4545   9–1D
*"In a sea of trendy bars", Will Ricker's "funky hotspot",
in "the heart of Shoreditch", still stands out, thanks to its "fantastic
Pan-Asian food" and its "superb cocktail list".
/ www.rickerrestaurants.com; 11 pm; closed Sat L & Sun.*

Great Nepalese NW1   £24   ❷❸④
48 Eversholt St   7388 6737   8–3C
*This Nepalese veteran, besides Euston station, is "a notch above"
your average Indian; it offers "good staples done well, plus a few
interesting dishes to try on an adventurous day".
/ www.great-nepalese.co.uk; 11.30 pm; closed Sun.*

Great Queen Street WC2 NEW   £36   ❷❸④
32 Great Queen St   7242 0622   4–1D
*This new Covent Garden dining room – largely backed by the same
people as the legendary Anchor & Hope – is "an object-lesson
in understatement"; our early-days experience of its "pared-down
British menu" was good rather than amazing, but early reporters
say the place is a "triumph". / 10.30 pm; closed Mon L & Sun; no Amex.*

Green & Blue SE22   £19   ❸❸❷
38 Lordship Ln   8693 9250   1–4D
*"One of the most unusual wine lists you will ever encounter"
rewards visitors to this East Dulwich wine shop; drink your choice
at a "very modest mark-up", with some simple but "good-value"
pies, salads and cheese. / www.greenandbluewines.com; 11 pm, Fri & Sat
midnight, Sun 10.30 pm; no Amex.*

Green & Red Bar & Cantina E1   £38   ❶❸❷
51 Bethnal Green Rd   7749 9670   1–2D
*"1,000,000 miles away from Tex-Mex yukiness" – this "cool"
cantina, near Brick Lane, serves Mexican food that's the
"real thing" (and better than anything else in town); there's also
"an amazing selection of tequilas" – "it's worth a visit for that
alone". / www.greenred.co.uk; 11 pm; Mon-Fri closed L, Sat & Sun closed D.*

Green Chilli W6 NEW   £27   ❷❸④
220 King St   8748 0111   7–2B
*"In an area crowded with curry houses", this "modern"
Hammersmith newcomer is "among the best"; the cuisine
is essentially "traditional", but comes "with a twist".
/ www.greenchilliltd.co.uk; midnight.*

The Green Olive W9   £38   ❸❷❸
5 Warwick Pl   7289 2469   8–4A
*"Elegantly-presented" cooking and service that's often "excellent"
win praise for this Little Venice Italian. / 10 pm; Mon-Thu D only, Fri-Sun
open L & D; no Amex; booking: max 20.*

Green's SW1 £55 ❸❷❷
36 Duke St 7930 4566 3–3D
"Expense be damned!", say fans of Simon Parker Bowles's "club-like but unstuffy" bastion of St James's – a "charming", "old-school" fixture that promises "no surprises", just "marvellous fish and nursery food", "professionally" served. / www.greens.org.uk; 11 pm, Sun 9 pm; May-Sep closed Sun.

The Greenhouse W1 £87 ❸❸❸
27a Hays Mews 7499 3331 3–3B
The "tucked-away" location is "lovely", the food can be "stunning" and the wine list is "immense", yet the "staid" régime at Marlon Abela's Mayfair mews spot does not invariably please reporters; perhaps it would help if prices weren't so "extortionate". / www.greenhouserestaurant.co.uk; 11 pm; closed Sat L & Sun; booking: max 6-10; set weekday L £53 (FP).

Greig's W1 £54 ④④⑤
26 Bruton Pl 7629 5613 3–2B
For its fans, this "good Mayfair steakhouse" is a "clubby" sort of place, where the food is occasionally "fantastic"; it's a "strange, long, narrow room", though, and a fair few critics find it "distinctly average" all round. / www.greigs.com; midnight; set weekday L £25 (FP).

Grenadier SW1 £37 ④④❶
18 Wilton Row 7235 3074 5–1D
This "hidden jewel" of a pub, in a Belgravia mews, is in every tourist guide, and you pay accordingly if you want to eat in its "cosy" dining room; those in the know opt for a sausage and a Bloody Mary – both house specialities – at the bar. / 9.30 pm.

The Greyhound NW10 £33 ❸❸❸
64-66 Chamberlayne Rd 8969 8080 1–2B
This Queen's Park gastropub is the sort of place that does "great fish 'n' chips"; a particular feature is the "nice courtyard garden". / www.breadandhoney.net; 10.30 pm, Sun 6 pm; closed Mon L & Sun D.

The Greyhound at Battersea SW11 £45 ❸❷❸
136 Battersea High St 7978 7021 10–1C
This Battersea backstreet operation – "not a gastropub, but a restaurant in a pub space" – has a "sensational wine list of biblical proportions"; the food can be "interesting" too. / www.thegreyhoundatbattersea.co.uk; 10 pm; closed Mon & Sun D.

Grissini SW4 £31 ❸④❸
31 Abbeville Rd 8675 6260 10–2D
"Hilarious" staff add to the appeal of this well-established Clapham trattoria (which has changed its name from Antipasto e Pasta). / 11 pm.

Ground W4 NEW £26 ❷❷❸
217-221 Chiswick High Rd 8747 9113 7–2A
"It thrashes GBK", say fans of this Chiswick "newcomer to the upmarket burger scene", where "great courgette fries" are a top tip from the "fantastic" menu; it's certainly more "atmospheric". / Mon-Sat 11 pm.

The Grove W6 £35 ❸❷❸
83 Hammersmith Grove 8748 2966 7–1C
"A little way from the bustle and grime of Hammersmith Broadway", this attractive corner-pub offers "simple" and "varied" food, usually realised to a very tolerable standard. / www.groverestaurants.co.uk; 11 pm; no Amex.

Grumbles SW1 £35 ④❷❸
35 Churton St 7834 0149 2–4B
A "cosy" and "old-fashioned" Pimlico bistro with a certain "steady" charm; "we used to eat here 35 years ago – it's still perfectly acceptable". / www.grumbles.co.uk; 11 pm; set weekday L £23 (FP).

The Guinea Grill W1 £52 ❷❸❸
30 Bruton Pl 7409 1728 3–3B
"Great steaks" and "brilliant pies" ("with crust to die for, and rich gravy") fly the flag for traditional British cuisine at this "squashed" but "cosy" pub-cum-grill, hidden-away in Mayfair; all this, and "a very decent pint" in the bar too. / www.theguinea.co.uk; 10.30 pm; closed Sat L & Sun; booking: max 8.

The Gun E14 £42 ❷❸❷
27 Coldharbour Ln 7515 5222 11–1C
This "brilliant", "chilled-out" Thames-side boozer may be "wretched to get to", but it's worth the trek for its "fabulous comfort food" and the "great views of the Dome"; there's also a terrace for the summer, and "roaring fires" in winter. / www.thegundocklands.com; 10.30 pm.

Gung-Ho NW6 £34 ❸❷❷
328-332 West End Ln 7794 1444 1–1B
Traditionally rated "a cut-above a 'local' Chinese", this West Hampstead all-rounder took more flak than usual this year from critics who find it "nothing special". / www.stir-fry.co.uk; 11.30 pm; no Amex.

Haandi SW7 £36 ❷❷❸
7 Cheval Pl 7823 7373 5–1C
"Shame they lost the front door" (almost opposite Harrods), but last year's refurb has really perked up this "reasonably-priced" Indian – its back (mews) entrance is well worth finding! / www.haandi-restaurant.com; 11 pm, Fri-Sat 11.30 pm.

Haché NW1 £24 ❷❸❷
24 Inverness St 7485 9100 8–3B
"Eclipsing the various gastro-burger chains", this "cosy" Camden Town two-year-old boasts, for many reporters, "the best burgers in London", and "brisk but friendly" service too. / www.hacheburgers.co.uk; 10.30 pm.

Hadley House E11 £40 ❸❸④
27 Wanstead High St 8989 8855 1–1D
This busy local is big news down Wanstead way; its "reasonable" food is consistently well rated – service and ambience less so. / 10.30 pm; no Amex.

Haiku W1 NEW £60 ④⑤⑤
15 New Burlington Pl 7494 4777 3–2C
"Choice is almost impossible" – so vast and miscellaneous is the "whirlwind" of a pan-oriental menu – at this "dark and moody" three-story newcomer, off Savile Row; dishes are "well-executed", but still seem "overpriced", and early-days service has been "intolerably poor". / 10.30 pm; closed Sun.

HAKKASAN W1 £76 ③④❷
8 Hanway Pl   7927 7000   4–1A
*"For sheer WOW! factor", it's hard to beat Alan Yau's "sexy",
"dark" and "moody" West End basement-oriental, and the cuisine
(especially dim sum) is "incredible" too; on the downside,
the location is "grim", prices are "astronomical", and service
is definitely "cooler-than-thou". / 11.30 pm, Fri-Sat 12.30 pm.*

Halepi W2 £35 ④❷❸
18 Leinster Ter   7262 1070   6–2C
*It may be "in its own special time warp", but this "'60s" Greek
"shack" in Bayswater is – for fans – "as reliable as ever"; others
are baffled by its alleged appeal. / www.halepi.co.uk; midnight.*

Hamburger Union £21 ③④④
25 Dean St, W1   7437 6004   4–2A
64 Tottenham Court Rd, W1   7636 0011   2–1C NEW
4-6 Garrick St, WC2   7379 0412   4–3C
Irving St (off Leicester Sq), WC2   7839 8100   4–4B NEW
341 Upper St, N1   7359 4436   8–3D NEW
1 South End Rd, NW3   7794 7070   8–2A NEW
*"Quality" burgers – "juicy, but not greasy, and generously-sized too"
– win many votes for this growing chain; overall, though, reporters
rate the scoff some way behind the market leader, GBK.
/ www.hamburgerunion.com; 10.30 pm; no Amex; no booking.*

Hammersmith Café W6 £15 ③③④
1a Studland St   8748 2839   7–2B
*For the very "essence of greasy breakfasts", this "shabby"-looking
Hammersmith caff is the place; from lunch onwards, however,
it becomes a BYO Thai, serving "great-value" dishes at low,
low prices. / 10.30 pm; closed Sun L; no credit cards.*

Hara The Circle Bar SE1 £40 ❶❷⑤
Queen Elizabeth St   0845 226 9411   9–4D
*"Wow!", the food is "stunning", at this "inventive" Indian bar
(downstairs)/restaurant (upstairs), hidden-away near Tower Bridge;
its location "doesn't do it justice", though, and it's too often
"empty". / www.hararara.co.uk; midnight.*

Harbour City W1 £26 ③③④
46 Gerrard St   7439 7859   4–3B
*"Some of the very best dim sum, and definitely the best value" wins
praise for this otherwise "basic" Chinatown fixture. / 11.30 pm, Fri &
Sat midnight, Sun 10.*

Hard Rock Café W1 £36 ④❸❷
150 Old Park Ln   7629 0382   3–4B
*Amazingly, this "very noisy" tourist-trail "Golden Oldie" can still
make "a great place to chill out"; the American fare may generally
be "mediocre", but the burgers "rarely disappoint".
/ www.hardrock.com; 12.30 am; need 10+ to book.*

Hardy's W1 £42 ❸❸❸
53 Dorset St   7935 5929   2–1A
*"Honest" British cooking and "friendly" service draw many loyal
regulars to this civilised Marylebone veteran; "it's supposed to be
a wine bar", but you eat "brasserie-style". / www.hardys-wl.com;
10.30 pm; closed Sat L & Sun; no Amex.*

Hare & Tortoise £21 ④④④
15-17 Brunswick Sq, WC1 7278 4945 2–1D
373 Kensington High St, W14 7603 8887 7–1D
38 Haven Grn, W5 8610 7066 1–2A
296-298 Upper Richmond Rd, SW15 8394 7666 10–2B
You get "solid"-quality food – "really cheap", and in "generous helpings" too – at this "useful" sushi-to-noodles chain; at the more popular branches, "there's usually a queue".
/ www.hareandtortoise-restaurants.co.uk; 10.45 pm; W14 no bookings.

Harlem W2 £42 ④④③
78 Westbourne Grove 7985 0900 6–1B
"Cracking cocktails" and "excellent American brunch menus" are key strengths of this "buzzing" Bayswater "hotspot"; when it's busy, though, service can be "slow" (and "despite the name, the place is actually full of Euro-bankers, juggling their BlackBerrys").
/ www.harlemsoulfood.com; 2 am, Sun midnight.

Harrison's SW12 NEW £40
15-19 Bedford Hill 8675 6900 10–2C
As this guide was heading towards the press, it emerged that Nick Jones had sold the Balham Bar & Grill (RIP) to Sam Harrison; the site is to be relaunched as a sibling to Sam's Brasserie, and in a broadly similar style, in late-2007.

Harry Morgan's NW8 £33 ④④⑤
31 St John's Wood High St 7722 1869 8–3A
"No other deli comes close", say fans of this Jewish "institution" in St John's Wood, who hail its "chicken soup like mama used to make" and "massive portions of salt beef"; the unconvinced, however, find it an "ordinary" place, charging "rip-off" prices.
/ www.harryms.co.uk; 10.30 pm.

The Hartley SE1 £35 ❸❸❷
64 Tower Bridge Rd 7394 7023 1–3C
A mile or so south of Tower Bridge, a very "decent" gastropub – it's "far better than others nearby". / www.thehartley.com; 10 pm, Sun 7 pm.

The Hat & Feathers EC1 NEW £40 ④④④
2 Clerkenwell Rd 7490 2244 9–1B
This formal – and "slightly sterile" – dining room makes a rather "strange" find on the first floor of a newly-converted Clerkenwell boozer; some dishes are of "high quality", but reports overall are mixed. / www.hatandfeathers.com; 10.30 pm; closed Sat L & Sun.

The Havelock Tavern W14 £35 ❷⑤❸
57 Masbro Rd 7603 5374 7–1C
"Back with a vengeance" – post-fire, this famous Olympia backstreet gastropub is again dishing up some "fantastic" and "innovative" dishes; even if the food is perhaps a touch more "hit-and-miss" than it was, the service – "rudeness elevated to a fine art" – provides reassuring continuity. / www.thehavelocktavern.co.uk; 10 pm; no credit cards; no booking.

The Haven N20 £36 ❸❷❷
1363 High Rd 8445 7419 1–1B
Despite an unlikely Whetsone location, this "excellent" five-year-old draws fans from across north London with its "interesting" cuisine and its "ebullient" atmosphere. / www.haven-bistro.co.uk; 10.30 pm; no Amex; set weekday L £23 (FP).

Hawksmoor E1   £52   ❷❸❸
157 Commercial St   7247 7392   9–1D
*"Brilliant", "man-sized" steaks, "truly award-winning chips",
and cocktails that are the "real thing" have won instant acclaim for
this "loud" yearling, just north of Spitalfields.*
/ www.thehawksmoor.co.uk; 10.30 pm; closed Sat L & Sun.

Haz   £32   ❸❷❷
9 Cutler St, E1   7929 7923   9–2D
6 Mincing Ln, EC3   7929 3173   9–3D **NEW**
*"Good-quality food" is served in "smart and slick" surroundings
at these "vibrant" Turkish ventures, whose large City outlets are
"usually jam-packed at lunchtime".* / 11.30 pm.

Hazuki WC2   £32   ❸❷④
43 Chandos Pl   7240 2530   4–4C
*"For a light snack or full meal" that's both central (by the 'Trafalgar
Square' Post Office) and "affordable", this unpretentious and
"consistent" Japanese is "one of the best".* / www.hazukilondon.co.uk;
10.30 pm, Sun 9 pm; closed Sun L.

Hellenik W1   £31   ❸❶❸
30 Thayer St   7935 1257   2–1A
*"The world moves on, leaving the odd gem like this in its wake…";
it may be an "anachronism", but this veteran Marylebone Greek
offers retro-charm of a sort it's "pitifully hard to find" nowadays,
and "you eat well for a good price".* / 10.45 pm; closed Sun; no Amex.

Henry J Beans SW3   £33   ⑤④④
195-197 King's Rd   7352 9255   5–3C
*This "formulaic" burger veteran seems "well past its sell-by"
nowadays; it does, however, boast the largest garden in Chelsea
(or so it has always claimed).* / www.henryjbeans.com; 10.30 pm.

Hereford Road W2 **NEW**   £45
3 Hereford Rd   7727 1144   6–1B
*As this guide goes to press, Tom Pemberton – ex-head chef
of St John Bread & Wine – is striking out alone, in a former
Bayswater butcher's shop; there are a few gastropubs succeeding
with 'school-of-St-John' cooking – perhaps this will be one of the
first restaurants to do so; price given is our guesstimate.*
/ www.herefordroad.org.

The Herne Tavern SE22 **NEW**   £35   ❸❸❸
2 Forest Hill Rd   8299 9521   1–4D
*A "very relaxed" new Herne Hill gastroboozer; early reports say
it offers "restaurant-standard" food, and service that's "very friendly
and efficient".* / www.hernetavern.co.uk; 9.45 pm; no Amex.

Hibiscus W1 **NEW**   £65
29 Maddox St   7629 2999   3–2C
*Claude Bosi is very close to the pinnacle of UK gastronomy , and –
though little-known in the capital – achieved survey ratings among
the country's very best when he was cooking in Ludlow; in late-
2007, he opens in Mayfair with the same team (and same prices!)
that won him fame in Shropshire – could be the début of the year.*

High Road Brasserie W4 £44 ❸❷❷
162-166 Chiswick High Rd   8742 7474   7–2A
This "cool" and "buzzy" new member of Nick 'Soho House' Jones's
empire has proved "an excellent addition to Chiswick";
the brasserie fare "isn't going to win any Michelin stars", but it
is "well-prepared and thought-out" (and brunch is "fabulous"). / www.highroadhouse.co.uk; 10.45 pm, Fri & Sat 11.45 pm; set weekday L £28 (FP).

The Hill NW3 £40 ❸❹❸
94 Haverstock Hill   7267 0033   8–2B
"Funky" styling helps create a "classy" vibe at this former Belsize
Park boozer; sometimes, though, its performance seems
"amateurish". / 10 pm; no Amex.

Hilliard EC4 £24 ❶❶❸
26a Tudor St   7353 8150   9–3A
"It's odd to see barristers polishing off bottles of claret in a
sandwich shop!", but this "gastro-café", by Inner Temple, is a
"magnificent" place, which uses "fantastic" ingredients to create
some "top-class" bites. / www.hilliardfood.co.uk; 6 pm; closed Sat & Sun.

Hokkien Chan EC2 NEW £35 ❹❹❹
85 London Wall   7628 5772   9–2C
An oriental basement formerly known as Sri Siam City (RIP);
we thought its pan-Asian menu pretty dull on our early-days visit,
but other (limited) feedback is more upbeat. / Rated on Editors' visit;
www.orientalrestaurantgroup.co.uk; 10.30 pm; closed Sat & Sun.

Hole in the Wall W4 £38 ❸❸❸
12 Sutton Lane North   8742 7185   7–2A
"Hidden-away in a quiet backstreet", south of Turnham Green,
this "friendly" gastropub offers "good-value" cooking, and it boasts
an "ace garden" too. / 9.45 pm.

Holly Bush NW3 £35 ❸❹❶
22 Holly Mount   7435 2892   8–1A
A "fabulous old-world" interior ensures that this countrified boozer,
just 100 yards from Hampstead tube, is often "crowded"
(so "get there early"); it serves a hearty menu of "better-than-basic
pub fare". / www.hollybushpub.com; 10 pm; no Amex.

Homage
Waldorf Hilton WC2 £50 ❹❹❷
22 Aldwych   7759 4080   2–2D
It may have a "lovely" setting in a "glamorous" ex-ballroom,
but this grand Aldwych brasserie remains largely unknown; those
who go for the "excellent-value set menus" (lunchtime or pre-
theatre), however, say it's "a great find". / www.homagerestaurant.co.uk;
10 pm; closed Sat L & Sun L; booking: max 6.

Home EC2 £42 ❹❹❸
100-106 Leonard St   7684 8618   9–1D
A "trendy" Shoreditch hang-out, combining a "retro" basement bar
with a ground-floor restaurant; it's often acclaimed for its
"innovative" cooking, but this year's reports included more "let-
downs" than usual. / www.homebar.co.uk; 11 pm; closed Sat L & Sun.

The Horseshoe NW3 NEW £32 ❷❸❷
28 Heath St 7431 7206 8–2A
You get "simple" British food "served with flair" at this new heart-of-Hampstead gastropub; "there are so few good places roundabouts", though, that it's "constantly rammed", and service can be "erratic". / www.thehorseshoehampstead.com; 10 pm; no Amex; set weekday L £18 (FP).

Hot Stuff SW8 £20 ❶❶❸
19 Wilcox Rd 7720 1480 10–1D
"Sensational" curries, "astoundingly cheap" prices, and "the friendliest" service – a formula that wins adulation for this "crowded, downmarket and wonderful" South Lambeth Indian; BYO. / www.eathotstuff.com; 10 pm; closed Sun.

The House N1 £45 ❸④❸
63-69 Canonbury Rd 7704 7410 8–2D
"High-end gastro-grub, served with panache" has won a big fan club for this Islington boozer (which is "really a restaurant" nowadays); even fans say it's "overpriced", though, and service tends to be "lackadaisical". / www.inthehouse.biz; 10.30 pm; closed Mon L; no Amex.

Hoxton Apprentice N1 £37 ❸❷❸
16 Hoxton Sq 7739 6022 9–1D
"It doesn't get the same publicity as Fifteen", but this "cool" Hoxton training-restaurant "deserves to be more widely known"; the grub is "cheap" and "surprisingly good", and service is "enthusiastic" and "charming" (in an "up-and-down" sort of way). / www.hoxtonapprentice.com; 11 pm; no Amex.

The Hoxton Grille EC2 NEW £38 ④❷❷
81 Great Eastern St 7739 9111 9–1D
Views on the cooking at this new "budget-chic" design-hotel range from "great" to "very average", so a safer attraction is "soaking up the Hoxton vibe"; breakfast here also has its fans. / www.grillerestaurants.com; 10.30 pm, Fri & Sat 11.30 pm.

Hoxton Square Bar & Kitchen N1 £36 ④④❷
2-4 Hoxton Sq 7613 0709 9–1D
"Full of trendy types", this stylish Hoxton bunker offers "good people-watching", and a tolerable bar menu. / www.hoxtonsqbarandkitchen.com; 11pm, Sun 8 pm; no Amex.

Hudson's SW15 £32 ④④❷
113 Lower Richmond Rd 8785 4522 10–1A
A "heaving Putney local", still widely tipped for its "great hangover-cure" brunch, and "great buzz"; this year, though, saw more flak for "uncaring" service and "food that's average, when prices are not". / 10.30 pm.

Hugo's £39 ❸❸❸
51 Prince's Gate, SW7 7596 4006 5–1C
25 Lonsdale Rd, NW6 7372 1232 1–2B
"Wholesome" dishes (with "lots of organic choice") – not least "excellent burgers" and "chunky chips" – help make the Goethe Institute's annexe "one of the best options near the Albert Hall"; there's also a "cute" branch for Queen's Park "yummy mummies". / SW7 10 pm, NW6 10 pm.

Hummus Bros £14 ❸❷④
88 Wardour St, W1   7734 1311   3–2D
37-63 Southampton Row, WC1   7404 7079   2–1D **NEW**
*For a "fast" and "healthy" pit stop, this "cheap and very cheerful"
(almost "studenty") new chain is excellent; "you do have to like
hummus", of course, but "with all the various combos, it's not
boring at all!"* / www.hbros.co.uk; WC1 & W1 10 pm.

Hunan SW1 £46 ❶❶④
51 Pimlico Rd   7730 5712   5–2D
*"Do as you're told, and eat what you're given" – that's the way
to get the best out of Mr Peng's "stellar", but "unpretentious" and
"friendly", Pimlico Chinese, which remains among
"the best in London".* / 11.30 pm; closed Sun.

Huong-Viet
An Viet House N1 £22 ❷⑤④
12-14 Englefield Rd   7249 0877   1–1C
*This "always-packed" Vietnamese canteen in De Beauvoir Town
offers "a quality of food way out of line with its interior", and at
"fantastic prices"; "the bad service is part of the charm".*
/ www.huongviet.co.uk; 11 pm; closed Sun; no Amex.

Hush W1 £55 ④④❸
8 Lancashire Ct   7659 1500   3–2B
*"A great location" – "tucked-away" from the bustle of Bond Street,
and with "fabulous outside tables" – helps draw a "lively" crowd
to this "trendy" bar/brasserie; for the price, however, the food
is "patently unexceptional", and service likewise.* / www.hush.co.uk;
10.30 pm; closed Sun; booking: max 12; set pre theatre £34 (FP).

I Thai
The Hempel W2 £65 ⑤⑤④
31-35 Craven Hill Gdns   7298 9001   6–2C
*This once-glamorous, Zen-minimalist fusion basement in Bayswater
attracts very limited and mixed feedback nowadays, mostly of the
"disappointing" variety.* / www.the-hempel.co.uk; 10.30 pm; D only,
closed Sun.

Las Iguanas
Royal Festival Hall SE1 **NEW** £35 ④④④
Unit 14, Festival Walk, Belvedere Rd   7620 1328   2–3D
*A "nice location" (with "great outside tables") is a prime draw
to this "lively" new South American, by the Royal Festival Hall;
feedback on the food – including "interesting-sounding" tapas –
is very mixed, though.* / www.iguanas.co.uk; 11 pm.

Ikeda W1 £68 ❶❸⑤
30 Brook St   7629 2730   3–2B
*Mrs Ikeda's stalwart Mayfair Japanese doesn't look much,
and provokes little feedback nowadays, but its fans "are happy for
others to nominate lesser places" – "it makes it easier to get
a table here", to enjoy the "extraordinary sushi".* / 10.15 pm; closed
Sat L & Sun; set weekday L £31 (FP).

Ikkyu W1 £30 ❸④❸
67a Tottenham Court Rd   7636 9280   2–1C
*"Like a student restaurant in Japan"; this "easy-to-miss" basement,
by Goode Street tube, may have a setting notably "lacking
in glamour", but the authentic, if basic, food "more than makes
up for it".* / 10 pm; closed Sat & Sun L.

Il Bacio £28 ❸❸❸
61 Stoke Newington Church St, N16   7249 3833   1–1C
178-184 Blackstock Rd, N5   7226 3339   8–1D
"Excellent pizzas" are the star turn at this "rightly popular" duo of "friendly" north London Italians; the Sardinian specialities are also "worth trying". / N5 & N16 11 pm; N5 Mon-Thu L - N16 Mon-Fri L; no Amex.

Imli W1 £25 ❸❸④
167-169 Wardour St   7287 4243   3–1D
"Tasty Indian snacks at bargain prices" have won a big following for this "bright" and "busy" Soho yearling; service, though, can be "patchy". / www.imli.co.uk; 11 pm.

Imperial China WC2 £37 ❷❸❸
25a Lisle St   7734 3388   4–3B
A large but "hidden-away" Chinatown "oasis" that's "a bit smarter than average", and offers food that's "reliable and fairly-priced"; "superb dim sum" too. / 11.30 pm.

Imperial City EC3 £41 ❸❸❷
Royal Exchange, Cornhill   7626 3437   9–2C
"Good food, and comfortable, despite its large size" – this "hidden" Chinese "gem" (in the cellars of the Royal Exchange) has long been one of the City's better all-rounders. / www.orientalrestaurantgroup.co.uk; 10.30 pm; closed Sat & Sun.

Inaho W2 £31 ❶⑤⑤
4 Hereford Rd   7221 8495   6–1B
"Tiny" and "eccentric", this "Swiss chalet"-style shack in Bayswater is the unlikely venue for some of "the best sushi in town"; be prepared for "very long waits" for service, though. / 11 pm; closed Sat L & Sun L; no Amex or Maestro.

Incognico WC2 £50 ❸❸❸
117 Shaftesbury Ave   7836 8866   4–2B
In the heart of Theatreland, this "rather formal" brasserie makes a natural pre-show destination; it's also tipped as a useful business-lunch haunt. / www.incognico.com; 11 pm; closed Sun.

L'Incontro SW1 £55 ④④❸
87 Pimlico Rd   7730 6327   5–2D
This "slick" Pimlico Italian is, say fans, "one of the best in town" – "albeit at a hefty cost"; as ever, though, critics say it charges "absurd prices for utterly ordinary cooking". / www.lincontro-restaurant.com; 11.30 pm, Sat & Sun 10.30 pm.

India Club
Strand Continental Hotel WC2 £21 ④④④
143 Strand   7836 0650   2–2D
This "astonishingly cheap", "no-frills" Aldwych institution is – for better or worse – "just like a real canteen in Delhi"; BYO. / 10.45 pm; no credit cards; booking: max 6.

Indian Ocean SW17 £25 ❷❶❸
216 Trinity Rd   8672 7740   10–2C
"Consistently good" and "well-priced" cooking (with fish a speciality) makes this "welcoming" and "lavishly-staffed" Indian very popular, down Wandsworth way; "they also have a super take-away service". / 11.30 pm.

Indian Zing W6 £29 ❷⓿❸
236 King St   8748 5959   7–2B
The "fantastic" food is full of "fresh, crisp flavours", at Manog
Vasaikar's "classy" (if unglamorously-located) and "personable"
Hammersmith yearling – "a modern take on the traditional
neighbourhood Indian". / www.indianzing.co.uk; 10.30 pm.

Indigo
One Aldwych WC2 £55 ❸❷❷
I Aldwych   7300 0400   2–2D
"Overlooking a buzzing bar", this "smart" and "spacious"
mezzanine restaurant – part of a "hip hotel" near Covent Garden
– is a "classy" venue with "attentive" service and "reliable" cuisine;
it's most popular for business and pre-theatre. / 11.15 pm.

The Inn at Kew Gardens
Kew Gardens Hotel TW9 £32 ❸④❷
292 Sandycombe Ln   8940 2220   1–4A
An "atmospheric" conversion of an old Kew tavern; the food
is "surprisingly good", but service can sometimes be "a little too
laid-back". / www.theinnatkewgardens.com; 10 pm.

Inn the Park SW1 £45 ④⑤④
St James's Pk   7451 9999   2–3C
What a "waste" – Oliver Peyton's St James's Park venture may
have a "lovely design" and "beautiful park views", but the service
is "appallingly incompetent", and the British food is "average" and
"overpriced"; for a "tasty" breakfast fry-up, though, the place still
has its attractions. / 10 pm, Winter 9 pm.

Inshoku SE1 £25 ④④⑤
23-24 Lower Marsh   7928 2311   9–4A
"Shabby" Waterloo Japanese, usually praised for its "reliably cheap
but good-quality" noodles and sushi; even some fans, though,
fear "the food has slipped" of late. / 10.30 pm; closed Sat L & Sun.

Inside SE10 £38 ⓿❸④
19 Greenwich South St   8265 5060   1–3D
The settling may be "like someone's front room", and service can
get "confused", but the food at Guy Awford's "unassuming"
Greenwich gaff is "phenomenally good" – possibly
"the best in South East London". / www.insiderestaurant.co.uk; 10.30 pm,
Fri-Sat 11pm; closed Mon & Sun D.

Isarn N1 £34 ❷⓿❷
119 Upper St   7424 5153   8–3D
With its "careful cooking", this Islington two-year-old, "stands apart
from your run-of-the-mill Thais"; it's a "stylish" place, too, with
notably accomplished and "friendly" service. / www.isarn.co.uk; 11 pm.

Ishbilia SW1 £38 ❷❷④
9 William St   7235 7788   5–1D
"As you can see from the number of Arabs who dine here",
this "oasis among the Knightsbridge shops" is "authentically
Lebanese"; "wonderful mezze" is a highlight. / www.ishbilia.com;
11.30 pm.

Ishtar W1 £29 ❷❸❸
10-12 Crawford St   7224 2446   2–1A
"Consistent" and "reasonably-priced" cuisine makes this "buzzy"
Turkish venture, in Marylebone, popular with all who comment
on it. / www.ishtarrestaurant.com; midnight; no Amex.

The Island NW10 — £35 — ❸❸❸
123 College Rd   8960 0693   1–2B
"A welcome change to the Kensal Green landscape"; this year-old
gastropub is a "relaxed" sort of place which looks as if it would
be more at home in southern Spain – its food is "somewhat out-of-
the-ordinary" too. / www.islandpubco.com; 10.30 pm; closed Mon L;
no Amex.

Island
Royal Lancaster Hotel W2 — £46 — ④④④
Lancaster Ter   7551 6070   6–2D
A strikingly-designed Bayswater venture (where some tables have
impressive Kensington Gardens views); it hasn't lived up to its initial
promise – it's "a better-than-average hotel restaurant, but not
worth a detour". / www.islandrestaurant.co.uk; 11 pm.

Isola del Sole SW15 — £38 — ❷❷❸
16 Lacy Rd   8785 9962   10–2B
"A lovely, cosy Sicilian restaurant, in the heart of Putney", where
"very friendly and laid-back" staff serve up "good and original"
cooking. / www.isoladelsole.co.uk; 10.30 pm; closed Sun; no Amex.

Itsu — £26 — ❷❸❸
1 Hanover Sq, W1   7491 9799   3–2C
103 Wardour St, W1   7479 4790   3–2D
118 Draycott Ave, SW3   7590 2400   5–2C
28a Jubilee Pl, E14   7512 9650   11–1C
Level 2, Cabot Place East, E14   7512 5790   11–1C
These "efficient" conveyor-sushi cafés attract higher ratings than
most rivals, thanks to their "fantastic range" of "fresh" sushi and
sashimi, and "good noodle-soups" too. / www.itsu.co.uk; 11 pm,
E14 10 pm; Cabot Pl closed Sat & Sun; no booking.

THE IVY WC2 — £54 — ❸❷❷
1 West St   7836 4751   4–3B
"For a touch of glamour and a damn good time", this world-famous
Theatreland icon is still a "classic" destination; but for how much
longer? – realisation of its "comfort food" menu seems ever-more
"average", and some reporters feel the place is now "best left
to the WAGs". / www.the-ivy.co.uk; midnight; booking: max 6.

Izgara N3 — £24 — ❷❷❸
11 Hendon Lane   8371 8282   1–1B
"A local Godsend" – this "genuine" Turkish café/take-away,
in Finchley, offers some "wonderfully tasty" food, and maintains
a "thoughtful" level of service, even though it's often "packed".
/ midnight; no Amex.

Jaan
The Howard WC2 — £59 — ❷❸④
12 Temple Pl   7300 1700   2–2D
"Hints of the Fat Duck" permeate the "bizarre" but interesting
menu at this "smart" and "competent" – and often-overlooked –
dining room, in an hotel by Temple tube; it also boasts
an unexpected courtyard, which is "great in summer".
/ www.swissotel.com; 10.30 pm; closed Sat L & Sun.

Jade Garden W1 — £28 — ❸④❸
15 Wardour St   7437 5065   4–3A
A Chinatown veteran, known for its "high-quality and attractively
priced dim sum". / www.londonjadegarden.co.uk; 11 pm.

Jashan £21 ❶❷⑤
1-2 Coronet Pde, Ealing Rd, HA0   8900 9800   1–1A
19 Turnpike Ln, N8   8340 9880   1–1C
*For an exotic meal that's truly "cheap and cheerful", these friendly
south Indian canteens are very hard to beat.*
/ www.jashanrestaurants.co.uk; 10.45 pm; N8 D only, closed Mon; no Amex;
no weekend bookings; set weekday L £7 (FP).

Jenny Lo's Tea House SW1 £25 ❷❷④
14 Eccleston St   7259 0399   2–4B
*"Steaming noodles and stir-frys" that taste "fresh! fresh! fresh!" are
the sort of "easy, fun and quick" sustenance you find at this
"loud and hectic" Belgravia canteen.* / 10 pm; closed Sat L & Sun;
no credit cards; no booking.

Jerk City £18 ❸④⑤
189 Wardour St, W1   7287 2878   3–1D **NEW**
112 Wandsworth High St, SW18   8704 4770   10–2B **NEW**
*You "pay at the counter, scramble for a chair and wait for your
dishes", at these fun little Caribbean caffs (which previously traded
as Mr Jerk); "fab jerk chicken, curried goat and plantains" make for
an "excellent cheap eat".* / 11 pm, Sun 8 pm.

Jin Kichi NW3 £35 ❶❷④
73 Heath St   7794 6158   8–1A
*It feels "just like being in Tokyo", at this "very cramped"
Hampstead "hide-away", which is "packed nightly", thanks to its
"simple" but "fantastic" yakitori and sushi, at great prices.*
/ www.jinkichi.com; 11 pm; closed Mon, Tue-Fri D only, Sat & Sun open L & D.

Joanna's SE19 £34 ❸❷❷
56 Westow Hill   8670 4052   1–4D
*"A winner every time" – that's the local verdict on this low-lit
Crystal Palace "favourite", which boasts a "lovely" atmosphere,
"really friendly" service and "consistently good" food.*
/ www.joannas.uk.com; 11 pm.

Joe Allen WC2 £40 ④❸❶
13 Exeter St   7836 0651   4–3D
*It's the "light-hearted Theatreland vibe" that makes this Covent
Garden basement such an enduring favourite, and (especially late-
night) it's "still frequented by the odd celeb" – the American food
can be "truly awful", but the off-menu burgers have their fans.*
/ www.joeallen.co.uk; 12.45 am.

Joe's Brasserie SW6 £33 ❸❷❷
130 Wandsworth Bridge Rd   7731 7835   10–1B
*"The best-value wine in London" (from merchant/restaurateur John
Brinkley) is the special plus-point of this "buzzing" brasserie,
in deepest Fulham, but the food is often surprisingly "tasty" too.*
/ www.brinkleys.com; 11 pm.

Joe's Café SW3 £55 ④④❸
126 Draycott Ave   7225 2217   5–2C
*"A fun place to watch ladies-who-lunch pushing their food around
their plates" – this "perfect rendezvous", near Brompton Cross,
offers a "light" and "simple" menu (on which "great burgers" are,
curiously, a highlight).* / www.joseph.co.uk; 11 pm; closed Sat D & Sun D;
no booking at weekends.

Joy King Lau WC2 £24 ❷❸④
3 Leicester St 7437 1132 4–3A
A "staple" Cantonese, just off Leicester Square, that's "always busy with Chinese customers"; its cuisine, not least dim sum, is always "well-prepared". / 11.30 pm.

Julie's W11 £46 ⑤④❶
135 Portland Rd 7229 8331 6–2A
This "inventively-decorated" Holland Park survivor – a maze of "wonderful, romantic nooks and crannies" – holds fond memories for many reporters; it's a shame, then, that service is "amateurish", and the food is sometimes plain "rubbish". / www.juliesrestaurant.com; 11pm.

The Junction Tavern NW5 £34 ❸❷❷
101 Fortess Rd 7485 9400 8–2B
"Good beers", "extremely friendly service", a "great garden" and "uncomplicated", filling food – these are the virtues of this "airy" Kentish Town gastropub "favourite". / www.junctiontavern.co.uk; 10.30 pm; no Amex.

Just Falafs £16 ❷❷④
155 Wardour St, W1 7734 1914 3–1D NEW
27b Covent Garden Piazza, WC2 7240 3838 4–3D NEW
"Superb" falafel (and "great coffee" too) wins raves for this "miniscule" Covent Garden newcomer – on the edge of the Market, and with outside tables, it's much better than most of the tourist traps nearby; there is also now a branch in Soho. / www.justfalafs.com; WC2 9 pm, W1 10 pm, Fri & Sat 11 pm; W1 closed Sun; no credit cards.

Just Oriental SW1 £34 ❸❸❸
19 King St 7930 9292 3–4D
A "handy" basement bar/restaurant, in St James's, worth knowing about for its competent grub and competitive prices. / www.justoriental.com; 11 pm; closed Sat L & Sun.

Just St James SW1 £48 ④⑤④
12 St James's St 7976 2222 3–4D
"A bit of a waste of space… which considering they have so much to spare is a shame" – this "cavernous" ex-banking hall, in St James's, suffers from "poor" service and "unmemorable" food; as a business rendezvous, though, it has its fans. / www.juststjames.com; 11.30pm; closed Sat L & Sun.

K10 EC2 £30 ❷④❸
20 Copthall Ave 7562 8510 9–2C
"Still the best sushi canteen in the City" – for "top-end conveyor belt eating" (with "a Western twist"), this basement oriental hits the mark; "for lunch, get there early". / www.k10.net; L only, closed Sat & Sun; no booking.

Kai Mayfair W1 £57 ❷❷④
65 South Audley St 7493 8988 3–3A
The "de luxe" décor may not be to all tastes, but this "formal" Mayfair oriental continues to impress reporters with its "excellent" (if "slightly precious") Chinese fare; "make sure you sit upstairs". / www.kaimayfair.com; 10.45 pm.

Kaifeng NW4 £47 ④④④
51 Church Rd 8203 7888 1–1B
Although it is traditionally regarded as "the best kosher Chinese in London", this Harrow veteran continues to inspire unsettled reports – some say it's "a guaranteed success", others that "it's not as good as it used to be". / www.kaifeng.co.uk; 10.30 pm; closed Fri & Sat.

Kandoo W2 £22 ❸❸④
458 Edgware Rd 7724 2428 8–4A
"Fresh food" and "friendly" service win praise for this BYO Persian, not far from Lords; "on a summer evening, the garden is great". / www.kandoorestaurant.co.uk; midnight.

kare kare SW5 £34 ❷❷❸
152 Old Brompton Rd 7373 0024 5–2B
"The unsung hero of the Brompton Road Indians"; though overshadowed by the famous 'Star', it's consistently praised for its "refreshingly different" cuisine and "good service". / www.karekare.co.uk; 11 pm; set weekday L £17 (FP).

Karma W14 £27 ❷❷⑤
44 Blythe Rd 7602 9333 7–1D
The "refreshing" cooking at this year-old Olympia Indian is often "very impressive indeed", so it's a shame that, like its predecessor Cotto (long RIP), it "suffers from its out-of-the-way location and thus poor ambience". / www.k-a-r-m-a.co.uk; 11.30 pm.

Kastoori SW17 £22 ❶❷④
188 Upper Tooting Rd 8767 7027 10–2C
Don't be fooled by the "dingy" decor or the "cr*p" location – they're "more than offset" by the "incredible-value" "voyage of discovery" offered by the menu of this family-run Tooting veteran, where the "ever-changing" east African/south Indian cuisine is nothing short of "sublime". / 10.30 pm; closed Mon L & Tue L; no Amex or Maestro; booking: max 12.

Kasturi EC3 £32 ❷❷❸
57 Aldgate High St 7480 7402 9–2D
"A little different in style from the operations in nearby Brick Lane" – this well-presented contemporary City Indian is a good all-rounder. / www.kasturi-restaurant.co.uk; 11 pm, Sat 9.30 pm; closed Sun L.

Katana
The International WC2 £33 ④④❸
116 St Martin's Ln 7655 9810 4–4B
This reasonably "competent" pan-Asian dining room, above a bar on Trafalgar Square, can make a useful West End stand-by (especially "pre-Coliseum"). / www.theinternational.uk.com; 11.30 pm, Sun 9.30 pm.

Kaz Kreol NW1 £26 ❸❷❸
35 Pratt St 7485 4747 8–3C
London's only Seychellois restaurant – in a former Camden Town pub – attracted only modest coverage in its first full year of operation; fans insist it's a "friendly" place, offering "lovely and interesting" food. / 11 pm, Sun 7 pm.

Kazan SW1 £34 ➋○○

93-94 Wilton Rd   7233 7100   2–4B

Cleaning up at the Victoria end of Pimlico – this "invaluable" Turkish restaurant is a "buzzy" sort of place with notably "pleasant" service; the food (including "brilliant" mezze) is "delicious" and "reasonably-priced" too. / 11.45 pm, Sun-Tue 10.30 pm; no Amex.

Ken Lo's Memories SW1 £49 ➌➋➌

67-69 Ebury St   7730 7734   2–4B

This "smart" (if "faded") Belgravia veteran is oft-cited as a "reliable" favourite, with "chirpy" service and "classic" Chinese cooking; this year, however, saw more reports of the "can't-see-what-the-fuss-is-about" variety. / www.memories-of-china.co.uk; 11 pm; closed Sun L.

Ken Lo's Memories of China W8 £48 ➊➋➌

353 Kensington High St   7603 6951   7–1D

"All-round excellent food and service" win many fans for this "dependable" and "understated" fixture, near Olympia; it "beats many more high-profile Chinese places" (including its Belgravia parent). / www.memories-of-china.co.uk; 11 pm; closed Sun L.

Kennington Tandoori SE11 £29 ➌➌④

313 Kennington Rd   7735 9247   1–3C

"Wonderful" curries (including "plenty of unusual options"), and "calm" and "efficient" service win much local approval for this "neighbourhood stalwart". / www.kenningtontandoori.co.uk; midnight, Fri & Sat 12.30 am.

Kensington Place W8 £54 ④➌④

201-209 Kensington Church St   7727 3184   6–2B

In its day this "goldfish bowl" of a place was a ground-breaking 'Modern' British restaurant; it's still "busy", but it's a "well-past-its-prime" neighbourhood favourite nowadays – are new owners D&D London (fka Conran Restaurants) the right people to pep it up? / www.egami.co.uk; 10.45 pm; set weekday L £35 (FP).

Kensington Square Kitchen W8 NEW £40

9 Kensington Sq   awaiting tel   5–1A

On a small, tucked-away Kensington site that was briefly Lillo e Franco (RIP), this new bar/restaurant is set to open in late-2007; chef/patron Sara Adams has a good CV and promises to deliver 'seasonal, British-inspired' food in 'an atmosphere of breezy urban chic'; price given is our guesstimate.

**(Brew House)
Kenwood House NW3** £24 ④④➊

Hampstead Heath   8341 5384   8–1A

"Unbeatable on a fine day" – the superb garden of this café by Hampstead Heath is ideal for brunch, Sunday lunch or afternoon tea; "a walk afterwards is obligatory". / www.companyofcooks.com; 6 pm (summer), 4 pm (winter).

Kenza EC2 NEW £40

10 Devonshire Sq   7929 5533   9–2D

Under the same ownership as Pasha, this ambitious new Middle Eastern restaurant – in the potentially very atmospheric cellar-site formerly occupied by Satu (RIP), near Liverpool Street station – opens in the autumn of 2007; price given is our guesstimate.

Kettners W1 £36 ④❸❷
29 Romilly St 7734 6112 4–2A
*For "sheer class", it's hard – as PizzaExpresses go, anyway –
to beat the décor of this "opulent" Soho institution (originally
established by the ex-chef to Napoleon III), which comes complete
with an ("overpriced") champagne bar; its "standard" fare –
from an "extended menu", including burgers – is "far from
a bargain". / www.kettners.com; midnight, Thu-Sat 1am; need 7+ to book.*

Kew Grill TW9 £48 ❸④④
10b Kew Grn 8948 4433 1–3A
*"Great steaks" are the highlight of the "meaty" cooking at Wozza's
"casual" Kew two-year-old; service is "off-hand", though, conditions
are "rather cramped"… and "does it have to cost this much?"
/ www.awtonline.co.uk; 10.30 pm; closed Mon L; set weekday L £27 (FP).*

Khan's W2 £15 ❸④④
13-15 Westbourne Grove 7727 5420 6–1C
*"Great curries, dirt cheap… what more could you want?", say fans
of this cavernous but crowded Bayswater stalwart; no alcohol!
/ www.khansrestaurant.com; 11.45 pm.*

Khan's of Kensington SW7 £28 ❸❸④
3 Harrington Rd 7581 2900 5–2B
*"A good local Indian"… er, that's about the whole story on this
"reliable", "cheap and cheerful" South Kensington fixture.
/ www.khansofkensington.com; 11 pm; set weekday L £16 (FP).*

Khoai N8 £24 ❸④④
6 Topsfield Pde 8341 2120 1–1C
*"Delicious Vietnamese street food at very reasonable prices" has
won a more-than-local fan club for this "friendly" but "noisy"
Crouch End café. / 11.30 pm; no Amex.*

Khyber Pass SW7 £26 ❸❷④
21 Bute St 7589 7311 5–2B
*"A good stand-by, near South Kensington tube"; its subcontinental
cuisine is "nothing particularly memorable", but still "good and
cheap". / midnight; need 4+ to book.*

Kiasu W2 NEW £25 ❷④④
48 Queensway 7727 8810 6–2C
*"Something different, in a street crowded with Cantonese
restaurants"; this "busy" new Bayswater café gets a strong thumbs-
up for its "delicious" Malaysian food – "about as authentic as you'll
find in London". / www.kiasu.co.uk; 11 pm.*

Kicca SW3 NEW £40 ④④❸
100 Draycott Ave 7823 7887 5–2C
*The pink 'n' black cocktail-bar-style décor is a "designer's delight",
at this new Italian near Brompton Cross; it opened too late in 2007
to attract much survey commentary, but early signs are that it's
more a 'scene' than a serious culinary destination. / Rated on Editors'
visit; www.kiccalondon.com; 11 pm.*

Kiku W1 £50 ❷❸④
17 Half Moon St 7499 4208 3–4B
*"Great-value set lunches", in particular, make it worth braving the
"harsh lighting" at this minimalist Mayfair Japanese.
/ www.kikurestaurant.co.uk; 10.15 pm; closed Sun L.*

King Eddie's
King Edward VII E15 £30 ❸④❸
47 Broadway   8534 2313   1–1D
"One of the nicest pubs in the area" – this "cosy" Stratford spot (revamped in early-2006) wins praise for the "dependable" grub served in its "comfortable back room". / www.kingeddie.co.uk; 10 pm; no Amex.

Koba W1 £44 ❷0❸
11 Rathbone St   7580 8825   2–1C
"Unlike many Koreans", this Fitzrovia yearling is decked out in a "trendy" style; "brilliant young staff" guide you through the "interesting" BBQ dishes, which are "impressively cooked at your table". / 11 pm; closed Sun L.

Kobe Jones WC1 **NEW** £49 ④④④
112 Gt Russell St   7300 3250   2–1C
Views divide on this "original", "East-meets-West" newcomer in a Bloomsbury basement – fans say it's a "cool" scene with "well cooked and presented" California/Japanese dishes, whereas doubters just find it "disappointing". / www.kobejones.com.au; 10 pm; closed Sat L & Sun L.

Kolossi Grill EC1 £24 ④0❷
56-60 Rosebery Ave   7278 5758   9–1A
"A throwback, but none the worse for that" – this "basic", "honest" and "consistently friendly" Clerkenwell Greek veteran is a "reliable" sort of place (and it can be "great fun" too). / www.kolossigrill.com; 11 pm; closed Sat L & Sun; set weekday L £14 (FP).

Konditor & Cook £19 0❸④
Curzon Soho, 99 Shaftesbury Ave, W1   7292 1684   4–3A
46 Gray's Inn Rd, WC1   7404 6300   9–1A
10 Stoney St, SE1   7407 5100   9–4C
22 Cornwall Rd, SE1   7261 0456   9–4A
"Terrifyingly tempting" snacks – from "decadent cakes" to "fantastic soups" – inspire many ecstatic reports on this "wonderful" chain of café/take-aways. / www.konditorandcook.com; W1 11 pm; SE1 closed Sun; no Amex; no booking.

Konstam at the Prince Albert WC1 £38 ❸0❸
2 Acton St   7833 5040   8–3D
This "wacky" King's Cross outfit has made quite a name with its "valiant efforts to utilise local produce" (from within the M25); results are a bit hit-and-miss, but, for most reporters, this is "a great idea, fantastically delivered". / www.konstam.co.uk; 10.30 pm; closed Sat L & Sun.

Kovalam NW6 £21 ❷❷④
12 Willesden Ln   7625 4761   1–2B
It "may not look that inviting", but this Kilburn-fringe spot is universally tipped for its "tasty and authentic" south Indian food. / www.kovalamrestaurant.co.uk; 11 pm.

Kruger E14 **NEW** £30 ④④④
Cabot Place West   7719 1629   11–1C
Related to a well-reputed Canary Wharf take-away, this bright new brasserie makes a handy rendezvous for an informal lunch; on our visit, though, the uninspired menu was realised to an unimpressive standard. / Rated on Editors' visit.

Kulu Kulu £25 ❷④⑤
76 Brewer St, W1   7734 7316   3–2D
51-53 Shelton St, WC2   7240 5687   4–2C
39 Thurloe Pl, SW7   7589 2225   5–2C
*They look "a bit shabby", but – on a good day – you get some
of "the best Kaiten-Zushi in town" at these "fast, cheap, no-fuss"
Japanese cafés; there's "always a queue". / 10 pm, SW7 10.30 pm;
closed Sun; no Amex; no booking.*

Kurumaya EC4 £30 ❷❸❸
76-77 Watling St   7236 0236   9–2B
*Fans say this Kaiten-Zushi outfit is "better than some of the bigger
names" – it gets "very busy at lunchtimes". / www.kurumaya.co.uk;
9.30 pm; closed Sat & Sun.*

Kwan Thai SE1 £37 ❸❸④
Unit 1, Hay's Galleria   7403 7373   9–4D
*You get "great views, if you can nab a window table", at this South
Bank river-sider; the food is "tasty" too, if "no better than many
cheap and cheerful Thais". / www.kwanthairestaurant.co.uk; 10.30 pm;
closed Sat L & Sun.*

L-Restaurant & Bar W8 £42 ④④④
2 Abingdon Rd   7795 6969   5–1A
*This odd Kensington yearling inspires limited and mixed feedback;
fans find its modern, glazed dining room a "beautiful" place serving
"very good" Spanish-influenced dishes – critics say the cooking
"lacks flair". / www.l-restaurant.co.uk; 10.30 pm, Sun 9 pm; closed Mon D;
set weekday L £26 (FP).*

The Ladbroke Arms W11 £37 ❷④❷
54 Ladbroke Rd   7727 6648   6–2B
*It may be "frustratingly full" (and "a bit squished"), but that's only
because this "really cosy" Notting Hill boozer offers "top-quality"
grub, and the terrace is nice too. / www.thecapitalpubcompany.com;
9.45 pm; no booking after 7.30 pm.*

Ladurée £50 ❸④❸
Harrods, 87-135 Brompton Rd, SW1   7730 1234   5–1D
71-72 Burlington Arc, Piccadilly, W1   7491 9155   3–3C **NEW**
*"The best macarons and people-watching!" are prime attractions
of this "jewelbox-like" operation, which imports some of the spirit
of the famous Parisian pâtisserie into deepest Knightsbridge
(and, more recently, to a tiny outlet on Piccadilly). / W1 6 pm - SW1
9 pm, Sun 6 pm.*

Lahore Kebab House E1 £22 ❶④⑤
2-4 Umberston St   7488 2551   11–1A
*"A dive, but a must-try!"; this "not-for-the-faint-hearted" East End
"institution" may have all the ambience of a "transport caff"
(refurb notwithstanding), but it serves "stunningly authentic"
Pakistani scoff at "unbelievable" prices; BYO. / midnight; need 8+
to book.*

Lamberts SW12 £42 ❶❶❷
2 Station Pde   8675 2233   10–2C
*"An excellent alternative to Chez Bruce" – this "chic", "friendly"
and "imaginative" Balham spot is an "unbeatable" local, whose
standards, say fans, are "not far behind" those of its legendary
rival; perhaps its recent refurbishment will draw even wider acclaim.
/ www.lambertsrestaurant.com; 10.30 pm, Sun 9 pm; closed Mon; no Amex.*

(Winter Garden)
The Landmark NW1   £60   ❸❸❶
222 Marylebone Rd   7631 8000   8–4A
The "stunning" setting – a "tranquil", palm-filled atrium – helps make this Marylebone hotel a popular business lunching destination; those paying their own way tend to tip it for a "classy" breakfast (or Sunday brunch), or afternoon tea.
/ www.landmarklondon.co.uk; 11 pm; booking: max 12.

Lanes
East India House E1   £48   ④④⑤
109-117 Middlesex St   7247 5050   9–2D
For fans, this City-fringe basement still offers "delicious" fare in an ambience that's "ideal for a business lunch"; in recent times, however, there has been a spate of gripes about "uninspiring" food and "indifferent" service. / www.lanesrestaurant.co.uk; 10 pm; closed Sat L & Sun.

(The Conservatory)
The Lanesborough Hotel SW1   £79   ④❸❶
Hyde Park Corner   7259 5599   5–1D
"There's nothing actually wrong with the food", in the grand conservatory of this OTT hotel, but "it's just eye-wateringly expensive for what it is"; for a "decadent brunch" or a "fabulous afternoon tea", however, "you feel special just sitting there".
/ www.lanesborough.com; 11 pm; set dinner £51 (FP).

Langan's Bistro W1   £34   ④❷❷
26 Devonshire St   7935 4531   2–1A
This pint-sized bistro was here long before Marylebone became trendy; its "straightforward" cuisine can seem "tired" nowadays, but its "cosy" ambience and "charming" service are still going strong. / www.langansrestaurants.co.uk; 11 pm; closed Sat L & Sun.

Langan's Brasserie W1   £48   ④❸❷
Stratton St   7491 8822   3–3C
It has "a certain buzz" and is "a great place to people-watch" (or "poseurs' paradise", if you prefer), but there's "nothing else to shout about" at this "fading" Mayfair legend – least of all the "school-dinners" food ("and that's pre-Jamie"!).
/ www.langansrestaurants.co.uk; midnight; closed Sat L & Sun.

Langan's Coq d'Or Bar & Grill SW5   £40   ④❷④
254-260 Old Brompton Rd   7259 2599   5–3A
"Good and plain" or "distinctly average"? – both schools of thought show up in feedback on this Earl's Court brasserie stand-by; "you rarely need to book". / www.langansrestaurants.co.uk; 11 pm.

Langtry's
Cadogan Hotel SW1 **NEW**   £49   ④④❸
21 Pont St   7201 6619   5–1D
This off-beat Chelsea newcomer – in "lovely" period chambers – makes quite a brave stab at updating the 'traditional British' formula; service can be "over-familiar", though, and the food doesn't always come off. / www.langtrysrestaurant.com; 10.30 pm; closed Sun D.

The Lansdowne NW1 £39 ❸④❷
90 Gloucester Ave 7483 0409 8–3B
This "marvellous", "relaxed" gastropub (with a "nice upstairs restaurant") is a Primrose Hill linchpin, serving "great" and "crispy" pizza, plus an "ever-changing" range of blackboard dishes; "inattentive" service, though, can take the edge off the experience. / www.thelansdownepub.co.uk; 10 pm; no Amex.

La Lanterna SE1 £32 ❸❶❷
6-8 Mill St 7252 2420 11–2A
Just over Tower Bridge, this "very pleasant" backstreet Italian is well worth knowing about – the cooking is "good" (or better), and on a summer evening the courtyard is "wonderful". / www.pizzeriadelanterna.co.uk; 11 pm; closed Sat L.

The Larder EC1 NEW £38 ❸④④
91-93 St John St 7608 1558 9–1A
A spacious new bakery-cum-brasserie in Clerkenwell – an all-day operation offering anything from a bun to a full meal; on our early-days visit, the food was fine, but the willing service was much in need of tightening up. / Rated on Editors' visit; www.thelarderrestaurant.com; 10.30 pm; closed Sun.

Latium W1 £43 ❶❶❷
21 Berners St 7323 9123 3–1D
An "all-round-great Italian experience", north of Oxford Street, where "delightful" staff serve up some "wonderfully seasonal" cooking; if it has a flaw, it's that the "elegant" interior can seem a trifle "austere". / www.latiumrestaurant.com; 10.30 pm, Fri-Sat 11pm; closed Sat L & Sun.

Latymers W6 £23 ❸⑤⑤
157 Hammersmith Rd 8741 2507 7–2C
"The freshest Thai pub-fare for miles around" has long won fans for the rear dining room of this Hammersmith gin palace – "one you've fought for your table", though, "they can't wait for you to go"! / 10 pm; closed Sun D; no Amex; no booking at L.

Laughing Gravy SE1 £39 ④❸❷
154 Blackfriars Rd 7721 7055 9–4A
Obscurely located in deepest Southwark, this "friendly" local has a small fan club who tip it as an "unknown gem", with "eclectic" décor and "well-priced food". / www.thelaughinggravy.com; 10 pm; closed Sat L & Sun.

Launceston Place W8 £48 ④❸❸
1a Launceston Pl 7937 6912 5–1B
"It used to be a reliable backstreet gem", but the food at this "charming" Kensington townhouse "is no longer impressive"; in mid-2007 it was sold to the D&D London (fka Conran) group – it will be interesting to see if they're the right people to turn it around. / www.egami.co.uk; 11 pm; closed Sat L & Sun D.

Lavender £33 ④❸❷
112 Vauxhall Walk, SE11 7735 4440 2–4D
171 Lavender Hill, SW11 7978 5242 10–2C
24 Clapham Rd, SW9 7793 0770 10–1D
"Fun" and "friendly" south London pub-conversions, offering "reasonable" (some would say "boring") "comfort food". / 10.45 pm; SW11 closed Mon L, SE11 closed Sat L & Sun, SW9 closed Mon-Wed L.

Leadenhall Italian Restaurant EC3 NEW £45 ❸⓿❸
48-52 Leadenhall Mkt   7621 0709   9–2D
"Unfussy but well-executed Italian food" (and "reasonably-priced"
wine) make this "handily-located" and "friendly" City basement,
recently re-branded, a stand-by that's well worth knowing about.
/ www.leadenhallitalianrestaurant.co.uk; 9.30 pm; closed Sat & Sun.

The Ledbury W11 £69 ⓿⓿❷
127 Ledbury Rd   7792 9090   6–1B
"Elegant and restrained", this Notting Hill sibling of Chez Bruce
and The Square is a "superb" all-rounder, where Brett Graham's
"terrific" and "inventive" dishes are complemented by an
"outstanding" wine list; service is "impeccable" too.
/ www.theledbury.com; 10.30 pm; set weekday L £40 (FP).

Lemonia NW1 £31 ❹❷⓿
89 Regent's Park Rd   7586 7454   8–3B
"A very special place" – this Primrose Hill landmark is "always
busy", thanks to the "buzzy" and "cheerful" ambience created
by its long-serving staff; the "classic Greek fare" is "nothing special"
(but lunches offer "astonishing value"). / 11.30 pm; closed
Sat L & Sun D; no Amex; set weekday L £17 (FP).

Leon £24 ❷❸❸
275 Regent St, W1   7495 1514   3–1C NEW
35-36 Gt Marlborough St, W1   7437 5280   3–2C
73-76 The Strand, WC2   7240 3070   4–4D NEW
136 Old Brompton Rd, SW3   7589 7330   5–1D
3 Crispin Pl, E1   7247 4369   9–1D
12 Ludgate Circus, EC4   7489 1580   9–2A
"Good news for London that it's rapidly expanding", say the many
fans of this "upmarket fast-food" chain, where "wholesome" and
"healthy" dishes are served in a "functional" but "friendly" style.
/ www.leonrestaurants.co.uk; 10 pm; EC4 closed Sat & Sun, W1 closed Sun D;
no Amex.

Levant W1 £46 ❹❹⓿
Jason Ct, 76 Wigmore St   7224 1111   3–1A
A "loud" and "highly entertaining" Lebanese den, near the
Wigmore Hall, that's "fun for a group outing" (or "for a date");
the food is "enjoyable", but hardly the point. / www.levant.co.uk;
11.30 pm.

Levantine W2 £39 ❸❷❸
26 London St   7262 1111   6–1D
"An oasis from the hurly burly of Paddington" – this fun, souk-style
outfit pleases its tiny fan club with a menu of "Lebanese
favourites". / www.levant.co.uk; 11.30 pm.

The Light House SW19 £43 ❸❷❸
75-77 Ridgway   8944 6338   10–2B
"Wimbledon is short on good places", and this "trendy" (by local
standards) venture – with its consistent cooking and "helpful" staff
– stands out as the most "interesting" option locally.
/ www.lighthousewimbledon.com; 10.30 pm, Fri-Sat 10.45 pm; closed Sun D.

Lilly's E1 £35 ❸❸❷
75 Wapping High St   7702 2040   11–1A
Surprisingly "slick", and "friendly" too – this "value-for-money"
Wapping brasserie offers simple dishes that are "tasty and well-
prepared". / www.lillysrestaurant.co.uk; 11 pm.

Lime E14 £35 ❸❷❸
1 Regatta Point, Manilla St   7515 4500   11–2C
"Decent restaurants are few and far between in E14" –
this "modern-style" Indian, a short walk from Canary Wharf, is one
of 'em. / www.limerestaurant.co.uk; 11 pm, Fri-Sat 11.30 pm; set weekday L
£20 (FP).

Lindsay House W1 £76 ❸❸❷
11-15 Swallow St   7439 0450   4–3A
Richard Corrigan's "elegant" Soho townhouse still divides opinion;
for its many ardent fans, it offers "a wonderful experience",
with "impeccable cuisine" and its own "unique" and "cosy" charm
– to a disappointed minority, though, it's just a "hushed" place,
where the cooking is "ho-hum". / www.lindsayhouse.co.uk; 10.30 pm;
closed Sat L & Sun; set pre theatre £51 (FP).

Lisboa Pâtisserie W10 £5 ❶❸❸
57 Golborne Rd   8968 5242   6–1A
"The best coffee" and "delicious" Portuguese pastries – sweet and
savoury – win ongoing raves for this "authentic" and ever-crowded
North Kensington café. / 8 pm; L & early evening only; no booking.

Little Bay £26 ❸❷❷
140 Wandsworth Bridge Rd, SW6   7751 3133   10–1B
228 Belsize Rd, NW6   7372 4699   1–2B
228 York Rd, SW11   7223 4080   10–2B
171 Farringdon Rd, EC1   7278 1234   9–1A
"Exuberant" budget bistros (featuring "zany" decor and "OTT live
opera"), whose "flavoursome" fare delivers "amazing value for
money"; unsurprisingly, they're "always full". / www.little-bay.co.uk;
11.30 pm; no Amex, NW6 no credit cards.

Little Italy W1 £47 ④④❸
21 Frith St   7734 4737   4–2A
"In the heart of Soho", this pricey Italian has something of a local
following as a business destination; adjacent to Bar Italia
(same owners), it's also a bit of a late-night scene.
/ www.littleitalysoho.co.uk; 4 am, Sun midnight.

The Little Square W1 £40 ④④❸
3 Shepherd Mkt   7355 2101   3–4B
A "cosy" little corner spot, on Shepherd Market, offering "nice,
if unspectacular" bistro fare at "fair-value" prices. / 11 pm; set Sun L
£25 (FP).

Livebait £44 ④④④
21 Wellington St, WC2   7836 7161   4–3D
43 The Cut, SE1   7928 7211   9–4A
This "stark", white-tiled chain does have its fans, who praise its
"great fish", "enormous seafood platters" and "good value"; critics,
though, bemoan "dull" food and "cheeky" prices.
/ www.santeonline.co.uk; 11 pm, SE1 Sun 9 pm; WC2 closed Sun.

Living Room £36 ⑤④④
3-9 Heddon St, W1   0870 166 2225   3–2C
18-26 Essex Rd, N1   0870 442 2712   8–3D
Fans of the West End branch of this national chain say it's "not bad
for a business lunch" (or as a respite from shopping); some reports
on both it and its Islington sibling, though, say the food
is "dreadful". / www.thelivingroom.co.uk; W1 1 am, Sun midnight –
N1 11.30 pm, Thu midnight, Fri & Sat 2 am.

LMNT E8 £25 ④❸❶
316 Queensbridge Rd 7249 6727 1–2D
*"Bliss out like an Egyptian", at this "surreal" Hackney pub-
conversion; the food is "not the star of the show", but then – given
the "bizarre" décor – how could it be? /* www.lmnt.co.uk; 10.45 pm;
no Amex.

Lobster Pot SE11 £43 ❷❸❷
3 Kennington Ln 7582 5556 1–3C
*"It's worth the trek to deepest Kennington", to seek out the Régent
family's "so-kitsch-it's-cool" fixture, which mixes "bizarre ship's
cabin décor" with surprisingly "excellent" (but "pricey") Gallic
seafood; before too long, though, it's going to need a "facelift".
/* www.lobsterpotrestaurant.co.uk; 10.30 pm; closed Mon & Sun; booking:
max 8; set weekday L £27 (FP).

LOCANDA LOCATELLI
CHURCHILL INTERCONT'L W1 £57 ❷❷❷
8 Seymour St 7935 9088 2–2A
*With its "wonderfully fresh" Italian cuisine, its "professional" service
and its "cool but unobtrusive modern setting", Giorgio Locatelli's
Marylebone "all-rounder" is the "crème de la crème of the cat's
whiskers" for most reporters; disappointments are not unknown,
though, and a fair few find it "over-rated". /* www.locandalocatelli.com;
11 pm, Fri & Sat 11.30 pm; booking: max 8.

Locanda Ottomezzo W8 £57 ❸❷❸
2-4 Thackeray St 7937 2200 5–1B
*All reporters agree this comfortable Italian – "tucked-away behind
Kensington High Street" – offers "great food" and "friendly"
service; on the downside, however, it is "ridiculously expensive".
/* www.locandaottomezzo.co.uk; 10.30 pm; closed Sat L & Sun.

Loch Fyne £36 ④❸④
2-4 Catherine St, WC2 7240 4999 2–2D
175 Hampton Rd, TW2 8255 6222 1–4A
*Fans of these "low-key" fish 'n' seafood cafés say they make "staid
but reliably good" stand-bys; the food "doesn't light any fires",
though and overall the experience is "unmistakably chain-like".
/* www.lochfyne.com; 10 pm-11 pm.

The Lock Dining Bar N17 £40 ❷❷❸
Heron Hs, Hale Wharf, Ferry Ln 8885 2829 1–1C
*With its "unexpectedly good" food and "efficient" service,
this Tottenham yearling is maintaining the standards of its
predecessor on this obscure site (Mosaica at the Lock, RIP).
/* www.thelock-diningbar.com; 10.30 pm; closed Mon D, Sat L & Sun D;
no Amex; set weekday L £20 (FP).

Lola Rojo SW11 NEW £30 ❷❸④
78 Northcote Rd 7350 2262 10–2C
*"Exquisite" tapas – "with a gourmet twist" – have inspired excited
feedback from locals on this small, "stark" Battersea newcomer.
/* 10.30 pm.

The Lord Palmerston NW5 £35 ❸⑤④
33 Dartmouth Park Hill 7485 1578 8–1B
*This Dartmouth Park gastropub still wins praise for its "interesting"
cuisine, but its purchase by Geronimo Inns seems to have "led to
a real drop in standards" (especially on the service and ambience
fronts). /* www.geronimo-inns.co.uk; 10 pm; no Amex; no booking.

Lots Road SW10 £36 ❸❸❸
114 Lots Rd 7352 6645 5–4B
A "low-key" hang out, on the way in to Chelsea Harbour; fans say
it's "relaxing" style and "good portions" are "just what you want"
from a gastropub – doubters find it "nothing special". / 10 pm.

Lotus Chinese Floating Restaurant E14 £33 ❹❹❸
38 Limeharbour 7515 6445 11–2C
A large and rather "'70s" floating Chinese fixture, near the London
Arena; its food "has gone down a bit of late", but it's still
a recommended destination "for dim sum", and "group get-
togethers". / www.lotusfloating.co.uk; 10.30 pm.

Lou Pescadou SW5 £42 ❸❹❹
241 Old Brompton Rd 7370 1057 5–3A
With its "authentic Côte d'Azur atmosphere", this "fiercely Gallic"
Earl's Court seafood veteran can still be a winner; its fare
is "well prepared", but the service "could be more charming",
which rather dampens enthusiasm. / midnight; closed Mon & Sun;
set weekday L £21 (FP).

Louvaine SW11 £34 ❸❷❷
110 St John's Hill 7223 8708 10–2C
"A lovely local", say Wandsworth types reporting on this "friendly"
and "intimate" little spot (with its "romantic nooks and crannies");
"the menu doesn't vary greatly, but it's all freshly cooked".
/ www.louvaine.co.uk; 10.30 pm; closed Mon, weekday L & Sat L.

Love India SW3 £37 ❷❷❹
153 Fulham Rd 7589 7749 5–2C
Near pricey Brompton Cross, this basement Indian (long called the
Tandoori of Chelsea) deserves to be better known; service can be a
touch "eccentric", but some of the "spicy" dishes are "particularly
fine". / 11.30 pm.

Lowiczanka
Polish Social & Cultural Assoc'n W6 £29 ❹❹❹
238-246 King St 8741 3225 7–2B
"For an out-of-the-ordinary experience that won't break the bank",
try this "little bit of Poland", in Hammersmith; "good portions"
of food and "plenty of vodka" come at "good-value" prices. / 11 pm,
Fri 12 pm, Sat 1 am; set Sun L £19 (FP).

Luc's Brasserie EC3 NEW £41 ❸❹❹
17-22 Leadenhall Mkt 7621 0666 9–2D
It's "too tightly-packed for serious business", but this re-launched
City bistro has already won a fair following with its "good",
traditional Gallic fare; service, though, can be "haphazard".
/ www.lucsbrasserie.com; 8.30 pm; closed Sat & Sun.

Luciano SW1 £57 ❹❹❹
72-73 St James's St 7408 1440 3–4D
As is his fashion, MPW's year-old St James's Italian divides
reporters; to fans, it's a "glamorous" place, serving "beautiful"
contemporary cuisine – critics, though, just find it "cavernous",
"gloomy" and "self-satisfied". / www.lucianorestaurant.co.uk; 10.30 pm;
closed Sun.

Lucio SW3 £49 ❸❸❸
257 Fulham Rd   7823 3007   5–3B
For fans, this is a "beautiful" Chelsea Italian, with "interesting" cooking and "friendly" service; other feedback, though, tends to hint it "could do better". / 11 pm.

Lucky Seven
Tom Conran Restaurants W2 £33 ❷❸❷
127 Westbourne Park Rd   7727 6771   6–1B
"If you like American diners", Tom Conran's "tiny", "'50s-style" re-creation looks like "the real McCoy", and serves "great burgers, pancakes and shakes". / www.tomconranrestaurants.com; 11 pm; no Amex; no booking.

Luna Rossa W11 £35 ④⑤⑤
192 Kensington Park Rd   7229 0482   6–1A
"A real Neapolitan experience", or one that's "tacky, mediocre and overpriced"? – that can be disputed, but it's widely agreed that the "moody" service at this Notting Hill pizzeria is often "very poor". / 11.30 pm.

Lundum's SW7 £46 ❷❶❶
119 Old Brompton Rd   7373 7774   5–2B
This "civilised" (and "very romantic") spot in South Kensington offers an "utterly reliable" mix of "warm yet unfussy" service and "refreshingly different" Danish food (including some "excellent fish"); tips includes its "fantastic Sunday brunch buffet", and particularly nice "semi-private rooms". / www.lundum.com; 10.30 pm; closed Sun D.

Ma Cuisine £36 ❷❷❸
6 Whitton Rd, TW1   8607 9849   1–4A
9 Station Approach, TW9   8332 1923   1–3A
John McClements's wilfully retro "neighbourhood bistros" (in Kew and Twickenham) offer "a reliable nostalgia trip for anyone who was around in the '60s" – fortunately, "genial" staff and "good food at sensible prices" have a "timeless" appeal. / www.macuisinegroup.co.uk; 10.30 pm; TW1 closed Sun; no Amex.

Ma Goa £31 ❶❷❸
194 Wandsworth Bridge Rd, SW6   7384 2122   10–1B
244 Upper Richmond Rd, SW15   8780 1767   10–2B
"Exciting Goan cooking" and "brilliant" service combine to make this family-run Putney fixture not just a "lovely local" but also one of London's more interesting Indians; its deepest-Fulham spin-off is less well-known, but equally highly rated. / www.ma-goa.com; 11 pm; SW15 closed Mon & Sat L, SW6 closed Mon; SW6 no Amex.

Made in China SW10 £36 ❷❷⑤
351 Fulham Rd   7351 2939   5–3B
"Meals always seem to have been prepared individually", at this "very useful" Chelsea Chinese; staff are "friendly" too, though the design is not about to win any awards. / 11.30 pm.

Made in Italy SW3 £39 ❸④④
249 King's Rd   7352 1880   5–3C
"Authentic" pizza (by the metre), a real sense of "brio" and a "great summer roof-terrace" are undoubted plus-points of this "buzzing" Chelsea Italian; critics find it "cramped" and "noisy", though, and service can be "inattentive". / 11.30 pm; closed weekday L; no Amex.

Madhu's UB1 £34 **❶❶❷**
39 South Rd 8574 1897 1–3A
"I live in India, and this is where I eat when I'm back in London" –
this Southall subcontinental offers "excellent" food
(with "some dishes showing the owners' East African roots").
/ www.madhusonline.com; 11.30 pm; closed Tue, Sat L & Sun L.

Magdalen SE1 🆕 £40 **❶❶❷**
152 Tooley St 7403 1342 9–4D
This "stonking" newcomer (on the site of Fina Estampa, RIP) is
"a dream come true", in the thin area near Tower Bridge; its "solid"
but "beautiful-tasting" English food – "like the Anchor & Hope,
but a bit grander" – is served by "dedicated" staff in a "convivial"
setting. / 10.30 pm; closed Mon L & Sun.

Maggie Jones's W8 £44 **④❸❶**
6 Old Court Pl 7937 6462 5–1A
With its "cosy" and "country kitchen-ish" interior, this candlelit,
"70s rustic" joint, near Kensington Palace, "oozes warmth and
romance"; its "stodgy" comfort fare "won't win any awards" but
"does the job". / 11 pm.

Magic Wok W2 £26 **❸❸④**
100 Queensway 7792 9767 6–2C
"Fab food" and "friendly staff" win praise for this "no-nonsense"
and "reasonably-priced" Bayswater fixture – "you often have
to queue". / 11 pm.

Maison Bertaux W1 £9 **❸④❶**
28 Greek St 7437 6007 4–2A
"Anachronistic" but "very special" – this endearingly "grotty" Soho
"institution" (est 1871) is still very popular for its "lovely" cakes,
and "the best croissants in London". / 11 pm, Sun 7 pm; no credit cards;
no booking.

Malabar W8 £31 **❷❷❷**
27 Uxbridge St 7727 8800 6–2B
"High standards have been maintained over many years", at this
"low-key" Indian veteran, "tucked-away" off Notting Hill Gate;
the "inventive" food is "far from bog-standard", staff are
"very charming", and the setting is "relaxed but chic".
/ www.malabar-restaurant.co.uk; 11.30 pm.

Malabar Junction WC1 £40 **❸❷❷**
107 Gt Russell St 7580 5230 2–1C
"No rush and plenty of space" ("a refreshing change in central
London") – that's much of the appeal of this "large, light and airy"
Bloomsbury fixture; "reliable" south Indian food is an added bonus.
/ 11 pm; set weekday L £13 (FP).

Malmaison Brasserie EC1 £42 **❸❷❷**
18-21 Charterhouse St 7012 3700 9–1B
Surprisingly "pleasant" all-round for an hotel dining room –
this Clerkenwell basement makes a "buzzy", "friendly" and
"discreet" rendezvous, where the food doesn't usually let the side
down. / www.malmaison.com; 10.30 pm.

Mamounia W1 £59 ④④❸
37a Curzon St 7629 2211 3–4B
*"Fun to go, bad to eat"; this Mayfair Moroccan – complete with
belly dancing – attracts a glossy Middle Eastern crowd, despite
cuisine that's often "bland and uninteresting".*
/ www.mamounialounge.com; 12.30 pm, Sun midnight; closed Sat L & Sun L.

La Mancha SW15 £36 ④④❸
32 Putney High St 8780 1022 10–2B
*"Nothing special, but consistently OK" – still the verdict on this
large and "lively" Putney tapas bar. / www.lamancha.co.uk; 11 pm;
need 6+ to book; set weekday L £22 (FP).*

Mandalay W2 £23 ❸②④
444 Edgware Rd 7258 3696 8–4A
*"Brilliant-value" Burmese food and "the best" service usually inspire
rave reviews of the Ally brothers' simple café, near Edgware Road
tube; by comparison it's been "very ordinary" this year – doubtless
the strain of opening a nearby hotel – let's hope for quick a return
to form. / 11 pm; closed Sun.*

Mandarin Kitchen W2 £33 ❶④④
14-16 Queensway 7727 9012 6–2C
*"You just can't beat the lobster noodles", at this "frenetic" and
fantastically grungy Bayswater veteran, which is known for its
"amazing" Chinese seafood; waits can be "dreadful", though,
even if you've booked. / 11.30 pm.*

Mangal Ocakbasi E8 £17 ❷④④
10 Arcola St 7275 8981 1–1C
*This Dalston BYO "dive" is known for its "huge" and "succulent"
grills at "astonishing" prices; some locals, though, say: "it's good,
but others locally are better". / www.mangal1.com; midnight; no credit
cards.*

Mango Room NW1 £35 ❸❸②
10-12 Kentish Town Rd 7482 5065 8–3B
*"Easily the best Caribbean in town" – this "busy" Camden Town
favourite is a "great-night-out" destination, with its "fantastic buzz",
"great cocktails" and "consistently delicious" food.
/ www.mangoroom.co.uk; 11 pm.*

Mango Tree SW1 £50 ❸❸④
46 Grosvenor Pl 7823 1888 2–4B
*This "hangar-like" space (at the foot of a swanky Belgravia-fringe
office block) has many fans for its "fresh and flavoursome" Thai
fare; it also takes a fair bit of flak, though, for "very average"
or "exorbitantly-priced" meals (so it's "worth looking out for
offers"). / www.mangotree.org.uk; 11 pm, Thu-Sat 11.30 pm.*

Manicomio SW3 £47 ④④❸
85 Duke of York Sq 7730 3366 5–2D
*With its "lovely summer terrace" and its handy location, this "calm"
Chelsea Italian (with deli attached) provides a "haven from the
King's Road crowds"; fans say the dishes are of "fantastic quality",
but critics find them "unoriginal". / www.manicomio.co.uk; 10.30 pm.*

Manna NW3 £36 ❸❸④
4 Erskine Rd   7722 8028   8–3B
Fans of this "homely" Primrose Hill veggie (the UK's oldest, est. 1968) swear by its "imaginative and seasonal food" and "honest prices", although others find the cooking "hit-and-miss"; a revamp is planned for late-2007. / www.manna-veg.com; 11 pm; closed weekday L; no Amex.

The Mansion SE27 £32 ❸❸❷
255 Gipsy Rd   8761 9016   1–4D
With its "decent" food and "very nice" garden, this Gypsy Hill boozer is "so good you can't get a seat at the weekends!" / 10 pm, Fri & Sat 10.30, Sun 9 pm; no Amex.

Mao Tai SW6 £42 ❷❸❸
58 New King's Rd   7731 2520   10–1B
The revamp "has made it a little more trendy", but "prices are up" at this long-established Fulham oriental; fans insist that the impressively "consistent" – if not especially authentic – pan-Asian fare is still "worth it". / 11.30 pm.

Marine Ices NW3 £27 ④❷❸
8 Haverstock Hill   7482 9003   8–2B
"An institution in North London for over 40 years"; this "lively, family-friendly" (and family-run) veteran still pumps out "very reliable" pizza and pasta, and "excellent" home-made ices. / www.marineices.co.uk; 11 pm; closed Mon; no Amex.

Maroush £40 ❸④④
I) 21 Edgware Rd, W2   7723 0773   6–1D
II) 38 Beauchamp Pl, SW3   7581 5434   5–1C
III) 62 Seymour St, W1   7724 5024   2–2A
IV) 68 Edgware Rd, W2   7724 9339   6–1D
V) 3-4 Vere St, W1   7493 3030   3–1B
'Garden') 1 Connaught St, W2   7262 0222   6–1D
For a "great" quick bite, try the lamb or chicken shawarmas – or other "fresh, delicious and healthy Lebanese fare" – in the café/take-away sections of this well-known chain (at branches I, II & V); "the adjoining restaurants are much more expensive and vary in quality". / www.maroush.com; 12.30 am-5 am.

The Marquess Tavern N1 £38 ❷❷❸
32 Canonbury St   7354 2975   8–2D
An "always-welcoming" gastropub "gem", "in the heart of Canonbury"; it offers an unusually "delicious" menu, which is "heavy on meat and traditional British fare". / www.marquesstavern.co.uk; 10.30 pm; closed Sun D; set always available £24 (FP).

Masala Zone £26 ❸❸❸
9 Marshall St, W1   7287 9966   3–2D
147 Earl's Court Rd, SW5   7373 0220   5–2A
80 Upper St, N1   7359 3399   8–3D
"You can zip in and zip out", at these "fun and buzzing" curry "warehouses", where the speciality is a "good selection of thalis"; fans say the food is "fresh", "authentic", and "keenly-priced", but others fear it's becoming "unremarkable". / www.realindianfood.com; 11 pm; no Amex; no booking unless over 10.

F S A

The Mason's Arms SW8   £35   ❷❷❸
169 Battersea Park Rd   7622 2007   10–1C
A "noisy" Battersea boozer whose "busy" kitchen is once again
turning out "modern basics" with "above-average success".
/ www.london-gastros.co.uk; 10 pm; set Sun L £22 (FP).

Matsuba TW9   £43   ❷❷④
10 Red Lion St   8605 3513   1–4A
"The best sushi to the west of London" is to be had, say fans,
at this "simple but effective" restaurant, on the edge of Richmond
town-centre; it offers "an excellent range of Japanese and Korean
dishes". / 11 pm; closed Sun.

Matsuri   £60   ❷❷④
15 Bury St, SW1   7839 1101   3–3D
Mid City Place, 71 High Holborn, WC1   7430 1970   2–1D
"High-quality sushi" and "attentive" service have helped win a big
following for these Japanese establishments in St James's and
Holborn; their interiors can seem a touch "sterile" (but, in SW1,
the teppan-yaki offers "great theatre"). / www.matsuri-restaurant.com;
SW1 10.30 pm, WC1 10 pm; WC1 closed Sun.

Maxwell's WC2   £33   ④④❸
8-9 James St   7836 0303   4–2D
Fans of this "buzzy" Covent Garden burger joint say it "does what
it says on the tin", offering food that may be "overpriced",
but which is "always pleasant"; the long-established Hampstead
branch is no more. / midnight.

MAZE W1   £55   ❷❸❸
10-13 Grosvenor Sq   7107 0000   3–2A
Jason Atherton's "fabulous", "creative" food – served tapas-style –
helps make this "hip" Ramsay-group Mayfair dining room
an "amazing" destination for most reporters; service is a bit
"patchy", though, and prices can seem "outrageous".
/ www.gordonramsay.com/maze; 10.30 pm.

Medcalf EC1   £40   ④④❸
40 Exmouth Mkt   7833 3533   9–1A
Fans still applaud the "innovative and good value" Brit-retro food
at this "cool" Clerkenwell bar/restaurant; others feel "it's starting
to slip" since it expanded, though, or "is it just that the school-
dinner-fodder-made-trendy thing can seem a bit of a cliché
nowadays?" / www.medcalfbar.co.uk; 10 pm, Sat 10.30 pm; closed
Fri D & Sun D; no Amex.

Mediterraneo W11   £44   ❷❸❸
37 Kensington Park Rd   7792 3131   6–1A
This "bustling" and "cramped" corner spot is still a "benchmark
local Italian", down Notting Hill way; these days, however, it strikes
the odd reporter as "a bit run-down".
/ www.mediterraneo-restaurant.co.uk; 11.30 pm; booking: max 10;
set weekday L £22 (FP).

Mekong SW1   £23   ④④⑤
46 Churton St   7630 9568   2–4B
A "very cheap" Pimlico oriental (primarily Vietnamese), long praised
by regulars as a "friendly" and "consistent" stand-by; it "could
do with a spruce-up", though. / 11.30 pm.

Mela WC2 £32 ❸④④
152-156 Shaftesbury Ave 7836 8635 4–2B
*For a "cheap, fast, and convenient" bite – made more "interesting"
by an "unusual" Indian menu – this handy Theatreland café retains
many fans; "over the years", though, "standards have been
slipping". / www.melarestaurant.co.uk; 11.15 pm; set pre theatre £21 (FP).*

Melati W1 £29 ④❸④
21 Gt Windmill St 7437 2745 3–2D
*"For a quick fill-me-up dinner", this Soho Malay/Indonesian canteen
has long been a "value-for-money" stand-by, just off Piccadilly
Circus; beware the upstairs, though: it "can get claustrophobic".
/ 11.30 pm.*

Memories of India SW7 £29 ❸②④
18 Gloucester Rd 7581 3734 5–1B
*This "modest"-looking South Kensington curry house retains a loyal
fan club, and its cooking is "always to a high standard". / 11.30 pm.*

Memsaheb on Thames E14 £28 ❷❷❸
65/67 Amsterdam Rd 7538 3008 11–2D
*A "great riverside location" boosts the appeal of this "excellent" –
if little-known – Indian, on the Isle of Dogs. / www.memsaheb.com;
11.30 pm; closed Sat L; set weekday L £15 (FP).*

Menier Chocolate Factory SE1 £33 ④❷❷
51-53 Southwark St 7407 4411 9–4B
*A "cute" and "quirky" space adjacent to a Southwark theatre;
even if the "kitchen hasn't lived up to its initial promise", a meal-
plus-show here is usually "a fun overall experience".
/ www.menierchocolatefactory.com; 11 pm; closed Mon & Sun D.*

Le Mercury N1 £24 ④❷❷
140a Upper St 7354 4088 8–2D
*An archetypal "cheap and cheerful" Gallic bistro, near Islington's
Almeida Theatre, where everyone "crams in to a dark, candle-lit,
garlic-scented fug"; "the prices seem to have stayed the same for
years". / www.lemercury.co.uk; 1 am.*

Meson don Felipe SE1 £26 ❸❸❶
53 The Cut 7928 3237 9–4A
*"It looks Spanish, and it feels Spanish", at this "totally reliable" and
"hard-to-get-into" tapas bar, near the Old Vic, which remains
"as crowded and frantic as ever"; NB: "the guitarist can be very
loud". / 11 pm; closed Sun; no Amex; no booking after 8 pm.*

Meson los Barilles E1 £26 ❸❸❸
8a Lamb Street 7375 3136 9–1D
*"Fresh-tasting tapas" and a "buzzy" ambience make this Spanish
bar/restaurant, near Spitalfields Market, a popular stand-by.
/ 10.30 pm; closed Sat & Sun D.*

Mestizo NW1 £29 ❸❸④
103 Hampstead Rd 7387 4064 8–4C
*It's "London's truest Mexican", say fans of this "lively" and
"inexpensive" joint, near Warren Street tube; there's a feeling
though, that "with a bit more inspiration, it could be a lot better".
/ www.mestizomx.com; 11.30 pm.*

Le Metro SW3   £31
28 Basil St   7591 1213   5–1D
*"A decent basement bistro, close to Harrods" – just before this
guide went to press, this useful all-day destination emerged from
a total revamp, which may raise its profile. / www.lemetro.co.uk;
9.30 pm; closed Sun D; need 5+ to book.*

Metro SW4   £39   ④④❷
9a Clapham Common S'side   7627 0632   10–2D
*An "OK" Clapham fixture, of note for its "beautiful hidden garden"
– thanks to the "charming ivy-clad greenhouse", a visit can be a
surprisingly "heady and magical" experience. / www.metromotel.co.uk;
11 pm; closed weekday L; no Amex.*

Metrogusto N1   £44   ④❷❷
13 Theberton St   7226 9400   8–3D
*A "lively" Islington venture, where owner Ambro is "more than
happy to share his knowledge" of an Italian wine list that's "second
to none"; other places, however, "do just as good food for less
money". / www.metrogusto.co.uk; 10.30 pm, Thu-Sat 11-30 pm;
Mon-Thu D only; booking: max 8, Sat & Sun.*

Mews of Mayfair W1   £62   ④④④
10-11 Lancashire Ct, New Bond St   7518 9388   3–2B
*Fans of this would-be fashionable Mayfair yearling praise its "sleek"
design, and feel the chef is "capable of great things"; a fair few
reporters are unconvinced, though, finding it "nothingy" and
"overpriced". / www.mewsofmayfair.com; 11 pm, Sun 8.30 pm; booking:
max 8.*

Meza W1   £34   ⑤④❸
100 Wardour St   7314 4002   3–2D
*Some reporters claim this huge Soho tapas bar (above Floridita)
is a "buzzy" and "fun" venue; as a place to eat, though, "forget it"
– the service is so-so, and the kitchen "seems to know nothing
of Spanish cuisine". / www.mezabar.co.uk; 1.30 am; closed Sun L.*

Mezzanine
Royal National Theatre SE1   £36   ④④④
Southbank Centre, Belvedere Rd   7452 3600   2–3D
*"You know you'll get to the theatre on time!", if you eat at the
RNT's in-house eatery; many reporters note a "huge improvement"
in recent times, but it can still seem "uninspiring and tense".
/ www.nationaltheatre.co.uk; 11 pm; D only, except Sat open L & D,
closed Sun.*

Michael Moore W1   £48   ❸❸❸
19 Blandford St   7224 1898   2–1A
*Michael Moore is an "entertaining" host and "fine" chef, whose
"pleasurable" cooking inspired many positive reports on this fusion-
Fitzrovian; the setting is "cramped", though, and service "can be
erratic". / www.michaelmoorerestaurant.com; 10.30 pm; closed Sat L & Sun.*

Mildred's W1   £30   ❷❸❷
45 Lexington St   7494 1634   3–2D
*"Who needs meat?", when you can eat at this "inspiring" Soho
"veggie stronghold"; "get there early", as there's no booking, and it
can get "ultra-crowded". / www.mildreds.co.uk; 11 pm; closed Sun;
only Maestro; no booking.*

Mimmo d'Ischia SW1 £50 ④❸❸
61 Elizabeth St   7730 5406   2–4A
A "rather dated" Belgravia Italian which fans (typically of a certain age) find "fun" and "romantic"; the food is still "good", but even supporters say it's "very pricey". / www.mimmodischia.co.uk; 11.30 pm; closed Sun.

Mini Mundus SW17 £34 ❸①❷
218 Trinity Rd   8767 5810   10–2C
A "great local", in Wandsworth, where the "authentic" Gallic cooking includes "melt-in-the-mouth" steaks. / 10.30 pm; closed Mon L.

Mint Leaf SW1 £51 ❸④❸
Suffolk Pl, Haymarket   7930 9020   2–2C
This "chic", "dark" and "sultry" Theatreland basement looks every bit like "the Indian version of Hakkasan"; most reporters still find it "pricey but good", but doubters say it risks becoming "pretentious". / www.mintleafrestaurant.com; 11 pm; closed Sat L & Sun.

Mirabelle W1 £60 ④❸❸
56 Curzon St   7499 4636   3–4B
Though still quite "glamorous", MWP's Mayfair classic is becoming ever more "bland" – "nothing is actually wrong, but it seems so tired these days"; for both business and romance, however, it still has its fans, and the wine list is "incredible". / www.whitestarline.org.uk; 11.30 pm.

Miraggio SW6 £31 ④❷❸
510 Fulham Rd   7384 9774   5–4A
"Personal" service makes for a "cheerful" experience at this small, family-run Italian, near Parson's Green; fans say it's the epitome of a good, "cheap" local (and you can BYO for £3 corkage), but this year also saw some disappointments. / www.miraggio.co.uk; midnight.

Mirch Masala £21 ①❸④
171-173 The Broadway, UB1   8867 9222   1–3A
1416 London Rd, SW16   8679 1828   10–2C
213 Upper Tooting Rd, SW17   8767 8638   10–2D
111 Commercial Rd, E1   7247 9992   9–2D
"Forget the drab surroundings" – you get "astonishing food" at "unbelievable" prices at these "bustling" Pakistani "caffs"; BYO. / midnight.

Misato W1 £23 ❷④④
11 Wardour St   7734 0808   4–3A
"The queues out of the door attest to the popularity" of this "cramped" and "über-cheap" Chinatown spot; "for good portions of decent Japanese food, it certainly offers value for money". / 11.30 pm; no credit cards.

Missouri Grill EC3 £43 ❸❸❸
76 Aldgate High St   7481 4010   9–2D
Opposite Aldgate tube, a little-followed American restaurant that's worth remembering – service can be slow, but fans insist its crab-cakes, steaks and burgers are "the best in the City". / www.missourigrill.com; 11 pm; closed Sat & Sun.

Mitsukoshi SW1 £55 ❸❷⑤
Dorland Hs, 14-20 Lower Regent St   7930 0317   3–3D
*"Ignore the space" – concentrate on the "great sushi" at the
counter, say fans of this "drab" department store basement, in the
heart of the West End; not everyone is equally wowed, but the
"early-bird dinners" and other specials certainly offer "great value".*
/ www.mitsukoshi-restaurant.co.uk; 10 pm.

Miyabi EC2 £38 ❸❷❸
Liverpool St   7618 7100   9–2D
*A "small, cramped and crowded" Japanese, by Liverpool Street
station; fans praise its "high-quality" sushi and other dishes – others
say the food is "not particularly memorable".* / www.miyabi.co.uk;
10.30 pm; closed Sat L & Sun; booking: max 6.

Miyama W1 £60 ❷❷⑤
38 Clarges St   7499 2443   3–4B
*Its ambience is "dire", but this Japanese veteran, in Mayfair, offers
"delicious and subtle" food and "helpful and courteous" service
(plus "one of the best-value lunches in the West End").*
/ www.miyama.co.uk; 10.30 pm; closed Sat L & Sun L.

Mju
Millennium Knightsbridge SW1 £45 ❸❸⑤
16-17 Sloane St   7201 6330   5–1D
*"Superbly creative" fusion cuisine (typically with myriad courses)
makes this an "undiscovered jewel"… in the very heart
of Knightsbridge! – unfortunately, however, its airport lounge-style
dining room seems to discourage much of a following.*
/ www.mju-restaurant.co.uk; 11 pm; closed Sun.

Mocotó SW1
145 Knightsbridge
*As this guide goes to press, we hear that the "many millions spent"
on this ambitious Knightsbridge Brazilian were in vain – it made its
last service in early-August 2007.*

Mohsen W14 £26 ❷❷④
152 Warwick Rd   7602 9888   7–1D
*For "good-quality, simple Persian cuisine" (including "delicious
freshly-made flat-breads"), it's worth seeking out this "welcoming"
and "inexpensive" family-run spot, opposite the Olympia branch
of Homebase; BYO.* / midnight; no credit cards.

Molloy's EC2 NEW £50 ④❸④
48 Gresham St   7600 4799   9–2B
*Near the Guildhall, this plain newcomer – presided over by the
former manager of Sweetings – opened in the summer of 2007;
on our early-days visit, prices seemed high, and we weren't quite
convinced the club-classics-with-a-twist cuisine really lived up.* / Rated
on Editors' visit; www.molloysrestaurant.co.uk.

Momo W1 £55 ④⑤❸
25 Heddon St   7434 4040   3–2C
*Fans are "transported to the Arabian Nights!" – especially after
a visit to the "intoxicating" basement bar – on visits to Mourad
Mazouz's party-Moroccan, off Regent Street; for too many
reporters, though, it's "an absolute rip-off", with "shoddy" food and
"the most condescending service ever".* / www.momoresto.com; 11 pm;
closed Sun L; set weekday L £26 (FP).

Mon Plaisir WC2 £45 ④❸❷
19-21 Monmouth St 7836 7243 4–2B
This "little corner of France" – "a bustling warren of small rooms" –
has been a "trusty favourite" in Covent Garden for half a century
(and is particularly popular for its "excellent-value pre-theatre
meals"); in recent years, though, its "classic" bistro fare has
"gone off the boil"; now open all day. / www.monplaisir.co.uk; 11.15 pm;
closed Sat L & Sun; set weekday L £26 (FP).

Mona Lisa SW10 £21 ❸❷④
417 King's Rd 7376 5447 5–3B
"Ladies-who-lunch and workmen" eat shoulder-to-shoulder at this
"genuinely cheap and cheerful" Italian greasy spoon, at World's
End; "the sardines are especially good". / 11 pm; closed Sun D;
no Amex.

Monmouth Coffee Company £10 ❶❷❷
27 Monmouth St, WC2 7379 3516 4–2B
2 Park St, SE1 7645 3585 9–4C
"What more could you want?" ("apart from a few more
branches"), say fans of these "enthusiastic" pit stops, which offer
"world-class" coffee and "tempting" pastries; at Borough Market,
"you can sit around eating bread and jam" too – more popular
than you might think! / www.monmouthcoffee.co.uk; L & afternoon tea only;
closed Sun; no Amex; no booking.

Montpeliano SW7 £59 ⑤④④
13 Montpelier St 7589 0032 5–1C
Diehard fans "have never understood the complaints" about this
long-established Knightsbridge trattoria, finding it "welcoming" and
"very reliable" – critics though, say it's "going downhill fast" and
wonder: "how on earth does it stay in business?" / midnight.

Monty's W5 £29 ❸④④
1 The Mall 8567 8122 1–2A
There are five Ealing curry houses of this name, not all under the
same ownership – this is arguably the flagship, but fortunately they
are "all good". / www.montystandoori.co.uk; midnight; set weekday L
£15 (FP).

Mooli SW4 £37 ④❷❷
36a Old Town 7627 1166 10–2D
Fans say this "neighbourhood" yearling, in Clapham Old Town,
serves "truly interesting" Italian food; others, though find it simply
"uninspired". / www.moolirestaurant.com; 11 pm.

Morel SW4 £42 ④❸⑤
14 Clapham Park Rd 7627 2468 10–2D
Blame it, perhaps, on the "sterile" décor, but this ambitious
Clapham two-year-old still doesn't inspire many reports – these rate
the food everything from "very good" to "average".
/ www.morelrestaurant.co.uk; 10.30 pm; D only, ex Sun open L & D; no Amex.

The Morgan Arms E3 £40 ❷❸❷
43 Morgan St 8980 6389 1–2D
"Always-interesting" food draws crowds to this "lively" Bow boozer;
fans say it's "perfect" – well, it would be if it weren't getting
"too popular with the locals". / www.geronimo-inns.co.uk; 10 pm; closed
Sun D; no Amex; booking: max 10.

Morgan M N7 £50 ❶❷④
489 Liverpool Rd 7609 3560 8–2D
Morgan Meunier's "inspired" Gallic venture offers "ravishing" cuisine at "unbeatable" prices; his north-Islington premises are "miles from anywhere", but have recently (too late to be reflected in the survey) been given a "warmer look". / www.morganm.com; 9.30 pm; closed Mon, Tue L, Sat L & Sun D; no Amex; booking: max 6.

MORO EC1 £42 ❶❷❷
34-36 Exmouth Mkt 7833 8336 9–1A
Sam and Samantha Clark's "stunning" and "interestingly different" (Spanish/North African) cuisine helps maintain their "seriously buzzing" Clerkenwell "canteen" as a perennial favourite; the noise level, though, can be "unbearable". / www.moro.co.uk; 10.30 pm; closed Sun; booking essential.

Moroccan Tagine W10 £20 ❸❷❸
95 Golborne Rd 8968 8055 6–1A
"Cheerful" staff lend an "easy" atmosphere to this "no-frills" Moroccan, amidst the bric-a-brac stalls of (north) Portobello Market. / 11 pm; no Amex; set weekday L £12 (FP).

Mosaica
The Chocolate Factory N22 £37 ❷❷❸
Unit C005, Clarendon Rd 8889 2400 1–1C
"It's always worth the trek", say fans of this stylish – if "very noisy" – factory-conversion, whose location is obscure even by Wood Green standards. / www.mosaicarestaurants.com; 9.30 pm; closed Mon, Sat L & Sun D.

Mosaico W1 £56 ❸❸❸
13 Albemarle St 7409 1011 3–3C
Your classic "efficient" Mayfair business-Italian – it's "very expensive", but its basement premises are "packed at lunch" nonetheless. / www.mosaicorestaurant.co.uk; 10.30 pm; closed Sat L & Sun.

Moshi Moshi £26 ❸④❸
Waitrose, Canada Pl, E14 7512 9201 11–1C
Unit 24, Liverpool St Station, EC2 7247 3227 9–2D
"It's not the most exciting formula, but they get the job done", say fans of this long-established conveyor-sushi chain, which is still dishing out "fresh and generous sushi" (and other Japanese dishes). / www.moshimoshi.co.uk; E14 8.30 pm, Sun 5.30 pm; Liverpool St 9.45 pm; Broadgate 4 pm; EC2 closed Sat & Sun; no Amex; E14 & Broadgate no booking.

Motcombs SW1 £51 ④④❸
26 Motcomb St 7235 6382 5–1D
There are "always fun people" on show at this "relaxed" and "buzzy" stalwart, on an ever-trendier Belgravia corner; the food, though, is not much more than "satisfactory", and service likewise. / www.motcombs.co.uk; 11 pm; closed Sat L & Sun; set dinner £34 (FP).

Moti Mahal WC2 £51 ❸④④
45 Gt Queen St 7240 9329 4–2D
"Quality", "nouvelle Indian" cuisine wins praise for this "posh" Covent Garden two-year-old – an outpost of a restaurant empire based in the subcontinent. / www.motimahal-uk.com; 11.30 pm; closed Sun; set weekday L £28 (FP).

Mr Chow SW1 £65 ❸❸④
151 Knightsbridge 7589 7347 5–1D
"It's a throwback to the '60s, but what's wrong with that?",
say supporters of this Knightsbridge "relic", where Italian waiters
serve up "Chinese comfort food"; even fans, though warn of staff
"pushing you to order more than you want", and doubters find the
place "poor all-round". / www.mrchow.com; midnight.

Mr Kong WC2 £26
21 Lisle St 7437 7341 4–3A
"The last Governor of Hong Kong" was spotted this year among
diners at this "invariably consistent" Chinatown linchpin; as this
guides goes to press, it is closed for a total revamp
(and expansion), scheduled for completion in late-2007. / 2.45 am,
Sun 1.45 am.

Mr Wing SW5 £42 ❸❸❶
242-244 Old Brompton Rd 7370 4450 5–2A
"Get a seat downstairs" – "with tropical fish swimming by" –
best to enjoy this atmospheric and "very romantic" Earl's Court
"old favourite"; the "fairly traditional Chinese" food is "reliable",
if arguably "rather pricey" for what it is. / www.mrwing.com; midnight.

Mugen EC4 NEW £38 ❸❸❸
26 King William St 7929 7879 9–3C
"A useful City location"; this Japanese newcomer, near Monument
– on the former site of Noto (RIP) – may not set the world on fire,
but it offers decent food at "non-City" prices. / Rated on Editors' visit;
10.30 pm; closed Sat & Sun.

Mulberry Street W2 NEW £31 ❸④❸
84 Westbourne Grove 7313 6789 6–1B
"The decor is all-New York and the staff all-Italian" – a "great
mix", say all early reporters on this Bayswater newcomer, where
"huge" pizzas (which may be shared) are the highlight.
/ www.mulberrystreet.co.uk; midnight, Sun 11 pm.

Nagomi W1 NEW £30 ❸❷❸
4 Blenheim St 7165 9506 3–2B
A "cosy" Japanese newcomer, near the top end of Bond Street;
it's nothing startling, but offers "good" food that's "well presented".
/ 10.30 pm; closed Sun.

Nahm
Halkin Hotel SW1 £77 ④⑤⑤
5 Halkin St 7333 1234 2–3A
Fans of David Thompson's much-fêted Belgravia Thai rave about his
"wonderful" cooking, and its "mind-blowing textures and tastes";
far too many reporters, though, find a meal here to be a total turn-
off – a "cold" place with "snooty" service, serving "pretentious"
fare that's "grossly overpriced". / www.nahm.como.bz; 10.30 pm; closed
Sat L & Sun L; set always available £48 (FP).

Naked Turtle SW14 £43 ④❸❷
505 Upper Richmond Rd 8878 1995 10–2A
"Talented musicians" (including the waiters and waitresses) help
make for "a great buzz" – and "a good night out" – at this "fun"
Sheen stalwart; the food, though, could be "one notch better".
/ 11 pm; D only, ex Sun open L & D; no Amex.

Nam Long SW5 £35 ⑤④④
159 Old Brompton Rd   7373 1926   5–2B
The food is "distinctly average", service can be "rude", and the setting is "cramped and noisy" – this Vietnamese bar/restaurant, in South Kensington, can still be "fun", though, particularly "for a late drink and nibbles". / 11.30 pm; D only, closed Sun.

Namo E9 £27 ❷❸❸
178 Victoria Park Rd   8533 0639   1–2D
"Amazingly good Vietnamese food" makes it worth truffling out this "out-of-the-way" oriental, near Victoria Park – it's "more a restaurant than the usual café-style operation hereabouts". / 11 pm; closed Mon, Tue L & Wed L.

Nancy Lam's Enak Enak SW11 £35 ❸❷④
56 Lavender Hill   7924 3148   10–1C
"Nancy's entertaining visits" are the draw to this TV chef's "modernised and extended" Battersea HQ; however, even fans of her "yummy" – if "not particularly inventive" – oriental cuisine can find it "a bit pricey nowadays". / www.nancylam.com; 10.30 pm; D only, closed Mon & Sun.

Nando's £21 ④④④
Branches throughout London
"If you're going to eat fast food", many reporters feel the Portuguese chicken at this popular chain "feels healthier, somehow"; beware, though: "when they say a sauce is hot, they mean it!" / www.nandos.co.uk; 11.30 pm; no Amex; no booking.

Nanglo SW12 £26 ❷⓿❸
88 Balham High Rd   8673 4160   10–2C
"Much better than your average local", this "pleasant" Balham Nepalese offers some "interesting" dishes, and the staff "couldn't be more charming". / 11.30 pm; D only.

Napket SW3 NEW £35 ❷❸❸
342 King's Rd   7352 9832   5–3C
The "super-stylish" surroundings aren't to all tastes, but early reporters praise the "amazing bread and sandwiches" and "superb coffee" at this self-consciously hip new café, in Chelsea. / www.napket.com; 9 pm, Fri-Sun 10 pm.

Napulé SW6 £35 ❷④④
585 Fulham Rd   7381 1122   5–4A
"Wonderful antipasti" and "great pizzas" are the top reasons to seek out this "jolly" and "busy" Italian, near Fulham Broadway. / 11.30 pm; closed weekday L; no Amex.

The Narrow E14 NEW £37 ❷④❸
44 Narrow St   7592 7950   11–1B
Gordon Ramsay's "cute" new Docklands riverside inn – his first in a planned string of gastro-boozers – impresses many reporters with its "tasty" British classics; some, though, feel it's "no better than it should be, at the prices", and service, in particular, "could be improved". / 10 pm.

The National Dining Rooms
National Gallery WC2   **£48**   ④④④
Sainsbury Wing, Trafalgar Sq   7747 2525   2–2C
*This "spacious" year-old venue, overlooking Trafalgar Square,
makes an OK business rendezvous; early-days excitement about its
"pricey" British food has faded, though, and service still "hasn't got
its act together"; (there's also a snack bar section, which gets better
reports). / www.thenationaldiningrooms.co.uk; Wed 8.30 pm; Thu-Tue closed
D; no Amex.*

National Gallery Café
National Gallery WC2 NEW   **£38**   ④⑤❸
East Wing, Trafalgar Sq   7747 5945   4–4B
*With its elegant interior, this "potentially outstanding"
café/brasserie – which has its own street entrance, and is open
in the evening – is a useful new option for a light meal
(or "tempting cake") in the West End; as with many Oliver Peyton
operations, though, service can be "bad", and the food "average
and overpriced". / www.thenationaldiningrooms.co.uk; 11 pm.*

Natural Burger Co & Grill NW8 NEW   **£28**   ❸❸⑤
12 Blenheim Terrace   7372 9065   8–3A
*"A welcome addition to the area" – this small new St John's Wood
bistro attracts consistent praise in early reports, not least for its
"high-quality" burgers. / 11 pm; no Amex.*

Nautilus NW6   **£25**   ❶❷④
27-29 Fortune Green Rd   7435 2532   1–1B
*A "crowded" kosher chippy in West Hampstead, which fans tip
as "the best in North London"; "portions are huge"; BYO. / 10 pm;
closed Sun L; no Amex.*

Navarro's W1   **£26**   ❸❸❷
67 Charlotte St   7637 7713   2–1C
*An "always-bustling" Fitzrovia bar, with a "lovely tiled interior";
it's known as an "authentic" spot offering "very good tapas",
but declining ratings confirm it's "gone down" a bit of late.
/ www.navarros.co.uk; 10 pm; closed Sat L & Sun.*

Nazmins Balti House SW18   **£26**   ❸❸④
398 Garratt Ln   8944 1463   10–2B
*An Earlsfield curry house veteran of over 40 years' standing, where
the food can be "brilliant"; it's "inconsistent", though.
/ www.nazmins.com; midnight.*

New Culture Revolution   **£23**   ⑤④⑤
305 King's Rd, SW3   7352 9281   5–3C
157-159 Notting Hill Gate, W11   7313 9688   6–2B
42 Duncan St, N1   7833 9083   8–3D
43 Parkway, NW1   7267 2700   8–3B
*Supporters still praise the "reasonable prices" of this basic oriental
chain; sceptics, though, insist it's "gone downhill", and find it very
"formulaic" nowadays. / www.newculturerevolution.co.uk; 10.30 pm;
need 4+ to book.*

New Mayflower W1   **£28**   ❷④④
68-70 Shaftesbury Ave   7734 9207   4–3A
*"Go with a Chinese-speaker", to get the best out of this
"unremarkable"-looking fixture, on the fringe of Chinatown;
some dishes are "brilliant" (but "many of them don't seem
to appear on the menu"). / 4 am; D only; no Amex.*

New Tayyabs E1 £20 ❶④❸
83 Fieldgate St 7247 9543 9–2D
"Absolutely astounding" Pakistani food ensures this *"cheap-as-chips"* (and BYO) Whitechapel canteen is always *"rammed full"*; indeed, the only real criticism is that it's *"too popular"*! / www.tayyabs.co.uk; 11.30 pm.

New World W1 £28 ❸❸❸
1 Gerrard Pl 7734 0396 4–3A
"Trolleys of dim sum go buzzing past", during the popular and *"fun"* lunchtime service at this *"garish"* Chinatown leviathan; as a dinner-destination, it inspires hardly any reports. / 11.45 pm; no booking, Sun L.

Newton's SW4 £36 ④④④
33 Abbeville Rd 8673 0977 10–2D
A Clapham *"neighbourhood"* spot which even fans admit has become more *"hit-and-miss"* of late; the food is *"not mind-blowing"*. / www.newtonsrestaurants.co.uk; 6 pm; set weekday L £19 (FP).

Nicole's W1 £57 ④④④
158 New Bond St 7499 8408 3–3C
"For a light shopping lunch", this Mayfair fashion store basement veteran remains a *"daytime favourite"* for some reporters; perhaps unsurprisingly, it's *"not quite as exciting as when it first opened"*. / www.nicolefarhi.com; 5.30 pm; L & afternoon tea only, closed Sun.

No 77 Wine Bar NW6 £31 ④❸❷
77 Mill Ln 7435 7787 1–1B
"Still going strong" – this *"relaxed"* West Hampstead stalwart may have no gastronomic pretensions, but it remains a *"perfect local wine bar"*. / 11.30 pm; no Amex.

NOBU METROPOLITAN HOTEL W1 £88 ❷④④
Old Park Ln 7447 4747 3–4A
For its army of fans, the *"sensational"* dishes at this legendary Mayfair Japanese/Latin American still make it the *"Gold Standard"* for oriental-fusion cuisine; its ratings are *"fading"*, though, and it's *"sooooooo expensive"* that doubters feel it's plain *"lost it"*. / 10.15 pm; booking: max 12.

Nobu Berkeley W1 £88 ❷④❸
15-16 Berkeley St 7290 9222 3–3C
With its *"fun and trashy"* crowd, the newer of the Mayfair Nobus is *"much the more happening of the two"*, and its *"gorgeous"* but *"outrageously pricey"* oriental fare now risks overhauling that at the original. / www.noburestaurants.com; 1.30 am; D only, closed Sun.

La Noisette SW1 £76 ⑤④⑤
164 Sloane St 7750 5000 5–1D
"What a disaster!"; Bjorn van Der Horst's food at the latest addition to Ramsay's London empire may sometimes be *"superb"*, but it's too often *"hit-and-miss"* – this might not be so bad if it were not for the *"brown and forgettable"* décor and the sometimes *"non-existent"* service, and all at *"eye-watering"* prices. / 10.30 pm; closed Sat L & Sun; set weekday L £38 (FP).

Noodle Noodle   **£22**   ④❸④
18 Buckingham Palace Rd, SW1   7931 9911   2–4B
Vauxhall Bridge Rd, SW1   7630 1778   2–4B
"Need a quick bite near Victoria?" – seek out one of these "cheap"
caffs, where the oriental fare is "tasty" and "filling".
/ www.noodle-noodle.co.uk; 10.45 pm; Buckingham Palace Rd closed Sun.

Noor Jahan   **£33**   ❷❷❸
2a Bina Gdns, SW5   7373 6522   5–2B
26 Sussex Pl, W2   7402 2332   6–1D
"Seriously good" Indian food – "nothing fancy or trendy", mind –
has long made this "reliable" curry house an Earl's Court institution;
its Bayswater spin-off is less known, but even better. / 11.30 pm.

Nordic Bakery W1 NEW   **£12**   ❷❷❸
14 Golden Sq   3230 1077   3–2D
An impressively spacious and airy new cafe, with a calming view
of Soho's Golden Square; service is charming, and the short menu
of Scandinavian snacks is realised to a high standard.
/ www.nordicbakery.com; 10 pm, Sat 7 pm; closed Sat D & Sun; no booking.

The Norfolk Arms WC1 NEW   **£29**   ❸❸❷
28 Leigh St   7388 3937   8–4C
This Bloomsbury newcomer – a "lovely restoration of a Victorian
pub", with "an interesting Spanish-themed menu" – is generally
hailed as a "very welcome" arrival. / www.norfolkarms.co.uk; 10.15 pm.

North China W3   **£25**   ❷❷❸
305 Uxbridge Rd   8992 9183   7–1A
"Hidden-away in Acton", this long-established, family-owned oriental
has earned a very "loyal clientele", thanks to its "unfailing" service
and its "high-quality" Chinese cooking. / www.northchina.co.uk; 11 pm;
set dinner £16 (FP).

The North London Tavern NW6   **£37**   ❸④❸
375 Kilburn High Rd   7625 6634   1–2B
"A wonderful-feeling gastropub, with the right ambitions, in a still-
dodgy area" – this new venture may be "nothing fancy",
but pleases all who comment on it. / www.realpubs.co.uk; 10.30 pm;
no Amex.

North Sea Fish WC1   **£28**   ❷❷④
7-8 Leigh St   7387 5892   8–4C
"Exemplary" fish 'n' chips draw many admirers to this "old-style"
chippy, hidden away in Bloomsbury. / 10.30 pm; closed Sun.

Northbank EC4 NEW   **£45**
1 Paul's Walk   awaiting tel   9–3B
In late-2007, Christian Butler, former manager of Baltic, is set
to open a new establishment in the hitherto under-exploited
riverside premises formerly known as Just The Bridge (RIP), which
have brilliant views; the aim, apparently, is a 'quintessentially
English' one; price given is our guesstimate.

The Northgate N1   **£33**   ④❸❸
113 Southgate Rd   7359 7392   1–1C
"Still a great place", say fans of this De Beauvoir town "favourite",
who hail it as a "great local gastropub"; reports of "poor"
standards, however, have not quite gone away. / 10.30 pm; closed
Mon L; no Amex.

Nosh TW1 £35 ④❸❸
139 St Margarets Rd 8891 4188 1–4A
It may be "basic", but this "local bistro" makes a tolerable option in the culinary wastelands of St Margaret's. / 10.30 pm; closed Sun.

Notting Grill W11 £58 ④⑤④
123a Clarendon Rd 7229 1500 6–2A
Standards "have slipped dramatically" at AWT's Holland Park hide-away; some reporters still praise its "divine" burgers and "great" steaks, but there are too many reports of "dreadful" cooking and "shocking" service – surely Wozza can do better than this? / www.awtonline.co.uk; 10.30 pm; closed Mon L.

Notting Hill Brasserie W11 £53 ❶❶❷
92 Kensington Park Rd 7229 4481 6–2B
"Romantic... special... gorgeous"; this "highly polished" restaurant (not brasserie) offers a "really lovely", "all-round" experience – Mark Jenkel's "very accomplished" food is served by "slick" staff, in a townhouse setting that's "elegant but not stuffy"; "great live jazz" too. / 11 pm; closed Sun D.

Noura £49 ④④④
122 Jermyn St, SW1 7839 2020 3–3D
16 Hobart Pl, SW1 7235 9444 2–4B
2 William St, SW1 7235 5900 5–1D
16 Curzon St, W1 7495 1050 3–4B
A "posh Lebanese" chain; it's "consistent" enough nowadays, but some reporters who remember how "fabulous" the initial Belgravia branch once was now regard it as "a shadow of its former self". / www.noura.co.uk; 11.30 pm.

Nozomi SW3 £66 ④④❸
15 Beauchamp Pl 7838 1500 5–1C
A "very self-conscious" Japanese for Knightsbridge "beautiful people"; it's sometimes "fun", but even fans concede it's "overpriced", and critics would settle for nothing less than "a massive overhaul of the kitchen". / www.nozomi.co.uk; 11.30 pm; closed Sun L.

Numero Uno SW11 £33 ❸❶❶
139 Northcote Rd 7978 5837 10–2C
"Always full, and deservedly so", this "very friendly" and "buzzy" family-run Battersea Italian pleases many fans with its "consistently good" food; "good value" too. / 11.30 pm; no Amex.

Nuovi Sapori SW6 £38 ❷❷④
295 New King's Rd 7736 3363 10–1B
"Passionate" cooking and "chatty" service have established this "buzzy" Fulham two-year-old as a "proper neighbourhood Italian"; it is "cramped", though, and the occasional reporter feels it's "over-rated". / 11 pm; closed Sun.

Nutmeg SW1 £24 ❷❷❸
147 Lupus St 7233 9828 5–3D
"Trying really hard in an awkward location" – this year-old Pimlico spot offers some "unusual" Bangladeshi dishes, realised to "above-average" standards. / www.nutmegbarrestaurant.co.uk; 11 pm.

Nyonya W11 £28 ❷❸④
2a Kensington Park Rd   7243 1800   6–2B
"Excellent for Malaysian one-plate dishes" – a "very modern",
"canteen-style" Notting Hill corner-spot, serving "authentic,
affordable and tasty" fare. / 10.30 pm.

O'Conor Don W1 £34 ④④❸
88 Marylebone Ln   7935 9311   3–1A
"A pleasant place to spend a long lunchtime" – the upstairs dining
room of this Irish pub in Marylebone offers "hearty", if rather
"clichéd", "Irish-themed" fare in "comfortable" surroundings.
/ www.oconordon.com; 10 pm; closed Sat & Sun.

O'Zon TW1 £24 ❸❶④
33-35 London Rd   8891 3611   1–4A
A supremely friendly pan-Asian restaurant in downtown
Twickenham, where the "eat-all-you-like menu" is "really good
value". / www.ozon.co.uk; 11 pm.

The Oak W2 £35 ❷❷❶
137 Westbourne Park Rd   7221 3355   6–1B
"Finally re-opened after the fire", this "well-loved" Notting Hill pub-
conversion has made a "welcome return" – its "relaxed" ambience
still "can't be beaten" and the pizza is "even better than before".
/ www.theoaklondon.com; 10.30 pm, Sun 9 pm; Mon-Thu closed L; no booking.

Odette's NW1 £68 ❸④❸
130 Regent's Park Rd   7586 8569   8–3B
Ex-rock promoter Vince Power's re-launch (without the trademark
mirrors) of this "romantic" Primrose Hill classic divides opinion –
fans acclaim a "lovely refurbishment" that's "impossible to fault",
but critics find the wallpaper "scary", and think that, given the
"high" prices, the food is rather "pedestrian". / 10.30 pm; closed
Mon & Sun D; set weekday L £42 (FP).

Odin's W1 £47 ❸❶❶
27 Devonshire St   7935 7296   2–1A
"Beautiful art" (the late Peter Langan's collection) and "unruffled"
service add to the "classy" charm of this "dignified" Marylebone
"old favourite"; it makes a good choice for business or romance...
"so long as you are happy with old-school British cooking".
/ www.langansrestaurant.co.uk; 11 pm; closed Sat L & Sun; booking: max 10.

Okawari W5 £22 ❸❸❸
13 Bond St   8566 0466   1–3A
With its "fun ground-level seating at the rear", this Japanese café
in the heart of Ealing offers "simply put-together" dishes (including
sushi) at "value-for-money" prices. / www.okawari.co.uk; 11 pm.

The Old Bull & Bush NW3 £35 ④❸❷
North End Rd   8905 5456   8–1A
This ancient Hampstead inn was revamped in 2006, and has
inspired quite a few reports, mostly suggesting that it offers
a "good variety" of food (often "meaty"), that's generally "well-
prepared". / www.thebullandbush.co.uk; 9.30 pm.

Old Parr's Head W14 £19 ❸❸④
120 Blythe Rd   7371 4561   7–1C
"Just what every neighbourhood needs" – this "Thai in a pub",
near Olympia, offers "freshly-prepared" scoff that's "tasty and
cheap". / 10 pm; no Amex.

Old Vic Brasserie SE1 £45
Mercury Hs, Waterloo Rd   awaiting tel   9–4A
*This new sibling to the Cheyne Walk Brasserie – first trailed
in these pages 12 months ago! – is finally set to open in late-2007;
the formula that's pleased the Chelsea glitterati is going to need
a bit of tweaking to thrive in gritty Waterloo – we've reflected this
in our price guesstimate, as shown.*

Ye Olde Cheshire Cheese EC4 £32 ⑤④❶
145 Fleet St   7353 6170   9–2A
*"The cosy coal fire and Dickensian setting here is very romantic...
if you like that kind of thing!"; the food at this wonderful old City
tavern can be "awful", though – "I feel sorry for the tourists!"*
/ www.yeoldecheshirecheese.com; 9.30 pm; closed Sun D; no booking,
Sat & Sun.

Olive Tree W6 £35 ❸❷❸
2 Perrers Rd   8600 0550   7–1B
*This Hammersmith "secret" – an "idiosyncratic" conversion of a
backstreet pub – serves good-value staples in a "friendly"
atmosphere.* / www.olivetreepeople.com; 10 pm.

Oliveto SW1 £43 ❷❸④
49 Elizabeth St   7730 0074   2–4A
*A "noisy" and "hard-edged" Belgravian, serving "first-rate pizza";
it's a great "neighbourhood" option, even if "it feels a bit fraught
when they're busy".* / 11 pm; booking: max 7 at D.

Olivo SW1 £44 ❷❷④
21 Eccleston St   7730 2505   2–4B
*It's "cramped and noisy", but this "long-time favourite" attracts
a "very smart" Belgravia crowd, and it's always "buzzing", thanks
to its "consistently fresh" Sardinian cooking and "very friendly"
service.* / 11 pm; closed Sat L & Sun L.

Olivomare SW1 NEW £47 ❷❶❸
10-12 Lower Belgrave St   7730 9022   2–4B
*This summer-2007 spin-off from Olivo, also of Belgravia, has been
hailed in the press as one of the best openings of recent times,
and we see no reason to disagree – a chic Italian seafood specialist,
it scores across the board.* / Rated on Editors' visit; 11 pm; closed Sun.

Olley's SE24 £31 ❷❷④
67-69 Norwood Rd   8671 8259   10–2D
*"South London's finest chippy" – occupying a railway arch
overlooking Brockwell Park.* / www.olleys.info; 10.30 pm; closed Mon L.

1 Blossom Street E1 £46 ❷❸❸
1 Blossom St   7247 6530   9–1D
*Don't be put off by the "inauspicious exterior" of this "tucked-
away" City-fringe Italian; it's "a very enjoyable place to do
business", thanks to its "simple, consistent-quality" cooking,
its "chunky" wine list and, in summer, its "beautiful garden".*
/ www.1blossomstreet.com; 9 pm; closed Sat & Sun.

1 Lombard Street EC3   £75   ④④④
1 Lombard St   7929 6611   9–3C
A location in the very heart of the City makes this "cavernous" classic – a former banking hall – "an archetypal choice for a business lunch" (and so, of course, "totally over-priced"); those paying their own way may wish to head for the "noisy" but (somewhat) cheaper brasserie area. / www.1lombardstreet.com; 9.45 pm; closed Sat & Sun; no trainers; booking essential.

One-O-One
Sheraton Park Tower SW1   £75
101 Knightsbridge   7290 7101   5–1D
Pascal Proyart's cooking of fish is often reckoned "the best in London", but the design of this Knightsbridge dining room has infamously never lived up – it was re-opening, after a major shake-up, as this guide went to press. / www.oneoone.com; 10 pm.

The Only Running Footman W1 NEW £44
5 Charles St   7499 2988   3–3B
Scheduled to launch in late-2007, an ambitious new Mayfair gastropub (and more) venture, from the same backers as the House and the Bull – precedent suggests it will be good but pretty expensive; price given is our guesstimate. / www.therunningfootman.biz.

Ooze W1 NEW   £32   ④④⑤
62 Goodge St   7436 9444   2–1B
"A great idea, poorly executed"; this Fitzrovia risotto bar is "a fun concept" with "good prices", but the décor is "bleak" and some meals are "very average". / www.ooze.biz; 11 pm; closed Sun; set weekday L £22 (FP).

Orange Tree N20   £37   ④④❷
7 Totteridge Ln   8343 7031   1–1B
With its "lovely green location" – "by some ponds", in Totteridge – and its "nice garden" too, this "smart pub/eating house" looks "great"; sadly, it's too often "otherwise disappointing". / www.theorangetreetotteridge.co.uk; 9.30 pm, Sun 8 pm.

L'Oranger SW1   £80   ❸❷❷
5 St James's St   7839 3774   3–4D
This "elegant" and "welcoming" St James's fixture offers a "really classy" all-round experience; its "classic" cuisine is "a notch below the Ramsays of the world", but typically inspires "few complaints". / www.loranger.co.uk; 11 pm; closed Sat L & Sun; booking: max 8; set weekday L £48 (FP).

The Oratory SW3   £31   ④④❷
232 Brompton Rd   7584 3493   5–2C
As at all John Brinkley's ventures, it's "bargain wine" that draws reporters to this "quirky" brasserie near the Brompton Oratory – the "hearty but unimaginative" food plays second fiddle. / www.brinkleys.com; 11 pm.

Oriel SW1   £34   ⑤⑤❸
50-51 Sloane Sq   7730 2804   5–2D
"So much potential, so badly executed" – this "Parisian-style" brasserie, at the heart of the Sloane world, thrives on "people-watching", not its "poor" food and "dreadful" service; if you must visit, breakfast is the best time. / www.tragusholdings.com; 11 pm; no booking.

Oriental City Food Court NW9 £23 ❷⑤⑤
399 Edgware Rd 8200 1188 1–1A
For "cheap, no-frills dining at its best", try the food court of this oriental shopping centre, in Colindale, whose many stalls offer "very authentic" pan-Asian dishes at knock-down prices; "shame they may be about to pull it down" (but not before May 2008, apparently). / 11 pm; L & early evening only; no Amex.

Origin Asia TW9 £35 ❷❷④
100 Kew Rd 8958 0509 1–4A
*"Imaginative", "Indian-with-a-twist" cuisine wins rave reviews from local fans of this bright and "friendly" Richmond spot.
/ www.originasia.co.uk; 11 pm.*

Original Tajines W1 £30 ❸❸❸
7a Dorset St 7935 1545 2–1A
"A lovely little Moroccan", hidden-away in Marylebone; it serves "great couscous and tagines" and "really succulent lamb", at "decent prices". / 11 pm; closed Sat L & Sun; no Amex.

Orrery W1 £68 ❸❷❸
55 Marylebone High St 7616 8000 2–1A
*"The best Conran by far" (even if the group is now officially called 'D&D London'), offering "pricey" modern French cooking that's often "surprisingly good"; the interior can seem "sterile", but some of the larger tables – overlooking a churchyard – are "lovely".
/ www.orreryrestaurant.co.uk; 10.30 pm, Thu-Sat 11 pm; booking: max 12.*

Orso WC2 £43 ④❷④
27 Wellington St 7240 5269 4–3D
"I still love this restaurant as much as ever", say long-term fans of this "buzzy" and "efficient" basement Italian, in Covent Garden – perennially hailed in some quarters as a "hidden gem". / midnight; set pre theatre £25 (FP).

Ortega £30 ④⑤❸
55 Charterhouse St, EC1 7253 1612 9–2A **NEW**
27 Leadenhall Mkt, EC3 7623 1818 9–2D **NEW**
*We quite enjoyed a visit to this new tapas 'concept' from the Tragus (Café Rouge, etc) people; initial ratings are very up-and-down, though, especially service-wise – "allow plenty of time!"
/ www.ortegatapas.co.uk; EC1 11 pm, Sat midnight - EC3 11 pm; EC1 Sun L - EC3 Sat & Sun.*

Oscar
Charlotte Street Hotel W1 £58 ④④④
15 Charlotte St 7806 2000 2–1C
"A buzzing bar" adds to the atmosphere at this attractive Fitzrovia rendezvous; popular for breakfast, it's otherwise – like most Firmdale Hotel operations – "expensive and nothing special". / www.charlottestreethotel.com; 10.30 pm; closed Sun L.

Oslo Court NW8 £46 ❷①❷
Charlbert St, off Prince Albert Rd 7722 8795 8–3A
To the delight of its many mature patrons (and the odd young whippersnapper too), "old-fashioned" dishes come in "epic" portions (especially puds, from the trolley) at this "bizarre" time warp, at the foot of a Regent's Park apartment block; it's "the most endearing waiters ever", though, who really make the occasion. / 11 pm; closed Sun.

Osteria Antica Bologna SW11   £37   ④❸❸
23 Northcote Rd   7978 4771   10–2C
A "closely-packed", rustic old-timer in Clapham, with a "homely"
feel; fans hail its "proper" Italian dishes – doubters find the cuisine
"tired". / www.osteria.co.uk; 11 pm.

Osteria Basilico W11   £40   ❷❸❷
29 Kensington Park Rd   7727 9957   6–1A
"Fun", "noisy" and "crowded" – this rustic Italian has been
a linchpin of Notting Hill life for 15 years, thanks not least to its
"great pasta" and "lovely pizza"; sometimes, though, the "truly
Italian" staff "could be friendlier". / www.osteriabasilico.co.uk; 11.30 pm;
no booking, Sat L.

Osteria dell'Arancio SW10   £51   ❸❷❸
383 King's Rd   7349 8111   5–3B
An "astonishingly detailed regional wine list" and "authentic"
cuisine make this "friendly" and "buzzy" World's End Italian
a "favourite" destination for numerous reporters; it's "not that
cheap", though, and results can be "a bit unpredictable".
/ www.osteriadellarancio.co.uk; 11 pm.

Ottolenghi   £37   ❶❸❸
63 Ledbury Rd, W11   7727 1121   6–1B
1 Holland St, W8   7937 0003   5–1A
287 Upper St, N1   7288 1454   8–2D
"You're tantalised the moment you enter" these "über-trendy"
cafés, which offer a "vibrant" selection of salads, and "stunningly
beautiful cakes and confections"; the food can initially seem "vastly
overpriced", but fortunately it's all just as "scrummy" as it looks.
/ www.ottolenghi.co.uk; 10.15 pm; W11 8pm, Sun 6 pm; N1 closed Sun D,
Holland St takeaway only; W11 no booking, N1 booking for D only.

(BRASSERIE)
OXO TOWER SE1   £60   ⑤⑤❸
Barge House St   7803 3888   9–3A
The views may be "breathtaking", but the food in the "noisy"
brasserie section of this "crammed-in" South Bank landmark dining
room is "very, very average" – for too many reporters, this place
"feels like one big con". / www.harveynichols.com; 11 pm; booking: max 8;
set weekday L £30 (FP).

(RESTAURANT)
OXO TOWER SE1   £72   ⑤⑤❸
Barge House St   7803 3888   9–3A
"Pound-for-pound, is this the worst restaurant in the world?";
"even the view cannot make up for the poor and pricey food",
on the 8th floor of this South Bank landmark – yet again the
survey's top nomination for both overpricing and disappointment.
/ www.harveynichols.com; 11 pm; booking: max 14.

Ozer W1   £32   ④❸❸
4-5 Langham Pl   7323 0505   3–1C
A large and "bustling" Turkish restaurant, just north of Oxford
Circus; the food seems ever-more "standard", but some reporters
still find this a handy "all-rounder". / www.sofra.co.uk; 11 pm.

Pacific Bar and Grill W6   £38   ④④❷
320 Goldhawk Rd   8741 1994   7–1B
"Food and service are a bit sloppy and pricey", but a "captive" local
market sustains this attractive, vaguely "US-style" operation,
near Stamford Brook tube. / 11.30 pm.

Pacific Oriental EC2 NEW   £45
52 Threadneedle St   7621 9988   9–2C
*A large City pan-Oriental, scheduled for a lavish (re)launch on a
new site in late-2007; price given is our guesstimate.*
/ www.orientalrestaurantgroup.co.uk; 9 pm; closed Sat & Sun.

Page in Pimlico SW1   £29   ❸❸❸
11 Warwick Way   7834 3313   2–4B
*"A half-decent pub Thai", in the heart of Pimlico – an area in which
even half-decent places are worth knowing about!*
/ www.frontpagepubs.com; 10 pm.

Il Pagliaccio SW6   £31   ④❷❷
182-184 Wandsworth Bridge Rd   7371 5253   10–1B
*"Italy meets Fulham", at this "atmospheric" local veteran, which
offers the "best pizza for kids and family", at low prices.*
/ www.paggs.co.uk; midnight; no Amex.

Le Pain Quotidien   £23   ❸④❷
18 Gt Marlborough St, Turner Bdg, W1   7486 6154   3–2C NEW
72-75 Marylebone High St, W1   7486 6154   2–1A
201-203A Kings Rd, SW3   7486 6154   5–3C NEW
Royal Festival Hall, Festival Ter, Southbank Centre, Belvedere
Rd, SE1   7486 6154   2–3D NEW
9 Young St, W8   7486 6154   5–1A NEW
*The arrival of these "top communal-tables Belgian bakeries"
is universally welcomed by reporters – attractions include
"wholesome" bread and pastries, "lovely" coffee and a "great
range of breakfast and brunch dishes".* / W1U 9 pm, Sun 8 pm;
SW3 10 pm, Sun 7 pm; W8 8 pm, Sun & Mon 7 pm; SE1 11 pm,
Sun 10 pm; W1F 10 pm, Sun 7 pm.

The Painted Heron SW10   £45   ❶❷❸
112 Cheyne Walk   7351 5232   5–3B
*"Unique" cuisine that's "as good as you'll find in London" makes
it worth seeking out this "posh Indian", tucked-away by the Chelsea
Embankment; it deserves to be better known.*
/ www.thepaintedheron.com; 11 pm; closed Sat L.

Le Palais du Jardin WC2   £46   ❸④❸
136 Long Acre   7379 5353   4–3C
*With its "lovely, bright and airy" premises, this large Covent Garden
stalwart can still seem quite a "glamorous" Theatreland destination;
it's rather "tired" and "lazy", though, and a bad trip here can
be simply "dire".* / www.lpdj.co.uk; 11.30 pm.

The Palmerston SE22   £36   ❷④④
91 Lordship Ln   8693 1629   1–4D
*Thanks to the "really good food", you "must book well ahead" for
this "fantastic neighbourhood restaurant", in a former East Dulwich
boozer; the pressure can make service "hit-and-miss", though,
and "too keen to rush you through".* / www.thepalmerston.co.uk;
10.30 pm, Fri-Sat 11 pm, Sun 9 pm; no Amex.

Pampa   £40   ❷❸❸
4 Northcote Rd, SW11   7924 1167   10–2C
60 Battersea Rise, SW11   7924 4774   10–2C
*The "exquisite steaks" are "the best in South West London, if not
the whole of town", at these "friendly" Battersea Argentineans.*
/ 11 pm; D only; Battersea Rise closed Sun.

Pan-Asian Canteen
Paxton's Head SW1   £31   ②④④
153 Knightsbridge   7581 6256   5–1D
The "yummy fresh food" on offer on the first floor of this large
Knightsbridge boozer is "much better than typical pub-Thai" –
and surprisingly "cheap and cheerful" for this part of town. / 10 pm;
no Amex.

Paolina Café WC1   £16   ②②④
181 Kings Cross Rd   7278 8176   8–3D
"Very tasty Thai food at incredibly cheap prices" and
"the friendliest" service commend this small BYO oriental caff,
in King's Cross, to reporters. / 10 pm; closed Sun; no credit cards.

Papageno WC2   £38   ⑤④②
29-31 Wellington St   7836 4444   4–3D
The décor – a "camp, OTT explosion" – sits "in strange contrast"
to the "unremarkable" (and sometimes "horrible") food on offer
at this "theatrical" Covent Garden experience (which could equally
well have been called The Son of Sarastro).
/ www.papagenorestaurant.com; 11.45 pm.

Papillon SW3   £50   ③②②
96 Draycott Ave   7225 2555   5–2C
Soren Jessen's "sophisticated but friendly" Belle Epoque-style
yearling has been "a happy addition to the Chelsea scene"; it offers
"competent" Gallic fare, plus an "overwhelming" (and, perhaps,
"overpriced") wine list. / www.papillonchelsea.co.uk; midnight, Sun 10 pm;
set weekday L £30 (FP).

Pappa Ciccia   £27   ②②②
105-107 Munster Rd, SW6   7384 1884   10–1B
41 Fulham High St, SW6   7736 0900   10–1B
90 Lower Richmond Rd, SW15   8789 9040   10–1A
These "great-value, local pizza places" are "fun" and "lively"
destinations with a strong regular following; you can BYO too
(Fulham High St, wine only). / www.pappaciccia.com; 11 pm; no Amex.

Pappagallo W1   £52   ③②③
54-55 Curzon St   7629 2742   3–4B
Near Shepherd Market, a Mayfair Italian on the site some still
remember from its Ristorante Italiano days; it's never set the world
alight, but service is notably "attentive", and the cooking
is "reliable". / 11 pm; closed Sat L & Sun L; set weekday L £32 (FP).

Paradise by Way of Kensal Green W10   £35   ②②①
19 Kilburn Ln   8969 0098   1–2B
A "characterful building" is the star of the show at this long-running
favourite; the food is still consistently "good", though, and service
is "attentive" too; major changes are afoot for 2008.
/ www.theparadise.co.uk; 10.30 pm, 9pm; no Amex.

Paradiso Olivelli   £28   ④④④
3 Gt Titchfield St, W1   7436 0111   3–1C
9 St Christopher's Pl, W1   7486 3196   3–1A
35 Store St, WC1   7255 2554   2–1C
61 The Cut, SE1   7261 1221   9–4A
"It's average, but I go back because it's always OK" – that's the
deal at these "speedy" pizza joints, which are "better than many
of the chains". / www.ristoranteparadiso.co.uk; midnight; W1 11pm;
WC1 11.30 pm; WC1 Sun.

El Parador NW1 £26 ❷❷④
245 Eversholt St   7387 2789   8–3C
*"If it wasn't in a grotty part of town, it would be impossible to get
a table", at this "shabby" but "cheerful" Spanish veteran,
near Euston – the food is "basic", but it's "cheap" and "full of
taste". / www.elparadorlondon.com; Mon-Sat 11 pm, Sun 9.30 pm; closed
Sat L & Sun L; no Amex.*

The Parsee N19 £34 ❸❷⑤
34 Highgate Hill   7272 9091   8–1C
*Most reports say the cooking at Cyrus Todiwala's sterile-feeling
Highgate Indian is still "fantastic", but feedback
is modest in volume nowadays, and somewhat mixed.
/ www.the-parsee.com; 10.45 pm; D only, closed Sun.*

Pasha SW7 £48 ④④❶
1 Gloucester Rd   7589 7969   5–1B
*A "sexy and sultry" atmosphere pervades the "numerous nooks
and crannies" of this South Kensington Moroccan;
new management, though, has yet to pep up its food and service,
which are still sometimes "terrible". / www.pasha-restaurant.co.uk;
midnight, Thu-Sat 1 am; booking: max 10 at weekends.*

Passione W1 £58 ❸❸④
10 Charlotte St   7636 2833   2–1C
*Fans of Gennaro Contaldo's "relaxed" Fitzrovia venture say that –
with its "real" food and its "superb" wine – it's "one of the
best Italians in London"; critics find it only "pleasant enough",
though, and mightily "over-priced" (especially given the rather
"harsh" setting). / www.passione.co.uk; 10.15 pm; closed Sat L & Sun.*

Pasta Brown £36 ④④⑤
31-32 Bedford St, WC2   7836 7486   4–3C
35-36 Bow St, WC2   7379 5775   4–2D
*They look touristy, but – "for a carbo-fix" – these "fast" and
"noisy" Covent Garden pasta stops have their fans.
/ www.pastabrown.com; 11 pm, Fri & Sat 11.30 pm, Sun 7 pm; closed Sun D;
no Sat booking.*

Patara £45 ❷❷❸
15 Greek St, W1   7437 1071   4–2A
3-7 Maddox St, W1   7499 6008   3–2C
181 Fulham Rd, SW3   7351 5692   5–2C
9 Beauchamp Pl, SW3   7581 8820   5–1C
*"Stunningly-presented and delicious" dishes, "very polite and
professional" staff, and "calm" and "comfortable" branches –
that's the formula which has created a large fan club for these
"elegant" Thai oases. / www.pataralondon.com; 10.30 pm.*

Paternoster Chop House EC4 £56 ④④④
Warwick Ct, Paternoster Sq   7029 9400   9–2B
*This "phenomenally noisy" D&D London (fka Conran) outfit,
near St Pauls, is "handy for informal business meals" (and has
some nice outside tables too); service is "indifferent", though,
and critics decry a "poor-value" performance overall.
/ www.paternosterchophouse.co.uk; 10.30 pm; closed Sat & Sun D.*

Patio W12 £26 ④❷❷
5 Goldhawk Rd   8743 5194   7–1C
"*Solid, stodgy, Polish fare is served with enthusiasm*" *(and free vodka!) at this* "*eccentric*" *and* "*entertaining*" *venture by Shepherd's Bush Green; it's all a bit* "*hit-and-miss*", *but prices are* "*very fair*". / 11.30 pm; closed Sat L.

Pâtisserie Valerie £28 ④④❸
17 Motcomb St, SW1   7245 6161   5–1D
Hans Cr, SW1   7590 0905   5–1D
105 Marylebone High St, W1   7935 6240   2–1A
162 Piccadilly, W1   7491 1717   3–3C
44 Old Compton St, W1   7437 3466   4–2A
215 Brompton Rd, SW3   7823 9971   5–1C
Duke of York Sq, SW3   7730 7094   5–2D
27 Kensington Church St, W8   7937 9574   5–1A
37 Brushfield St, E1   7247 4906   9–2D
This "*cosmopolitan*"*-feeling chain was sold to ex-PizzaExpresss entrepreneur Luke Johnson in late-2006; its* "*fail-safe*" *breakfasts,* "*gorgeous cakes*" *and* "*dependable*"*other bites have won it many fans – let's hope the formula survives the dreaded 'roll-out' (coming soon to a high street near you). / www.patisserie-valerie.co.uk; 7 pm, Old Compton St 7.30 pm, 10.30 pm Wed-Sat, Brushfield St 8 pm, Hans Cr 11.30 pm; minimum £5 using Amex; no booking.*

Patterson's W1 £60 ❷❷④
4 Mill St   7499 1308   3–2C
"*You get very good value, especially for Mayfair*", *at this* "*very sound*" *family-run venture –* "*warm and personal*" *service helps offset the rather* "*bland*" *and* "*crowded*" *interior, and the cuisine is sometimes* "*outstanding*". / www.pattersonsrestaurant.com; 11 pm; closed Sat L & Sun.

Paul £28 ❸④④
115 Marylebone High St, W1   7224 5615   2–1A
29-30 Bedford St, WC2   7836 3304   4–3C
73 Gloucester Rd, SW7   7373 1232   5–2B
43 Hampstead High St, NW3   7794 8657   8–1A
147 Fleet St, EC4   7353 5874   9–2A
"*Irresistible pastries*", "*crusty*" *breads and* "*delicious coffee*" *make this* "*surprisingly characterful*" *chain of café/pâtisseries popular with most reporters (even if staff do add* "*a good dose of Gallic indifference*"). / www.paul-uk.com; 7 pm-8.30 pm; no Amex; no booking.

Pearl WC1 £70 ❸❸❸
252 High Holborn   7829 7000   2–1D
"*Airy*" *and* "*well-spaced*", *this former Holborn banking hall is ideal for a* "*glamorous*" *business dinner (and also tipped for romance), thanks not least to Jan Tanaka's* "*classy*" *cuisine and the* "*superb*" *wine list; it's* "*expensive*", *though, and the* "*beautiful*" *décor can sometimes seem* "*cold*". / www.pearl-restaurant.com; 10 pm; closed Sat L & Sun.

Pearl Liang W2 🆕 £35 ❷❸❸
8 Sheldon Sq   7289 7000   6–1C
"*Delicate and divine dim sum*" *– and other* "*very authentic*" *Chinese cooking – has carved out an instant reputation for this opium den-style newcomer,* "*hidden-away*" *in the bowels of the huge new Paddington Basin development. / www.pearlliang.co.uk; 11 pm.*

The Peasant EC1 £40 ❸❸❸
240 St John St 7336 7726 8–3D
*Fans of this "eclectic but traditional" Clerkenwell gastropub say
it has "greatly improved" of late; downstairs there's a "cheap"
tapas option – upstairs "isn't bad either", serving a full menu that
"borders on the adventurous". / www.thepeasant.co.uk; 10.30 pm,
Sun 9 pm.*

Pellicano SW3 £44 ❷❷❸
19-21 Elystan St 7589 3718 5–2C
*"Very much back on form" – this "friendly" Chelsea backstreet
Italian is an "attentive" sort of place, offering "attractively-
presented" dishes. / 11 pm.*

E Pellicci E2 £14 ❸❷❶
332 Bethnal Green Rd 7739 4873 1–2D
*A "stunning" Art Deco interior would make this landmark East End
greasy spoon notable, irrespective of any other virtues; however,
its "brilliant Full English breakfasts" – served with "passion" –
are "worth crossing town for". / 5pm; L only, closed Sun; no credit cards.*

Peninsular
Holiday Inn Express SE10 £30 ❷④④
85 Bugsbys Way 8858 2028 1–3D
*Though oddly-situated within an hotel, this Chinese restaurant
in Greenwich is "always buzzing" with "a largely oriental clientele";
"be prepared to queue" for its "fresh and delicious" Sunday dim
sum. / www.peninsular-restaurant.co.uk; 11 pm.*

The Pepper Tree SW4 £20 ❸❷❸
19 Clapham Common S'side 7622 1758 10–2D
*A "lively young crowd" tucks into "good, simple Thai fare" at this
"cheap" but "dependable" fixture, by Clapham South tube; expect
queues. / www.thepeppertree.co.uk; 11 pm; no Amex; no booking at D.*

Perc%nto EC4 £47 ⑤④⑤
26 Ludgate Hill 7778 0010 9–2B
*An "anonymous-feeling" Italian City basement, where standards are
"not good", and prices are "highly inflated".
/ www.etruscarestaurants.com; 10 pm.*

Père Michel W2 £42 ❷❸④
11 Bathurst St 7723 5431 6–2D
*"Good quality" – "if uninspired" – Gallic dishes win a loyal older
following for this "unchanging" Bayswater bistro, where fish and
seafood are specialities. / 11 pm; closed Sat L & Sun.*

Perla £32 ④④❸
11 Charlotte St, W1 7436 1744 2–1C
28 Maiden Ln, WC2 7240 7400 4–4D
*"Cheap" and "very jolly" – these Mexican cantinas in Covent
Garden and Fitzrovia offer "tasty" grub that's "better than it needs
to be, considering the effects of their margaritas".
/ www.cafepacifico.co.uk; 10 pm-11 pm; WC2 Sun D only; no Sat bookings.*

Pescatori £43 ④④④
11 Dover Street, W1 7580 3289 3–3C
55-57 Charlotte St, W1 7580 3289 2–1C
*These West End Italian fish "old-timers" go down well with some
traditionalists, who praise their "honest food and cheerful service";
they can seem "overpriced", though, and their critics are not at all
impressed. / 11 pm; closed Sat L & Sun.*

Petek N4 £25 ❷❷❷
96 Stroud Green Rd   7619 3933   8–1D
*"More than your bog-standard Turkish café" – this Finsbury Park
yearling is a "friendly" place, offering a good "cheap and cheerful"
experience (and a wide-ranging menu, including non-Turkish
dishes). / 11 pm; closed Sun.*

Petersham Nurseries TW10 £54 ❸④❷
Off Petersham Rd   8605 3627   1–4A
*"Absurd" prices colour many reports on this "genuinely odd" but
"romantic" garden centre café (where "you sit in a greenhouse,
amongst the plants"); thanks to Skye Gingall's "top-notch" cuisine,
though, it's still hard to book – early, if you can, as "they quickly run
out". / www.petershamnurseries.com; Wed-Sun L only, closed Mon & Tue.*

La Petite Auberge N1 £28 ④❸❸
283 Upper St   7359 1046   8–2D
*On Islington's trendy main drag, this "cosy and reliable" bistro offers
"honest" food and "friendly" service; it's all "very basic", though.
/ 11 pm, Fri-Sat 11.30 pm; set weekday L £17 (FP).*

La Petite Maison W1 🆕 £64 ❸❸❷
54 Brooks Mews   7495 4774   3–2B
*Co-owned with Zuma, this new Mayfair re-creation of a fashionable
Nice outfit looks set to become one of the beau-monde hits
of 2007; it's certainly a light and handsome room, and on our
early-days visit, the pricey Provençal 'tapas' were generally of high
quality. / Rated on Editors' visit; www.lpmlondon.co.uk; 10.45 pm; closed Sun.*

PÉTRUS
THE BERKELEY SW1 £89 ❶❶❷
Wilton Pl   7235 1200   5–1D
*How long before Marcus Wareing's "brilliant" cuisine overtakes that
at his boss Gordon Ramsay's Royal Hospital Road flagship?; looking
at the whole experience – and factoring in the charm of the
"classy, plush and opulent" surroundings – this Knightsbridge dining
room is already rated by the survey as the better all-round choice;
the wine list is "simply astounding" too. / www.marcuswareing.com;
10.45 pm; closed Sat L & Sun; no jeans or trainers; booking: max 10;
set always available £50 (FP).*

Pham Sushie EC1 £23 ❶❷❸
155 Whitecross St   7251 6336   9–1B
*Some of "the best-value-for-money sushi" in town – "superbly fresh
every time" – draws many fans to this "basic" spot, in a
"backwater" near the Barbican. / 10 pm; closed Sat L & Sun.*

Philpotts Mezzaluna NW2 £38 ❸❷❸
424 Finchley Rd   7794 0455   1–1B
*"It's a winner every time", say fans of David Philpott's "good",
"solid" and "unpretentious" Child's Hill Italian.
/ www.philpotts-mezzaluna.com; 11 pm; closed Mon & Sat L; no Amex.*

Pho EC1 £22 ❸❷❸
86 St John St   7253 7624   9–1A
*"Pho is the future", say fans of this Vietnamese noodle-outfit
in Clerkenwell, which benefits from "personable" service and "good-
value" prices; a new branch opens in Fitzrovia in late-2007.
/ www.phocafe.co.uk; 10 pm; closed Sun.*

The Phoenix SW1 NEW £31 ④④❸
14 Palace St 7828 8136 2–4B
A "cosy" gastropub, behind the new Cardinal Place development,
by Victoria Station – fans say it offers "good food at reasonable
prices", but its handy location is arguably its biggest plus. / 10 pm.

The Phoenix SW3 £35 ④④❸
23 Smith St 7730 9182 5–2D
A "dependable" and "well-attended" gastropub, just off the King's
Road; "it's not that cheap, but this is Chelsea".
/ www.geronimo-inns.co.uk; 9.45 pm; closed Sun D; no Amex.

Phoenix Bar & Grill SW15 £43 ❷❷❷
162-164 Lower Richmond Rd 8780 3131 10–1A
"Very good in recent times" – this "buzzy" Putney brasserie serves
up some "high-quality" Mediterranean dishes (not least "the best-
ever pasta"); "nice terrace" too. / www.sonnys.co.uk; 10.30 pm, 11 pm.

Phoenix Palace NW1 £30 ❷④④
3-5 Glentworth St 7486 3515 2–1A
"Judging by the number of Chinese diners", this "busy" oriental,
near Baker Street tube, deserves its reputation for "authentic" food
(particularly "great dim sum"); service, though, can be "erratic".
/ 11.15 pm.

Picasso's SW3 £28 ⑤④④
127 King's Rd 7352 4921 5–3C
Now the Chelsea Kitchen has gone, this "nostalgic" Italian coffee
shop is one of the King's Road last remnants of the swinging '60s;
it's most popular for breakfast – "they'll cook anything you want,
any way you want it". / 11.15 pm.

Piccolino £31 ④④④
21 Heddon St, W1 7287 4029 3–2C NEW
27-29 Bellevue Rd, SW17 8767 1713 10–2C
38 High St, SW19 8946 8019 10–2B
Some reporters feel the London branches of this NW England-
based Italian chain offer "poor value for money", but we enjoyed
our (post-survey) visit to its large new branch off Regent Street
(formerly Zinc, RIP), which has a notably smart terrace. / 11 pm.

Pick More Daisies N8 £30 ❷❷❷
12 Crouch End Hill 8340 2288 8–1C
"Fantastic all-American breakfasts", "serious salads" and "succulent
burgers to die for" are among features that make this "chilled" and
"child-friendly" hang-out a smash hit, up Crouch End way.
/ www.pickmoredaisies.com; 10 pm; no Amex.

PIED À TERRE W1 £84 ❷❷❸
34 Charlotte St 7636 1178 2–1C
Shane Osborn's "magnificent" cuisine and an "astonishing" wine
list maintain David Moore's Fitzrovia townhouse as a Mecca for
serious foodies; its "relaxed and informal" style, though,
can sometimes give a rather "uneventful" impression.
/ www.pied-a-terre.co.uk; 11 pm; closed Sat L & Sun; booking: max 6;
set weekday L £53 (FP).

The Pig's Ear SW3 £39 ❸❸❷
35 Old Church St   7352 2908   5–3C
A "very buzzy" and "very Chelsea" pub, with a "crammed" downstairs bar, and a more "civilised" dining room upstairs; its combination of a "cosy" British ambience with "Frenchified" fare is making it very popular. / www.thepigsear.co.uk; 10 pm.

Pigalle Club W1 £48 ⑤❸❷
215-217 Piccadilly   7734 8142   3–3D
It's "a great place to party", but the "unimaginative" food at this year-old Mayfair supper club is very much a side-show – "go to the bar, and enjoy the music from there". / www.thepigalleclub.com; 11.30 pm; D only, closed Sun.

The Pilot W4 £33 ④❸❷
56 Wellesley Rd   8994 0828   7–2A
A "safe", if "standard", gastropub stand-by in an area – near Gunnersbury tube – without many alternatives; it's a "lively" place, and has a "nice" beer garden too. / 10 pm.

ping pong £26 ④④❷
10 Paddington St, W1   7009 9600   2–1A
29a James St, W1   7034 3100   3–1A **NEW**
45 Gt Marlborough St, W1   7851 6969   3–2C
48 Eastcastle St, W1   7079 0550   3–1C **NEW**
48 Newman St, W1   7291 3080   3–1C **NEW**
74-76 Westbourne Grove, W2   7313 9832   6–1B
Southbank Centre, SE1   7960 4160   2–3D **NEW**
"A fab concept" – these "sleek" and "affordable" hang-outs offer a dim sum formula (plus "lovely cocktails and jasmine tea") conducive to "great social eating"; the chain is growing "at a frantic pace", though, and you increasingly "take pot luck on the quality of the product". / www.pingpongdimsum.com; Newman St Mon-Sat 10.45 pm, Sun 10.15 pm; midnight, Sun 10.30 pm.

La Piragua N1 £26 ❷❸❷
176 Upper St   7354 2843   8–2D
"A true Latin American experience in the heart of Islington" – highlights include "fantastic Argentinian steaks, and real salsa dancing after 11pm". / 11.30 pm (Fri club till 6 am); no Amex.

El Pirata W1 £32 ❸❷❷
5-6 Down St   7491 3810   3–4B
For "a jolly meal in Mayfair" that "won't break the bank", this "buzzy" tapas bar is worth knowing about; "the '70s décor is great" too. / www.elpirata.co.uk; 11.30 pm; closed Sat L & Sun.

Pissarro's W4 £41 ❸❸❶
Corney Reach Way   8994 3111   10–1A
This "relaxed" Thames-side spot, near Chiswick House, doesn't just rely on the "lovely" charms of its "conservatory overlooking the river" – it serves "surprisingly good" traditional scoff.
/ www.pissarro.co.uk; 10.30 pm.

Pizza Metro SW11 £32 ❶❷❷
64 Battersea Rise   7228 3812   10–2C
"Is it the best pizza in London?" – this "really authentic" and "good-value" Neapolitan joint, in Battersea, has a better claim than most; it's "really fun and buzzy" too. / www.pizzametro.com; 11 pm; closed Mon, Tue-Fri D only, Sat & Sun open L & D; no Amex.

Pizza on the Park SW1 £34 ④④❷
11 Knightsbridge   7235 5273   5–1D
It's the "superb jazz" that's the draw to the club-basement of this upmarket PizzaExpress, near Hyde Park Corner; the airy ground floor is also an "enjoyable" destination, although "the food is nothing to write home about". / www.pizzaonthepark.co.uk; 11 pm, Fri & Sat midnight.

Ciro's Pizza Pomodoro £31 ④④❷
51 Beauchamp Pl, SW3   7589 1278   5–1C
7-8 Bishopsgate Churchyard, EC2   7920 9207   9–2D
The "happening" late-night atmosphere is the raison d'être of these "fun" pizzerias (especially the "grotto"-like Knightsbridge original); both the food and the "hit-and-miss" service are rather incidental. / SW3 1 am, EC2 midnight; SW3 D only, EC2 closed Sat/Sun.

PizzaExpress £25 ④❸❸
Branches throughout London
"Often imitated, but never beaten"; the UK's original mid-market chain – est 1965 – is still a "steadfast" stand-by for many Londoners (and its "friendly" staff are famously "helpful with children"); it "still hasn't bounced back", though, to its best standards of yesteryear. / www.pizzaexpress.co.uk; 11.30 pm-midnight; most City branches closed all or part of weekend; no booking at most branches.

Pizzeria Oregano N1 £30 ❷❸④
19 St Albans Pl   7288 1123   8–3D
Tucked-away off Islington's Upper Street, this "authentic '80s Italian" serves "enormous pizzas with mountains of toppings"; it is, however, "not a place you go for ambience". / 10.45 pm; closed Mon, Tue-Fri D only, Sat & Sun open L & D; no Amex.

PJ's SW3 £47 ⑤⑤④
52 Fulham Rd   7581 0025   5–2C
The food "has gone from bad to worse", at this "happening" South Kensington scene; if you want "Sunday lunch surrounded by the Euro-set", though, this is the place. / 11.45 pm.

The Place Below EC2 £18 ❷④❸
St Mary-le-Bow, Cheapside   7329 0789   9–2C
In the crypt of one of the Square Mile's most impressive churches, this veggie canteen offers "a more-interesting-than-usual City eating experience"; "the food is healthy, and prices are low". / www.theplacebelow.co.uk; L only, closed Sat & Sun; no Amex; need 15+ to book.

Planet Hollywood W1 £47 ⑤⑤⑤
13 Coventry St   7287 1000   4–4A
Time to roll the credits on this "tacky", movie-themed West End landmark? – the food is "expensive" and "not very nice". / www.planethollywoodlondon.com; 1 am.

Plateau E14 £69 ④④④
Canada Pl   7715 7100   11–1C
With its "great location, and view of Canary Wharf", this fourth-floor vantage point is "one of the few real choices" for business entertaining in the area; it's "strictly for expense-accounts", though, and can seem "uninspiring", "snotty" and "overpriced" – the brasserie (price £53) is probably a better bet. / www.plateaurestaurant.co.uk; 10 pm; closed Sat L & Sun D; set dinner £45 (FP).

Poissonnerie de l'Avenue SW3   £57   ❷❷❸
82 Sloane Ave   7589 2457   5–2C

"An old-fashioned fish restaurant, in the best sense" – this "grown-up" Brompton Cross "institution" is notable for its "consistent quality" over many years; younger bloods, though, may find its clientele a touch "geriatric". / www.poisonneriedelavenue.co.uk; 11.15 pm; closed Sun.

(Ognisko Polskie)
The Polish Club SW7   £39   ④❷❶
55 Prince's Gate, Exhibition Rd   7589 4635   5–1C

The "unique" atmosphere offers "reason enough to visit" this "time-warp" émigrés' club, which benefits from "gracious" South Kensington premises (and a "wonderful balcony" for the summer); the hearty Polish fare, though, is "undistinguished". / www.ognisko.com; 11 pm.

Pomegranates SW1   £50   ④❷❷
94 Grosvenor Rd   7828 6560   2–4C

"Eccentric, '70s décor" adds to the "quirky" charm of Patrick Wynn Jones's "clubby" Pimlico basement; the "eclectic" menu is similarly a "throwback" – part of an overall experience that's "enjoyable, if pricey". / 11.15 pm; closed Sat L & Sun.

Le Pont de la Tour SE1   £66   ④④❸
36d Shad Thames   7403 8403   9–4D

"Only for the view of Tower Bridge"; otherwise, this D&D London (formerly Conran) veteran – with its "bored" staff and its "boring" food – often seems "a bit of a rip-off"; optimists insist it's "getting better", though, and they have (modest) support from the ratings. / www.danddlondon.com; 11 pm; closed Sat L.

Le Pont de la Tour Bar & Grill SE1   £50   ❸❷❷
36d Shad Thames   7403 8403   9–4D

"Better value than big brother next door"; this (somewhat) cheaper brasserie-style operation – sharing the "top view" and "beautiful" wines of its neighbour – is a "lively and buzzing scene", where the food is generally "enjoyable". / www.lepontdelatour.co.uk; 11 pm; no booking.

Popeseye   £38   ❸❸④
108 Blythe Rd, W14   7610 4578   7–1C
277 Upper Richmond Rd, SW15   8788 7733   10–2A

These basic bistros – in Olympia and Putney – are still widely tipped as "a carnivore's delight", offering "fantastic steaks" washed down by "amazing-value red wines"; the occasional critic, though, fears they've "lost their touch". / www.popeseye.com; 10.30 pm; D only, closed Sun; no credit cards.

La Porchetta Pizzeria   £23   ❸④❸
33 Boswell St, WC1   7242 2434   2–1D
141-142 Upper St, N1   7288 2488   8–2D
147 Stroud Green Rd, N4   7281 2892   8–1D
74-77 Chalk Farm Rd, NW1   7267 6822   8–2B
84-86 Rosebery Ave, EC1   7837 6060   9–1A

"Happy, almost a bit slapdash" – thanks to their "enormous" pizzas (and other "generous" Italian fare), these "boisterous and engaging" Italians are usually forgiven any "rough edges"; the Finsbury Park original is particularly "exuberant". / 10.30-midnight; WC1 closed Sat L & Sun, N1 Mon-Thu closed L, N4 closed weekday L; no Amex; need 5+ to book.

Portal EC1 £59 ❸❸❷
88 St John St   7253 6950   9–1B
*"The roomy rear conservatory" makes a "great space" for eating,
at this Clerkenwell two-year-old; for the most part, its "personal"
service, "cracking" wine list and "very interesting" Portuguese-
influenced cuisine win approval too, but – on the food front –
some critics "can't see what the fuss is about".*
/ www.portalrestaurant.com; 10.15 pm; closed Sat L & Sun.

La Porte des Indes W1 £56 ❸❸❶
32 Bryanston St   7224 0055   2–2A
*"You'd never guess you're only a block from Marble Arch", at this
"dramatic", "tropical-themed" basement, which comes complete
with waterfall; it can seem "overpriced", but its "eclectic, French-
Indian fusion" fare is usually "very enjoyable" (and the Sunday
buffet is "splendid").* / www.pilondon.net; 11.30 pm; closed Sat L.

Porters English Restaurant WC2 £30 ⑤⑤⑤
17 Henrietta St   7836 6466   4–3D
*It may be "loved by foreigners who think this is English food", but –
according to the modest volume of feedback from reporters –
this "too touristy" Covent Garden stalwart is "just terrible".*
/ www.porters.uk.com; 11.30 pm; no Amex.

Il Portico W8 £42 ❸❷❷
277 Kensington High St   7602 6262   7–1D
*A "homely" Kensington Italian "staple" – now run by the third
generation of the Chiavarini family – to which "the faithful return
time-after-time".* / www.ilportico.co.uk; 11.15 pm; closed Sun, & Bank
Holidays.

The Portrait
National Portrait Gallery WC2 £51 ④④❷
St Martin's Pl   7312 2490   4–4B
*"Fantastic views" – "over rooftops and Nelson on his column" –
are the key feature of this "bright and airy" venue, atop the
galleries; the food is "by numbers", though, and you take "pot luck"
on the service.* / www.searcys.co.uk; Thu-Fri 8.30 pm; Sat-Wed closed D.

Potemkin EC1 £40 ④⑤⑤
144 Clerkenwell Rd   7278 6661   9–1A
*"A remarkable vodka selection" is a key feature of this
"uninspired"-looking bar (upstairs)/restaurant (cellar)
in Clerkenwell, which has sometimes seemed "quiet" of late;
the food's "stodgy" ("authentic"), and service can be "surly".*
/ www.potemkin.co.uk; 10.30 pm; closed Sat L & Sun; set weekday L £26 (FP).

LA POULE AU POT SW1 £50 ❸❸❶
231 Ebury St   7730 7763   5–2D
*"Take someone you love" to this "quirky" and "romantically dark"
candlelit bit of "rustic France", in Pimlico – yet again, the survey's
top tip for a date; the cuisine is "simple" and generally "well-
cooked", but the "idiosyncratic" service has sometimes seemed
"arrogant" of late.* / 11 pm; set weekday L £32 (FP).

Pret A Manger £10 ❸❷④
Branches throughout London
"Still the sarnie-benchmark" – this "ubiquitous but totally reliable" chain is praised by legions of reporters for its "flavour-packed and always fresh" food (and "decent" coffee too); plus, of course, its "unnaturally cheerful" staff. / www.pret.com; 4 pm-6 pm, Trafalgar Sq 8 pm, St. Martin's Ln 9 pm; closed Sun (except some West End branches), City branches closed Sat & Sun; no credit cards; no booking.

Prima EC3 NEW £40 ❸❷❸
14 New London St 7264 1240 9–3D
"Snappy service" and "decent food" have made this chichi new first-floor bar/restaurant, near Fenchurch Street, a useful addition to the City – it's becoming "increasingly crowded at lunchtimes". / www.barprima.com; midnight, Thu & Fri 2 am; closed Sat.

The Prince Arthur E8 NEW £35
95 Forest Rd awaiting tel 1–1D
Due to open in late-September 2007, this London Fields gastropub is the fifth venture from the Gun people; very simple British fare, done well, is promised; price given is our guesstimate.

The Princess EC2 £40 ❷❷❸
76 Paul St 7729 9270 9–1C
This Shoreditch two-year-old (sibling to Farringdon's Easton) wins nothing but praise for its "sophisticated gastropub fare"; the stylish small dining room is up a spiral staircase, over the main bar. / 10 pm; closed Sat L & Sun.

Princess Garden W1 £50 ❷❷④
8 North Audley St 7493 3223 3–2A
For an "upmarket" (if slightly "sterile") Chinese experience, this "comfortable" Mayfair spot – with its "remarkably helpful" service and its "consistently good" food – is often tipped as "pricy but worth it". / www.princessgardenofmayfair.com; 11.15 pm; set weekday L £29 (FP).

Priory House W14 £28 ❸❷❷
58 Milson Rd 7371 3999 7–1C
This "stylish" bar, in the backstreets behind Olympia, gets a big thumbs-up for its "warm" ambience, its "charming" staff and its "good-quality" tapas. / www.priorybars.com; 10 pm; no Amex.

Prism EC3 £70 ④④⑤
147 Leadenhall St 7256 3888 9–2D
Some reporters do tip Harvey Nics's City outpost as a "decent" business venue; prices for the "formulaic" cuisine are "outrageous", though, and the setting – a converted banking hall – can seem "stilted" and "echoey". / www.harveynichols.com; 10 pm; closed Sat & Sun.

The Providores W1 £55 ❷❸④
109 Marylebone High St 7935 6175 2–1A
Peter Gordon's "wacky combinations of ingredients" and some "great Kiwi wines" make this "unusual" (and "cramped") first-floor Marylebone dining room something of a foodie Mecca; for critics, though, the food can be "rich and overcomplicated". / www.providores.co.uk; 10.30 pm; booking: max 12.

(Tapa Room)
The Providores W1 £35 ❷④④
109 Marylebone High St   7935 6175   2–1A
*"Unusual combos that work really well" create a "yummy" choice
of "imaginative" tapas at this popular Marylebone hang-out, where
"unbeatable Kiwi brunches" and "splendid NZ wines" are
highlights; it's "a tight squeeze", though, and "mad" when busy.
/ www.theprovidores.co.uk; 10.30 pm.*

The Pumphouse N8 £42 ④❸❶
1 New River Ave   8340 0400   1–1C
*"The location is the star", at this "funky" converted pumping
station, in Hornsey; not infrequently, though, the food "fails to live
up to the interesting setting". / www.phn8.co.uk; 9.30 pm; closed Mon.*

Pure California W1 £18 ❸④④
47 Goodge St   7436 3601   2–1C
*"Aimed at size-zero types", this fast-food mini-chain (in Soho and
Fitzrovia) wins praise for its "great range of fresh and healthy
drinks, sandwiches, salads and desserts". / www.purecalifornia.co.uk;
6 pm; closed Sat & Sun; no booking.*

Putney Station SW15 £33 ④❸❸
94-98 Upper Richmond Rd   8780 0242   10–2B
*For an "enjoyable evening out", this Putney wine bar – offering John
Brinkley's trademark "great value-for-money" wine deal – can be
worth a try, despite its "cooking-by-numbers" cuisine.
/ www.brinkleys.com; 11 pm.*

Quadrato
Four Seasons Hotel E14 £64 ❸❸❸
Westferry Circus   7510 1857   11–1B
*A "spacious" dining room, off the lobby of a Canary Wharf hotel,
that's occasionally voted a business "favourite"; feedback is modest,
but a couple of reporters say the place does "the best buffet
brunch spread in town". / www.fourseasons.com; 10.30 pm.*

Quaglino's SW1 £54 ⑤⑤⑤
16 Bury St   7930 6767   3–3D
*Hopefully Des & David (the 'new' captains of the outfit formerly
called Conran Restaurants) will eventually get around to sorting out
this "cavernous" St James's "factory" – with its "poor" service and
"formulaic" brasserie fare, it continues to "live off its reputation".
/ www.quaglinos.co.uk; midnight, Fri & Sat 1 am; set pre theatre £33 (FP).*

The Quality Chop House EC1 £38 ❸❸❸
94 Farringdon Rd   7837 5093   9–1A
*For "comfort food of an elevated kind", this lovingly-restored
'Working Class Caterer', in Clerkenwell, remains a "quirky"
favourite; it's "not cheap", though, and "watch out for the narrow
bench seating" (which "can make lingering uncomfortable").
/ www.qualitychophouse.co.uk; 11 pm; closed Sat L; set weekday L £24 (FP).*

Queen's Head W6 £30 ④❸❶
13 Brook Grn   7603 3174   7–1C
*A huge, "charming" tavern on Brook Green, with a "fantastic" rear
garden – "it's such a pity that the gigantic menu is stuck in the
'70s". / 10 pm; no booking.*

Queen's Head & Artichoke NW1   £38   ❸❸❸
30-32 Albany St   7916 6206   8–4B
*This "off-the-beaten-track" boozer, near Regent's Park, serves
"interesting" tapas, plus more "hearty" fare that's "better than
anything else nearby"; choose between "the formal upstairs room
or the busy downstairs bar".* / www.theartichoke.net; 10.15 pm.

The Queens Arms W6 NEW   £33   ❸❸❷
171 Greyhound Rd   7386 5078   7–2D
*"A very nice surprise", in the thin backstreets of Baron's Court;
this new pub-conversion has a notably light and airy interior,
and serves food that's mainly "good" (if "occasionally hit-and-
miss").* / 10 pm.

Le Querce SE23 NEW   £29   ❶❷④
66-68 Brockley Rise   8690 3761   1–4D
*"Well worth the trip to SE23" – this totally unexpected (and very
modest) newcomer, in the backwoods of Lewisham, serves
"the best" Italian food you'll find for the money, including some
"excellent home-made pasta"; (option to BYO for £2 corkage).*
/ Rated on Editors' visit; 10.30 pm; no Amex; set weekday L £18 (FP).

Quilon SW1   £47   ❷❷④
41 Buckingham Gate   7821 1899   2–4B
*It's worth braving the "slightly cold" setting of this subcontinental
in the "barren" area near Buckingham Palace – service
is "courteous" and the south Indian cuisine shows "great subtlety
and lightness of touch".* / www.thequilonrestaurant.com; 11 pm; closed
Sat L & Sun; set Sun L £20 (FP).

Quirinale SW1   £55   ❷❶④
North Ct, 1 Gt Peter St   7222 7080   2–4C
*"Plenty of rotund MPs" add to the businesslike vibe of this
"discreet" Westminster basement; it's a shame the setting can
seem rather "characterless" – the service is "slick", and Stefano
Favio's Italian cooking is often "superb".* / www.quirinale.co.uk;
10.30 pm; closed Sat L & Sun.

Quo Vadis W1   £51   ④④④
26-29 Dean St   7437 9585   4–2A
*Supporters of this MPW-branded Soho veteran say it's
an "imaginative" place which "never fails to please" – there are,
however, almost as many critics, who just find the whole experience
"very disappointing".* / www.whitestarline.org.uk; 11 pm; closed
Sat L & Sun.

Racine SW3   £48   ❷❶❸
239 Brompton Rd   7584 4477   5–2C
*"Just sit back and pretend you're in Paris", at this "wonderful"
(if "very crowded and noisy") Knightsbridge brasserie, where Henry
Harris is in charge of the "particularly well-executed" cuisine,
and Eric Garnier oversees "attentive but unobtrusive" service that's
"close to perfect".* / 10.30 pm.

Ragam W1   £30   ❶❷⑤
57 Cleveland St   7636 9098   2–1B
*Forget the "grotty" décor and the "crowded and noisy" conditions –
this "low-key Fitzrovia classic" delivers "astoundingly good" South
Indian dishes (mostly veggie) at prices that "can't be beaten";
BYO at modest corkage.* / www.mcdosa.co.uk; 11 pm; set weekday L
£13 (FP).

Rainforest Café W1 £35 ⑤④❷
20 Shaftesbury Ave 7434 3111 3–3D
"Dire food, but the kids love it" – this West End theme-extravaganza may be a "shockingly bad tourist trap", but "where else can you have burgers with elephants?"; "NB: some under-3s are scared by the thunderstorm". / www.therainforestcafe.co.uk; 10 pm, Fri & Sun 8 pm.

Rajasthan £29 ❸❷❸
38-41 Houndsditch, EC3 7626 0033 9–2D NEW
49 Monument St, EC3 7626 1920 9–3C
8 India St, EC3 7488 9777 9–2D
"Fast and friendly" service helps win support for this "reliable and popular" chain of City curry houses. / 11 pm; closed Sat & Sun.

Ran W1 £37 ❸❷❸
58-59 Great Marlborough St 7434 1650 3–1D
A "pleasant" north-Soho fixture, worth knowing about for its "good service" and OK Korean BBQ fare. / www.ranrestaurant.com; 10.30 pm; closed Sun L.

Randa W8 £36 ❸❷④
23 Kensington Church St 7937 5363 5–1A
"Very professional and welcoming staff" inject some (necessary) va-va-voom into this glitzy but dull-looking Kensington yearling (part of the Maroush Group); the food – from an open grill – is "fresh" and "consistent". / www.maroush.com; midnight.

Randall & Aubin £39 ❸❸❷
16 Brewer St, W1 7287 4447 3–2D
329-331 Fulham Rd, SW10 7823 3515 5–3B
"A fantastic buzz" animates this "super-groovy" Soho pit stop, and – once you've secured your perch – you can enjoy top people-watching, plus some "excellent" (if "not cheap or ambitious") seafood; Chelsea – a more standard brasserie operation – "lacks the fizz of W1". / www.randallandaubin.co.uk; 11 pm; SW10 no Amex; W1 no booking.

Rani N3 £26 ❸❷④
7 Long Ln 8349 4386 1–1B
"You eat well and so cheaply", from the "fun" veggie buffet of this "out-of-the-way" North Finchley Indian; it's a "slightly shabby" place, but service is "attentive". / www.raniuk.com; 10 pm; D only, ex Sun open L & D.

Ranoush £31 ❸④④
22 Brompton Rd, SW1 7235 6999 5–1D
338 King's Rd, SW3 7352 0044 5–3C
43 Edgware Rd, W2 7723 5929 6–1D
86 Kensington High St, W8 7938 2234 5–1A
"Hard to beat for tasty and healthy fast food" – this "authentic" Lebanese chain dishes up "fantastic" shawarmas and "great juices". / www.maroush.com; 1 am-3 am.

Ransome's Dock SW11 £47 ❸❷❸
35 Parkgate Rd 7223 1611 5–4C
"One of the country's best-selected, widest-ranging and most fairly-priced wine lists" draws fans from far and wide to Martin & Vanessa Lam's "cramped" but "reliable" Battersea restaurant; the cuisine is "well-executed", but plays rather a supporting rôle. / www.ransomesdock.co.uk; 11 pm; closed Sun D.

Raoul's Café £38 ④④❸
105-107 Talbot Rd, W11 7229 2400 6–1B
13 Clifton Rd, W9 7289 7313 8–4A
*These Maida Vale and Notting Hill cafés have quite a name
in some quarters as "the best places in town for brunch"
(and that's "in spite of the cramped conditions, the staff that never
catch your eye and the noisy neighbours on adjacent tables");
egg dishes are a highlight. / www.raoulsgourmet.com; 10 pm.*

Rapscallion SW4 £37 ❸④❸
75 Venn St 7787 6555 10–2D
*"A cute place in Clapham" that's "ideal for lazy weekend brunch"
(if you can get a table); "service is slow, but it doesn't seem
to matter". / 11 pm; no Amex; booking: max 6.*

Rasa N16 £24 ❶❶❸
55 Stoke Newington Church St 7249 0344 1–1C
*The "Stokey original" is "still the best" of this superb Indian group;
its "passionate" staff are "exceptionally friendly", and its veggie
Keralan fare is "superlative" – so "fresh", so "interesting", and at
such "incredibly low" prices. / www.rasarestaurants.com; 10.30 pm; closed
weekday L.*

Rasa £35 ❶❶④
5 Charlotte St, W1 7637 0222 2–1C
6 Dering St, W1 7629 1346 3–2B
Holiday Inn Hotel, 1 Kings Cross, WC1 7833 9787 8–3D
56 Stoke Newington Church St, N16 7249 1340 1–1C
*With its "wonderful South Indian cuisine" at "incredibly low prices",
this Keralan mini-chain stands in "a class apart"; Dering Street and
N16 (Travancore) serve meat, while the Charlotte Street branch
(Samudra) offers "amazing seafood curries" and the like; (see also
Rasa N16). / www.rasarestaurants.com; 10.45 pm; N16 Mon-Fri closed
L, Dering St W1 closed Sun, N16 D only Mon-Sat, N1 L only Mon-Fri.*

RASOI VINEET BHATIA SW3 £74 ❶❷❸
10 Lincoln St 7225 1881 5–2D
*Vineet Bhatia's "incredible" cuisine – "a superb synthesis
of traditional and modern styles" – makes this Chelsea townhouse
"arguably the best Indian restaurant in the world"; its interior can
"lack buzz", but this year it has seemed more "intimate" and
"elegant". / www.vineetbhatia.com; 11 pm; closed Sat L & Sun; set weekday L
£42 (FP).*

Ratchada SE3 £26 ❸④⑤
129 Lee Rd 8318 0092 1–4D
*In Blackheath, a "great local stand-by", praised for its "tasty and
reasonably authentic Thai fare"; the atmosphere, though,
in "unimpressive". / www.ratchda.co.uk; 11 pm; closed Sun; no Amex.*

Raviolo SW12 NEW £25 ④④④
1 Balham Station Rd 8778 4499 10–2C
*This "casual" and "basic" pasta-specialist is – on most accounts –
a "good concept", and "a great addition to the Balham scene";
it's early days, though, and reports are not consistent.
/ www.raviolo.co.uk; 10 pm.*

F S A

The Real Greek N1 £35 ④④❸
15 Hoxton Market   7739 8212   9–1D
*Hoxton's original 'nouvelle Greek' outfit is now a "formulaic" –
if still sometimes "fun" – place, where service can be "dismal";
even so, it's "far better than its decidedly second-rate spin-off
chain". / www.therealgreek.com; 10.30 pm; closed Sun; no Amex.*

The Real Greek Souvlaki & Bar £25 ⑤⑤④
56 Paddington St, W1   7486 0466   2–1A
60/62 Long Acre, WC2   7240 2292   4–2D
1-2 Riverside Hs, Southwark Br Rd, SE1   7620 0162   9–3B
31-33 Putney High St, SW15   8788 3270   10–2B
140-142 St John St, EC1   7253 7234   9–1A
*"Not a patch on the Hoxton original" – the Clapham House
group's "inexcusably poor" chain incites far too many reports
of "truly awful" Greek "tapas", and "obnoxious" service.
/ www.therealgreek.co.uk; 10.45 pm; WC2 11 pm; EC1 closed Sun; no Amex;
WC2 no bookings .*

Rebato's SW8 £30 ❸①①
169 South Lambeth Rd   7735 6388   10–1D
*"As if by magic, you're transported to Seville", at this "comforting"
and "old-fashioned" Vauxhall veteran, where "great" staff oversee
the "buzzing" tapas bar, and an amiably "cheesy" restaurant.
/ www.rebatos.com; 10.45 pm; closed Sat L & Sun.*

Red Fort W1 £60 ❷❸❸
77 Dean St   7437 2525   4–2A
*"An interesting slant on Indian cooking of the highest quality"
retains quite a following for this grand and slightly "staid" Soho
veteran. / www.redfort.co.uk; 11.15 pm; closed Sat L & Sun L.*

The Red Pepper W9 £36 ❷❸❸
8 Formosa St   7266 2708   8–4A
*"Top-quality" pizza and "other interesting dishes" have long won
popularity for this "cramped" Maida Vale spot. / 11 pm; closed
weekday L; no Amex.*

Redmond's SW14 £46 ❸❷❸
170 Upper Richmond Rd West   8878 1922   10–2A
*"Accomplished" food and "interesting" wines have made Redmond
& Pippa Hayward's "smart" (for East Sheen) fixture quite a local
destination; ratings this year were undercut, though, by a few
'off' reports. / www.redmonds.org.uk; 10 pm; D only, closed Sun; no Amex.*

Refettorio
The Crowne Plaza Hotel EC4 £52 ❸❸④
19 New Bridge St   7438 8052   9–3A
*"Wonderful antipasti" and "genuine" regional Italian dishes can
come as an "unexpected" find at this "comfortable" refectory,
near Blackfriars Tube; the style is a bit "cold", but "great for a light
business lunch". / 10.30 pm; closed Sat L & Sun; booking: max 8.*

Refuel
Soho Hotel W1 £54 ④④❸
4 Richmond Mews   7559 3007   3–2D
*In the heart of Soho, this "glamorous" design-hotel bar/brasserie
is a "great place to see and be seen"; it's "pricey", though,
and "food and service need to try harder". / 10.45 pm; set always
available £35 (FP).*

Le Relais de Venise L'Entrecôte W1   £33   ❸④❷
120 Marylebone Ln   7486 0878   2–1A
"No messing, just steak-frites and secret sauce" – that's the
formula winning support for this "Parisian import", in Marylebone;
after a shaky start, it's now finding more favour for "doing what
it says on the packet". / www.relaisdevenise.com; 10.45 pm.

Le Rendezvous du Café EC1   £40   ❸❸❷
22 Charterhouse Sq   7336 8836   9–1B
A "typical" Gallic bistro, in Clerkenwell – as you'd hope, there's
nothing fancy, just "good, simple food" and a setting that "turns
on the charm". / 10.30 pm; closed Sat L & Sun; no Amex.

Retsina NW3   £35   ❸❷④
48-50 Belsize Ln   7431 5855   8–2A
A recent arrival on this Belsize Park site formerly called Halepi
(RIP) – a handy Greek stand-by, offering food that's "good,
if somewhat standard". / 11 pm; no Amex.

Reubens W1   £43   ❸④④
79 Baker St   7486 0035   2–1A
This '80s-style, kosher deli and restaurant in Marylebone – known
for its salt beef sandwiches – inspired very limited feedback this
year, but all positive. / www.reubensrestaurant.com; 10 pm; closed
Fri D & Sat.

Rhodes 24 EC2   £62   ❸❸❷
25 Old Broad St   7877 7703   9–2C
"If conversation flags, you can always discuss the view", at Gary
Rhodes's 24th-floor City eyrie, which "hits all the right spots for
business entertaining"; fans say his trademark "English staples with
a twist" are equally "fabulous", but others have found them
increasingly "pedestrian" of late. / www.rhodes24.co.uk; 9 pm; closed
Sat & Sun; booking essential.

Rhodes W1 Brasserie
Cumberland Hotel W1   £53   ⑤⑤⑤
Gt Cumberland Pl   7479 3838   2–2A
"Is it a bar, a trendy disco or an airport hangar?" – however you
describe it, Gary Rhodes's "unadventurous" and "overpriced"
Oxford Street brasserie can be "very disappointing"; if you're
organising a "screechy hen night", however, it may be just the
place. / www.garyrhodes.com; 10.30 pm; set always available £34 (FP).

Rhodes W1 Restaurant W1 NEW   £71
Gt Cumberland Pl   7479 3737   2–2A
We sadly didn't get to visit Gary Rhodes's new (mid-2007) fine
dining room, near Marble Arch, before this guide went to press;
newspaper reviews have hailed the very high quality of its Gallic
cuisine, but commentary on the décor is more mixed.
/ www.rhodesw1.com; 10.30 pm; closed Mon, Sat L & Sun; no trainers.

Rib Room
Jumeirah Carlton Tower Hotel SW1   £80   ❸④④
2 Cadogan Pl   7858 7251   5–1D
It's a shame about the "greatly inflated prices" of this "luxurious"
(but staid) Knightsbridge grill room, as – on a good day – it offers
"the best thick-cut roast beef in town", and very good oysters and
fowl too. / www.jumeirah.com; 10.30 pm.

RIBA Café
Royal Ass'n of Brit' Architects W1   £34   ④④**❶**
66 Portland Pl   7631 0467   2–1B
A "soaring" Art Deco interior, and one of the
best (and least discovered) terraces in London dominate
commentary on this Marylebone café; "you hardly notice the food".
/ www.riba-venues.com; L only, closed Sun.

Riccardo's SW3   £38   **❸❸❸**
126 Fulham Rd   7370 6656   5–3B
A "bubbly" family-run Chelsea fixture offering "well-priced Italian-
tapas dishes" – "right for a date, for a group of friends, or with the
parents". / www.riccardos.it; 11.30 pm.

Richoux   £35   ⑤⑤④
172 Piccadilly, W1   7493 2204   3–3C
41a South Audley St, W1   7629 5228   3–3A
86 Brompton Rd, SW3   7584 8300   5–1C
3 Circus Rd, NW8   7483 4001   8–3A
For fans, these "swish" and "quaint" (if "touristy") café/diners are
"good for lunch or coffee"; sceptics, though, say they've "eaten
better at motorway service stations". / 11 pm, SW3 7.30 pm, W1 Sat
11.30 pm.

Rick's Café SW17   £31   **❸❸❷**
122 Mitcham Rd   8767 5219   10–2C
Thanks to its "excellent, well-priced food", this "cramped" Tooting
spot is an ever-"busy" local; results, though, seemed more "patchy"
this year (and included the odd disaster). / 11 pm, Sun 8 pm; no Amex.

El Rincón Latino SW4   £28   **❸❶❶**
148 Clapham Manor St   7622 0599   10–2D
"Incredibly friendly" service, and "wonderful" tapas make this
family-fun Clapham stalwart "extremely popular" – "visit during the
day if you want to avoid the noise". / 11.30 pm; closed Mon,
Tue-Fri D only, Sat & Sun open L & D.

Ristorante Semplice W1 NEW   £45   ❷❸④
10 Blenheim St   7495 1509   3–2B
Opinion divides rather oddly on this "gleaming" small Italian
newcomer, in Mayfair; the more general view is to emphasise the
"brilliant" cooking, but some "very disappointing" experiences are
also recorded – it may be because: "the centre tables offer
an experience completely different from the cramped and
claustrophobic banquettes". / 10.30 pm; closed Sun.

The Ritz W1   £93   ④❷❶
150 Piccadilly   7493 8181   3–4C
"There is no more romantic room in London" than this "ornate,
Louis XVI-style" chamber; unless you're looking for the "ne plus
ultra of formal breakfasts", the food has generally been lacklustre
for decades, but better survey ratings are – at last! – beginning
to support those who say it's "improved" of late.
/ www.theritzlondon.com; 10.30 pm; jacket & tie required; set weekday L
£53 (FP).

Riva SW13   £48   ❷❷④
169 Church Rd   8748 0434   10–1A
Fans find "no gimmicks, just unpretentious and perfectly-cooked
dishes", at Andreas Riva's "outstanding" Barnes Venetian; it's a
pretty "basic" place, though, and some reporters feel it's "better for
those who know the patron". / 10.30 pm; closed Sat L.

The River Café W6 £64 ❷❸❸
Thames Wharf, Rainville Rd   7386 4200   7–2C
"Still a winner after all these years" – this "casual" Hammersmith legend is still the "epitome" of haute-rustic Italian style (and its hard-to-find riverside location can be "inspirational" on a summer's day); prices, though, can seem "obscene". / www.rivercafe.co.uk; 9 pm; closed Sun D.

Riviera
Gabriels Wharf SE1 £37 ⑤④④
56 Upper Ground   7401 7314   9–3A
"A great location, but food standards are slipping" – the prime reason to visit this riverside brasserie is to "sit upstairs", and enjoy the brilliant views of the City and St Paul's. / 11.30 pm.

The Rivington Grill SE10 £46 ④⑤⑤
178 Greenwich High Rd   8293 9270   1–3D
The Caprice Group's Greenwich outpost is a "perfect local" for some reporters, but also draws a lot of flak for being "variable", "lacklustre", and "overpriced" – it's hard to see how it fits in among the investments of Mr Trophy Asset (aka Richard Caring). / www.rivingtongrill.co.uk; 11 pm; closed Mon, Tue L & Wed L.

The Rivington Grill EC2 £45 ❸④❸
28-30 Rivington St   7729 7053   9–1C
This "bright" and "trendy" Shoreditch brasserie earns (diminishing) praise for its "traditional British food from well-sourced ingredients"; "arrogant" service, though, can contribute to a feeling that it "doesn't really fit into the Caprice empire". / www.rivingtongrill.co.uk; 11 pm.

Roast
The Floral Hall SE1 £50 ④⑤❸
Stoney St   7940 1300   9–4C
With its "lovely" Borough Market location, and its "wonderfully spacious interior", Iqbal Wahhab's ambitious two-year-old is "a real opportunity thrown away" – service is "so poor", and the traditional British fare comes at "barmy" prices. / www.roast-restaurant.com; 10.30 pm, Sat 11 pm; closed Sun D.

Rock & Sole Plaice WC2 £23 ❸④④
47 Endell St   7836 3785   4–1C
"Scrumptious" fish 'n' chips wins fans for this "reliable" and "traditional" chippy; its "sit-down option isn't very good", but you'll struggle to find many cheaper places near Covent Garden (which makes this a handy group rendezvous), / 11 pm; no Amex.

The Rocket W3 £35 ❸❸❷
11-13 Churchfield Rd   8993 6123   7–1A
"A real jewel" for the area (near Acton Central BR), this "laid-back gastropub" has quite a local name for its "tasty" and "reasonably-priced" food. / www.therocketw3.co.uk; 10.15 pm; closed Mon L.

Rocket £36 ④④❸
4-6 Lancashire Ct, W1   7629 2889   3–2B
Putney Wharf, Brewhouse St, SW15   8789 7875   10–2B
6 Adams Ct, EC2   7628 0808   9–2C **NEW**
"Great locations" off Bond Street, and on the Thames at Putney – and now also "tucked-away" in the City – help make these popular pizzerias "a good place for meeting friends"; standards, though, have seemed rather "tired" of late. / www.rocketrestaurants.co.uk; 10.45 pm; W1 closed Sun; E6 closed Sat & Sun.

Rodizio Rico £35 ④④④
111 Westbourne Grove, W2 7792 4035 6–1B
77-78 Upper St, N1 7354 1076 8–3D
*"Help yourself" – as much as you like – at these "huge" Brazilian
buffets, which specialise in "plentiful servings" of BBQ meat; they're
often made "hectic" by "noisy groups" though, and quantity comes
at the expense of quality. / www.rodizio.co.uk; W2 11.30 pm,
N1 midnight; closed weekday L.*

The Roebuck W4 NEW £38 ④❸❷
122 Chiswick High Rd 8995 4392 7–2A
*"The garden lends extra kudos" to this "spacious and airy"
gastropub newcomer, which many locals tip as "a great addition"
to Chiswick; standards can be "variable", though. / 10.15 pm.*

Roka W1 £51 ❶❸❷
37 Charlotte St 7580 6464 2–1C
*With its "non-stop buzz", its "sexy" bar and its "brilliant" Japanese
fare – largely from the central robata grill – this Fitzrovia "goldfish
bowl" arouses almost as much excitement as its grander sibling
Zuma; portions, though, "suit size-zero supermodels".
/ www.rokarestaurant.com; 11.15 pm; booking: max 8.*

Ronnie Scott's W1 £45 ⑤④❶
47 Frith St 7439 0747 4–2A
*"You don't go to Ronnie Scott's for the food", which is just as well –
"it's all about the jazz", and the "superb" atmosphere.
/ www.ronniescotts.co.uk; 3 am, Sun midnight; D only.*

Rooburoo N1 NEW £27 ❷❷❸
21 Chapel Mkt 7278 8100 8–3D
*"More-imaginative-than-usual dishes" make it "worth the trek"
to this new modern-Indian, rather "rough" Islington location
notwithstanding. / www.rooburoo.com; 11 pm; closed Mon L.*

Rosemary Lane E1 £44 ❷❷④
61 Royal Mint St 7481 2602 11–1A
*"A hidden gem on the fringes of the City" (in an "unpromising"-
looking ex-boozer, near the DLR track, a few minutes' walk
east of Tower Hill); staff are extremely "friendly" and the cooking
is "surprisingly good". / www.rosemarylane.btinternet.co.uk; 10 pm; closed
Sat L & Sun; set always available £28 (FP).*

The Rosendale SE21 NEW £42
65 Rosendale Rd 8670 0812 1–4D
*Unfortunately, we didn't make it to distant West Dulwich in time
to check out this new (summer-2007) gastropub, which features
a garden and a barbecue; it's the second venture from the
Greyhound SW11 people, suggesting that it will be particularly
popular with wine-lovers. / www.therosendale.co.uk; 10 pm; closed Mon,
Tue-Thu closed L, Sun closed D; no Amex.*

Rosmarino NW8 £48 ⑤④④
1 Blenheim Terrace 7328 5014 8–3A
*Still "slipping" – this once-popular St John's Wood Italian attracts
too many complaints of "mediocre" cooking and "tiny" portions;
on a sunny day, though, the terrace is "stunning".
/ www.rosmarino.co.uk; 10.30 pm; closed Mon, Tue L & Wed L.*

Rossopomodoro £28 ❸④❸
214 Fulham Rd, SW10   7352 7677   5–3B
184a Kensington Park Rd, W11   7229 9007   6–1A **NEW**
*"Excellent" wood-fired pizza – and other "authentic" fare –
has created an instant fan club for this "fun" Neapolitan group;
service can be "variable", though, and critics dismiss this
as just "a typical chain". / W11 & SW10 midnight.*

The Rôtisserie £35 ❸❸④
316 Uxbridge Rd, HA5   8421 2878   1–1A
1288 Whetstone High Rd, N20   8343 8585   1–1B **NEW**
82 Fortune Green Rd, NW6   7435 9923   1–1B **NEW**
87 Allitsen Rd, NW8   7722 7444   8–3A
*"Wonderful steaks" and other "good", "simple" dishes are the
mainstay of this "pleasant" grill chain which – after years
of retrenchment – is again expanding. / www.therotisserie.co.uk;
10.30 pm; closed L ex Sat; no Amex (except HA5).*

Rôtisserie Jules £27 ❸④⑤
6-8 Bute St, SW7   7584 0600   5–2B
133 Notting Hill Gate, W11   7221 3331   6–2B
*These "useful" pit stops "do what it says on the can", and serve
"hot and juicy chicken" (and not much else); they're little more than
"glorified" caffs, though, and quite "tired"-looking ones at that.
/ 10.30 pm.*

Roundhouse Café NW1 £31 ④❸❸
Chalk Farm Rd   0870 389 9920   8–2B
*Camden Town's revitalised arts venue boasts an "attractive" café;
reports on its "varied and unusual" menu, though, are up-and-
down. / www.roundhouse.org.uk; 10.30 pm; closed Sun D.*

ROUSSILLON SW1 £68 ❶❶❸
16 St Barnabas St   7730 5550   5–2D
*A "classy" Pimlico "hidden gem" that's "not to be missed";
few places can match its "elegant and interesting" Gallic cuisine,
its "outstanding" wine list (with "very knowledgeable" selections
from SW France) or its "superb" service. / www.roussillon.co.uk;
10.30 pm; closed Mon L, Sat L & Sun; booking: max 11; set weekday L
£39 (FP).*

Rowley's SW1 £55 ④④④
113 Jermyn St   7930 2707   3–3D
*"It gets a lot of stick", but this "smart" St James's veteran achieved
a rating around the "not-that bad" level this year; prices may still
be "too much", but – "for an uncomplicated meal, in a convenient
central location" – its "good steak 'n' chips" still have their fans.
/ www.rowleys.co.uk; 11 pm.*

Royal Academy W1 £33 ④④❸
Burlington Hs, Piccadilly   7300 5608   3–3C
*"Useful if you're in W1 and don't want to spend a fortune
on lunch" – the Academy's self-service café (off the foyer of its
"stunning" building) offers "quality dishes" in a "pleasant" setting.
/ www.royalacademy.org.uk; 8.15 pm; L only, except Fri & Sat open L & D;
no booking at L.*

Royal China Club W1 £55 ❸❸④
40-42 Baker St 7486 3898 2–1A

In its first full year, the Royal China group's "upmarket" flagship isn't lived up to its initial promise – critics say "it's not much different from the rest of the chain... except the steep prices". / www.theroyalchinaclub.co.uk; 11 pm; set weekday L £32 (FP).

Royal China £37 ❶❸④
24-26 Baker St, W1 7487 4688 2–1A
805 Fulham Rd, SW6 7731 0081 10–1B **NEW**
13 Queensway, W2 7221 2535 6–2C
68 Queen's Grove, NW8 7586 4280 8–3A
30 Westferry Circus, E14 7719 0888 11–1B

"Stunning" dim sum – and other "authentic" Chinese dishes – make this "consistent" chain a true culinary benchmark; "only lovers of '70s clubbing will like the décor", though (and beware "shocking" Sunday queues, especially at the Bayswater branch). / 10.45 pm, Fri & Sat 11.15 pm; E14 no bookings Sat & Sun L; SW6 no bookings Sat & Sun L.

Royal China SW15 £35 ❷❸④
3 Chelverton Rd 8788 0907 10–2B

You'd never know this Putney veteran is nowadays run separately from the famous chain it spawned – it has the same "'black-lacquered" night-club décor, and similarly offers "dependably delicious" Chinese fare (including "very fine dim sum"). / 10.30 pm; only Amex.

Royal Court Bar
Royal Court Theatre SW1 £28 ④❸❷
Sloane Sq 7565 5061 5–2D

"Very reasonable prices" ("for Chelsea") make it worth knowing about this "spacious" bunker; the food is unremarkable, but includes some "healthy" options. / www.royalcourttheatre.com; 11 pm; closed Sun; no Amex.

The Royal Exchange Grand Café
The Royal Exchange EC3 £46 ④⑤❷
Cornhill 7618 2480 9–2C

This "buzzy" seafood bar – at the heart of this "fabulous" City building – is "a typical Conran, with a great location, ordinary food, and poor service"; will it get any better, now that Sir Tel's group is called 'D&D London'? / www.royalexchangegrandcafeandbar.com; 11 pm; closed Sat & Sun; no booking.

Royal Oak E2 £37 ❸❷❶
73 Columbia Rd 7729 2220 1–2D

"A lovely buzz" permeates this characterful East End boozer, where you can eat in the "attractive" upstairs room (overlooking Columbia Road Flower Market) or the downstairs bar; the food is "well done" too. / www.royaloaklondon.com; 10 pm; closed Mon, Tue-Sat D only, Sun L only.

RSJ SE1 £39 ❸❷⑤
33 Coin St 7928 4554 9–4A

"The food is okay, but the amazing Loire wine list is the star", at this "durable" – if "ambience-free" – South Bank "old-favourite"; now, "if only they would redecorate..." / www.rsj.uk.com; 11 pm; closed Sat L & Sun.

Rudland & Stubbs EC1 £44 ④④⑤
35-37 Greenhill Rents, Cowcross St 7253 0148 9–1A
This "plain" Smithfield seafood parlour inspired limited reports
in the first year of its new régime; fans find the food "fresh and
well-presented" – others think it "mediocre".
/ www.rudlandstubbs.co.uk; 10 pm; closed Sat & Sun; booking: max 10.

La Rueda £30 ④④❸
102 Wigmore St, W1 7486 1718 3–1A
642 King's Rd, SW6 7384 2684 5–4A
66-68 Clapham High St, SW4 7627 2173 10–2D
"Efficient service, even when busy" helps win praise for this lively
Spanish chain, which realises its "all-the-usual-suspects tapas
menu" to a satisfactory standard; it does not, however, inspire the
affection it once did. / 11.30 pm, Sat & Sun midnight; SW6 1 am.

Rules WC2 £55 ❸❸❶
35 Maiden Ln 7836 5314 4–3D
"A magnet for well-heeled Americans", it may be, but few reporters
hold that against this "charming and remarkable" Covent Garden
"survivor" (London's oldest, 1798); to a surprising extent,
its "classic" and "hearty" meat and game menu "still delivers".
/ www.rules.co.uk; 11.30 pm.

Running Horse W1 £33 ❷❸❷
50 Davies St 7493 1275 3–2A
"Simple food, made with quality ingredients and presented well" –
it's a good formula, but seems to inspire remarkably little feedback
on this "lovely" Mayfair pub. / www.therunninghorselondon.co.uk;
9.30 pm; closed Sun; need 8+ to book.

S & M Café £22 ④④❸
268 Portobello Rd, W10 8968 8898 6–1A
4-6 Essex Rd, N1 7359 5361 8–3D
48 Brushfield St, E1 7247 2252 9–1D
If you're after "good old sausage 'n' mash", fans say these "upbeat
'50s-style" greasy spoons "do exactly what they say on the tin";
increasingly, though, critics find them "nothing special".
/ www.sandmcafe.co.uk; 11 pm; no Amex; W10 no booking Fri-Sun;
N1 no booking at L, E1 no booking Fri & Sat.

Sabor N1 £32 ❸❷❸
108 Essex Rd 7226 5551 8–3D
"Zingy" Latino fare makes a visit to this Islington "oasis" quite
a "stimulating" experience; the "curiously long and narrow" room
can feel "a bit soulless", but it's jazzed up by a "wonderfully
committed host". / www.sabor.co.uk; 10.45 pm; closed Mon; no Amex.

Le Sacré-Coeur N1 £34 ❸❸❷
18 Theberton St 7354 2618 8–3D
"Like a real Parisian bistro", this "gem" – just off Islington's Upper
Street – offers "basic but always palatable" food at notably
"reasonable" prices; "get there early for the best dishes". / 11 pm,
Sat 11.30 pm.

Sagar £25 **❷❷**④
157 King St, W6   8741 8563   7–2C
27 York St, TW1   8744 3868   1–4A
"Spectacular-value" vegetarian cuisine – "delicately-spiced" but "hearty" – has made a name for this "no-frills" Hammersmith south Indian; last year's opening of a "fantastic" Twickenham spin-off seems to have produced a slight slip in ratings. / Sun-Thu 10.45 pm, Fri & Sat 11.30 pm.

Saigon Saigon W6 £31 **❸❸❸**
313-317 King St   8748 6887   7–2B
"Good-value, honest Vietnamese food, and friendly service" – a formula that's currently winning high approval for this "homely" Hammersmith spot. / www.saigon-saigon.co.uk; 11 pm; closed Mon; no Amex.

St Alban SW1 NEW £55 **❸❷**④
4-12 Lower Regent St, Rex Hs   7499 8558   3–3D
Fans "love the vibe", but critics just scratch their heads at the "weird", "'70s airport lounge" interior of this Theatreland newcomer; its Mediterranean food inspires mixed feelings too – can the place ever hope to live up to the "über-maestro" reputation of its backers Corbin and King (who also run the Wolseley)? / www.stalban.net; midnight, Sun 11 pm.

St Germain EC1 NEW £32 ④**❷❸**
89-90 Turnmill St   7336 0949   9–1A
A "cool" brasserie newcomer, near Farringdon tube; shame the "unexceptional" fare is the weakest part of the operation. / www.stgermain.info; 10.30 pm; closed Sun D.

ST JOHN EC1 £48 **❷❷❸**
26 St John St   7251 0848   9–1B
"Inspiring" cooking – that's "distinctively British", "confidently straightforward" and "offaly good" – has made this "utilitarian" Smithfield "institution" a "place of pilgrimage for chefs worldwide"; its ratings slipped a bit this year, though, and staff risk becoming a bit "self-important". / www.stjohnrestaurant.com; 11 pm; closed Sat L & Sun.

St John Bread & Wine E1 £40 **❷❷**④
94-96 Commercial St   7392 0236   9–1D
"The best bacon sandwich you'll ever eat" is typical of the "simple, traditional British fare" on offer at this "noisy" canteen, by Spitalfieds Market (a worthy spin-off from the EC1 "mothership"); for some of the more "robust" dishes, though, "you need a strong stomach". / www.stjohnbreadandwine.com; 10.30 pm; closed Sun D.

St Johns N19 £35 **❷❷❶**
91 Junction Rd   7272 1587   8–1C
"A beautiful interior" adds to the "shabby-chic" charm of this large and very popular Archway gastropub – an all-round "favourite", it offers "rustic" scoff that's "always on the interesting side of reliable", and "helpful" service. / 11 pm, Sun 9.30 pm; Mon-Thu D only, Fri-Sun open L & D; booking: max 12.

Le Saint Julien EC1 £47 **❸**④④
62-63 Long Ln   7796 4550   9–1B
A straight-up "classic" Gallic brasserie, "in the shadow of Smithfield"; for the prices, though, the experience is rather "unremarkable". / 10 pm; closed Sat & Sun.

St Moritz W1 £42 ❸❸❸
161 Wardour St 7734 3324 3–1D
*"You feel as if you're in a mountain-top chalet", at this "romantic"
Soho stalwart; its "excellent" fondues and "lovely Swiss wines" are
"better than many people expect". / www.stmoritz-restaurant.co.uk;
11.30 pm; closed Sat L & Sun.*

Sake No Hana SW1 NEW £100
23 St James's St awaiting tel 3–4C
*Alan Yau (of Hakkasan and Yauatcha fame) is set to open his
most 'serious' venture yet in the autumn of 2007; this time,
it's Japanese cuisine that's getting the Yau treatment, in the striking
St James's building which formerly housed Shumi (RIP).*

Saki Bar & Food Emporium EC1 £44 ❷❸④
4 West Smithfield 7489 7033 9–2A
*"Vibrant, extremely high-quality dishes (with fusion touches)" win
a huge thumbs-up for this Japanese two-year-old; prices are a little
"gourmet", though, and the basement setting can "lack ambience".
/ www.saki-food.com; 10.30 pm; closed Sat L & Sun; no Amex; set weekday L
£28 (FP).*

Sakonis HA0 £18 ❷④⑤
129 Ealing Rd 8903 9601 1–1A
*A "cheap and cheerful" classic – this Wembley canteen offers
a mix "of authentic" Gujarati dishes with "Indo-Chinese" fare;
the best value is to be had from the stupendous buffet. / 9.30 pm;
no Amex; set weekday L £11 (FP).*

Sakura W1 £25 ❷⑤⑤
9 Hanover St 7629 2961 3–2C
*Fear not if the premises seem "depressing", or the staff "rude"
("when they aren't ignoring you", that is) – this "chaotic" Mayfair
basement offers a "full-on Japanese experience", including
a "good selection of dishes" at "excellent" prices. / 10 pm.*

Salaam Namaste WC1 NEW £27 ❷❸④
68 Millman St 7405 3697 2–1D
*Most reporters hail this Bloomsbury backstreet newcomer as a
"cracking Indian eating experience", and it's quickly become
"very popular"; the odd "bland" dish, however, is not unknown.
/ 11.30 pm.*

Salade £15 ❸④④
52 Stratton St, W1 7499 6565 3–3C NEW
3 Old Bailey, EC4 7248 6612 9–2A NEW
*"You pick, they mix" – that's the deal at these "great" new pit
stops, which are praised by all for their "super range" of "perfect"
salads; they're "certainly not cheap", though. / www.salade.co.uk; L only;
closed Sat & Sun; no Amex.*

Sale e Pepe SW1 £45 ❸❸❷
9-15 Pavilion Rd 7235 0098 5–1D
*"Little changes" at this "dated" but "entertaining" trattoria,
near Harrods, where "mad" staff enliven the "cramped" setting.
/ www.saleepepe.co.uk; 11.30 pm; closed Sun.*

The Salisbury Tavern SW6 £38 ④④④
21 Sherbrooke Rd 7381 4005 10–1B
*This "smart" Fulham boozer has a name for "above-average" scoff;
its recent make-over has its fans, but the more general view is that
it's taken the place "downhill". / www.thesalisbury.com; 11 pm.*

Salloos SW1 £43 ❷❸④
62-64 Kinnerton St   7235 4444   5–1D
*"Pakistani food at its best" compensates for the "iffy" service and
"waiting-room ambience" of this quirky stalwart, hidden-away in a
Knightsbridge mews. / 11 pm; closed Sun.*

Salt House NW8 £39 ④④❷
63 Abbey Rd   7328 6626   8–3A
*"When it gets things right", this "really buzzing and laid-back"
St John's Wood gastropub can be "one of the best in London"
(and it has a "fantastic" summer terrace); unfortunately, however,
it's "inconsistent". / www.thesalthouse.co.uk; 10.30 pm.*

Salt Yard W1 £36 ❶❷❸
54 Goodge St   7637 0657   2–1B
*The "exciting" tapas – "a twist on traditional Spanish and Italian
dishes" – at this "un-flashy" Fitzrovia two-year-old are among
London's best; "despite its popularity", it remains a "friendly"
destination. / www.saltyard.co.uk; 11 pm; closed Sat L & Sun.*

The Salusbury NW6 £35 ❸❷❸
50-52 Salusbury Rd   7328 3286   1–2B
*A "lovely pub, with a smallish restaurant tacked on", in Queen's
Park; it serves "interesting", mainly Mediterranean cuisine.
/ 10.15 pm; closed Mon L; no Amex.*

Sam's Brasserie W4 £42 ④❸❸
11 Barley Mow Pas   8987 0555   7–2A
*"Sam is still much in evidence", at this large and "casual" all-day
yearling – a "funky" place (by Chiswick standards), where
"the atmosphere makes up for any failings on the food front".
/ www.samsbrasserie.co.uk; 10.30 pm; booking: max 12; set weekday L
£25 (FP).*

San Carlo N6 £39 ⑤④④
2 Highgate High St   8340 5823   8–1B
*"Locals are up in arms" at the "Footballers' Wives"-style refit
of this Highgate stalwart; the food may be "cheaper" than before,
but it's "not worth the money", and service can be "amateur" too.
/ wwww.sancarlohighgate.co.uk; 11 pm.*

San Daniele del Friuli N5 £32 ❸❷❷
72 Highbury Park   7226 1609   8–1D
*"Generous Italian dishes" – with game a speciality – are served
up by "friendly" staff at this "ever-reliable" Highbury "favourite".
/ 10.30 pm; closed Mon L, Tue L, Sat L & Sun; no Amex.*

San Lorenzo SW3 £55 ⑤④④
22 Beauchamp Pl   7584 1074   5–1C
*This "iconic" '60s Knightsbridge trattoria is still "full of people-
watchers and self-conscious celebs wanting to be seen"; otherwise,
"everything about it is average, apart from the ridiculous prices".
/ 11.30 pm; closed Sun; no credit cards.*

San Lorenzo Fuoriporta SW19 £45 ④④④
38 Wimbledon Hill Rd   8946 8463   10–2B
*Fans of this rather '70s Wimbledon Town Italian say it "never
disappoints"; there are echoes of its more famous Knightsbridge
cousin, though, as a few critics say its "OK" cuisine is "not worth
the price". / www.sanlorenzo.com; 10.45 pm; set pre theatre £29 (FP).*

San Remo SW13 £42 ④❸④
195 Castelnau 8741 5909 7–2C
"A convenient local Italian", in the thin area south of Hammersmith
Bridge; *"staff are so friendly and welcoming, you can forgive them
anything"*. / 11 pm; closed Sun.

Santa Lucia SW10 £36 ❸❷❷
2 Hollywood Rd 7352 8484 5–3B
"Haphazard but fun" – this *"buzzy"* Chelsea-fringe Italian has
quite a name for its *"proper pizza"* and *"good pasta"*.
/ www.madeinitalygroup.co.uk; 11.30 pm; closed weekday L; no Amex.

Santa Maria del Buen Ayre E8 £34 ❷❸❶
50 Broadway Mkt 7275 9900 1–2D
"Totally packed every night", this *"proper and authentic"*
Argentinean parrilla (grill) offers an experience *"like a small
restaurant in Buenos Aires"*, including *"steaks to die for"*.
/ www.buenayre.co.uk; 10.30 pm; closed weekday L.

Santa Maria del Sur SW8 NEW £34 ❷❸④
129 Queenstown Rd 7622 2088 10–1C
A new sibling for the *"classic"* 'del Buen Ayre' original –
this Battersea parrilla similarly offers *"great steak"* and *"awesome
chips"* (if in a setting with *"rather less atmosphere"* than in E8).
/ www.buenayre.co.uk; 10.30 pm; closed weekday L.

Santini SW1 £60 ⑤④④
29 Ebury St 7730 4094 2–4B
With its *"shockingly poor"* cooking and *"preposterous"* prices,
this *"pretentious"* Belgravia Italian *"seems to trade on its history"*.
/ www.santini-restaurant.com; 11 pm; closed Sat L & Sun L.

Sapori WC2 £30 ④❸❸
43 Drury Ln 7836 8296 4–2D
A *"simple"* Italian stand-by, just a minute's walk from the Royal
Opera House; it provides *"very standard"* food, but service
is *"friendly"* and prices *"reasonable"*. / 11.30 pm; no Amex.

Saran Rom SW6 £40 ④❸❸
Imperial Wharf 7751 3111 5–4B
The Thai menu may be *"standard"*, but the cooking is usually
"competent", at this *"expensively-decorated"* but *"strangely
soulless"* Fulham yearling – the *"apparent emptiness"* of the
surrounding Imperial Wharf development really doesn't help.
/ www.saranrom.com; midnight.

Sarastro WC2 £37 ⑤⑤❸
126 Drury Ln 7836 0101 2–2D
This *"wonderfully colourful, vibrant, and fun opera-restaurant"*,
near Covent Garden, can be *"a great place to go in a group"*;
the food, though, is *"just dire"*, and service little better.
/ www.sarastro-restaurant.com; 11.30 pm.

Sardo W1 £43 ❷❸④
45 Grafton Way 7387 2521 2–1B
"Very distinctive" food that's *"authentic and unusual"* (plus some
"hard-to-find Italian wines") makes it worth seeking out this
unpretentious Fitzrovia Sardinian. / www.sardo-restaurant.com; 11 pm;
closed Sat L & Sun.

Sardo Canale NW1 £44 ❸❸❷
42 Gloucester Ave 7722 2800 8–3B
*Despite an obscure Primrose Hill location – a "lovely" spot
by (but with no views of) Regent's Canal – this "relaxed" (if "noisy")
venture has won an impressive following; its Sardinian cooking
is usually "interesting" too, but there were also some
"very average" meals this year.* / www.sardocanale.com; 10 pm; closed
Mon L.

Sargasso Sea N21 £48 ❷❸❸
10 Station Rd 8360 0990 1–1C
*"A top-notch restaurant in the suburbs"; this Winchmore Hill spot
may be "as expensive as a top West End joint", but it serves
up fish dishes which are often "stunning".* / www.sargassosea.co.uk;
10.30 pm; closed Mon, Tue L, Wed L, Sat L & Sun D; set Sun L £29 (FP).

Sarracino NW6 £38 ❷❷❸
186 Broadhurst Gdns 7372 5889 1–1B
*The pizza – sold be the metre, with "heavenly crusts" and "tangy"
toppings – is "the real deal", at this "cramped" and "genuinely
friendly" West Hampstead Italian.* / www.sarracinorestaurant.co.uk;
11 pm.

Sartoria W1 £55 ❸❸④
20 Savile Row 7534 7000 3–2C
*"Tailor-made for business" – this would-be "stylish" Mayfair Italian
may be "a bit of a barn", but its "well-spaced" tables help make
it an "ideal" rendezvous for discussions; those paying their own way
may find it a fraction "overpriced".* / www.danddlondon.co.uk; 11 pm;
closed Sun.

Satay House W2 £30 ❸❷④
13 Sale Pl 7723 6763 6–1D
*Winning wider acclaim after a recent refurb' – this long-established
(1967) Bayswater Malaysian attracts consistent support for its
"tasty" dishes (including, but by no means limited to,
"the best satay in central London").* / www.satay-house.co.uk; 11 pm.

Satsuma W1 £27 ❸④❸
56 Wardour St 7437 8338 3–2D
*"Waga-who?" – slap bang in the middle of Soho, this "fun" canteen
offers "better food all-round than the other Japanese-on-benches
places".* / www.osatsuma.com; 11 pm; no booking.

Sauterelle
Royal Exchange EC3 £53 ④❸❸
Bank 7618 2483 9–2C
*A "wonderful" location – "overlooking the central lobby of the
Exchange" – makes this heart-of-the-City location a "reliable venue
for entertaining", even if the food is "unmemorable".*
/ www.restaurantsauterelle.co.uk; 10 pm; closed Sat & Sun.

La Saveur SW14 NEW £43 ❷❸❸
201 Upper Richmond Road West 8876 0644 10–2A
*"It's just what East Sheen needs!", say fans of this cramped new
bistro "from the Brula stable"; it shares its parent's restrained Gallic
styling and "sensible prices", but – given the locale – staff seem
strangely uptight around kids.* / 10.30 pm; set weekday L £25 (FP).

(Savoy Grill)
Savoy Hotel WC2 £84
Strand 7592 1600 4–3D
This famously "high-powered" business "bastion" (annexed by the Ramsay empire in recent years) seems almost certain to be closed throughout 2008, while the hotel undergoes a much-needed total revamp. / www.marcuswareing.com; 11 pm; jacket required; set weekday L £51 (FP).

Scalini SW3 £58 ❸❸❷
1-3 Walton St 7225 2301 5–2C
"Tooooo noisy, and sooooo expensive" – situation normal, then, at this "squashed-in" Knightsbridge Italian, which is "always packed" with a glossy international crowd. / midnight.

Scarlet Dot E1 £39 ④④④
4 Crispin Sq 7375 0880 9–1D
Fans say it's "worth a visit, after a few beers", but this year-old "modern Indian" mostly inspires more muted feedback; its semi-al fresco tables, though, have a good view of the "happening" Spitalfields scene. / www.scarletdot.co.uk; 11 pm; set weekday L £20 (FP).

Scarpetta TW11 £32 ❷❷❷
78 High St 8977 8177 1–4A
"Bringing life to central Teddington" – this "great" neighbourhood Italian offers "imaginative" pasta and "delicious" pizza in a "tasteful" setting; service is "utterly charming" too. / www.scarpetta.co.uk; 11 pm; no shorts.

The Scarsdale W8 £32 ④④❶
23a Edwardes Sq 7937 1811 7–1D
A "beautiful" setting – "tucked-away in a leafy square", just off Kensington High Street – sets the scene for this "lovely" boozer (plus small garden); "it's one of the few non-trendy, non-gastro pubs left", and serves food that's "hearty" and "honest". / 10 pm.

Scoffers SW11 £35 ④❸❶
6 Battersea Rise 7978 5542 10–2C
Sitting under a fig tree, it's "hard to remember you're actually in the conservatory" of this "friendly" Battersea local; the food is "nothing special", though – perhaps why the place is especially popular for brunch. / www.scoffersrestaurant.co.uk; 11 pm.

SCOTT'S W1 £58 ❷❷❶
20 Mount St 7495 7309 3–3A
"A triumphant return"; this revived Mayfair fish veteran – the survey's most commented-on 'newcomer' – is a "smart", "stylish" and "totally professional" operation that already bears comparison with stable-mate J Sheekey; as even a sceptic admits: "the hype is justified". / www.scotts-restaurant.com; 11 pm.

The Sea Cow £31 ❸❸❸
67 Stoke Newington Church St, N16 7249 6566 1–1C **NEW**
37 Lordship Ln, SE22 8693 3111 1–4D
57 Clapham High St, SW4 7622 1537 10–2D
These "post-modern chippies" win much praise for their "ethical" policies, their "incredibly fresh fish" ("cooked how you want it") and their "wonderful chips"; ratings this year dipped a little though – "perhaps they're spreading themselves too thin too quickly?" / www.theseacow.co.uk; 10.30 pm, Sun 8.30 pm; SW4 & N16 closed Mon.

Seabass W2 NEW £32
9 Sheldon Sq, Paddington Central   7286 8000   6–1C
*The latest member of the – generally surprisingly good – collection
of restaurants in the new Paddington Basin development,
ten minutes' walk from the railway station; as at its longer-
established sibling at 40 James St W1, the menu mixes seafood
with some Middle Eastern dishes. / www.seabassrestaurants.com; 10 pm.*

Seafresh SW1 £28 ❸❷④
80-81 Wilton Rd   7828 0747   2–4B
*For "slap-up fish 'n' chips" – and "inexpensive" seafood too –
this recently revamped Pimlico chippy remains a popular
destination for a diverse ("cabbie-to-yuppie") crowd. / 10.30 pm;
closed Sun.*

Seaport W1 NEW £35 ❸④⑤
24 Seymour Pl   7724 4307   2–2A
*This "unprepossessing" Marylebone newcomer – "a fish restaurant
with a fresh fish shop attached" – is too like Fishworks for some
tastes, but most reporters say it offers "first-class" fish and
"outstanding" seafood.*

Searcy's Brasserie EC2 £50 ④❸❸
Level 2, Barbican Centre   7588 3008   9–1B
*"Fantastic views across the City" compensate for "a lack
of ambience" at this "quiet" brasserie, where the food
is "acceptable, rather than thrilling". / www.searcys.co.uk; 10.30 pm;
closed Sat L & Sun.*

Seashell NW1 £32 ❷④⑤
49 Lisson Grove   7224 9000   8–4A
*Take-away is the way to go, at this famous Marylebone chippy –
the fish is "succulent" and the chips are "heavenly", but the dining
room is "horrible". / www.seashellrestaurant.co.uk; 10.30 pm; closed Sun.*

Serafino W1 £46 ④❸④
8 Mount St   7629 0544   3–3B
*It's the "good, cheap and cheerful" basement which is particularly
worth knowing about at this Mayfair Italian; the ground floor
is "indifferent" (but can make a handy business venue).
/ www.finos.co.uk; 10.45 pm; closed Sat L & Sun.*

Seven Stars WC2 £28 ❸④❷
53 Carey St   7242 8521   2–2D
*Roxy Beaujolais's "tiny" boozer behind the Royal Courts of Justice
is something of a "hidden gem", even if the service is rather "take-
it-or-leave-it". / 11 pm.*

Shampers W1 £35 ❸❷❷
4 Kingly St   7437 1692   3–2D
*"An unpretentious place that never disappoints" – this "friendly"
wine bar "time warp", in Soho, is usually "packed", thanks to its
"simple" and "good-quality" bistro fare and its "eclectic" wine list.
/ www.shampers.net; 11 pm; closed Sun (& Sat in Aug).*

Shanghai E8 £28 ❷❷❸
41 Kingsland High St   7254 2878   1–1C
*A "great setting" – "the front room is exactly how it was when
it was a pie and eel shop" – adds distinction to this "really nice"
Dalston hang-out; dim sum which are "better than Chinatown" is a
highlight of the consistently "good" Chinese food.
/ www.wengwahgroup.com; 11 pm.*

Shanghai Blues WC1 £45 ❷❸❷
193-197 High Holborn   7404 1668   4–1D
It's "a bit pricey for what it is" (and sometimes dismissed as a
"Hakkasan wannabe"), but this "smart-looking" Holborn Chinese –
in an "interesting renovation" of a former civic building – scores
very highly for its "superb dim sum" and its "sexy and fun" style.
/ www.shanghaiblues.co.uk; 11.30 pm; set weekday L £29 (FP).

J SHEEKEY WC2 £59 ❶❷❷
28-32 St Martin's Ct   7240 2565   4–3B
"Oozing class", this "traditional" and "glamorous" Theatreland
"classic" yet again inspired more survey reports than anywhere else
in town; an "unbeatable" fish pie heads up the "brilliant" but
"unfussy" fish-and-seafood menu served in its "cosy" panelled
rooms. / www.j-sheekey.co.uk; midnight.

Shepherd's SW1 £46 ④❷❸
Marsham Ct, Marsham St   7834 9552   2–4C
"Oodles of British comfort food" is realised to a "boring but decent"
standard at this "discreet" Westminster establishment, whose
panelled parlour is something of a favourite with "lobbyists" and
"people in power". / www.langansrestaurants.co.uk; 11 pm; closed
Sat & Sun.

Shikara SW3 £26 ❷❸④
87 Sloane Ave   7581 6555   5–2C
For a "first-rate" and quite inexpensive curry, this Indian two-year-
old is worth bearing in mind; given its Brompton Cross location,
it remains surprisingly little-known. / www.shikara.com; 11.30 pm;
set weekday L £16 (FP).

Shimo EC4 NEW £40 ④❷❸
17-18 Tooks Ct   7404 1818   9–2A
A Holborn back alley newcomer, which wins a general thumbs-up
for its "excellent" service and its "satisfying" cuisine; Japanese
purists, though, may find it a touch "impressive". / 10 pm; closed
Sat & Sun; set weekday L £15 (FP).

The Ship SW18 £31 ❸④❷
41 Jews Row   8870 9667   10–2B
The "great" terrace of this "lovely" Thames-side pub,
by Wandsworth Bridge, is "an ideal sunshine spot", which hosts
"great and busy" summer BBQs; standards here have held up well
since management reverted to Young's in recent times.
/ www.theship.co.uk; 10 pm; no booking, Sun L.

Shish £28 ④④❸
75 Bishops Bridge Rd, W2   7229 7300   6–1C
2-6 Station Pde, NW2   8208 9290   1–1A
313 Old St, EC1   7749 0990   9–1D
"Posh kebabs" are the speciality of this smart, small chain – it's still
"fairly reliable", but in danger of becoming "a bit expensive for
what it is". / www.shish.com; 11.30 pm; need 6+ to book.

Shogun W1 £56 ❷❷④
Adam's Row   7493 1255   3–3A
Despite the odd claim that it's "over-rated", this Japanese "step-
back-in-time", in a Mayfair basement, can still deliver some
"excellent" dishes, including (say fans) "the best sushi in town".
/ 11 pm; D only, closed Mon.

Signor Sassi SW1 £44 ❸❷❸
14 Knightsbridge Grn   7584 2277   5–1D
*"Boisterous" service, "good" Italian food and a "buzzy"
atmosphere still commend this "cramped" Knightsbridge
"old favourite" to most reporters. / 11.30 pm; closed Sun.*

Signor Zilli W1 £46 ❸❷❸
41 Dean St   7734 3924   4–2A
*The food may be "no better than many simple, old-style trattorias",
but TV-chef Aldo Zilli's original Soho venture is still rated a "reliable
central London stand-by". / 11.30 pm; closed Sat L & Sun.*

Silks & Spice £28 ❸❸❸
95 Chiswick High Rd, W4   8995 7991   7–2B
28 Chalk Farm Rd, NW1   7482 2228   8–2B
Temple Ct, 11 Queen Victoria St, EC4   7248 7878   9–2C
*Fans insist you get "top-quality" Thai food for "very reasonable
prices", at this small chain; compared to its glory-days, though,
its following is now very modest. / www.silksandspice.net; 11 pm,
EC4 Thu & Fri 2 am; EC4 closed Sat & Sun, W4 L only Mon-Fri.*

Simply Lebanese SW7 £38 ❸❸④
68 Old Brompton Rd   7584 5805   5–2B
*"Very approachable staff" add to the appeal of this "reliable and
authentic" South Kensington Lebanese (which previously traded
as Al Bustan). / www.simplylebanese.com; 10.30 pm.*

Simpson's Tavern EC3 £26 ④④❶
38 1/2 Ball Ct, Cornhill   7626 9985   9–2C
*A "unique" Dickensian "institution", which is "a joy" for "City suits",
who relish its "boarding school" staples and its "fun" and "chaotic"
atmosphere. / www.simpsonstavern.co.uk; L only, closed Sat & Sun.*

Simpsons-in-the-Strand WC2 £57 ④④❷
100 Strand   7836 9112   4–3D
*This "ultra-traditional" but "touristy" Edwardian temple
to roast beef can still make a "satisfying" destination for business
or breakfast (or both combined), though "bad experiences" sour some
reports, though, even from long-term fans.
/ www.fairmont.com/simpsons; 10.45 pm, Sun 9 pm; no jeans or trainers.*

Singapore Garden NW6 £38 ❷❷❷
83a Fairfax Rd   7624 8233   8–2A
*"Looking good" – in every respect – since its refurbishment,
this Swiss Cottage fixture is roundly praised for its "authentic"
Malaysian/Singaporean dishes, its "polite" service, and its
"very comfortable" décor. / www.singaporegarden.co.uk; 11 pm, Fri-Sat
11.30 pm.*

Singapura £34 ❸❸④
78-79 Leadenhall St, EC3   7929 0089   9–2D
1-2 Limeburner Ln, EC4   7329 1133   9–2A
*"White walls, white floors, white tablecloths, white plates...";
though it's "a bit clinical", this "stalwart" mini-chain continues
to serve up some "extremely reliable" oriental fare.
/ www.singapuras.co.uk; 10.30 pm; closed Sat & Sun, EC2 & EC3 L only.*

Sitaaray WC2 NEW £30 ❷❷❷
167 Drury Ln 7269 6422 4–1C
*"An amusing and different place to go with a group of mates" –
there's little not to like at this Bollywood-themed Covent Garden
newcomer, which offers "great" Indian food at "reasonable" prices.
/ www.sitaaray.com; 1 am.*

606 Club SW10 £40 ❹❹❶
90 Lots Rd 7352 5953 5–4B
*"Even if the food is bad" – which it isn't, always – this hard-to-find
jazz speakeasy, in a cellar near Chelsea Harbour, is "worth a visit".
/ www.606club.co.uk; midnight; D only; booking essential.*

06 St Chad's Place WC1 £36 ❸❸❸
6 St Chad's Pl 7278 3355 8–3D
*"A hidden oasis in the King's Cross wasteland" – this "interestingly-
located" and "airy" former railway workshop is worth knowing
about for its "proficient" and "reasonably-priced" food.
/ www.6stchadsplace.com; 9.30 pm; closed Sat & Sun; no Amex.*

**(Lecture Room)
Sketch W1** £134 ❹❸❹
9 Conduit St 0870 777 4488 3–2C
*Even many fans of Parisian über-chef Pierre Gagnaire's "complex"
cuisine can't get over the "absurd" prices at this ultra-luxurious
first-floor dining room, in Mayfair; ratings improved a bit this year,
but feedback on the food is still eclipsed by that for the "bling-
tastic" loos. / www.sketch.uk.com; 10.30 pm; closed Mon, Sat L & Sun;
booking: max 8.*

**(Gallery)
Sketch W1** £57 ❹❹❹
9 Conduit St 0870 777 4488 3–2C
*"So poor, it's not even ironic...", "I felt my wallet had been
raped...", "one visit was enough..." – in the survey, critics of this
"massively overpriced" Mayfair style-scene outnumber fans
by about four to one; "the egg-loos are pretty good, though".
/ www.sketch.uk.com; 1 am; D only, closed Sun; booking: max 12.*

**(Parlour)
Sketch W1** £34 ❹❸❸
9 Conduit St 0870 777 4488 3–2C
*Fans say this "Alice in Wonderland" parlour is a "gorgeous" spot for
tea (or a light lunch); for critics, though, it's almost as "overpriced"
and "disappointing" as the rest of this Mayfair palazzo.
/ www.sketch.uk.com; 10 pm; closed Sun; no booking.*

**Skylon
South Bank Centre SE1** NEW £56 ❸❸❷
Southbank Centre, Belvedere Rd 7654 7800 2–3D
*An elegant (Conran) revamp has made the Thames-facing chamber
of the revamped Festival Hall (formerly The People's Palace,
RIP) one of the capital's most striking dining rooms; we enjoyed our
early-days visit to the (not inexpensive) brasserie – there's also
a fine dining section, and a bar. / Rated on Editors' visit;
www.danddlondon.com; 10.45 pm.*

Slurp SW19 £16 ②③④
138 Merton Rd   8543 4141   10–2B
*"A bit like Wagamama" – but "combining Chinese and Japanese
dishes" – this "canteen-style" Wimbledon spot wins nothing but
praise for its "fresh and healthy" oriental fare. / 11 pm; no Amex;
no booking.*

(Top Floor)
Smiths of Smithfield EC1 £58 ③③②
67-77 Charterhouse St   7251 7950   9–1A
*"Great rooftop views of St Pauls and Old Bailey" distinguish the
"more spacious and less noisy" top floor of this Smithfield landmark
– an ideal spot for "power" entertaining over some "great steak";
it's "priced for expense-accounters", though, and standards are
sometimes "underwhelming". / www.smithsofsmithfield.co.uk; 10.45 pm;
closed Sat L; booking: max 10.*

(Dining Room)
Smiths of Smithfield EC1 £35 ③④④
67-77 Charterhouse St   7251 7997   9–1A
*"Sturdy" staples (not least "tasty burgers") help make the second-
floor brasserie of this Smithfield complex "a good stand-by for
a casual business lunch"; its style is a bit "clinical", though, and at
night the place gets "deafeningly noisy". / www.smithsofsmithfield.co.uk;
10.45 pm; closed Sat L & Sun.*

(Ground Floor)
Smiths of Smithfield EC1 £23 ④④②
67-77 Charterhouse St   7251 7950   9–1A
*Weekend mornings "can't start better", than by "lounging" around
in the "cool and fun" ground floor bar of this large warehouse-
conversion, enjoying the "great and varied" brunch selection;
"too bad the service doesn't live up". / www.smithsofsmithfield.co.uk;
L only.*

Smollensky's £36 ⑤⑤④
105 Strand, WC2   7497 2101   4–3D
Hammersmith Broadway, W6   8741 8124   7–2C
Unit 1 Reuters Plaza, Canary Wharf, E14   7719 0101   11–1C
22 Wapping High St, E1   7680 1818   11–1A
*Some reporters insist they're "fun with kids", but this "soulless"
American-style chain is hard to tip – the food sometimes seems
"very processed", and service can be "comically erratic".
/ www.smollenskys.co.uk; 10.30 pm, W6 Mon-Thu 11 pm, Fri & Sat 2 am,
Sun 10.30; E1 10 pm; W6 & E14 closed Sun; E1 D only and closed Mon;
TW1 closed L.*

Snazz Sichuan NW1 NEW £35 ②②③
37 Chalton St   7388 0808   8–3C
*"Superb" Sichuanese cuisine – "the real thing" – inspires a few
ecstatic early-days reports on this Euston newcomer.
/ www.newchinaclub.co.uk.*

Snows on the Green W6 £42 ③③③
166 Shepherd's Bush Rd   7603 2142   7–1C
*Most reports say Sebastian Snow's long-standing fixture on Brook
Green is "a wonderful, welcoming local"; if there is a criticism,
it's that the whole experience can seem a bit "neutral".
/ www.snowsonthegreen.co.uk; 10.45 pm; closed Sat L & Sun.*

So W1 NEW £37 ❸❷❸
3-4 Warwick St   7292 0767   3–2D
This "conceptual" ("à la Nobu") Japanese newcomer is an
"elegantly simple" ("stark") Soho spot, offering some "innovative"
dishes; service is "excellent" too. / www.sorestaurant.com; 10.30 pm;
closed Sun.

Sofra £30 ④④④
1 St Christopher's Pl, W1   7224 4080   3–1A
18 Shepherd St, W1   7493 3320   3–4B
36 Tavistock St, WC2   7240 3773   4–3D
11 Circus Rd, NW8   7586 9889   8–3A
21 Exmouth Mkt, EC1   7833 1111   9–1A
Though still often tipped as "reliable" stand-bys, these "affordable"
Turkish cafés have "really gone downhill" in recent years;
they suffer from "complacent" service and often-"boring"
(and sometimes "dire") food. / www.sofra.co.uk; 11 pm-midnight,
EC1 10.30 pm.

Soho Japan W1 £25 ❷❸④
52 Wells St   7323 4661   2–1B
"A basic place that can't be beaten" – this "welcoming" (north)
Soho pub-conversion ("it even has the toucan signs") serves
"very authentic Japanese dishes", including "great sushi".
/ www.sohojapan.co.uk; 10.30 pm; closed Sat L & Sun; set weekday L £16 (FP).

Soho Spice W1 £34 ④❸④
124-126 Wardour St   7434 0808   3–1D
This modern Soho Indian offers food of "predictable" quality; it can,
though, seem a little "tired" nowadays. / www.sohospice.co.uk; midnight,
Fri-Sat 1.30 am, Sun 10.30 pm; set weekday L £21 (FP).

Solly's Exclusive NW11 £31 ❸④④
148 Golders Green Rd   8455 0004   1–1B
"Fab shawarma, hummus and falafal" are to be had at this "busy"
and kitschy Golder's Green Israeli; downstairs, there's a lively
café/take-away – upstairs a "more formal" restaurant. / 10.30 pm;
closed Fri D & Sat L; no Amex.

Somerstown Coffee House NW1 £36 ④❸④
60 Chalton St   7691 9136   8–3C
A rather unusual pub – run by two sisters from Normandy – that's
tipped by some reporters as an "oasis" near the British Library;
the food is reliable, but only "pleasant". / 11 pm; closed Sat & Sun.

Sông Quê E2 £24 ❷⑤⑤
134 Kingsland Rd   7613 3222   1–2D
The space may be "charmless" and the service "comically poor",
but the "fresh" and "authentic" Vietnamese cuisine at this "cheap"
Shoreditch "canteen" still wins many fans. / 11 pm.

Sonny's SW13 £43 ④❸❸
94 Church Rd   8748 0393   10–1A
This Barnes institution is – say fans – the epitome of "high-quality
neighbourhood dining"; it's "suffered from chef-turnover" in recent
years, though, and cynics say locals have become "blind to the
failings" of its "very average" food. / www.sonnys.co.uk; 10.30 pm; closed
Sun D.

Sophie's Steakhouse SW10 £34 ❸❸❶
311-313 Fulham Rd   7352 0088   5–3B
*"The no-reservation policy is a total pain" – "at weekends, it can
take up to two hours to get a table" – but most reporters feel it's
"worth the wait" for this "always fun and buzzy" Chelsea hang-out,
where the steaks and burgers are "fab".* / www.sophiessteakhouse.com;
11.45 pm; no booking.

Sotheby's Café W1 £44 ❷❶❷
34 New Bond St   7293 5077   3–2C
*"People-watch while you eat", at this "all-round classy" café, off the
foyer of the famous Mayfair auction house; the "imaginative" food
is "excellent for a light lunch", and service is "consummately good".*
/ www.sothebys.com; L only, closed Sat & Sun.

Souk WC2 £32 ④④❷
27 Litchfield St   7240 1796   4–3B
*It's "about as authentic as a Chinese chippy", but this "fun" and
"really atmospheric" party-Moroccan, near the Ivy, "transports you
to another world"; it's "romantic" too ("as long as the belly dancer
isn't around").* / www.soukrestaurant.co.uk; midnight.

Souk Medina WC2 £32 ④❷❶
1A Short Gdns   7240 1796   4–2B
*"Staff may be Eastern European rather than Arabic", but this
"chaotic", "dark" and "exotic" party-Moroccan – sibling to Souk –
is still "quite a crowd-pleaser"; it's also "inexpensive".*
/ www.soukrestaurant.co.uk; midnight.

Spacca Napoli W1 £28 ❷④❸
101 Dean St   7437 9440   3–1D
*"The best pizza in Soho" (sold by the metre) and other "genuine"
staples ensure this "very Italian-feeling" joint, just off Oxford Street,
is always "noisy and bustling"; service, though, is sometimes "below
par".* / www.spaccanapoli.co.uk; 11 pm.

Spago SW7 £29 ④❸❸
6 Glendower Pl   7225 2407   5–2B
*Most feedback still hails this "cheap and cheerful" South
Kensington Italian as "a gem"; this year, however, saw a couple
of reports of the "no-redeeming-features" variety.* / 11.30 pm.

Spaniard's Inn NW3 £26 ④④❷
Spaniards Rd, Hampstead Heath   8731 6571   8–1A
*This "ancient" inn – with large garden – makes a charming stop-off
after a walk on Hampstead Heath (and is often "packed");
the atmosphere "just about makes up" for grub that "should
be better".* / 10 pm.

The Spencer Arms SW15 £38 ④❸❸
237 Lower Richmond Rd   8788 0640   10–1B
*Results can be "sometimes a bit slapdash", but when this "relaxed"
Putney Heath gastropub is on form it offers an "enterprising" menu
of "traditional" British dishes.* / www.thespencerarms.com; 10 pm;
no Amex.

Spianata £12 ❷④④
41 Brushfield St, E1   7655 4411   9–1D
20 Holborn Viaduct, EC1   7248 5947   9–2A
73 Watling St, EC4   7236 3666   9–2B
"Italian expats come in droves" to these City take-aways, and their
yummy toasted sandwiches (spianata) – made from "pizza-style"
bread, and with "unusual fillings" – please native reporters too.
/ L only; closed Sat & Sun, except E1 open Sun; no credit cards.

La Spiga W1 £42 ❸④❸
84-86 Wardour St   7734 3444   3–2D
"Authentic" pizza (and other "tasty" dishes) makes this "buzzing"
Soho Italian a useful stand-by; at night, it can get very noisy.
/ 11 pm; closed Sun.

The Spread Eagle SE10 £46 ❸❸❸
1-2 Stockwell St   8853 2333   1–3D
The "sympathetic renovation" of this ancient Greenwich tavern –
with its "well-executed" French cuisine and "beautiful" decor –
has been a big hit with most reporters; a few critics, though, find it
"frigid" and "pretentious". / www.spreadeaglerestaurant.com; 10 pm,
Sat & Sun 11 pm; no Amex; set weekday L £29 (FP).

THE SQUARE W1 £101 ❷❷❸
6-10 Bruton St   7495 7100   3–2C
Philip Howard's cuisine can be "astonishing", and it's complemented
by an "ultra-comprehensive" wine list and "discrete" service at this
Mayfair luminary, whose "formal" style particularly appeals
to "corporate types". / www.squarerestaurant.com; 10.45 pm; closed
Sat L & Sun L.

Square Pie Company £15 ❸④④
Unit 9, The Brunswick Centre, WC1   7837 6207   8–4C NEW
1 Canada Sq, Jubilee Line Mall, E14   7519 6071   11–1C
16 Horner St, Old Spitalfields Mkt, E1   7377 1114   9–1D
"A good choice", "great pies", "reasonable prices" – there's not
much to add about this no-frills eat-in/take-away chain.
/ www.squarepie.com; E14 Mon-Wed 4 pm, Thu & Fri 7 pm, Sat 6.30 pm;
E1 3pm, Sun 6 pm; E1 closed Sat, E14 closed Sun; no Amex; no bookings.

Sree Krishna SW17 £20 ❷❷❸
192-194 Tooting High St   8672 4250   10–2C
"No matter how hard you try, it's impossible to break the bank",
at this Tooting south Indian veteran, where the "reliable" cooking
"just goes on year after year". / www.sreekrishna.co.uk; 10.45 pm, Fri &
Sat midnight.

Sri Nam E14 £35 ❸❸④
10 Cabot Sq   7715 9515   11–1C
This two-level operation – one of the more useful options in Canary
Wharf – relaunched in spring 2007; it has a "grab-a-bite" pan-
Asian downstairs, and a slower-paced Thai restaurant above,
both of which are praised for their "tasty" dishes.
/ www.orientalrestaurantgroup.co.uk; 10.30 pm; closed Sat & Sun.

Standard Indian Restaurant W2 £22 ❸❸④
21-23 Westbourne Grove   7229 0600   6–1C
"Plentiful and satisfying food for a reasonable outlay" is still the
"reliable" promise of this aptly-named Bayswater "old faithful".
/ 11.45 pm.

Stanza W1 NEW £41 ④④④
93-107 Shaftesbury Ave   7494 3020   4–3A
*On the first-floor West End site that was Teatro Restaurant
(long RIP, but the adjoining club continues), this summer-2007
newcomer offers a straightforward menu, in a style that might suit
purposeful business meetings; we couldn't see any other reason,
though, why one might seek it out.* / Rated on Editors' visit;
www.stanzalondon.com; 11 pm; closed Sat L & Sun.

Star Café W1 £25 ❸②❸
22 Gt Chapel St   7437 8778   3–1D
*If you're looking for a "nicely-cooked fry-up", down Soho way – or
a snack at any time – seek out this "unique, old-style café" –
a treasured "haunt" of ad-land types.* / www.thestarcafesoho.com; L only,
closed Sat & Sun.

Star of India SW5 £39 ❷②❸
154 Old Brompton Rd   7373 2901   5–2B
*After a (much-needed) "contemporary" revamp (leaving the "odd"
Italianate frescoes intact), this "upmarket" Earl's Court "stalwart"
remains a firm favourite, not least for its "interesting and delicious"
subcontinental fare.* / 11.45 pm.

Starbucks £11 ④❸❸
Branches throughout London
*"They're taking over the world!", but – with its "mellow" branches
and coffee that's "often too nice to resist" – Uncle Sam's
"ubiquitous" chain incites a "shameful love" in many reporters;
the food, though, "could be more interesting".* / www.starbucks.com;
6.30 pm-11 pm; most City branches closed all or part of weekend; no booking.

Stein's TW10 £20 ❸④❸
Towpath (Rear of 55 Petersham Rd)   8948 8189   1–4A
*"A German Biergarten on the Thames", near Richmond Bridge;
it's only open in summer, and offers "good-quality Wurst (and other
German specialities) with proper German beer", in a leafy setting –
"what more could you want?"* / www.stein-s.com; 10.30 pm.

The Sterling EC3 £37 ④⑤④
30 St Mary Axe   7929 3641   9–2D
*A prominent location at the foot of the 'Gherkin' is the main feature
distinguishing this "light and airy" bar/restaurant; "service is hit-
and-miss and the food is nothing special".* / www.lewisandclarke.com;
11 pm; closed Sat & Sun.

Stick & Bowl W8 £19 ❸④⑤
31 Kensington High St   7937 2778   5–1A
*"If you're on a budget" – or "missing Chinese street food" –
this "tired"-looking oriental canteen is still "hard to beat".* / 11 pm;
no credit cards; no booking.

Sticky Fingers W8 £37 ⑤④❸
1a Phillimore Gdns   7938 5338   5–1A
*For fans, this old Kensington rocker is still a "fun" venue with
"great" burgers; service can be iffy, though, and some critics dismiss
the fare as "deep-fried rubbish".* / www.stickyfingers.co.uk; 11.30 pm.

Stock Pot   £15   ④❸❸
40 Panton St, SW1   7839 5142   4–4A
18 Old Compton St, W1   7287 1066   4–2A
273 King's Rd, SW3   7823 3175   5–3C
"Cheap and cheerful" is the exact definition of these studenty,
'60s "old-faithfuls", which serve "basic but edible" comfort food
at "absurdly inexpensive" prices. / 11 pm-midnight; SW1 Sun 10 pm;
W1 no credit cards, SW3 no Amex; some booking restrictions apply.

Stone Mason's Arms W6   £33   ❸②②
54 Cambridge Grove   8748 1397   7–2C
"A great find" on a busy Hammersmith highway, this "casual"
boozer is a "warm" and "friendly" place, offering food that's "well-
executed and occasionally adventurous". / 11 pm.

The Stonhouse SW4 NEW   £33   ④④②
165 Stonhouse St   7819 9312   10–1D
Some Clapham locals do welcome this new brasserie – prettily
hidden-away in Old Town – as a "solid" arrival; from the Cinnamon
Cay team, though, one might have hoped for more, and some visits
have been "disappointing". / www.thestonhouse.co.uk; 11 pm.

Story Deli
The Old Truman Brewery E1   £23   ❶❸②
3 Dray Walk   7247 3137   1–2D
"Unbeatable" pizza and "interesting" décor win rave reviews for
this shabby-chic East End hang-out; at weekends, though, it "can be
too popular". / 10 pm during summer (D only during summer); L only.

Strada   £32   ④④❸
Branches throughout London
"Maybe preferable to PizzaExpress, but only maybe"; for "decent"
Italian fare, this "reliable" upstart chain marginally beats its longer-
established rival – service and ambience, though, have now slipped
behind. / www.strada.co.uk; 11 pm; some booking restrictions apply.

Stringray Globe Café E2   £23   ②④④
109 Columbia Rd   7613 1141   1–2D
The "crispy" pizzas are "very good indeed" – and "enormous" too
– at this "cheery" but "chaotic" East End Italian. / 11 pm.

Sugar Hut SW6   £43   ④④❶
374 North End Rd   7386 8950   5–3A
"Exotic" décor lends an "illicit" and "undoubtedly romantic"
ambience to this "beautiful" Fulham Thai; the food is "pleasant",
but some reporters feel prices verge on the "ridiculous".
/ www.sugarhutgroup.com; midnight; D only.

Sugar Reef W1   £32   ⑤⑤④
42-44 Gt Windmill St   7851 0800   3–2D
A Soho nite-club/bar/restaurant, where the food is "generally rather
poor"; discount deals are regularly advertised, though, which can
be "surprisingly good". / www.sugarreef.co.uk; 1 am; D only, closed Sun.

Suka
Sanderson W1 NEW   £67   ⑤⑤⑤
50 Berners St   7300 1444   3–1D
Fans of this "wannabe" newcomer, in a design-hotel north
of Oxford Street, say it's "miles better than Spoon+" (RIP); whether
that's saying much is debatable and, to detractors, it's just a "flashy
disappointment" – "you can get much better Malaysian food for
a fraction of the price". / 12.30 am Sun 10.30 pm.

Sukho Thai Cuisine SW6 £37 **❶❶❷**
855 Fulham Rd   7371 7600   10–1B
"Tucked-away in deepest Fulham", this "outstanding neighbourhood oriental" is a "classy" and "courteous" sort of place, where the "non-clichéd" Thai cooking is rated by reporters as "the best in London". / 11 pm.

Sumosan W1 £75 **❸❹❹**
26b Albemarle St   7495 5999   3–3C
It's "minimalist" and "wallet-breakingly pricey", but fans claim this Mayfair Japanese is "as good as Nobu, just less hyped"; service can be poor, though, and the place sometimes has all the ambience of a "mausoleum". / www.sumosan.com; 11.45 pm; closed Sat L & Sun L.

The Sun & Doves SE5 £26 **❸❹❷**
61 Coldharbour Ln   7733 1525   1–4C
There are still only thin pickings down Camberwell way, so it's worth knowing about this "relaxing" and "spacious" hang-out (which is "noted for its child-friendliness"); the food is "regular pub fare, cooked well". / www.sunanddoves.co.uk; 10 pm; no Amex; need 10+ to book.

Le Suquet SW3 £51 **❷❹❸**
104 Draycott Ave   7581 1785   5–2C
It "really does feel like Cannes", at this "comfortable" Chelsea old-timer; for "a great seafood experience", it's very hard to beat. / 11.30 pm; set weekday L £33 (FP).

Sushi Hiroba WC2 £25 **❷❷❸**
50-54 Kingsway   7430 1888   2–2D
This Korean-backed Kaiten-Zushi yearling, near Holborn tube, is praised for its "keen" service and its "inventive" and "beautifully-presented" sushi; some doubters, though, say it's "over-rated". / www.sushihiroba.co.uk; 11 pm; closed Sun L.

Sushi-Hiro W5 £37 **❶❷⑤**
1 Station Pde   8896 3175   1–3A
"I used to live in Tokyo, and I rate this place 100%"; despite "the most unlikely of locations" (and "no ambience at all"), this diner near Ealing Common tube is "much patronised by Japanese people", thanks to its "amazingly fresh" sushi. / 9 pm; closed Mon; no credit cards.

Sushi-Say NW2 £37 **❶❶④**
33b Walm Ln   8459 7512   1–1A
"Staff make you feel very welcome", at this "outstanding", family-run fixture in Willesden Green, which is known for its "beautiful, fresh sushi and traditional Japanese dishes". / 10.30 pm; closed Mon.

Suzie Wong W1 NEW £32 **❸❸❸**
16 Old Compton St   7434 3544   4–2A
An "improvement" on its predecessor, Sri Thai Soho (RIP), this camp pan-Asian newcomer makes a handy West End stand-by; it doesn't purport to be a gourmet destination, but the food can be "surprisingly good". / www.orientalrestaurantgroup.co.uk; 11 pm.

The Swag & Tails SW7 £43 **❸❷❶**
10-11 Fairholt St   7584 6926   5–1C
"If you can find it", this "posh pub" – "just five minutes from Harrods" – has "no tourists", and serves "above-average" food in an "energetic" setting; at quiet times, it can feel a touch "cliquey". / www.swagandtails.com; 10 pm; closed Sat & Sun.

The Swan
Shakespeare's Globe SE1   **£38**
New Globe Walk   7928 9444   9–3B
It's early days for this recently-revamped (and re-named) dining room in the South Bank landmark; it's a "stunning" setting though, and initial reports (too few for a rating) suggest the operation has been "revitalised". / 10.30 pm.

The Swan W4   **£33**   ❸❷❷
119 Acton Ln   8994 8262   7–1A
A "brilliant local gastropub", "tucked-away" in "deepest Chiswick" (and with a "heaven-sent" garden for the summer); the "Mediterranean-influenced" food is "a bit less good than it was", but "still recommended". / 10.30 pm; closed weekday L; no Amex; no booking.

Sweetings EC4   **£43**   ❷❷❶
39 Queen Victoria St   7248 3062   9–3B
"They should slap a preservation order" on this "legendary City stalwart" – where "old-school fish dishes" are served in a "quaint" Dickensian setting; it's "loved by business types young and old", so "arrive early to avoid disappointment". / L only, closed Sat & Sun; no booking.

Tabaq SW12   **£30**   ❸④④
47 Balham Hill   8673 7820   10–2C
The setting is "unpretentious" ("think traditional curry house"), but this Balham Indian has a keen local following for its "delicious curries, that go beyond the norm"; service, though, can be "brusque". / www.tabaq.co.uk; 11.30 pm; closed Sun.

Taberna Etrusca EC4   **£43**   ④④❸
9 Bow Churchyard   7248 5552   9–2C
As a business venue "to enjoy, rather than to endure", this "conveniently-located" Italian of long standing still has quite a fan club, despite charging "high prices for average food". / www.etruscarestaurants.com; L only, closed Sat & Sun.

The Table SE1   **£30**   ④④❸
83 Southwark St   7401 2760   9–4B
Part of the offices of a leading architectural practice, this year-old café is – say fans – "an asset to Borough", serving good, "fresh" fare; prices, though, sometimes seem "a little steep". / www.thetable.com; 11 pm; closed Sat D & Sun D; no Amex.

Taiwan Village SW6   **£28**   ❷❷❸
85 Lillie Rd   7381 2900   5–3A
"Fulham's best-kept secret!" – this "off-the-beaten-track" Chinese delivers "spicy" cooking that's "better value than most places in Chinatown"; "the leave-it-to-us feast is the way to go". / www.taiwanvillage.com; 11.30 pm; closed Mon L.

Tajima Tei EC1   **£27**   ❷❸④
9-11 Leather Ln   7404 9665   9–2A
A "slightly Spartan" canteen, near Hatton Garden; fans say it's "consistently overlooked", and praise its "traditional" Japanese scoff. / www.tajima-tei.co.uk.

Talad Thai SW15 £26 ❷❸⑤
320 Upper Richmond Rd 8789 8084 10–2A
"Superb food at pocket-money prices" still makes this "cheap and cheerful Thai" a "fabulous find" for many Putney folk (notwithstanding the odd report of a "poor patch" this year). / www.taladthai.co.uk; 10.30 pm; no Amex.

Taman Gang W1 £77 ⑤⑤❸
141 Park Ln 7518 3160 2–2A
Financial difficulties have contributed to a "disappointing" year for this "cool" pan-Asian basement near Marble Arch; what the future holds… it's hard to say. / www.tamangang.com; 11.30 pm; D only, closed Sun; booking: max 6.

Tamarai WC2 £49 ④④❸
167 Drury Ln 7831 9399 4–1C
It's "for cocktails, and for groups" that this new nightclub-style Covent Garden basement is of most interest; the pan-Asian food is incidental – "I was eating on a 50%-off promotion, and it was still overpriced!" / www.tamarai.co.uk; 11.30 pm; closed Sun.

Tamarind W1 £58 ❷❷❸
20 Queen St 7629 3561 3–3B
Alfred Prasad's "refined" dishes – "cooked perfectly and presented immaculately" – still win rave reviews for this "stylish" Mayfair subcontinental (London's original 'haute Indian'); "shame it's in a basement", though. / www.tamarindrestaurant.com; 11.15 pm; closed Sat L; set weekday L £31 (FP).

tamesa@oxo
Oxo Tower SE1 £38 ⑤⑤④
2nd Fl, Oxo Tower Wharf, Barge House St 7633 0088 9–3A
It has a "superb river-view setting" (on the second floor), but this year-old South Bank brasserie can seem "dull" and "lacking identity" – at least it's "easier on the pocket than upstairs" (see Oxo Tower). / www.oxotower.co.uk/tamesa.html; 11.30 pm; closed Sun D.

Tampopo SW10 £27 ❸❸❸
140 Fulham Rd 7370 5355 5–3B
"Cheap and cheerful" but still quite "classy" – this Chelsea canteen is "conveniently located" for the cinema, and its oriental ("wok and Thai") cuisine rarely disappoints. / www.tampopo.co.uk; 11 pm, Fri-Sat 11.30 pm.

Tandoori Lane SW6 £26 ❷❷❸
131a Munster Rd 7371 0440 10–1B
"Every dish is distinctive, and there's no grease in sight", at this long-established, high-quality curry house, in the depths of Fulham. / 11.15 pm; no Amex.

Tandoori Nights SE22 £31 ❷❷❸
73 Lordship Ln 8299 4077 1–4D
The "fantastic" food is "always spot-on", at this "cramped" and "homely" curry house, which is world-famous among East Dulwich folk. / 11.30 pm; closed weekday L & Sat L.

Tangawizi TW1 £34 ❸❷❷
406 Richmond Rd 8891 3737 1–4A
*Despite an "unlikely" Twickenham location, this "crisp,
contemporary" yearling wins more-than-local acclaim for its
"interesting African twist on Indian cooking". / www.tangawizi.co.uk;
10.30 pm; D only, closed Sun.*

Tapas Brindisa SE1 £35 ❷❸❸
18-20 Southwark St 7357 8880 9–4C
*As you'd hope of somewhere owned by renowned Iberian food
importers, this Borough Market bar serves "some of the best tapas
in town" ; it's pretty "cramped", though, and can get "ridiculously
busy". / www.brindisa.com; 11 pm; closed Sun.*

Taqueria W11 £29 ❷❸④
139-143 Westbourne Grove 7229 4734 6–1B
*"Take friends, and expect to share (messily)", if you visit this
"unusually authentic and interesting" Bayswater Mexican;
the setting is "not memorable", but "strong margaritas" help fuel
a "laid-back" vibe. / www.coolchiletaqueria.co.uk; Mon-Thu 11 pm, Fri &
Sat 11.30 pm, Sun 10.30 pm; no Amex; no booking.*

Taro £22 ❸❸④
10 Old Compton St, W1 7439 2275 4–2B
61 Brewer St, W1 7734 5826 3–2D
*"For a quick bite in the West End", Mr Taro's "bustling and
somewhat cramped" Soho "pit stops" serve up "simple" and
"cheap" sushi (and so on). / www.tarorestaurants.co.uk; 10.30 pm,
Sun 9.30 pm; no Amex; no booking.*

Tartine SW3 £36 ❸❷❸
114 Draycott Ave 7589 4981 5–2C
*Hang with a "beautiful Chelsea crowd" at this "cosy yet buzzy"
spot, near Brompton Cross; on the menu – "an innovative range
of French open sandwiches at sensible prices", plus some
"good brunch items". / www.tartine.co.uk; 11 pm; need 6+ to book at D.*

Tas £27 ④❸❸
22 Bloomsbury St, WC1 7637 4555 2–1C
33 The Cut, SE1 7928 2111 9–4A
72 Borough High St, SE1 7403 7200 9–4C
97-99 Isabella St, SE1 7620 6191 9–4A
37 Farringdon Rd, EC1 7430 9721 9–1A
*For a "quick and friendly" bite, these "always-buzzing" Turkish
cafés "won't break the bank"; with expansion, though, "standards
have slipped" – the food "could do with a bit more sparkle",
nowadays. / www.tasrestaurant.com; 11.30 pm.*

Tas Pide SE1 £30 ④❸❸
20-22 New Globe Walk 7928 3300 9–3B
*"OK, it's not GREAT food", but for "honest" and "tasty" scoff
at "cheap" prices, this "retro"-rustic Anatolian-themed joint makes
a "useful" option near Shakespeare's Globe; it offers a pretty
standard Tas menu, spiced up with pide (Turkish pizza).
/ www.tasrestaurant.com; 11.30 pm.*

La Tasca £28 ⑤④❸
23-24 Maiden Ln, WC2   7240 9062   4–4C
404-406 Chiswick High Rd, W4   8994 4545   7–2A
21 Essex Rd, N1   7226 3272   8–3D
West India Quay, E14   7531 9990   11–1C
15-17 Eldon St, EC2   7256 2381   9–2C
Fans acclaim these "lively" Spanish-themed joints – with their
"mass-produced" tapas – as "useful "stand-bys; we're with those
who say that the fact that this is – financially at least – one of the
nation's most successful chains is nothing short
of "an embarrassment". / www.latasca.co.uk; 11 pm, E14 10.45 pm;
need 8+ to book.

Tate Britain SW1 £47 ④❸❷
Millbank   7887 8825   2–4C
"Stunning" Whistler murals and a "superb" wine list ("for price and
choice, simply the best in town") win enduring praise for this
"hidden-away" gallery dining room; fans feel the "basic" food
is "better than is often credited". / www.tate.org.uk; L & afternoon
tea only.

(Café, Level 2)
Tate Modern SE1 £32 ④④❸
Bankside   7401 5014   9–3B
This second-floor South Bank gallery café is a surprisingly
"interesting" spot for a "tasty" snack, especially if you "fight your
way through the crowds, and get a seat by the window". / Fri
9.30 pm; L & tea only, except Fri & Sat open L&D.

(Restaurant, Level 7)
Tate Modern SE1 £39 ⑤④❷
Bankside   7401 5020   9–3B
"Great views over the Thames" help make Tate Modern's "noisy"
7th-floor dining room popular with tourists and locals alike;
the "unimpressive" food, though, is "more an assembly-job than
cooking". / www.tate.org.uk; 9.30 pm; Sat-Thu closed D.

Tatsuso EC2 £80 ❸❸⑤
32 Broadgate Circle   7638 5863   9–2D
This "very pricey" Broadgate Japanese is "one of the
most prestigious City eateries", with a ground-floor teppan-yaki,
and basement restaurant; sliding ratings this year coincided with
a six month hiatus with no sushi chef – a new one was taken
on shortly before this guide went to press. / 10.15 pm; closed
Sat & Sun.

Tawana W2 £33 ❷❷④
3 Westbourne Grove   7229 3785   6–1C
Just off Queensway, a well-established spot notable for its
"consistently reliable and high-quality Thai dishes".
/ www.tawana.co.uk; 11 pm; no Amex.

Ten Ten Tei W1 £35 ❷❷⑤
56 Brewer St   7287 1738   3–2D
It's "ugly" and "a bit tatty", but this Soho Japanese is "very cheap,
very cheerful, and offers very authentic cooking"; set lunches,
in particular, are "excellent value". / 10 pm; closed Sun; no Amex;
set weekday L £18 (FP).

Tendido Cero SW5 £35 ❷❷❸
174 Old Brompton Rd 7370 3685 5–2B
"Fantastic" tapas draw a permanent crowd to this "buzzing" Earl's Court bar; there were a few quibbles this year – "can no longer BYO", "smaller portions", "new two-sittings policy" – but nothing sufficient to dent its reputation as a "classy" and "good-value" choice. / www.cambiodetercio.co.uk; 11 pm.

Tentazioni SE1 £51 ❷❷❸
2 Mill St 7394 5248 11–2A
Fans of this "little hidden-away spot", near Shad Thames, again tip it as "one of London's top Italians", and say "it's grown in confidence now the chef is the sole owner"; feedback was more mixed this year, though, with some reporters finding it "forgettable". / www.tentazioni.co.uk; 10.45 pm; closed Mon L, Sat L & Sun; set dinner £34 (FP).

The Tenth Restaurant & Bar
Royal Garden Hotel W8 £60 ❸❸❷
Kensington High St 7361 1910 5–1A
"Amazing views across London" add to the ambience at this top-floor dining room, by Kensington Gardens; even fans say "a little refurbishment" wouldn't go amiss, but – for a room with a view – the food is "rather good". / www.royalgardenhotel.co.uk; 10.30 pm; closed Sat L & Sun.

Terminus
Great Eastern Hotel EC2 £45 ⑤⑤⑤
40 Liverpool St 7618 7400 9–2D
This "antiseptic" City brasserie has not been improved by new ownership; its breakfasts make a "classy" start to the morning, but otherwise it's a "very noisy" place, serving "boring" food at "unjustified" prices. / www.terminus-restaurant.co.uk; 11 pm; set brunch £23 (FP).

The Terrace in the Fields WC2 £42 ④❸❸
Lincoln's Inn Fields 7430 1234 2–2D
This "bright" hut in the middle of leafy Lincoln's Inn Fields makes "a pleasant oasis"; the cooking, however, is "adequate" at best – they "should either focus on West Indian dishes exclusively, or improve the rest of the menu". / www.theterrace.info; 9 pm; closed Sun.

Texas Embassy Cantina SW1 £38 ⑤⑤⑤
1 Cockspur St 7925 0077 2–2C
"It has a great location", just off Trafalgar Square, but – with too many reports of "uninterested" service and "yuck" food – this busy Tex/Mex can sometimes be a "never-again" experience. / www.texasembassy.com; 11 pm.

Texture W1 NEW £60
34 Portman Sq 7224 0028 2–2A
Two staff (including an ex-head chef) from Raymond Blanc's famous 'Manoir' are launching this newcomer on the former site of Deya (RIP), just north of Oxford Street, in late-2007; their background – and the fact that much of the seating will be given over to a champagne bar – suggests this will be a pretty upmarket affair (reflected in the price-guesstimate shown).

TGI Friday's   £35   ⑤④⑤
25-29 Coventry St, W1   7839 6262   4–4A
6 Bedford St, WC2   7379 0585   4–4C
Fulham Broadway, SW6   7385 1660   5–4A
96-98 Bishops Bridge Rd, W2   7229 8600   6–1C
Pentravia Retail Pk, Watford Way, NW7   8203 9779   1–1B **NEW**
Fans of this All-American chain say it's "a formula that works";
critics, though, are scathing about its "over-friendly yet inept"
service, and its poorly-cooked "slop" – "even the children didn't like
it". / www.tgifridays.co.uk; 11.30 pm.

Thai Bistro W4   £26   ❸❷④
99 Chiswick High Rd   8995 5774   7–2B
"A simple but great-tasting menu" is "swiftly served" at the
communal seats of this "efficient" Chiswick Thai; even fans, though,
aren't necessarily impressed by the atmosphere. / 11 pm; closed
Tue L & Thu L; no Amex.

Thai Café SW1   £26   ❸❸⑤
22 Charlwood St   7592 9584   2–4C
"Plentiful" and "good-value" dishes maintain the appeal of this
"cheap" Pimlico Thai; the ambience, though, "lets it down a little".
/ 10.30 pm; closed Sat L & Sun L.

Thai Corner Café SE22   £22   ❸❸❸
44 North Cross Rd   8299 4041   1–4D
"Elbow-to-elbow" with your neighbours, you get "reliable" and
"very cheap" chow at this "tiny" BYO Thai in East Dulwich.
/ 10.30 pm; no credit cards.

Thai Elephant TW10   £33   ❸❶❸
1 Wakefield Rd   8940 5114   1–4A
"It may nestle beside an unattractive bus station", but this pleasant
Thai comes mainly well-recommended by Richmond folk for its
"delicious" cooking. / www.thaielephantrichmond.co.uk; 11 pm;
set weekday L £20 (FP).

Thai Garden SW11   £26   ❸❸④
58 Battersea Rise   7738 0380   10–2C
A "reliable" Battersea stalwart that's "like an old friend" to some
locals, thanks to its "good quality and reasonable prices". / 11 pm;
D only.

Thai on the River SW11   £37   ❸❸❸
2 Lombard Rd   7924 6090   5–4B
"A great location by the river" (with "brilliant al fresco dining")
is the star feature of this "out-of-the-way" Battersea spot;
its "delicate" Thai cuisine, however, is well rated too.
/ www.thaiontheriver.com; 11 pm; set weekday L £23 (FP).

Thai Pot WC2   £30   ④④⑤
1 Bedfordbury   7379 4580   4–4C
It has a handy location (behind the Coliseum), but this "once-
reliable" oriental has gone "downhill". / www.thaipot.biz; 11.15 pm;
closed Sun.

Thai Square £29 ④❸❸
21-24 Cockspur St, SW1   7839 4000   2–3C
5 Princes St, W1   7499 3333   3–1C
148 Strand, WC2   7497 0904   2–2D
19 Exhibition Rd, SW7   7584 8359   5–2C
347-349 Upper St, N1   7704 2000   8–3D
2-4 Lower Richmond Rd, SW15   8780 1811   10–1A
136-138 Minories, EC3   7680 1111   9–3D
1-7 Gt Thomas Apostle, EC4   7329 0001   9–3B
The glass-fronted Putney branch, with its "amazing river views",
is the best of the "exotic" – but still rather "clinical" – outlets
of this Thai chain; the food is "reliable" enough, in a "ho-hum" sort
of way. / www.thaisq.co.uk; between 10 pm and 11.30 pm, SW1 open till
1am Fri & Sat; EC3 & EC4 closed Sat & Sun, W1 & WC2 closed Sun.

Thailand SE14 £29 ❷①❷
15 Lewisham Way   8691 4040   1–3D
"Some of the best Thai/Laotian food in London" makes it worth
seeking out this "simple café" in New Cross; service is "very good"
too, but "it's a tight squeeze". / 11.30 pm.

The Thatched House W6 £32 ❸④❸
115 Dalling Rd   8748 6174   7–1B
An agreeably "stress-free" Hammersmith local (with a nice garden
in summer), serving "humungous portions of tasty, classic pub
grub". / www.thatchedhouse.com; 10 pm; no Amex.

Theo Randall
InterContinental Hotel W1 £65 ❷❷④
1 Hamilton Pl   7409 3131   3–4A
With its "stunning" cooking – from the ex-head chef of the River
Café – this Mayfair newcomer deserves to be hailed as one
of London's foremost Italians; it's blighted, though, by appallingly
"sterile" décor – "a bit like an airport lounge". / www.theorandall.com;
11 pm; closed Sun D; set weekday L £41 (FP).

Thomas Cubitt SW1 £52 ❸❸❷
44 Elizabeth St   7730 6060   2–4A
A "fun and really buzzy" vibe has helped this "lovely" boozer
become Belgravia's top hang-out, and it's "always packed";
downstairs, you get "excellent burgers" and so on – upstairs,
there's a more "formal" dining room. / www.thethomascubitt.co.uk;
10 pm.

The Three Crowns N16 NEW £36 ❸❸❸
175 Stoke Newington High St   7241 5511   1–1D
A large new gastropub that's already "very popular", up Stokie way;
it charges "restaurant prices", but fans say that's "justified by the
quality of the food". / www.threecrowns-n16.com; 10 pm; no Amex.

3 Monkeys SE24 £31 ④④④
136-140 Herne Hill   7738 5500   1–4C
"Formerly a great Indian", this "cavernous" Herne Hill spot has hit
a rocky patch of late; fans still hail its "delicious" and "interesting"
dishes, but quite a few critics now deride it as "pretentious" and
"overpriced". / www.3monkeysrestaurant.com; 11 pm; set weekday L
£18 (FP).

Tiffinbites £25 ❸④④
22-23 Jubilee Pl, E14   7719 0333   11–1C **NEW**
23 Russia Row (off Gresham St), EC2   7600 4899   9–2B **NEW**
*Is this ambitious new concept "a largely successful attempt to apply
the Starbucks principle to subcontinental food", or just "a fast-food
Indian with little to recommend it"? – initial commentary is mixed
(but we're more in the latter camp).*

Tiger Tiger SW1 £32 ⑤⑤❸
29 Haymarket   7930 1885   4–4A
*A vast West End pick-up scene, with its own red-in-tooth-and-claw
charm; it's "loud if you just want to eat and chat", though, and the
food is not good, and "not all that cheap". / www.tigertiger-london.co.uk;
10.30 pm.*

Timo W8 £51 ❸❷④
343 Kensington High St   7603 3888   7–1D
*This Kensington Italian "hasn't got everything quite right",
particularly the "lifeless" ambience, but it's still "recommended"
by some reporters for its "helpful" service and its "very competent"
cooking. / www.timorestaurant.net; 11 pm; closed Sun; booking: max 8;
set weekday L £31 (FP).*

Toff's N10 £28 ❷❷④
38 Muswell Hill Broadway   8883 8656   1–1B
*"Lovely fish 'n' chips, old-style" – and in "big portions" too –
draw "queues all year-round" to this "welcoming" Muswell Hill
veteran. / www.toffsfish.co.uk; 10 pm; closed Sun; no booking, Sat; set always
available £17 (FP).*

Toku
Japan Centre W1 £27 ❷❸⑤
212 Piccadilly   7255 8255   3–3D
*It's "not glamorous", but this cultural-centre café, by Piccadilly
Circus, is dead "authentic", and serves "decent food" (including
"amazing sushi") at "good prices". / www.japancentre.com; 10 pm,
Sun 8 pm; no Amex.*

Tokyo City EC2 £35 ❸④④
46 Gresham St   7726 0308   9–2B
*"The Japanese items are excellent" – "the rest of the menu is OK,
but not as good" – at this "reliable" oriental, near the Bank
of England. / www.tokyocity.co.uk; 10 pm; closed Sat & Sun.*

Tokyo Diner WC2 £17 ④❸❸
2 Newport Pl   7287 8777   4–3B
*"For a quick Japanese fix in Chinatown", this cosily grungy fixture
offers "honest" (if basic) nosh at "good prices"; staff are "helpful"
too (and "don't accept tips"). / www.tokyodiner.com; 11.30 pm; no Amex;
no booking, Fri & Sat.*

TOM AIKENS SW3 £82 ❷❷❸
43 Elystan St   7584 2003   5–2C
*Fans find Tom Aikens's "complex" cuisine nothing short
of "sublime", and his "Zen-like" Chelsea dining room is often touted
as "one of London's best"; more sceptical reporters, though,
continue to complain of "fiddly" dishes and "outrageous" prices.
/ www.tomaikens.co.uk; 11 pm; closed Sat & Sun; jacket and/or tie; booking:
max 8; set weekday L £42 (FP).*

Tom's W11   £26   ④④❷
226 Westbourne Grove   7221 8818   6–1B
"A great atmosphere for breakfast or brunch" is the special strength of Tom Conran's "cramped" and "buzzy" Notting Hill deli/diner… "if you can get a table". / 5.30pm; L only; no Amex; no booking.

Tom's Kitchen SW3   £50   ❸④④
27 Cale St   7349 0202   5–2C
Tom Aikens's "new kid on the Chelsea block" certainly "packs 'em in", and its "utilitarian", white-tiled interior is usually "overcrowded" (and often "very noisy"); service can be "haphazard", and the food – which, at its best, is "simple and delicious" – is likewise. / www.tomskitchen.co.uk; 11 pm.

Tom's Place SW3 NEW   £40
1 Cale St   awaiting tel   5–2C
In late-2007, Tom Aikens is set to open his 'ethical' chippy – just round the corner from his Chelsea HQ, on the former site of Monkey's (RIP); price indicated is our guesstimate.

Tootsies   £30   ④❸④
35 James St, W1   7486 1611   3–1A
177 New King's Rd, SW6   7736 4023   10–1B
107 Old Brompton Rd, SW7   7581 8942   5–2B
120 Holland Park Ave, W11   7229 8567   6–2A
148 Chiswick High Rd, W4   8747 1869   7–2A
196-198 Haverstock Hill, NW3   7431 3812   8–2A
1 Battersea Rise, SW11   7924 4935   10–2C
Putney Wharf, 30 Brewhouse St, SW15   8788 8488   10–2B
48 High St, SW19   8946 4135   10–2B
36-38 Abbeville Rd, SW4   8772 6646   10–2D
"Staple food for all ages" is the draw to these "bustling" family diners; though they're often tipped for "dependable burgers", sceptics say their cooking's "really not great" – you'd certainly never guess their owners also run the (vastly superior) GBK. / www.tootsiesrestaurants.co.uk; 11 pm; some booking restrictions apply.

Tosa W6   £28   ❷❸④
332 King St   8748 0002   7–2B
"Wonderful yakitori", "fresh sushi" and other "authentic" dishes – at "reasonable" prices – win high praise for this "compact" Japanese, a short walk from Stamford Brook tube. / www.tosatosa.net; 11 pm; no Amex.

Toto's SW1   £66   ❸❷❷
Lennox Gardens Mews   7589 0075   5–2C
"It's always a pleasure", for fans to visit this "lovely" and "romantic" Knightsbridge Italian (where the "garden is a delight for lunch in good weather"); staff are "formal but friendly", and the food is "delicious", and the only gripe is that "it's a bit expensive". / 11 pm.

Trader Vics
Hilton Hotel W1   £70   ⑤⑤④
22 Park Ln   7208 4113   3–4A
Like the heiress Paris, the basement tiki bar of the Park Lane Hilton "trades on its reputation" – the food can taste "like mass-produced cardboard", and service is "just as drab". / www.tradersvics.com; 12.30 am; closed Sat L & Sun L.

The Trafalgar Tavern SE10 £38 ⑤④❷
Park Row   8858 2909   1–3D
*It's impossible to beat the location – "right on the Thames" –
or the "beautiful dining room" of this "perfect" Georgian tavern;
and don't they know it – the food is "tragic". / 10 pm; closed Sun D;
no Amex; no booking, Sun L.*

Tree House SW13 £37 ④❸❸
73 White Hart Ln   8392 1617   10–1A
*This "jolly" Barnes pub-conversion – with "fairy lights" and a "lovely
garden" – is, in atmosphere terms, something of a "hidden gem";
on the food front, though, "quality varies". / www.treehousepeople.com;
10.30 pm; no Amex.*

Trenta W2 NEW £38 ④❸④
30 Connaught St   7262 9623   6–1D
*Opinions differ on this pint-sized (and somewhat "cramped")
Bayswater Italian newcomer; supporters say it's a "welcome
addition to the neighbourhood" – detractors that it's "amateurish"
and "pretentious". / 10.30 pm; closed Mon L & Sun.*

Trinity SW4 £46 ❷❸④
4 The Polygon   7622 1199   10–2D
*"It's great to have Adam Byatt back", say fans of Clapham's
favourite prodigal son, whose "highly accomplished" cuisine at this
"sombre" newcomer (on the site of Polygon, RIP) is "some of the
best south of the river"; prices are "high", though,
and disappointments not unknown. / www.trinityrestaurant.co.uk;
10.30 pm; closed Mon L.*

Trinity Stores SW12 £15 ❸❷❸
5-6 Balham Station Rd   8673 3773   10–2C
*A Balham deli yearling that's made "a good start"; aside from good
coffee, it serves "home-made soups and tasty sandwiches".
/ www.trinitystores.co.uk; 8pm, Sat 6.30pm, Sun 4pm; L only.*

Les Trois Garçons E1 £70 ④❸❶
1 Club Row   7613 1924   1–2D
*"Opulent and OTT" decor – "so madcap it's surreal" – helps set
up some "very seductive" vibes at this "kitsch" East End pub-
conversion; service can be "snooty", though, and the Gallic cuisine
seems "unnecessarily expensive". / www.lestroisgarcons.com; 9.30 pm;
D only, closed Sun.*

Trojka NW1 £27 ④④❷
101 Regent's Park Rd   7483 3765   8–2B
*"A good local haunt", in Primrose Hill, with a cosy and "unusual"
atmosphere; it serves "cheap" and "substantial" Eastern European
dishes (plus "the biggest range of vodkas"). / www.trojka.co.uk;
10.30 pm.*

LA TROMPETTE W4 £54 ❶❶❷
5-7 Devonshire Rd   8747 1836   7–2A
*"Tucked-away" in a Chiswick sidestreet, it may be, but Chez Bruce's
"stylish" sibling is "one of the very best places in London";
its "knowledgeable and passionate" staff deliver "sensational"
cuisine (including "legendary" cheese), plus a "really exciting" wine
list. / www.latrompette.co.uk; 10.30 pm; booking: max 6.*

Troubadour SW5 £32 ⑤❸❶
265 Old Brompton Rd 7370 1434 5–3A
This "kooky" Earl's Court coffee house has a "chilled" style all of its own; you "don't go there for the food", but – if you do – the "hangover-cure" breakfasts are the best bet.
/ www.troubadour.co.uk; 11.30 pm; no Amex.

La Trouvaille W1 £47 ❸❷❷
12a Newburgh St 7287 8488 3–2C
"It means 'a find' and it is!"; this "lovely" bar/restaurant occupies a small Georgian townhouse – "tucked-away in an atmospheric part of Soho" – where an "energetic team of young French staff" serve up some "unfamiliar" Gallic dishes. / www.latrouvaille.co.uk; 11 pm; closed Sun; set weekday L £30 (FP).

Truc Vert W1 £46 ④④❸
42 North Audley St 7491 9988 3–2A
With its "bare-board" décor, this "idiosyncratic" deli makes a "useful refuge from the madding crowds of Selfridges"; it offers "awesome breakfasts" – as well as other "delicious" treats – but prices can seem "OTT for a casual corner spot".
/ www.trucvert.co.uk; 10 pm; closed Sun D.

Tsar SW1 NEW £75
12 Waterloo Pl 7484 1355 2–3C
We keep hearing that the Russians are coming, but where are their restaurants? – this opulent autumn-2007 newcomer, on the former site of W'Sens (RIP), may be the answer; price given is our guesstimate.

Tsunami SW4 £37 ❶❸❷
1-7 Voltaire Rd 7978 1610 10–1D
"You get Nobu without the pretence and the prices", at Ken Sam's "truly exceptional" but "relaxed" Japanese-fusion five-year-old; "who knew somewhere in Clapham could be so good?" / www.tsunami.co.uk; 10.30 pm, Sun 9 pm; closed weekday L; set weekday L £20 (FP).

Tuttons WC2 £43 ④④④
11-12 Russell St 7836 4141 4–3D
"Much better than you'd expect for a tourist trap", this well-located spot, by Covent Garden Market, is quite a "friendly" place, with "nice outside tables" and generally "acceptable" food.
/ www.coventgardenrestaurants.com; 11.30 pm.

2 Amici SW1 NEW £33 ❸❸❸
48a Rochester Rw 7976 5660 2–4C
"A good addition to the Westminster culinary desert" – this "promising" new Italian offers "a warm welcome" and "honest" and "filling" fare, in a setting redolent of the '80s.
/ www.2amici.com; 11 pm; closed Sun.

Two Brothers N3 £27 ❷❷④
297-303 Regent's Park Rd 8346 0469 1–1B
"Friendly and slightly upmarket" – the Manzi Brothers' "old-favourite" Finchley chippy "runs like clockwork", and is "worthy of its high local reputation"; "the queues can get a bit long at times". / www.twobrothers.co.uk; 10.15 pm; closed Mon & Sun; no booking at D.

202

Nicole Farhi W11 £37 ❸❷❶
202 Westbourne Grove   7727 2722   6–1B
"Brilliant for brunch", this "very cool" diner-cum-clothes store is one
of Notting Hill's key see-and-be-seen weekend destinations –
its NYC twin is apparently "even better". / www.nicolefarhi.com; 4 pm;
L & afternoon tea only; no booking.

2 Veneti W1 NEW £47 ❷❷❸
10 Wigmore St   7637 0789   3–1B
A "thoroughly enjoyable" newcomer, where "very knowledgeable"
staff present "good and solid" Venetian cooking; it seems to have
mustered the "panache" which always eluded Eddalino (RIP) –
its predecessor on this site near the Wigmore Hall. / 10.30 pm; closed
Sat L & Sun.

Ubon E14 £91 ❸❹❹
34 Westferry Circus   7719 7800   11–1B
"Fantastic views over the Thames" jazz up the "bland" décor
at Nobu's E14 cousin, which is probably "Canary Wharf's top
restaurant"; bills are "super-sized" – for fans, "sublime" Japanese
fusion fare justifies such expense, but sceptics say standards are
getting "a little sloppy". / www.noburestaurants.com; 10.15 pm; closed
Sat L & Sun.

Uli W11 £29 ❷❶❸
16 All Saints Rd   7727 7511   6–1B
"Michael is still the most charming host", at this "wonderful
neighbourhood asset" in North Kensington, which serves "first-
class" oriental fare (and has a "great garden in summer");
this year, though, a few regulars found it "below expectations".
/ www.uli-oriental.co.uk; 11 pm; D only; no Amex.

Ultimate Burger £22 ❹❹❹
127 Tottenham Court Rd, W1   7436 5355   2–1B
334 New Oxford St, WC1   7436 6641   4–1C
"Tasty and meaty" burgers commend this small chain
to most reporters; it inspires only limited feedback, but rarely
attracts much flak. / www.ultimateburger.co.uk; 11.30 pm, Sun 10.45 pm;
no bookings.

Umu W1 £120 ❷❸❸
14-16 Bruton Pl   7499 8881   3–2C
"Unique" and "subtle", the Kyoto-style cuisine and "mouth-
watering" sushi at Marlon Abela's slickly-decorated Mayfair
Japanese inspire ever-more adulatory reviews; "unbelievable" prices,
though, are still a sore point. / www.umurestaurant.com; 10.30 pm; closed
Sat L & Sun; booking: max 14.

The Union W2 £32 ❹❹❸
13 Sheldon Sq   7289 3063   6–1C
After a stroll around Little Venice, this large gastropub – part of the
new Paddington Square development – provides a useful watering
hole, serving decent (if standard) fare. / Rated on Editors' visit;
www.theunionbar.co.uk; 10 pm.

The Union Café W1 £42 ❹❸❹
96 Marylebone Ln   7486 4860   3–1A
A "wide selection of wines at bargain prices" – backed up by some
"consistent" cooking – makes this "airy" and "unfussy" Marylebone
outfit a popular destination, especially at lunchtime.
/ www.brinkleys.com; 11 pm; closed Sun D.

Uno SW1   £38   ❸④④
1 Denbigh St   7834 1001   2–4B
*Most reporters find this "airy" Pimlico fixture a "reliable
neighbourhood Italian" – it's noisy, though, and service is "hit-and-
miss". / www.uno1.co.uk; 10.45 pm.*

Upper Glas N1   £39   ④❸④
359 Upper St   7359 1932   8–3D
*"SE1's loss is Islington's gain", say fans of this "interesting" Swedish
venture, now transplanted to the former site of Lola's (RIP);
something's been lost in translation, though – critics say food at the
new site's only "OK", and the décor's "a nightmare fusion of IKEA
and '60s psychedelia". / www.glasrestaurant.co.uk; 11 pm; closed
Mon L & Sun D.*

Upstairs Bar SW2   £35   ❶❶❷
89b Acre Ln (door on Branksome Rd)   7733 8855   10–2D
*"Through an unassuming door in a Brixton back street" lies this
"corker" of a restaurant; it's an "unfussy", sort of place –
intriguingly located on an upper floor – where Daniel Budden's food
is simply "excellent". / www.upstairslondon.com; 9.30 pm, Sat 10.30 pm;
closed Mon, Tue-Sat D only, closed Sun D.*

Le Vacherin W4   £41   ❷❸❸
76-77 South Pde   8742 2121   7–1A
*Malcolm John's "astonishingly authentic" bistro – "in an unlikely bit
of Chiswick" – "really is like a corner of provincial France";
most reports are a hymn of praise to its "classic" cuisine and
"interesting wine" – the place "can seem gloomy when empty",
though, and both food and service are a bit "variable".
/ www.levacherin.co.uk; 10.30 pm; closed Mon L; no Amex.*

Vama SW10   £43   ❷❷❸
438 King's Rd   7351 4118   5–3B
*This "closely-packed" World's End venture has won a formidable
reputation for its "memorable", "new-wave" Indian cuisine;
even some fans, though, have noted "occasionally average" results
of late. / www.vama.co.uk; 11 pm.*

Vasco & Piero's Pavilion W1   £44   ❸❷④
15 Poland St   7437 8774   3–1D
*This "cosy", "cramped" and "old-fashioned" Soho veteran – with its
"clean and simple" Umbrian cooking and its "lovely" staff –
has long held a reputation as a hidden "jewel"; some recent
reports, however, feature "nondescript" meals and "ropey" service.
/ www.vascosfood.com; 10.30 pm; closed Sat L & Sun.*

Veeraswamy W1   £50   ❷❸❷
Victory Hs, 99-101 Regent St   7734 1401   3–3D
*A stone's throw from Piccadilly Circus, London's oldest Indian is still
– for its fans – "the best"; that's probably overdoing it, but it does
offer "interesting" cooking (in essentially "traditional" style), and its
contemporary styling is "terrific". / www.realindianfood.com; 10.30 pm;
booking: max 12.*

El Vergel SE1   £17   ❶❷❸
8 Lant St   7357 0057   9–4B
*A "little South American in a Borough back street" that's "great
in so many ways" – its "entirely charming" staff serve "interesting"
dishes to a "cosmopolitan" crowd at "pocket-money" prices;
"shame it isn't open longer hours". / www.elvergel.co.uk;
breakfast & L only, closed Sat & Sun; no credit cards.*

Vertigo
Tower 42 EC2 £54 ⑤④❷
20-25 Old Broad St   7877 7842   9–2C
The "stunning" views are "ideal for impressing a date" (or a client),
but this 42nd-floor City eyrie is, itself, a "sterile" sort of place;
the food is a let-down too, and "eye-wateringly pricey" – "avoid
eating, just spend a fortune on fizz". / www.vertigo42.co.uk; 11 pm;
closed Sat & Sun; booking essential.

Via Condotti W1 £42 ❸❷❸
23 Conduit St   7493 7050   3–2C
"Authentic and fresh" Italian fare has made this yearling, off Bond
Street "a useful addition to the West End"; despite the odd let-
down, it usually delivers "excellent value in a pricey area".
/ www.viacondotti.co.uk; 11 pm; closed Sun.

Vic Naylors EC1 £41 ④❸❸
38 & 42 St John St   7608 2181   9–1B
"For dinner after work, and a few beers", this "cosy" Smithfield
hang-out can make a "very useful" option. / www.vicnaylor.com;
12.30 am; closed Sat L & Sun.

Il Vicolo SW1 £41 ❸❸⑤
3-4 Crown Passage   7839 3960   3–4D
"In the expense-account world of St James's", this "cramped" and
hidden-away old-timer is quite a "find" – its Sardinian cooking
offers "excellent value" (for this bit of town anyway). / 10 pm; closed
Sat & Sun.

The Victoria SW14 £41 ❸❸❸
10 West Temple   8876 4238   10–2A
"Great after a walk in Richmond Park"; this "obscurely-located"
Sheen gastropub offers a good "all-round" package, including
"consistent" food, "welcoming" service and an "attractive"
conservatory. / www.thevictoria.net; 10 pm.

Viet W1 £18 ❷⑤⑤
34 Greek St   7494 9888   4–3A
"A funny little place serving great pho" (pron. 'feu', noodles) –
this "fantastic" café delivers "punchy" Vietnamese flavours,
and BYO adds to the "amazing value for money". / 11 pm; no Amex.

Viet Garden N1 £25 ❸❸④
207 Liverpool Rd   7700 6040   8–2D
A "busy" Islington Vietnamese local, where the staff are "smiley",
and the cooking "tasty" and "fresh-tasting". / www.vietgarden.co.uk;
11 pm; no Amex.

Viet Hoa E2 £24 ❸④④
70-72 Kingsland Rd   7729 8293   1–2D
"It's losing ground in comparison to Sông Quê", but this bare café –
"the original Shoreditch Vietnamese" – is still a "friendly" place,
offering "good, cheap food"; BYO. / www.viethoarestaurant.co.uk;
11.30 pm.

Viet-Anh NW1 £19 ❸❶④
41 Parkway   7284 4082   8–3B
"Fresh and tasty food, friendly and efficient service and great value"
– that's the deal at this ever-popular Vietnamese café, in Camden
Town. / 11 pm; no Amex.

Vijay NW6 £28 ❷❷④
49 Willesden Ln 7328 1087 1–1B
*This "always-busy" Kilburn veteran offers a "consistently high
standard" of cooking – with "superb South Indian specialities" –
at "unbeatable-value" prices; you can BYO at modest corkage.
/ www.vijayindia.com; 10.45 pm, Fri-Sat 11.30 pm.*

Vijaya Krishna SW17 £19 ❷❷④
114 Mitcham Rd 9767 7688 10–2C
*"Light" and "delicious" Keralan food wins fans for this "reliable"
and "extremely good-value" Tooting south Indian. / 11 pm, Fri & Sat
midnight.*

Villa Bianca NW3 £50 ④❸❸
1 Perrins Ct 7435 3131 8–2A
*"In a very pretty cobbled lane, off the High Street", this long-
established Hampstead Italian is a cute-looking destination;
the menu, though, "doesn't seem to have changed since 1970".
/ www.villabiancanw3.com; 11.30 pm.*

Village East SE1 £40 ❸❷❷
171-173 Bermondsey St 7357 6082 9–4D
*"A stylish interpretation of the warehouse vernacular" has helped
this "bright" and "buzzy" yearling pull in a "trendy" Bermondsey
following; it generally serves "good food at reasonable prices" too.
/ www.villageeast.co.uk; 10.30 pm.*

Villandry W1 £42 ❸④❷
170 Gt Portland St 7631 3131 2–1B
*"The recent refurb was very welcome"; under the management
of the Hush team, this Marylebone deli-annexe is an "infinitely
better" destination (especially for breakfast, or "informal business");
service still has its blips, though, and the suitably "seasonal" menu
can still seem "overpriced". / www.villandry.com; 10.30 pm; closed Sun D;
booking: max 12.*

Vincent Rooms
Westminster Kingsway College SW1 £25 ❸④❸
Vincent Sq 7802 8391 2–4C
*"It's sometimes excellent, sometimes not so good", being a guinea
pig in the "pleasant" dining room of this Westminster chefs'
training school – either way, "at the prices, you don't complain".
/ www.westking.ac.uk; 7.15 pm; times vary; only term times; closed Mon D,
Wed D, Fri D, Sat & Sun; no Amex.*

The Vine NW5 £36 ❸❸❸
86 Highgate Rd 7209 0038 8–1B
*A "lovely" Kentish Town gastropub with dependable cooking, and a
"cosy" interior for the winter – for the summer, there's
an "attractive covered area". / www.thevinelondon.co.uk; 10.30 pm.*

Vingt-Quatre SW10 £41 ④❸❸
325 Fulham Rd 7376 7224 5–3B
*"Comfort food to aid recovery" is served – "whatever the time
of day or night" – at this "well-run" pit stop, on the Chelsea
'Beach'. / www.vingtquatre.co.uk; open 24 hours; no booking.*

Vino Rosso W4 NEW £49 ❷❸④
9 Devonshire Rd 8994 5225 7–2A
*"A really good addition to the crowded Chiswick scene" – this new
Italian attracts much praise for its "proper" cooking, with "top-
quality ingredients, simply prepared". / www.vinorosso.co.uk; 10.30 pm,
Fri & Sat 11 pm, Sun 9.30 pm; no Amex; set weekday L £29 (FP).*

Vinoteca EC1 £33 ❸❷❶
7 St John St 7253 8786 9–1B
*"A stand-out new wine bar" – this "delightful" (if "cramped") and
"buzzy" Clerkenwell yearling offers "simple" bistro fare
to complement a "massive" and "sensibly-priced" list; staff
"ooze enthusiasm" too.* / www.vinoteca.co.uk; 10 pm; closed Sun; no Amex.

Vivat Bacchus EC4 £43 ❸❶❸
47 Farringdon St 7353 2648 9–2A
*"An enormous glass-sided wine cellar" (where a "great South
African selection" is the highlight) dominates this "wonderful" City-
fringe basement spot, which also boasts a walk-in cheese room;
it pleases generally, but its best point is its "outstanding" service.*
/ www.vivatbacchus.co.uk; 9.30 pm; closed Sat & Sun; set weekday L £26 (FP).

Vivezza SW1 NEW £45 ❹❷❹
101 Pimlico Rd 7730 0202 5–2D
*A few months after opening, this Pimlico Italian dropped its pizzeria
menu, in preference for a more formal approach – not, in our view,
an improvement, and this remains a surprisingly lacklustre spin-off
from nearby Caraffini.* / Rated on Editors' visit; www.viveeza.co.uk; 11 pm.

Volt SW1 £40 ❸❸❸
17 Hobart Pl 7235 9696 2–4B
*Not far from Victoria, quite a glamorous, night-club-style hang-out
with better food (Italian) than you might expect; "it's possibly
best in a group".* / www.voltlounge.com; 11.15 pm; closed Sat L & Sun;
set always available £21 (FP).

Vrisaki N22 £29 ❷❷❸
73 Myddleton Rd 8889 8760 1–1C
*"I still can't finish it all!"; the mezze "just keep coming", at this
"fun" Bounds Green Greek veteran, where "a humble kebab shop
leads on to a cavernous dining room".* / midnight; closed Sun D.

Wagamama £23 ❹❸❹
8 Norris St, SW1 7321 2755 4–4A
Harvey Nichols, Knightsbridge, SW1 7201 8000 5–1D
101a Wigmore St, W1 7409 0111 3–1A
10a Lexington St, W1 7292 0990 3–2D
4a Streatham St, WC1 7323 9223 2–1C
1 Tavistock St, WC2 7836 3330 4–3D
14a Irving St, WC2 7839 2323 4–4B
26a Kensington High St, W8 7376 1717 5–1A
N1 Centre, 37 Parkfield St, N1 7226 2664 8–3D
11 Jamestown Rd, NW1 7428 0800 8–3B
Royal Festival Hall, Southbank Centre, SE1 7021 0877 2–3D
50-54 Putney High St, SW15 8785 3636 10–2B
46-48 Wimbledon Hill Rd, SW19 8879 7280 10–2B
Jubilee Place, 45 Bank St, E14 7516 9009 11–1C
1a Ropemaker St, EC2 7588 2688 9–1C
22 Old Broad St, EC2 7256 9992 9–2C
Tower Pl, EC3 7283 5897 9–3D
109 Fleet St, EC4 7583 7889 9–2A
30 Queen St, EC4 7248 5766 9–3B
*"Brisk", "affordable" and "healthy" – these hard-edged noodle
canteens still win high acclaim as handy pit stops (and child-friendly
ones too); the food has "gone the way of most chains", though,
and now risks becoming "formulaic" and "bland".*
/ www.wagamama.com; 10 pm-11 pm; EC4 & EC2 closed Sat & Sun;
no booking.

Wahaca WC2 NEW £26 ❸❷❷
66 Chandos Pl 7240 1883 4–4C
Mexican 'street food' is the theme of this new Covent Garden spot, which opened in a bright Covent Garden basement just as this guide was going to press; the food on our early-days visit was nothing remarkable, but we thought the place has all the makings of a really useful central rendezvous. / Rated on Editors' visit; www.wahaca.com; 11 pm; need 8+ to book.

Wakaba NW3 £45 ❸④⑤
122a Finchley Rd 7586 7960 8–2A
Mr Wakaba's ultra-stark survivor, opposite Finchley Road tube, has long been known for its quality Japanese fare – this year's feedback, however, was limited and rather mixed. / 11 pm; closed Sun.

The Wallace
The Wallace Collection W1 NEW £45 ❸④❶
Hertford Hs, Manchester Sq 7563 9505 3–1A
The "extraordinary" and "magical" atrium of this Marylebone palazzo has taken a huge step-up from its former incarnation (as Café Bagatelle, RIP), and it now serves some "delicious" Gallic dishes; it is a bit "pricey", though, and service can be iffy. / www.thewallacerestaurant.com; Fri & Sat 9 pm; Sun-Thu closed D.

The Walmer Castle W11 £32 ❸④❷
58 Ledbury Rd 7229 4620 6–1B
The "atmospheric" first-floor dining room of this Notting Hill pub remains "popular with the local twenty/thirty-somethings", attracted by its "solid" Thai cooking. / 10.30 pm; D only, ex Fri & Sat open L & D.

Walnut NW6 £31 ④④❸
280 West End Ln 7794 7772 1–1B
A well-established West Hampstead "local favourite"; it's often praised for its "helpful" staff and for food that's "a cut above", but there were also a couple of "really disappointing" reports this year. / www.walnutwalnut.com; 11 pm; closed Mon, Tue-Sun D only; no Amex.

Wapping Food E1 £47 ❸❸❶
Wapping Power Station, Wapping Wall 7680 2080 11–1A
"What a space!" – "a cavernous old hydraulic pumping station, complete with old machinery, and art shows" provides the "über-cool" setting for this "terrific" Docklands venture; the food's pretty good too, as is the "totally Aussie" wine list. / www.thewappingproject.com; 10.30 pm; closed Sun D.

The Warrington W9 NEW £37
93 Warrington Cr awaiting tel 8–4A
In late-2007, as 'brand Gordon' spreads ever further (and thinner), this vast Victorian tavern will re-open as the second member of Ramsay's expanding pub portfolio; (Dang from Ben's Thai – the former occupant of the site – is now down the road above The Robert Browning, 15 Clifton Road, tel 7266 3134).

The Waterway W9 £41 ❸④❷
54 Formosa St 7266 3557 8–4A
On a hot day, "getting a seat is worse than on a Ryanair flight", at this "lively" Little Venice spot, which has a "lovely" canal-side location; "you have to speak up to get any service", but the food is "good" when it arrives. / www.thewaterway.co.uk; 10.30 pm; booking: max 12.

The Well EC1 £38 ❸④❸
180 St John St 7251 9363 9–1A
*A popular Clerkenwell local: "it looks like a typical gastropub,
but the food is just a little better". / www.downthewell.com; 10.30 pm.*

The Wells NW3 £44 ❸❸❶
30 Well Walk 7794 3785 8–1A
*"A wonderful location" ("especially on the terrace in summer")
lends a "lovely" ambience to this gastropub near Hampstead
Heath; the odd reporter finds the cooking "mixed", but most say
it's "consistently good". / www.thewellshampstead.co.uk; 10.30 pm;
no Amex; booking: max 8.*

Weng Wah House NW3 £33 ④④④
240 Haverstock Hill 7794 5123 8–2A
*A "local Chinese" that remains popular with Belsize Park folk;
it's rather "dated", though, and the food "used to be great, but isn't
any more". / www.wengwahgroup.com; 11.30 pm, Sat midnight, Sun 11 pm.*

The Westbourne W2 £35 ❸④❶
101 Westbourne Park Villas 7221 1332 6–1B
*"Beautiful people" help "inject buzz" into this "bustling" Bayswater
"hotspot"; when the "aloof" staff do eventually bring the food,
it's often "unexpectedly good". / www.thewestbourne.com; 10.45 pm;
closed Mon L; no Amex; need 4+ to book.*

Wet Fish Cafe NW6 £38 ❸④❷
242 West End Ln 7443 9222 1–1B
*A West Hampstead café with quite a local following, thanks to its
"lovely" atmosphere and "carefully-prepared" (and not notably
fishy) fare; service, though, can "let it down".
/ www.thewetfishcafe.co.uk; 11 pm; closed Mon; no Amex.*

The Wharf TW11 £42 ④④❶
22 Manor Rd 8977 6333 1–4A
*"A fantastic setting overlooking the Thames" (with a big terrace)
is the star attraction at this modern bar/brasserie near Teddington
Lock; "if only the food was better…" / www.walk-on-water.co.uk; 10 pm;
closed Mon.*

White Horse SW6 £34 ❸❸❷
1-3 Parsons Grn 7736 2115 10–1B
*It has no 'gastro-' reputation, but Fulham's 'Sloaney Pony' delivers
a good all-round package of "wholesome food" – including popular
summer BBQs – "quality" beers (and wines) and a "lively"
atmosphere. / www.whitehorsesw6.com; 10.30 pm.*

The White Swan EC4 £40 ❸❸④
108 Fetter Ln 7242 9696 9–2A
*On the upper floor of a Holborn pub, a small dining room that's
made a name for its "surprisingly good" food; this year, however,
it seemed more "average" and "expensive" than previously.
/ www.thewhiteswanlondon.com; 10 pm; closed Sat & Sun.*

Whits W8 £44 ❷❶❸
21 Abingdon Rd 7938 1122 5–1A
*"Extremely helpful" service helps create a "cosy" atmosphere
at this Kensington bar/bistro, which serves "thoughtful" dishes
at "good-value" prices. / www.whits.co.uk; 10.30 pm; closed Mon,
Sat L & Sun.*

Wild Honey W1 NEW £44 ❸❷❷
12 St George St   7758 9160   3–2C
The summer-2007 offshoot of Arbutus offers essentially the same foodie-pleasing formula of well-priced cuisine, and interesting wines by the carafe, but in the more elegant surroundings of a panelled Mayfair dining room; on an early-days visit, the cooking was rather inconsistent. / Rated on Editors' visit; www.wildhoneyrestaurant.co.uk; 10.30 pm; set weekday L £28 (FP).

William IV NW10 £28 ❹❸❸
786 Harrow Rd   8969 5944   1–2B
For "great tapas in a culinary dessert", it's well worth knowing about this otherwise "typical" (and "loud") Kensal Green gastropub; it has a very pleasant courtyard garden. / www.williamivlondon.com; 10.30 pm, Thu-Sat 11 pm, Sun 9 pm.

Willie Gunn SW18 £38 ❹❹❹
422 Garratt Ln   8946 7773   10–2B
"It used to be a favourite local", but this "airy" Earlsfield spot has "gone downhill" in recent years; for brunch, though, it can still be "great". / 11 pm.

Wiltons SW1 £83 ❸❷❷
55 Jermyn St   7629 9955   3–3C
Traditionalists say "it doesn't get any better" than this "plush", "stuffy", and "very-old fashioned" St James's bastion, where the speciality is "splendid" seafood (and game); whether it's "reassuringly expensive", or just "hideously overpriced", remains a matter for debate. / www.wiltons.co.uk; 10.30 pm; closed Sat & Sun; jacket required.

The Windmill W1 £34 ❸❸❸
6-8 Mill St   7491 8050   3–2C
"Terrific pies", "doorstep sandwiches" and other "real pub food" makes it worth knowing about this traditional boozer, in the "heart of Mayfair". / www.windmillmayfair.co.uk; 9.30 pm; closed Sat D & Sun.

The Windsor Castle W8 £29 ❹❸❶
114 Campden Hill Rd   7243 9551   6–2B
This Notting Hill Gate "classic" – an 18th century coaching inn – feels just "like a country pub" (and comes complete with a lovely walled garden); it serves "traditional" pub food that's on the "good" side of "average". / 10 pm; no booking.

Wine Factory W11 £33 ❹❷❷
294 Westbourne Grove   7229 1877   6–1B
"Surprisingly good wine at fantastic prices" – as at all John Brinkley's joints, that's the lifeblood of this "cheap and cheerful" Notting Hill pizza joint. / www.brinkleys.com; 11 pm.

Wine Gallery SW10 £35 ❹❸❷
49 Hollywood Rd   7352 7572   5–3B
"A very good-value wine list" and a "super garden" are key selling points of John Brinkley's "cheap and cheerful" Chelsea perennial; it's "always busy". / www.brinkleys.com; 11 pm; booking: max 12.

The Wine Library EC3 £26 ⑤❸❷
43 Trinity Sq 7481 0415 9–3D
*"Don't eat, just drink!" – it's the "amazing wine selection"
("at prices a normal person can afford") which makes these
ancient City cellars of note; soak up your choice with its cheese and
pâté buffet. / www.winelibrary.co.uk; 8 pm, Mon 6 pm; L & early evening
only, closed Sat & Sun.*

Wódka W8 £42 ❸❸❷
12 St Alban's Grove 7937 6513 5–1B
*"An unsurpassed selection of vodkas" is soaked up by "hearty" and
"honest" Polish fare at this "boisterous" Kensington backwater spot;
this year's reports, however, were rather up-and-down.
/ www.wodka.co.uk; 11.15 pm; closed Sat L & Sun L.*

Wolfe's WC2 £35 ④⑤⑤
30 Gt Queen St 7831 4442 4–1D
*"Very '70s" (and "not in an ironic way"), this upmarket American
diner in Covent Garden inspires ever more mixed feedback; fans say
it's "pricey but good", whereas critics say the service is "dreadful"
and the food "rubbish". / www.wolfes-grill.net; 11 pm, Sun 9 pm.*

THE WOLSELEY W1 £52 ❸❷❷
160 Piccadilly 7499 6996 3–3C
*"The real joy is the room, and feeling part of it", at Messrs Corbin
and King's "loud" and "vibrant" grand-brasserie, by the Ritz –
an all-purpose favourite for many reporters (and now the survey's
No. 1 tip for a business meeting); leaving aside the "perfect tea
and breakfast", though, the food is often rather "ordinary".
/ www.thewolseley.com; midnight.*

Wong Kei W1 £22 ❸⑤④
41-43 Wardour St 7437 8408 4–3A
*For "quick, cheap, tasty" chow, this huge and "bustling" Chinatown
"legend" is "always a winner"; staff – although "a lot more polite
than they used to be!" – are still "so brusque it's entertaining".
/ 11 pm; no credit cards; no booking.*

Wood Street EC2 NEW £36 ④❸⑤
cnr of Fore St and Wood St 7256 6990 9–2B
*"A welcome opening in the Barbican Centre" – this new
bar/restaurant offers "a good selection of dishes" (and makes quite
an effort on its wine); despite some unexpected views of the 'lake',
though, "the ambience isn't all it might be". / www.woodstreetbar.com;
10 pm, Sun 5.30 pm; closed Sat & Sun D; no Amex.*

Woodlands £29 ❷❷④
37 Panton St, SW1 7839 7258 4–4A
77 Marylebone Ln, W1 7486 3862 2–1A
12-14 Chiswick High Rd, W4 8994 9333 7–2B
102 Heath St, NW3 7794 3080 8–1A
*"Light" and "tasty" south Indian food "at fair prices" still carves
a solid niche for this long-established, veggie chain; despite the
"superb" service, though, pizzazz is in short supply.
/ www.woodlandsrestaurant.co.uk; 10.45 pm; W4 Mon-Thu D only.*

Wright Brothers SE1 £37 ❷❷❷
11 Stoney St 7403 9554 9–4C
*"Brilliant" oysters are the highlight of the "very good" fish-and-
seafood menu at this "tremendously buzzy" Borough Market
yearling – the sort of place where "everyone appears to enjoy
themselves". / www.wrightbros.eu.com; 10.30 pm; closed Sun.*

XO NW3 £40 ④④❸
29 Belsize Ln   7433 0888   8–2A
Will Ricker's "hotly-anticipated" newcomer (on the site of The Belsize, RIP) has so far been a major (surprise) "disappointment"; it does have its fans, but there are far too many reports of "hit-and-miss" service and "badly-executed" pan-Asian fare.
/ www.rickersrestaurants.com; 11 pm.

Yakitoria W2 £48 ❸❷❷
25 Sheldon Sq   3214 3000   6–1C
An obscure location – "hidden in the depths of the Paddington Basin" – means this "beautifully designed" and "funky" oriental is too often a bit "empty"; fans say it's "just as good as Nobu and Zuma" – others that it can be "hit-and-miss". / www.yakitoria.co.uk; 11 pm; closed Sat D & Sun.

Yas W14 £30 ④⑤⑤
7 Hammersmith Rd   7603 9148   7–1D
A rather "shabby" Persian restaurant, opposite Olympia, that's only of interest for its late-late opening; "the staff specialise in being a bit grumpy, but the convenience makes up for it". / 5 am.

YAUATCHA W1 £50 ❶❸❷
Broadwick Hs, 15-17 Broadwick St   7494 8888   3–2D
"Unbeatable dim sum" – "like little parcels of joy" – and an "exciting" vibe have made a huge hit of Alan Yau's "groovy" Soho oriental; pity about the "rigid" 90-minute dining-slots, though, and the "unpredictable" service; NB as well as the "stylish" basement, there's an "elegant" upstairs section that also does tea and "funky cakes". / 11.30 pm.

Yelo £24 ❸❷④
136a Lancaster Rd, W11   7243 2220   6–1A
8-9 Hoxton Sq, N1   7729 4626   9–1D
"Everyone should have a Thai local" like these "cheap and cheerful" eat-in/take-aways (in Hoxton and near Ladbroke Grove tube); their scoff is "fresh, tasty and generous". / www.yelothai.com; N1 11 pm, W1 10.30 pm; no booking.

Yi-Ban £31 ❷❷❷
Imperial Wharf, Imperial Rd, SW6   7731 6606   5–4B
Regatta Centre, Dockside Rd, E16   7473 6699   11–1D
"Planes taking off from City Airport" add interest to the "great views" from this distant-Docklands waterside spot, and its Chinese fare (especially dim sum) is "surprisingly good" too; the Fulham branch attracts practically no feedback. / www.yi-ban.co.uk; 10.45 pm; SW6 closed Sun.

Yming W1 £33 ❷❶❸
35-36 Greek St   7734 2721   4–2A
"Un-typically good service" underpins the vast popularity of Christine Lau's "elegant" Soho Chinese, where the "interesting" cooking is sometimes tipped as "London's finest"; this year's reports, however, were a bit more up-and-down than usual. / www.yminglondon.com; 11.45 pm; closed Sun.

Yo! Sushi £28 ⑤⑤④
Branches throughout London
Standards "have really slipped" at this "once funky and futuristic" – but now "tired" – conveyor-sushi chain, where "dispiritingly bland" food is part of the "production-line" experience. / www.yosushi.co.uk; 10 pm-11 pm; no booking.

Yoshino W1 £38 ❷❷④
3 Piccadilly Pl 7287 6622 3–3D
*"A best-kept secret, just off Piccadilly"; this "packed" and
"authentic" Japanese pit stop offers "superb sushi" ("some of the
best in town") to a largely expatriate clientele. / www.yoshino.net;
10 pm; closed Sun.*

Yum Yum N16 £29 ❷❷❶
183-187 Stoke Newington High St 7254 6751 1–1D
*This "Stokey institution" moved a year ago to these new "mega-
sized" premises; inevitably, some old-timers "preferred it when
it was smaller" (and less "noisy"), but the general view is that the
new look is "amazing", that service is "intelligent" and that the
Thai food is "really lovely and fresh". / www.yumyum.co.uk; 11.30 pm;
set weekday L £19 (FP).*

Yumenoki SW10 NEW £40 ❸❷④
204 Fulham Rd 7351 2777 5–3B
*"Fresh, varied and authentically Japanese" scoff and "lovely" staff
have helped this Fulham newcomer quickly gather a "faithful
clientele of hungry locals". / www.yumenoki.co.uk; 10.30 pm; set always
available £25 (FP).*

Yuzu NW6 £34 ❸④❸
102 Fortune Green Rd 7431 6602 1–1B
*Service can be "a bit stretched" or "surly", but "the food
is consistently good" – with "really fresh" sushi the highlight –
at this "tiny" but "buzzy" West Hampstead Japanese.
/ www.yuzurestaurants.com; 10.30 pm; D only, closed Mon.*

ZAFFERANO SW1 £56 ❷❷❸
15 Lowndes St 7235 5800 5–1D
*Still often hailed as "the best Italian in London", this Belgravia
stalwart has become "a bit glitzier" (and less "crowded") since its
enlargement a couple of years ago; it can still seem "remarkably
unpretentious, given the sophistication of the food".
/ www.zafferanorestaurant.com; 11 pm.*

Zaffrani N1 NEW £32 ❷❷❷
47 Cross St 7226 5522 8–3D
*"A great new local Indian"; Islington reporters are very enthusiastic
about the "delicious" cuisine and "friendly" service offered by this
"excellent" contemporary-style spot. / 11 pm.*

Zaika W8 £50 ❷❸❸
1 Kensington High St 7795 6533 5–1A
*Thanks to Sanjay Dwivedi's "amazing" and "refined" cuisine, this is
still one of London's top "innovative" Indians; the ex-banking hall
setting (opposite Kensington Gardens) can sometimes seem a touch
"austere", but most reporters say it's "lovely".
/ www.zaika-restaurant.co.uk; 10.45 pm; closed Sat L.*

Zakudia SE1 £27 ④④❷
2a Southwark Bridge Rd 7021 0085 9–3B
*"You get standard bar food, but great cocktails and fabulous river-
views", at this useful South Bank bar, near Shakespeare's Globe.
/ www.zakudia.com; 11.30 pm.*

Zamzama NW1 £26 ❸④❸
161-163 Drummond St 7387 6699 8–4C
*This high-tech Little India curry house serves some "decent" dishes;
the "constant stream of Bollywood", though, "can be distracting".
/ www.zamzama.co.uk; 11.30 pm; closed Sat L & Sun.*

Zaytouna W1 NEW £34 ④④❸
45 Frith St 7494 9008 4–2A
Just off Soho's main drag, a "convenient" and quite inexpensive new townhouse-Moroccan; it hasn't attracted much feedback, but we agree with the reporter who found it "good, if slightly flat".
/ www.zaytouna.co.uk; 1 am, Sun midnight.

Zen Central W1 £43 ❷❸④
20-22 Queen St 7629 8089 3–3B
Presumably it's the "sterile" – '80s-period-piece – décor which discourages a wider following for this "polite" Mayfair Chinese; on most – if not quite all – reports, the food is "consistently good".
/ www.zencentralrestaurant.com; 11.15 pm.

ZeNW3 NW3 £37 ❸❸❸
83 Hampstead High St 7794 7863 8–2A
Considering it's a striking glazed-fronted venture in the heart of Hampstead, this long-established Chinese attracts astonishingly few reports; as ever, their theme is that it's "good" but a bit "pricey". / www.zenw3.com; 10.45 pm; no Amex.

Zero Degrees SE3 £27 ❸④❸
29-31 Montpelier Vale 8852 5619 1–4D
"Very industrial" and "hangar"-like, this Blackheath bar/microbrewery has a good "buzz", and offers "good pizza" and "great moules frites" (plus a variety of "decent home brews").
/ www.zerodegrees.co.uk; 11.30 pm.

Zero Quattro SW19 £44 ❸❸❸
28 Ridgway 8946 4840 10–2B
This "buzzy" year-old Italian has been "a great addition to Wimbledon Village", offering "good food and good fun".
/ www.zeroquattro.co.uk; midnight, Sun 11 pm.

The Zetter EC1 £43 ④④❸
St John's Sq, 86-88 Clerkenwell Rd 7324 4455 9–1A
This "light" boutique hotel dining room is "a great space" from which you can "watch the (Farringdon) world go by"; the food, though, can sometimes be "staggeringly poor". / www.thezetter.com; 11 pm, Sun-Wed, 10.30 pm.

Ziani SW3 £42 ❸❷❷
45-47 Radnor Walk 7352 2698 5–3C
"Everyone knows everyone else" at this "classic" Chelsea backstreet Italian; there may be a singular "lack of elbow room", but the "humorous" staff help ensure it's "always fun".
/ www.ziani.uk.com; 10.30 pm.

Zilli Fish W1 £58 ❷❸❸
36-40 Brewer St 7734 8649 3–2D
"Excellent-quality fish" is the main point of the menu at Aldo Zilli's "happy", "buzzy" and "tightly-packed" Soho corner-site; it's also "a good spot for people-watching on a sunny day". / www.zillialdo.com; 11.30 pm; closed Sun.

Zizzi £29 ④④④
Branches throughout London
Fans still find this once-promising pizza 'n' pasta chain a "reliable" option, especially with families in tow; overall, though, it seems ever-more "formulaic", and survey ratings slumped this year.
/ www.askcentral.co.uk; 11 pm; some booking restrictions apply.

Zuccato £30 ④❸④
02 Centre, 255 Finchley Rd, NW3 7431 1799 8–2A
41 Bow Ln, EC4 7329 6364 9–2C
*This oddly diverse pizzeria-duo – in the City and Finchley – still
make handy stand-bys; they're "a bit more individual than the big
chains, but no more expensive". / www.etruscarstaurants.com;
NW3 11.30 pm, EC4 10 pm; EC4 closed Sat & Sun.*

ZUMA SW7 £60 ❶❸❶
5 Raphael St 7584 1010 5–1C
*"Just a damn sexy experience, every time"; this über-"happening"
Knightsbridge oriental – complete with "Eurotrashy" bar –
has "taken over from Nobu" as London's top fusion-Japanese;
needless to say it's "mightily expensive", and the service can
sometimes be "abrasive". / www.zumarestaurant.com; 10.45 pm; booking:
max 8.*

INDEXES

BREAKFAST
(with opening times)

Central

Acorn House (6)
Amato (8, Sun 10)
Apostrophe: *Barrett St W1, Tott' Ct Rd W1, WC2 (7)*
Asia de Cuba (7)
Atrium (8)
Aubaine: *W1 (8, Sat 10)*
Automat (7)
Baker & Spice: *SW1 (7)*
Balans: *all branches (8)*
Bar Italia (7)
Benugo: *all central branches (7.30)*
Bistro 1: *Beak St W1 (Sun 11)*
Brasserie Roux (6.30, Sat & Sun 7)
Brian Turner (*Mon - Fri 6.30, Sat & Sun 7*)
Brown's Grill (7)
Brumus (7)
Café Bohème (8)
Café in the Crypt (Mon-Sat 8)
Caffè Vergnano: *WC2 (8, Sun 11)*
Caramel (7)
Cecconi's (7)
The Chelsea Brasserie (7)
Chez Gérard: *Chancery Ln WC2 (8)*
Christopher's (*Sat & Sun 11.30*)
The Cinnamon Club (Mon-Fri 7.30)
City Café (6.30, Sat & Sun 7)
The Club Bar & Dining (10.30)
Connaught (7)
The Contented Vine (*Sat & Sun 10*)
Crussh: *W1 (7)*
Daylesford Organics (8, Sun 11)
Diner: *all branches (8, Sat & Sun 9)*
Dorchester Grill (7, Sat & Sun 8)
Eagle Bar Diner (Sat 10, Sun 11)
Eat & Two Veg (9, Sun 10)
The Fifth Floor Café (*Mon-Sat 8, Sun 11*)
5 Cavendish Square (8)
Flat White (8, Sun 10)
Fortnum's, The Fountain (8.30)
Franco's (Mon-Fri 7, Sat 7.30)
La Fromagerie Café (*Mon 10.30, Tue-Fri 8, Sat 9, Sun 10*)
Fuzzy's Grub: *all branches (7)*
Galvin at Windows (7)
Giraffe: *all branches (7.45, Sat & Sun 9)*
The Goring Hotel (7)
Homage (9)
Hush (Mon-Fri 7.30)
Indigo (6.30)
Inn the Park (8)
Jaan (6.30, Sat 7)
Joe Allen (8)
Konditor & Cook: *WC1 (9.30); W1 (9.30, Sun 10.30)*
Ladurée: *W1 (9); SW1 (Mon - Sat 9)*
The Lanesborough (Conservatory) (7)

Langtry's (7)
Leon: *WC2 (7.30, Sat 9, Sun 10); Gt Marlborough St W1 (9.30, Sat & Sun 10.30)*
Living Room: *W1 (Mon-Sat 10)*
Loch Fyne: *all branches (9)*
Luciano (8.15)
Maison Bertaux (8.30, Sun 9)
Maroush: *Vere St W1 (8)*
Maxwell's (*Sat & Sun 9.30*)
Mju (7)
Monmouth Coffee Company: *WC2 (10)*
The National Dining Rooms (10)
National Gallery Café (10)
Nicole's (10)
Nordic Bakery (*Mon - Fri 10*)
Oriel (8.30, Sun 9)
Oscar (7, Sat & Sun 8)
Le Pain Quotidien: *Marylebone High St W1 (7, Sat & Sun 8); Great Marlborough St, Turner Building W1 (8, Sat & Sun 9)*
Pâtisserie Valerie: *all in W1: (7.30); Motcomb St SW1 (8); Hans Cr SW1 (8-8.30)*
Paul: *WC2 (7.30); W1 (7.30, Sat & Sun 8)*
Pearl (6.30)
The Portrait (10)
The Providores (9, Sat & Sun 10)
Providores (Tapa Room) (9, Sat & Sun 10)
Pure California (8)
Ranoush: *all branches (9)*
Refuel (7, Sun 8)
Rhodes W1 Brasserie (6.30, Sat & Sun 7)
Rib Room (7, Sun 8)
RIBA Café (8)
Richoux: *all central branches (7.30)*
The Ritz (7, Sun 8)
Royal Academy (10)
Salade: *all branches (7.30)*
Serafino (7)
Simpsons-in-the-Strand (*Mon-Fri 7.30*)
06 St Chad's Place (8)
Sketch (Parlour) (*Mon-Fri 8, Sat 10*)
Sotheby's Café (9.30)
Star Café (7)
Stock Pot: *SW1 (7); W1 (9)*
Tate Britain (10)
The Terrace (8)
Tootsies: *W1 (Sat & Sun 11)*
Truc Vert (7.30, Sun 9.00)
Tuttons (9.30)
The Union Café (Sun 11)
Villandry (Mon-Fri 8)
The Wallace (10)
The Wolseley (7, Sat & Sun 9)

West

Adams Café (7.30, Sat 8.30)
Annie's: *all branches (Tue-Sun 10)*
Aquasia (7)

213

Boiled Egg *(9)*
Le Bouchon Bordelais *(10)*
Brula *(9)*
Canteen: *all branches (8, Sat & Sun 9)*
Le Chardon *(Sat & Sun 9.30)*
The Duke's Head *(10 ex sun)*
Eco Brixton: *SW9 (8.30)*
Ferrari's *(10)*
Fuego Pizzeria *(9)*
Garrison *(8, Sat & Sun 9)*
Gastro *(8)*
Gazette *(8)*
Giraffe: *all branches (7.45, Sat & Sun 9)*
Green & Blue *(9, Sun 11)*
Hudson's *(10)*
The Inn at Kew Gardens *(7)*
Joanna's *(10)*
Loch Fyne: *all branches (9)*
Lola Rojo *(Sat & Sun 11)*
Monmouth Coffee
   Company: *SE1 (7.30)*
Le Pain Quotidien: *SE1 (8, Sun 9)*
Putney Station *(Sat & Sun 11)*
Rapscallion *(10.30)*
Raviolo *(8.30)*
El Rincón Latino *(Sat & Sun 11)*
The Rivington Grill *(8)*
Roast *(7)*
Scoffers *(10)*
The Table *(8, Sat 9, Sun 10)*
Tapas Brindisa *(Fri & Sat 9)*
Tate Restaurant *(10)*
Tate Café *(10)*
Tootsies: *SW19 (9); SW15, SW4 (Sat & Sun 10); SW11 (Sat & Sun 9.30)*
Trinity Stores *(8, Sat 9.30, Sun 10)*
El Vergel *(8.30)*
The Victoria *(7)*

East

Addendum *(Brasserie 7)*
Ambassador *(8.30, Sat & Sun 11)*
Apostrophe: *all east branches (7)*
Aurora *(7)*
Bar Capitale: *all branches (6)*
Benugo: *all east branches (7.30)*
Bleeding Heart *(7)*
Bonds *(7)*
Brick Lane Beigel Bake *(24 hrs)*
Canteen: *all branches (8, Sat & Sun 9)*
Chez Gérard: *EC2, EC4 (8)*
Club Mangia *(7)*
Cock Tavern *(6)*
Comptoir Gascon *(9)*
Coq d'Argent *(Mon-Fri 7.30)*
Crussh: *One Canada Sq E14, EC3 (7); Unit 21 Jubilee Pl E14, EC4 (7.30)*
Curve *(Mon 6.30)*
The Diner: *all branches (8, Sat & Sun 9)*
The Empress of India *(Mon-Fri 8, Sat & Sun 9)*
Flâneur *(8.30, Sat & Sun 10)*
Fuzzy's Grub: *all branches (7)*
Grazing *(7)*

The Gun *(Sat & Sun 10.30)*
Hadley House *(10)*
Hilliard *(8)*
The Hoxton Grille *(7)*
Leon: *EC4 (8); E1 (8, Sat 9, Sun 10)*
Lilly's *(Sat & Sun 11)*
Luc's Brasserie *(Mon - Fri 9.30)*
Malmaison Brasserie *(7, Sat & Sun 8)*
Ortega: *EC3 (8); EC1 (Mon - Fri 8)*
Paternoster Chop House *(Mon-Fri 10.30)*
Pâtisserie Valerie: *E1 (7.30)*
Paul: *EC4 (7)*
E Pellicci *(6.15)*
Perc%nto *(6.45)*
The Place Below *(7.30)*
Prism *(8)*
Quadrato *(6.30, Sat & Sun 8)*
The Rivington Grill *(8)*
The Royal Exchange *(8)*
S & M Café: *E1 (7.30, Sat & Sun 8.30)*
St Germain *(Sat & Sun 11)*
St John Bread & Wine *(9, Sat & Sun 10)*
Salade: *all branches (7.30)*
Scarlet Dot *(9)*
Shish: *all branches (Sat & Sun 10.30)*
Smiths (Ground Floor) *(7)*
Square Pie Company: *E14 (7)*
The Sterling *(7.30)*
Story Deli *(9)*
Terminus *(7, Sat & Sun 7.30)*
Wapping Food *(Sat & Sun 10)*
The Well *(Sat & Sun 10.30)*
The Zetter *(7, Sat & Sun 7.30)*
Zuccato: *EC4 (7.30)*

BRUNCH MENUS

Central

Amato
Aurora
Balans: *all branches*
Boisdale
Boulevard Bar & Dng Rm
Boxwood Café
Brasserie Roux
Le Caprice
Caramel
Cecconi's
Christopher's
City Café
Daylesford Organics
The Fifth Floor Café
La Fromagerie Café
Fuzzy's Grub: *SW1*
Galvin at Windows
Giraffe: *all branches*
Hush
Indigo
Inn the Park
The Ivy
Joe Allen
Ladurée: *SW1*

BUSINESS

BYO

*(Bring your own wine at no
or low – less than £3 – corkage.
Note for £5-£15 per bottle,
you can normally negotiate
to take your own wine to many,
if not most, places.)*

CHILDREN

*(h – high or special chairs
 m – children's menu
 p – children's portions
 e – weekend entertainments
 o – other facilities)*

ENTERTAINMENT
(Check times before you go)

Central

Cantina del Ponte
(live music, Thu)
Dish Dash: all branches
(belly dancing, first Wed of month)
Donna Margherita
(live music, weekly)
The Freemasons
(quiz night, Mon)
The Gowlett
(DJ, Sun)
Grafton House
(DJ, Fri & Sat)
The Hartley
(live music, Tue)
La Lanterna
(live music, Fri)
The Mansion
(live jazz, Sun)
Menier Chocolate Factory
(live jazz, third Thu of month)
Meson don Felipe
(guitarist, nightly)
Metro
(live jazz, 1st & 3rd Sunday of month)
Naked Turtle
(live jazz, Wed-Sat & Sun L)
Le Pont de la Tour
Bar & Grill
(pianist, nightly)
Rocket Riverside: SW15
(live music, Sun, Sept-June only)
La Rueda: SW4
(Spanish music & dancing, Fri & Sat; Sun L
live music)
Santa Maria del Sur
(live music, Mon)
The Ship
(live music, Sun, quiz Wed)
The Sun & Doves
(live music, Sun)
Tas: The Cut SE1, Borough High St SE1
(guitarist, nightly); Isabella St SE1
(live music, Mon-Sat)
Tas Pide
(guitarist, Mon-Sat)
Thai Square: SW15
(DJ, Fri & Sat)
Thailand
(karaoke, Thu-Sat)
Tree House
(live music, Tue)
The Wharf
(live music, first Thu of the month)
Zakudia
(DJ, Thu-Sat)

East
Aurora
(pianist, nightly)
The Bar & Grill
(live music, Thu & Fri)
Barcelona Tapas: EC4
(disco, Thu & Fri)
Bistrotheque

(transvestite show, varies; cabaret varies)
Café du Marché
(pianist & bass, nightly)
Cat & Mutton
(DJ, Sun)
(Ciro's) Pizza Pomodoro: EC2
(live music, Mon-Fri)
Club Mangia
(wine tasting once a month)
Coq d'Argent
(pianist, Sat; jazz, Fri & Sun L)
Cottons: EC1
(live music, Tue-Sun)
$
(DJ, Fri & Sat)
The Drunken Monkey
(DJ, Wed-Sun)
Elephant Royale
(live music, Thu-Sat)
Green & Red Bar & Cantina
(DJ, Thu-Sat)
Home
(DJ, Thu-Sat)
The Hoxton Grille
(DJ)
King Eddie's
(live music, Thu night)
LMNT
(opera, Sun)
Medcalf
(DJ, Fri)
1 Lombard Street
(jazz, Fri D)
Ortega: EC1
(live music Wed D L, DJ Fri D)
Pacific Oriental
(disco, Thu & Fri)
Le Rendezvous du Café
(jazz, nightly)
Shanghai
(karaoke, nightly)
Shish: EC1
(DJ, Thu & Fri)
Silks & Spice: EC4
(DJ, Thu & Fri)
Smiths (Ground Floor)
(DJ, Wed-Sat)
Smollensky's: E1
(live music, Sat)
Sri Nam
(disco, Fri)
Terminus
(live & unplugged, Sat-Sun brunch)
Thai Square City: EC3
(DJ, Fri)
Tokyo City
(karaoke, Thu & Fri)
The Well
(DJ, Fri)
Yi-Ban: E16
(live music, Fri & Sat)

LATE

(open till midnight or later as shown; may be earlier Sunday)

Central

Al Sultan
All Star Lanes: WC1 (Fri & Sat midnight)
Annex 3
Asia de Cuba (midnight, Thu-Sat 12.30 am)
Automat (1 am)
The Avenue
Balans: Old Compton St W1 (24 hours); Old Compton St W1 (5 am, Sun 1 am)
Bar Italia (open 24 hours, Sun 3 am)
Beiteddine
Bentley's
Bohème Kitchen
Boulevard
Boulevard Bar & Dng Rm
Browns: WC2
Café Bohème (2.45 am)
Café du Jardin
Café Lazeez (Fri & Sat 1.30 am)
Café Pacifico
Le Caprice
Cecconi's
China Tang
The Club Bar & Dining
Cyprus Mangal (Sun-Thu midnight, Fri & Sat 1 am)
Le Deuxième
Diner: W1 (12.30 am, Sun midnight)
Dover Street (2 am)
Eagle Bar Diner (Thu-Sat)
Ed's Easy Diner: both W1 (midnight, Fri & Sat 1 am)
Fakhreldine
Floridita (2 am)
The Forge
Gaby's
Gaucho Grill: W1
Golden Dragon
Goya: Lupus St SW1 (for tapas midnight)
Greig's
Hakkasan (midnight, ex Mon & Sun)
Harbour City (Fri & Sat midnight)
Hard Rock Café (12.30 am)
Ishtar
Itsu: all central branches (Fri & Sat midnight)
The Ivy
Joe Allen (12.45 am)
Just Oriental
Kazan
Kettners (midnight, Thu-Sat 1am)
Langan's Brasserie
Little Italy (4 am, Sun midnight)
Living Room: W1 (1 am)
Mamounia (12.30 am, Sun midnight)
Maroush: Vere St W1 (12.30 am)
Maxwell's
Melati, Gt Windmill St (Fri & Sat midnight)

Meza (1.30 am)
Moti Mahal
Mr Chow
Mr Kong (2.45 am, Sun 1.45 am)
New Mayflower (4 am)
Nobu Berkeley (1.30 am)
Noura: Jermyn St SW1, William St SW1; W1 (12.30 am); Hobart Pl SW1 (12.30am, Thu-Sat 1am)
Original Tajines
Orso
Ozer
Le Palais du Jardin
Papageno
Pappagallo
Paradiso Olivelli: all branches
ping pong: Gt Marlborough St W1, Paddington St W1
Pizza on the Park (Fri & Sat midnight)
Planet Hollywood (1 am)
Quaglino's (midnight, Fri & Sat 1 am)
Ranoush: SW1
Ronnie Scott's (3 am, Sun midnight)
La Rueda: all branches (Sat & Sun midnight)
Rules
St Alban
Sarastro
Satsuma (Fri & Sat midnight)
J Sheekey
Sitaaray (1 am)
Sketch (Gallery) (1 am)
Smollensky's: WC2 (Thu-Sat midnight 12.15 am)
Sofra: all branches
Soho Spice (midnight, Fri-Sat 1.30 am)
Souk
La Spiga (Wed-Sat midnight)
Stock Pot: W1
Sugar Reef (1 am)
Suka (12.30 am)
TGI Friday's: all central branches (Fri & Sat midnight)
Tokyo Diner
Trader Vics (12.30 am)
Volt
The Wolseley
Zaytouna (1 am)

West

Alounak: W14
Anarkali
Balans: W4, W8; SW5 (2 am)
Beirut Express: SW7; W2 (2 am)
Best Mangal
Big Easy (Fri & Sat 12.20 am)
Bistrot 190
Blue Elephant
Bowler Bar & Grill (midnight, Sat 1 am)
Brilliant (Fri & Sat midnight)
Bumpkin
Buona Sera: all branches
The Cabin

Cactus Blue
Chelsea Bun Diner
Cheyne Walk Bras'
Choys
(Ciro's) Pizza
  Pomodoro: *SW3 (1 am)*
Cochonnet *(pizza till midnight)*
Dish Dash: *all branches*
Duke on the Green
Green Chilli
The Grove
Halepi
Harlem *(2 am, Sun midnight)*
Henry J Beans
Kandoo
Khan's of Kensington *(Fri & Sat midnight)*
Khyber Pass
Lou Pescadou
Lowiczanka *(Sat 1 am)*
Maroush: *1) 21 Edgware Rd W2 (1.45 am); Edgware Rd W2 (12.30 am); SW3 (3.30 am)*
Miraggio
Mirch Masala: *UB1*
Mohsen
Montpeliano
Monty's
Mr Wing
Mulberry Street
Il Pagliaccio
Papillon
Pasha *(midnight, Thu-Sat 1 am)*
ping pong: *W2*
Randa
Ranoush: *SW3 ; W8 (1.30 am); W2 (2.30 am)*
Rossopomodoro: *all branches*
La Rueda: *all branches (Sat & Sun midnight)*
Saran Rom
Scalini
606 Club
Sticky Fingers
Sugar Hut
TGI Friday's: *all west branches (Fri & Sat midnight)*
Vingt-Quatre *(24 hours)*
Yas *(5 am)*

North

Ali Baba
Bacchus
Banners *(Fri midnight)*
Camino *(Thu-Sat 1 am)*
Emni *(Fri midnight)*
The Fox Reformed *(Sat & Sun midnight)*
Gallipoli: *all branches (Fri & Sat midnight)*
Gaucho Grill: *NW3*
Gem
Gilgamesh *(midnight, Fri & Sat 12.30 am)*
Izgara
Kovalam *(Fri & Sat midnight)*

Landmark (Winter Garden) *(1 am)*
The Living Room: *N1 (Thu midnight, Fri & Sat 2 am)*
Le Mercury *(1 am)*
Mestizo
La Piragua
La Porchetta Pizzeria: *all north branches*
Rodizio Rico: *N1*
Sofra: *all branches*
Solly's Exclusive *(Sat 1 am)*
Vrisaki
Weng Wah House *(Sat midnight)*

South

Bar Estrela
Bread & Roses *(Fri & Sat midnight)*
The Bridge
Buona Sera: *all branches*
The Dartmouth Arms *(12.30 am)*
Dish Dash: *all branches*
Everest Inn *(Fri & Sat midnight)*
Firezza: *SW11*
Fujiyama
Gastro
The Gowlett
Green & Blue *(Fri & Sat midnight)*
Hara The Circle Bar
Kennington Tandoori *(midnight, Fri & Sat 12.30 am)*
Metro *(midnight, Fri & Sat 2 am)*
Mirch Masala: *all south branches*
Nazmins Balti House
Paradiso Olivelli: *all branches*
La Rueda: *all branches (Sat & Sun midnight)*
Sree Krishna *(Fri & Sat midnight)*
Vijaya Krishna *(Fri & Sat midnight)*
Zero Degrees
Zero Quattro

East

Barcelona Tapas: *EC4 (2.30 am)*
Brick Lane Beigel Bake *(24 hours)*
Cellar Gascon
(Ciro's) Pizza Pomodoro: *EC2 (midnight)*
Clifton *(midnight, Sat & Sun 1am)*
The Diner: *EC2*
$
The Gaylord
Itsu: *Level 2, Cabot Place East E14 (Fri & Sat midnight)*
Lahore Kebab House
Mangal Ocakbasi
Ortega: *EC1 (Sat midnight)*
La Porchetta Pizzeria: *EC1*
Prima *(midnight, Thu & Fri 2 am)*
Sofra: *all branches*
Vic Naylors *(12.30 am)*

OUTSIDE TABLES
(* particularly recommended)

233

PRIVATE ROOMS
**(for the most comprehensive
listing of venues for functions –
from palaces to pubs – visit
www.hardens.com/party, or buy
*Harden's London Party, Event
& Conference Guide*, available
in all good bookshops)
* particularly recommended**

Fuego Pizzeria *(60)*
Fujiyama *(40,25)*
Garrison *(25)*
Gazette *(14, 40)*
The Greyhound at Battersea *(50)*
Hara The Circle Bar *(28)*
Hare & Tortoise: *SW15 (30)*
The Hartley *(70)*
The Herne Tavern *(125)*
Joanna's *(6)*
La Lanterna *(50,85)*
Lobster Pot *(20,28)*
Lola Rojo *(20)*
Louvaine *(22)*
Ma Cuisine: *TW1 (30)*
La Mancha *(60)*
Naked Turtle *(30,16,30)*
Nancy Lam's Enak Enak *(20)*
Nazmins Balti House *(80)*
Nosh *(24)*
Peninsular *(100)*
Le Pont de la Tour *(20)*
Le Pont de la Tour
   Bar & Grill *(20)*
Ratchada *(25)*
Raviolo *(40, 60)*
Rocket Riverside: *SW15 (28)*
The Rosendale *(150,20-40)*
RSJ *(24,30)*
San Lorenzo Fuoriporta *(20,30)*
San Remo *(25)*
Scarpetta *(25)*
Scoffers *(14)*
The Ship *(18)*
Sonny's *(20)*
The Spread Eagle *(12, 14)*
Sree Krishna *(50,60)*
The Swan *(14,70,200)*
tamesa@oxo *(28)*
Tentazioni *(25)*
Thai on the River *(40)*
Thailand *(40)*
3 Monkeys *(35)*
The Trafalgar Tavern *(200)*
Tree House *(60)*
The Victoria *(45)*
Village East *(18)*
The Wharf *(80)*
Zero Quattro *(10,20)*

East

Addendum *(60)*
Alba *(50)*
Arkansas Café *(20, 50)*
Bankside: *EC2 (120,40)*
Barcelona Tapas: *EC4 (30); Beaufort Hs,*
   St Botolph St EC3 (75)
Bevis Marks *(80)*
Bistrotheque *(40)*
Bleeding Heart *(20,35,45)*
Boisdale of Bishopsgate *(40)*
Bonds *(8,8,16)*
Brasserie Pierre *(150)*
Browns: *E14 (10); EC2 (30,30,60)*

Café du Marché *(30,60)*
Café Spice Namaste *(40)*
Cat & Mutton *(40)*
Cây Tre *(40)*
Cellar Gascon *(20)*
Chamberlain's *(60)*
The Chancery *(25, 25)*
Chez Gérard: *EC2 (12); EC3 (45)*
Cicada *(24)*
City Miyama *(4,4,8,10)*
The Clerkenwell Dining
   Room *(40)*
Clifton *(160)*
Club Mangia *(80)*
Cottons: *EC1 (70)*
Curve *(45)*
Dans le Noir *(25)*
$ *(12)*
The Don *(24,12)*
The Drunken Monkey *(10,30)*
Epicurean Lounge *(200)*
El Faro *(60)*
Faulkner's *(30)*
Fish Central *(60)*
The Fox *(10)*
Frocks *(30)*
George & Vulture *(14,16,24)*
The Gun *(18, 18)*
The Hat & Feathers *(40, 30)*
Hawksmoor *(14)*
Home *(16)*
The Hoxton Grille *(100)*
Imperial City *(14)*
King Eddie's *(32)*
Lanes *(28)*
The Larder *(20)*
Luc's Brasserie *(60)*
Malmaison Brasserie *(14)*
Missouri Grill *(14)*
Moro *(14)*
Mugen *(8)*
The Narrow *(14)*
New Tayyabs *(40)*
Ye Olde Cheshire Cheese *(15,50)*
1 Blossom Street *(8,12,26)*
1 Lombard Street *(50)*
Ortega: *EC1 (120); EC3 (50)*
Pacific Oriental *(40)*
The Peasant *(20)*
Perc%nto *(16,26,40,64)*
Plateau *(24)*
Portal *(15)*
Prima *(100, 250)*
Prism *(20,40)**
Rajasthan: *Monument*
   St EC3 (40); Houndsditch EC3 (50)
The Real Greek Souvlaki: *EC1 (30)*
Refettorio *(30)*
Le Rendezvous du Café *(30,60)*
The Rivington Grill *(26)*
Rosemary Lane *(40)*
Royal China: *E14 (15,20)*
Rudland & Stubbs *(12)*
S & M Café: *E1 (50)*

241

ROMANTIC

ROOMS WITH A VIEW

NOTABLE WINE LISTS

CUISINES

An asterisk (*) after an entry indicates exceptional or very good cooking

AMERICAN
Central
All Star Lanes (WCI)
Automat (WI)
Bodean's (WI)
Christopher's (WC2)
Hard Rock Café (WI)
Joe Allen (WC2)
Maxwell's (WC2)
Planet Hollywood (WI)
Pure California (WI)
Rainforest Café (WI)
Smollensky's (WC2)
TGI Friday's (WI,WC2)

West
All Star Lanes (W2)
Babes 'n' Burgers (WII)
Big Easy (SW3)
Bodean's (SW6)
Harlem (W2)
Lucky Seven (W2)*
Pacific Bar and Grill (W6)
PJ's (SW3)
Smollensky's (W6)
Sticky Fingers (W8)
TGI Friday's (SW6,W2)

North
Hoxton Square Bar & Kitchen (NI)
Pick More Daisies (N8)*
TGI Friday's (NW7)

South
Bodean's (SW4)

East
All Star Lanes (EI)
Arkansas Café (EI)*
Missouri Grill (EC3)
Smollensky's (EI, EI4)

AUSTRALIAN
East
The Princess (EC2)*

BELGIAN
Central
Belgo Centraal (WC2)

North
Belgo Noord (NWI)

BRITISH, MODERN
Central
About Thyme (SWI)
Acorn House (WCI)
Adam Street (WC2)
Alastair Little (WI)
Andrew Edmunds (WI)
Atrium (SWI)
Aurora (WI)

The Avenue (SWI)
Axis (WC2)
Bank Westminster (SWI)
Bellamy's (WI)
Blandford Street (WI)
Boulevard Bar & Dng Rm (WI)
Brian Turner (WI)
Brown's Grill (WI)
Café du Jardin (WC2)
Café Emm (WI)
Le Caprice (SWI)*
The Club Bar & Dining (WI)
The Contented Vine (WI)
The Cuckoo Club (WI)
Le Deuxième (WC2)
Dorchester Grill (WI)
The Easton (WCI)*
Ebury Wine Bar (SWI)
The Fifth Floor Restaurant (SWI)
Footstool (SWI)
French House (WI)
Homage (WC2)
Hush (WI)
Indigo (WC2)
Inn the Park (SWI)
The Ivy (WC2)
Just St James (SWI)
Konstam (WCI)
The Lanesborough (Conservatory) (SWI)
Langan's Brasserie (WI)
Langtry's (SWI)
Lindsay House (WI)
The Little Square (WI)
Mews of Mayfair (WI)
Nicole's (WI)
The Only Running Footman (WI)
Oscar (WI)
Patterson's (WI)*
The Phoenix (SWI)
Pigalle Club (WI)
The Portrait (WC2)
Quaglino's (SWI)
Refuel (WI)
Rhodes WI Brasserie (WI)
RIBA Café (WI)
Royal Court Bar (SWI)
Shampers (WI)
Sotheby's Café (WI)*
Stanza (WI)
Tate Britain (SWI)
The Terrace (WC2)
Thomas Cubitt (SWI)
Tuttons (WC2)
The Union Café (WI)
Villandry (WI)
Vincent Rooms (SWI)
Wild Honey (WI)
The Wolseley (WI)

West
The Abingdon (W8)
Admiral Codrington (SW3)
The Anglesea Arms W6 (W6)*
The Anglesea Arms SW7 (SW7)
Babylon (W8)
Beach Blanket Babylon (WII)
Belvedere (W8)

The Bentley Hotel *(SW7)*
Bibendum Oyster Bar *(SW3)*
Bistrot 190 *(SW7)*
Bluebird *(SW3)*
Bowler Bar & Grill *(SW3)*
The Brackenbury *(W6)*
Brinkley's *(SW10)*
Britannia *(W8)*
The Builder's Arms *(SW3)*
Bush Bar & Grill *(W12)*
Butcher's Hook *(SW6)*
Clarke's *(W8)**
The Collection *(SW3)*
Coopers Arms *(SW3)*
Crescent House *(W11)*
The Crown & Sceptre *(W12)*
Devonshire House *(W4)*
Duke on the Green *(SW6)*
Ealing Park Tavern *(W5)**
11 Abingdon Road *(W8)*
The Farm *(SW6)**
First Floor *(W11)*
Fish Hook *(W4)**
Formosa Dining Room *(W9)*
The Frontline Club *(W2)*
The Havelock Tavern *(W14)**
High Road Brasserie *(W4)*
Hole in the Wall *(W4)*
Island *(W2)*
Joe's Brasserie *(SW6)*
Joe's Café *(SW3)*
Julie's *(W11)*
Kensington Place *(W8)*
The Ladbroke Arms *(W11)**
Launceston Place *(W8)*
Lots Road *(SW10)*
Le Metro *(SW3)*
Notting Hill Brasserie *(W11)**
Olive Tree *(W6)*
The Oratory *(SW3)*
Paradise by Way of Kensal
   Green *(W10)**
The Phoenix *(SW3)*
The Pilot *(W4)*
Pissarro's *(W4)*
PJ's *(SW3)*
Queen's Head *(W6)*
The Queens Arms *(W6)*
Raoul's Café *(W9)*
The Rocket *(W3)*
The Roebuck *(W4)*
The Salisbury Tavern *(SW6)*
Sam's Brasserie *(W4)*
Snows on the Green *(W6)*
Sophie's Steakhouse *(SW10)*
Stone Mason's Arms *(W6)*
The Tenth Restaurant & Bar *(W8)*
The Thatched House *(W6)*
Tom's *(W11)*
Tom's Kitchen *(SW3)*
The Union *(W2)*
Vingt-Quatre *(SW10)*
The Warrington *(W9)*
The Waterway *(W9)*
The Westbourne *(W2)*
White Horse *(SW6)*
Whits *(W8)**

North

The Albion *(N1)*
Bacchus *(N1)*
The Barnsbury *(N1)*
Bradley's *(NW3)*
The Bull *(N6)*
Café Med *(NW8)*
The Chapel *(NW1)*
The Drapers Arms *(N1)*
The Duke of Cambridge *(N1)*
The Elk in the Woods *(N1)*
The Engineer *(NW1)*
Frederick's *(N1)*
Freemasons Arms *(NW3)*
The Garden Café *(NW1)*
The Greyhound *(NW10)*
The Haven *(N20)*
The Hill *(NW3)*
The Horseshoe *(NW3)**
The House *(N1)*
The Island *(NW10)*
The Junction Tavern *(NW5)*
The Lansdowne *(NW1)*
The Lock Dining Bar *(N17)**
The Lord Palmerston *(NW5)*
Mango Room *(NW1)*
Mosaica *(N22)**
No 77 Wine Bar *(NW6)*
The North London Tavern *(NW6)*
The Northgate *(N1)*
Odette's *(NW1)*
The Old Bull & Bush *(NW3)*
The Pumphouse *(N8)*
Roundhouse Café *(NW1)*
The Three Crowns *(N16)*
Walnut *(NW6)*
The Wells *(NW3)*
Wet Fish Cafe *(NW6)*
Landmark (Winter
   Garden) *(NW1)*

South

The Abbeville *(SW4)*
Alma *(SW18)*
Archduke Wine Bar *(SE1)*
The Aviary *(SW20)*
Bankside *(SE1)*
Benugo *(SE1)**
The Blue Pumpkin *(SW17)*
Blueprint Café *(SE1)*
Bread & Roses *(SW4)*
The Bridge *(SW13)*
The Brown Dog *(SW13)*
Buchan's *(SW11)*
Canteen *(SE1)*
Cantina Vinopolis *(SE1)*
The Castle *(SW11)*
Chapter Two *(SE3)**
Chez Bruce *(SW17)**
Cinnamon Cay *(SW11)*
The Clarence *(SW12)*
The Dartmouth Arms *(SE23)*
The Depot *(SW14)*
The Duke's Head *(SW15)**
Earl Spencer *(SW18)**
The East Hill *(SW18)*
Emile's *(SW15)**
The Fentiman Arms *(SW8)*

247

The Fire Stables *(SW19)*
Four O Nine *(SW9)**
Franklins *(SE11, SE22)*
The Freemasons *(SW18)*
Garrison *(SE1)*
The Glasshouse *(TW9)**
Grafton House *(SW4)*
The Greyhound at
  Battersea *(SW11)*
Harrison's *(SW12)*
The Hartley *(SE1)*
The Herne Tavern *(SE22)*
The Inn at Kew Gardens *(TW9)*
Inside *(SE10)**
Kew Grill *(TW9)*
Lamberts *(SW12)**
The Lavender *(SE11, SW11, SW9)*
The Mason's Arms *(SW8)**
Menier Chocolate Factory *(SE1)*
Mezzanine *(SE1)*
The Palmerston *(SE22)**
Petersham Nurseries *(TW10)*
Phoenix *(SW15)**
Le Pont de la Tour *(SE1)*
Ransome's Dock *(SW11)*
Redmond's *(SW14)*
Oxo Tower (Rest') *(SE1)*
The Rivington Grill *(SE10)*
The Rosendale *(SE21)*
RSJ *(SE1)*
Scoffers *(SW11)*
Skylon *(SE1)*
Sonny's *(SW13)*
The Spencer Arms *(SW15)*
The Sun & Doves *(SE5)*
The Swan *(SE1)*
The Table *(SE1)*
tamesa@oxo *(SE1)*
The Trafalgar Tavern *(SE10)*
Tree House *(SW13)*
Trinity *(SW4)**
The Victoria *(SW14)*
The Wharf *(TW11)*
Willie Gunn *(SW18)*

East

Addendum *(EC3)*
Ambassador *(EC1)*
Bankside *(EC2)*
The Bar & Grill *(EC1)*
Bar Bourse *(EC4)*
Beach Blanket Babylon *(E1)*
Bevis Marks *(EC3)*
Bistrotheque *(E2)*
Canteen *(E1)*
Cat & Mutton *(E8)*
The Chancery *(EC4)**
Club Mangia *(EC4)**
Coach & Horses *(EC1)*
The Don *(EC4)**
The Empress of India *(E9)*
The Fox *(EC2)*
Frocks *(E9)*
Gow's *(EC2)*
The Gun *(E14)**
Hadley House *(E11)*
The Hat & Feathers *(EC1)*
Hilliard *(EC4)**

Home *(EC2)*
The Hoxton Grille *(EC2)*
King Eddie's *(E15)*
Lanes *(E1)*
The Larder *(EC1)*
LMNT *(E8)*
Malmaison Brasserie *(EC1)*
Molloy's *(EC2)*
The Morgan Arms *(E3)**
Northbank *(EC4)*
1 Lombard Street *(EC3)*
The Peasant *(EC1)*
Prism *(EC3)*
Rhodes 24 *(EC2)*
The Rivington Grill *(EC2)*
Royal Oak *(E2)*
St Germain *(EC1)*
Searcy's Brasserie *(EC2)*
Smiths (Top Floor) *(EC1)*
Smiths (Ground Floor) *(EC1)*
The Sterling *(EC3)*
Terminus *(EC2)*
Vic Naylors *(EC1)*
Vinoteca *(EC1)*
Wapping Food *(E1)*
The Well *(EC1)*
The White Swan *(EC4)*
Wood Street *(EC2)*

BRITISH, TRADITIONAL

Central
Boisdale *(SW1)*
Chimes *(SW1)*
Fortnum's, The Fountain *(W1)*
Fuzzy's Grub *(SW1)**
The Goring Hotel *(SW1)*
Great Queen Street *(WC2)**
Green's *(SW1)*
Greig's *(W1)*
Grenadier *(SW1)*
The Guinea Grill *(W1)**
The National Dining
  Rooms *(WC2)*
Odin's *(W1)*
Porters *(WC2)*
Rib Room *(SW1)*
Rules *(WC2)*
Savoy Grill *(WC2)*
Scott's *(W1)**
Shepherd's *(SW1)*
Simpsons-in-the-Strand *(WC2)*
Square Pie Company *(WC1)*
Wiltons *(SW1)*
The Windmill *(W1)*

West
The Arbiter *(SW6)*
Bumpkin *(W11)*
The Fat Badger *(W10)*
Ffiona's *(W8)*
Hereford Road *(W2)*
Kensington Square Kitchen *(W8)*
Maggie Jones's *(W8)*
S & M Café *(W10)*
The Windsor Castle *(W8)*

North
Camden Bar & Kitchen *(NW1)*

The Flask *(N6)*
Holly Bush *(NW3)*
Kenwood (Brew House) *(NW3)*
The Marquess Tavern *(N1)**
S & M Café *(N1)*
St Johns *(N19)**

The Anchor & Hope *(SE1)**
Butlers W'f Chop-house *(SE1)*
Roast *(SE1)*
The Trafalgar Tavern *(SE10)*

Boisdale of Bishopsgate *(EC2)*
Cock Tavern *(EC1)*
Fuzzy's Grub *(EC2, EC3, EC4)**
George & Vulture *(EC3)*
Medcalf *(EC1)*
The Narrow *(E14)**
Ye Olde Cheshire Cheese *(EC4)*
Paternoster Chop House *(EC4)*
The Quality Chop House *(EC1)*
S & M Café *(E1)*
St John *(EC1)**
St John Bread & Wine *(E1)**
Simpson's Tavern *(EC3)*
Square Pie Company *(E1, E14)*
Sweetings *(EC4)**
The Wine Library *(EC3)*

CZECH
The Czech Restaurant *(NW6)*

DANISH
The Arbiter *(SW6)*
Lundum's *(SW7)**

EAST & CENT. EUROPEAN
Gay Hussar *(W1)*
The Wolseley *(W1)*

Trojka *(NW1)*

FISH & SEAFOOD
Back to Basics *(W1)**
Belgo Centraal *(WC2)*
Bentley's *(W1)*
Cape Town Fish Market *(W1)*
The Ebury *(SW1)*
Fishworks *(W1)*
Fung Shing *(WC2)**
Green's *(SW1)*
Livebait *(WC2)*
Loch Fyne *(WC2)*
Olivomare *(SW1)**
One-O-One *(SW1)*
Le Palais du Jardin *(WC2)*
Pescatori *(W1)*
Quaglino's *(SW1)*
Randall & Aubin *(W1)*
Rib Room *(SW1)*
Scott's *(W1)**

Seaport *(W1)*
J Sheekey *(WC2)**
Wiltons *(SW1)*
Zilli Fish *(W1)**

Big Easy *(SW3)*
The Cow *(W2)*
Deep *(SW6)**
Fish Hook *(W4)**
Fishworks *(SW10, SW6, W11, W4)*
Geale's *(W8)*
Lou Pescadou *(SW5)*
Mandarin Kitchen *(W2)**
Poissonnerie de l'Av. *(SW3)**
Seabass *(W2)*
Le Suquet *(SW3)**
Tom's Place *(SW3)*

Belgo Noord *(NW1)*
Bradley's *(NW3)*
La Brocca *(NW6)*
Chez Liline *(N4)**
Fishworks *(N1, NW1)*
Nautilus *(NW6)**
Sargasso Sea *(N21)**

Ev Restaurant, Bar & Deli *(SE1)*
Fish Club *(SW11)**
fish! *(SE1)*
Fishworks *(SW11, TW9)*
Gastro *(SW4)*
Livebait *(SE1)*
Lobster Pot *(SE11)**
Loch Fyne *(TW2)*
Le Pont de la Tour
 Bar & Grill *(SE1)*
Wright Brothers *(SE1)**

Chamberlain's *(EC3)*
Curve *(E14)*
Fish Central *(EC1)**
Fish Shop *(EC1)*
Fishmarket *(EC2)*
Gow's *(EC2)*
The Grapes *(E14)**
Rudland & Stubbs *(EC1)*
Sweetings *(EC4)**
Vertigo *(EC2)*
Wapping Food *(E1)*

FRENCH
The Admiralty *(WC2)*
Alain Ducasse *(W1)*
Annex 3 *(W1)*
Arbutus *(W1)**
L'Artiste Musclé *(W1)*
L'Atelier de Joel
 Robuchon *(WC2)**
Aubaine *(W1)*
Bellamy's *(W1)*
Beotys *(WC2)*
Boudin Blanc *(W1)*
Brasserie Roux *(SW1)*

249

Café Bohème *(W1)*
Café des Amis du Vin *(WC2)*
Le Cercle *(SW1)**
The Chelsea Brasserie *(SW1)*
Chez Gérard *(SW1,W1,WC2)*
Clos Maggiore *(WC2)*
Criterion Grill *(W1)*
Dover Street *(W1)*
Drones *(SW1)*
The Ebury *(SW1)*
Elena's L'Etoile *(W1)*
L'Escargot *(W1)**
L'Escargot (Picasso Room) *(W1)**
Foliage *(SW1)**
Galvin at Windows *(W1)*
Galvin Bistrot de Luxe *(W1)**
Le Gavroche *(W1)**
Gordon Ramsay at
 Claridge's *(W1)*
The Greenhouse *(W1)*
Hibiscus *(W1)*
Incognico *(WC2)*
Langan's Bistro *(W1)*
maze *(W1)**
Mirabelle *(W1)*
Mon Plaisir *(WC2)*
La Noisette *(SW1)*
L'Oranger *(SW1)*
Orrery *(W1)*
Le Palais du Jardin *(WC2)*
Pearl *(WC1)*
La Petite Maison *(W1)*
Pétrus *(SW1)**
Pied à Terre *(W1)**
La Poule au Pot *(SW1)*
Randall & Aubin *(W1)*
Le Relais de Venise *(W1)*
Rhodes W1 Restaurant *(W1)*
The Ritz *(W1)*
Roussillon *(SW1)**
Sketch (Lecture Rm) *(W1)*
Sketch (Gallery) *(W1)*
The Square *(W1)**
Texture *(W1)*
La Trouvaille *(W1)*
Villandry *(W1)*
The Wallace *(W1)*

Angelus *(W2)*
Aubaine *(SW3)*
Aubergine *(SW10)**
Belvedere *(W8)*
The Bentley Hotel *(SW7)*
Bibendum *(SW3)*
La Bouchée *(SW7)**
La Brasserie *(SW3)*
Brasserie St Quentin *(SW3)*
Le Café Anglais *(W2)*
The Capital Restaurant *(SW3)**
Charlotte's Place *(W5)*
Cheyne Walk Bras' *(SW3)*
Chez Kristof *(W6)*
Chez Patrick *(W8)*
Le Colombier *(SW3)*
11 Abingdon Road *(W8)*
L'Etranger *(SW7)*
Gordon Ramsay *(SW3)**

Langan's Coq d'Or *(SW5)*
The Ledbury *(W11)**
Lou Pescadou *(SW5)*
Notting Hill Brasserie *(W11)**
Papillon *(SW3)*
Père Michel *(W2)**
The Pig's Ear *(SW3)*
Poissonnerie de l'Av. *(SW3)**
Racine *(SW3)**
Randall & Aubin *(SW10)*
Rôtisserie Jules *(W11)*
Le Suquet *(SW3)**
Tartine *(SW3)*
Tom Aikens *(SW3)**
La Trompette *(W4)**
Le Vacherin *(W4)**
Whits *(W8)**

The Almeida *(N1)*
Les Associés *(N8)*
L'Aventure *(NW8)**
Bistro Aix *(N8)*
Bradley's *(NW3)*
La Cage Imaginaire *(NW3)*
Fig *(N1)**
Le Mercury *(N1)*
Morgan M *(N7)**
Oslo Court *(NW8)**
La Petite Auberge *(N1)*
Le Sacré-Coeur *(N1)*
Somerstown Coffee
 House *(NW1)*
The Wells *(NW3)*

Bar du Musée *(SE10)*
Le Bouchon Bordelais *(SW11)*
Brew Wharf *(SE1)*
Brula *(TW1)**
La Buvette *(TW9)*
Le Chardon *(SE22)*
Chez Gérard *(SE1)*
Chez Lindsay *(TW10)*
The Food Room *(SW8)**
Gastro *(SW4)*
Gazette *(SW11)*
Lobster Pot *(SE11)**
Louvaine *(SW11)*
Ma Cuisine *(TW1,TW9)**
Magdalen *(SE1)**
Mini Mundus *(SW17)*
Morel *(SW4)*
Old Vic Brasserie *(SE1)*
Rick's Café *(SW17)*
Riviera *(SE1)*
La Saveur *(SW14)**
The Spread Eagle *(SE10)*
Upstairs Bar *(SW2)**

Aurora *(EC2)*
Bistrotheque *(E2)*
Bleeding Heart *(EC1)**
Brasserie Pierre *(EC2)*
Café du Marché *(EC1)**
Cellar Gascon *(EC1)*
Chez Gérard *(EC2, EC3, EC4)*

Club Gascon *(EC1)**
Comptoir Gascon *(EC1)**
Coq d'Argent *(EC3)*
Dans le Noir *(EC1)*
The Gun *(E14)**
Luc's Brasserie *(EC3)*
Plateau *(E14)*
Le Rendezvous du Café *(EC1)*
Rosemary Lane *(E1)**
The Royal Exchange *(EC3)*
Le Saint Julien *(EC1)*
Sauterelle *(EC3)*
Les Trois Garçons *(E1)*

FUSION
Central
Archipelago *(W1)*
Asia de Cuba *(WC2)*
Bam-Bou *(W1)*
Jaan *(WC2)**
Mju *(SW1)*
Nobu *(W1)**
Nobu Berkeley *(W1)**
The Providores *(W1)**
Providores (Tapa Room) *(W1)**
So *(W1)*

West
Aquasia *(SW10)*
I Thai *(W2)*

South
Beauberry House *(SE21)*
Champor-Champor *(SE1)**
The Mansion *(SE27)*
Rapscallion *(SW4)*
Tsunami *(SW4)**
Village East *(SE1)*

East
Ubon *(E14)*

GAME
Central
Boisdale *(SW1)*
Rules *(WC2)*
Wiltons *(SW1)*

North
San Daniele *(N5)*

East
Boisdale of Bishopsgate *(EC2)*
Gow's *(EC2)*

GERMAN
South
Stein's *(TW10)*

GREEK
Central
Beotys *(WC2)*
Hellenik *(W1)*
Real Greek Souvlaki & Bar *(W1, WC2)*

West
Costa's Grill *(W8)*

Halepi *(W2)*

North
Daphne *(NW1)*
Lemonia *(NW1)*
The Real Greek *(N1)*
Retsina *(NW3)*
Vrisaki *(N22)**

South
Real Greek Souvlaki & Bar *(SE1, SW15)*

East
Kolossi Grill *(EC1)*
The Real Greek Souvlaki *(EC1)*

HUNGARIAN
Central
Gay Hussar *(W1)*

INTERNATIONAL
Central
Balans *(W1)*
Bedford & Strand *(WC2)*
Bohème Kitchen *(W1)*
Boulevard *(WC2)*
Boxwood Café *(SW1)*
Browns *(W1,WC2)*
Café in the Crypt *(WC2)*
Caramel *(SW1)*
City Café *(SW1)*
Cork & Bottle *(WC2)*
Eat & Two Veg *(W1)*
The Forge *(WC2)*
Giraffe *(W1)*
Gordon's Wine Bar *(WC2)*
Grumbles *(SW1)*
Hardy's *(W1)*
Living Room *(W1)*
Michael Moore *(W1)*
Motcombs *(SW1)*
National Gallery Café *(WC2)*
O'Conor Don *(W1)*
Ooze *(W1)*
Oriel *(SW1)*
Papageno *(WC2)*
Pomegranates *(SW1)*
Ronnie Scott's *(W1)*
Running Horse *(W1)**
Sarastro *(WC2)*
Seven Stars *(WC2)*
06 St Chad's Place *(WC1)*
Star Café *(W1)*
Stock Pot *(SW1,W1)*
Sugar Reef *(W1)*
Tiger Tiger *(SW1)*

West
The Academy *(W11)*
Annie's *(W4)*
Balans West *(SW5,W4,W8)*
Blakes *(SW7)*
Brompton Quarter Café *(SW3)*
The Cabin *(SW6)*
Café Laville *(W2)*
Chelsea Bun Diner *(SW10)*
Coopers Arms *(SW3)*

Electric Brasserie *(W11)*
The Enterprise *(SW3)*
Foxtrot Oscar *(SW3)*
The Gate *(W6)**
Giraffe *(W4,W8)*
Glaisters *(SW10)*
Mona Lisa *(SW10)*
The Scarsdale *(W8)*
606 Club *(SW10)*
Stock Pot *(SW3)*
The Swag & Tails *(SW7)*
202 *(W11)*
The Windsor Castle *(W8)*
Wine Factory *(W11)*
Wine Gallery *(SW10)*

North

The Arches *(NW6)*
Banners *(N8)*
Browns *(N1)*
The Fox Reformed *(N16)*
Giraffe *(N1, NW3)*
The Haven *(N20)*
Hoxton Apprentice *(N1)*
Kaz Kreol *(NW1)*
The Living Room *(N1)*
The Old Bull & Bush *(NW3)*
Orange Tree *(N20)*
Petek *(N4)**
Spaniard's Inn *(NW3)*

South

Annie's *(SW13)*
Bread & Roses *(SW4)*
Browns *(SE1)*
Tate Café *(SE1)*
Delfina Studio Café *(SE1)**
Duke of Cambridge *(SW11)*
Giraffe *(SE1, SW11)*
Green & Blue *(SE22)*
Hudson's *(SW15)*
Joanna's *(SE19)*
Laughing Gravy *(SE1)*
The Light House *(SW19)*
The Mansion *(SE27)*
Metro *(SW4)*
Morel *(SW4)*
Naked Turtle *(SW14)*
Newton's *(SW4)*
Nosh *(TW1)*
Putney Station *(SW15)*
Tate Restaurant *(SE1)*
The Ship *(SW18)*
The Wharf *(TW11)*

East

Browns *(E14, EC2)*
Club Mangia *(EC4)**
$ *(EC1)*
Kruger *(E14)*
Lilly's *(E1)*
Prima *(EC3)*
The Prince Arthur *(E8)*
Les Trois Garçons *(E1)*
Vivat Bacchus *(EC4)*

IRISH
Central
O'Conor Don *(W1)*

ITALIAN
Central
Al Duca *(SW1)*
Alloro *(W1)**
Amato *(W1)*
Aperitivo *(W1)*
Bertorelli's *(W1,WC2)*
Brumus *(SW1)*
Caffè Caldesi *(W1)*
Caffé Vergnano *(WC2)*
Caldesi *(W1)*
Camerino *(W1)*
Caraffini *(SW1)*
Caricatura *(W1)*
Cecconi's *(W1)*
Ciao Bella *(WC1)*
Cipriani *(W1)*
Como Lario *(SW1)*
Il Convivio *(SW1)*
Delfino *(W1)**
Diverso *(W1)*
5 Cavendish Square *(W1)*
Franco's *(SW1)*
Getti *(SW1,W1)*
Giardinetto *(W1)*
Gran Paradiso *(SW1)*
Incognico *(WC2)*
L'Incontro *(SW1)*
Latium *(W1)**
Little Italy *(W1)*
Locanda Locatelli *(W1)**
Luciano *(SW1)*
Mimmo d'Ischia *(SW1)*
Mosaico *(W1)*
Oliveto *(SW1)**
Olivo *(SW1)**
Orso *(WC2)*
Paolina Café *(WC1)**
Pappagallo *(W1)*
Paradiso Olivelli *(W1)*
Passione *(W1)*
Pasta Brown *(WC2)*
Pescatori *(W1)*
Piccolino *(W1)*
Pizza on the Park *(SW1)*
La Porchetta Pizzeria *(WC1)*
Quirinale *(W1)**
Quo Vadis *(W1)*
Ristorante Semplice *(W1)**
Sale e Pepe *(SW1)*
Salt Yard *(W1)**
Santini *(SW1)*
Sapori *(WC2)*
Sardo *(W1)**
Sartoria *(W1)*
Serafino *(W1)*
Signor Sassi *(SW1)*
Signor Zilli *(W1)*
Spacca Napoli *(W1)**
La Spiga *(W1)*
Theo Randall *(W1)**
Toto's *(SW1)*
2 Amici *(SW1)*
2 Veneti *(W1)**

Uno *(SW1)*
Vasco & Piero's Pavilion *(W1)*
Via Condotti *(W1)*
Il Vicolo *(SW1)*
Vivezza *(SW1)*
Volt *(SW1)*
Zafferano *(SW1)**
Zilli Fish *(W1)**

West

L'Accento Italiano *(W2)*
Aglio e Olio *(SW10)**
The Ark *(W8)*
Arturo *(W2)*
Assaggi *(W2)**
Brunello *(SW7)*
Buona Sera *(SW3)*
C Garden *(SW3)*
Carpaccio's *(SW3)*
Cibo *(W14)**
Cristini *(W2)*
Da Mario *(SW7)*
Daphne's *(SW3)*
De Cecco *(SW6)*
La Delizia *(SW3)*
Edera *(W11)*
11 Abingdon Road *(W8)*
Elistano *(SW3)*
Esenza *(W11)*
Il Falconiere *(SW7)*
La Famiglia *(SW10)*
Frankie's Italian Bar & Grill *(SW3)*
Frankie's Italian Bar & Grill *(W4)*
Frantoio *(SW10)*
Friends *(SW10)*
The Green Olive *(W9)*
Locanda Ottomezzo *(W8)*
Lucio *(SW3)*
Luna Rossa *(W11)*
Made in Italy *(SW3)*
Manicomio *(SW3)*
Mediterraneo *(W11)**
Miraggio *(SW6)*
Montpeliano *(SW7)*
Mulberry Street *(W2)*
Napulé *(SW6)**
Nuovi Sapori *(SW6)**
The Oak *(W2)**
Osteria Basilico *(W11)**
Osteria dell'Arancio *(SW10)*
Ottolenghi *(W11,W8)**
Il Pagliaccio *(SW6)*
Pappa Ciccia *(SW6)**
Pellicano *(SW3)**
Picasso's *(SW3)*
Il Portico *(W8)*
The Red Pepper *(W9)**
Riccardo's *(SW3)*
The River Café *(W6)**
Rossopomodoro *(SW10,W11)*
San Lorenzo *(SW3)*
Santa Lucia *(SW10)*
Scalini *(SW3)*
Spago *(SW7)*
Timo *(W8)*
Trenta *(W2)*
Vino Rosso *(W4)**
Ziani *(SW3)*

North

Artigiano *(NW3)*
L'Artista *(NW11)*
Il Bacio *(N16, N5)*
La Brocca *(NW6)*
Cantina Italia *(N1)**
Casale Franco *(N1)*
La Collina *(NW1)*
Fifteen Restaurant *(N1)*
Fifteen Trattoria *(N1)*
Florians *(N8)*
Fratelli la Bufala *(NW3)*
Marine Ices *(NW3)*
Metrogusto *(N1)*
Ottolenghi *(N1)**
Philpotts Mezzaluna *(NW2)*
Pizzeria Oregano *(N1)**
La Porchetta Pizzeria *(N1, N4, NW1)*
Rosmarino *(NW8)*
Salt House *(NW8)*
The Salusbury *(NW6)*
San Carlo *(N6)*
San Daniele *(N5)*
Sardo Canale *(NW1)*
Sarracino *(NW6)**
Villa Bianca *(NW3)*
Zuccato *(NW3)*

South

A Cena *(TW1)**
Al Forno *(SW15, SW19)*
Amici *(SW17)*
Antipasto & Pasta *(SW11)*
Arancia *(SE16)**
Buona Sera *(SW11)*
Cantina del Ponte *(SE1)*
Il Cantuccio di Pulcinella *(SW11)*
Castello *(SE16)**
Donna Margherita *(SW11)*
Enoteca Turi *(SW15)**
Ferrari's *(SW17)*
Frankie's Italian Bar & Grill *(SW15)*
Grissini *(SW4)*
Isola del Sole *(SW15)**
La Lanterna *(SE1)*
Mooli *(SW4)*
Numero Uno *(SW11)*
Ost. Antica Bologna *(SW11)*
Pappa Ciccia *(SW15)**
Piccolino *(SW17, SW19)*
Pizza Metro *(SW11)**
Le Querce *(SE23)**
Rick's Café *(SW17)*
Riva *(SW13)**
Riviera *(SE1)*
San Lorenzo Fuoriporta *(SW19)*
San Remo *(SW13)*
Scarpetta *(TW11)**
Tentazioni *(SE1)**
Zero Quattro *(SW19)*

East

Alba *(EC1)*
Amerigo Vespucci *(E14)*
Bertorelli's *(EC3, EC4)*
Il Bordello *(E1)**
Caravaggio *(EC3)*

253

La Figa *(E14)*
Flâneur *(EC1)*
Leadenhall Italian *(EC3)*
1 Blossom Street *(E1)**
E Pellicci *(E2)*
Perc%nto *(EC4)*
La Porchetta Pizzeria *(EC1)*
Quadrato *(E14)*
Refettorio *(EC4)*
Stringray Globe Café *(E2)**
Taberna Etrusca *(EC4)*
Zuccato *(EC4)*

MEDITERRANEAN

Central

About Thyme *(SW1)*
Connaught *(W1)*
Bistro 1 *(W1,WC2)*
The Fifth Floor Café *(SW1)*
Hummus Bros *(W1,WC1)*
Leon *(W1,WC2)**
Meza *(W1)*
La Noisette *(SW1)*
The Norfolk Arms *(WC1)*
Rocket *(W1)*
St Alban *(SW1)*
Salt Yard *(W1)**
Truc Vert *(W1)*
Tuttons *(WC2)*

West

The Atlas *(SW6)**
Cochonnet *(W9)*
Cross Keys *(SW3)*
Cumberland Arms *(W14)*
The Grove *(W6)*
Kicca *(SW3)*
Leon *(SW3)**
Little Bay *(SW6)*
Locanda Ottomezzo *(W8)*
Made in Italy *(SW3)*
Mediterraneo *(W11)**
Priory House *(W14)*
Raoul's Café *(W9)*
Raoul's Café & Deli *(W11)*
Snows on the Green *(W6)*
The Swan *(W4)*
Tom's *(W11)*
Troubadour *(SW5)*
William IV *(NW10)*

North

Café Med *(NW8)*
Café RED *(NW5)*
Camden Brasserie *(NW1)*
The Chapel *(NW1)*
Cru *(N1)*
The Little Bay *(NW6)*
The Pumphouse *(N8)*
Queen's Head & Artichoke *(NW1)*
The Vine *(NW5)*

South

Bar Estrela *(SW8)*
Bermondsey Kitchen *(SE1)*
Fish in a Tie *(SW11)*
The Fox & Hounds *(SW11)**
The Little Bay *(SW11)*

Oxo Tower (Brass') *(SE1)*
Raviolo *(SW12)*
Rocket Riverside *(SW15)*
The Stonhouse *(SW4)*
The Wharf *(TW11)*

East

Ambassador *(EC1)*
Bonds *(EC2)*
The Clerkenwell Dining
   Room *(EC1)*
The Eagle *(EC1)**
Eyre Brothers *(EC2)*
Flâneur *(EC1)*
Leon *(E1, EC4)**
The Little Bay *(EC1)*
The Peasant *(EC1)*
Portal *(EC1)*
Rocket *(EC2)*
Le Saint Julien *(EC1)*
Vinoteca *(EC1)*
The Zetter *(EC1)*

ORGANIC

Central

Daylesford Organics *(SW1)*

West

Babes 'n' Burgers *(W11)*
Bush Garden Café *(W12)*
Goodness *(W4)*

North

The Duke of Cambridge *(N1)*
Holly Bush *(NW3)*

South

The Hartley *(SE1)*

East

Smiths (Dining Rm) *(EC1)*
Story Deli *(E1)**

POLISH

West

Daquise *(SW7)*
Lowiczanka *(W6)*
Ognisko Polskie *(SW7)*
Patio *(W12)*
Wódka *(W8)*

South

Baltic *(SE1)*

PORTUGUESE

West

Lisboa Pâtisserie *(W10)**

South

Bar Estrela *(SW8)*

East

Portal *(EC1)*

RUSSIAN

Central

Tsar *(SW1)*

North
Trojka *(NW1)*

South
Zakudia *(SE1)*

East
Potemkin *(EC1)*

SCANDINAVIAN
Central
Garbo's *(W1)*
Nordic Bakery *(W1)**

West
Lundum's *(SW7)**

North
Upper Glas *(N1)*

SCOTTISH
Central
Albannach *(WC2)*
Boisdale *(SW1)*

South
Buchan's *(SW11)*

East
Boisdale of Bishopsgate *(EC2)*

SPANISH
Central
Barrafina *(W1)**
Café España *(W1)*
Cigala *(WC1)*
Fino *(W1)**
Goya *(SW1)*
Meza *(W1)*
Navarro's *(W1)*
The Norfolk Arms *(WC1)*
El Pirata *(W1)*
La Rueda *(W1)*
Salt Yard *(W1)**
La Tasca *(WC2)*

West
Cambio de Tercio *(SW5)**
Galicia *(W10)*
L-Restaurant & Bar *(W8)*
La Rueda *(SW6)*
La Tasca *(W4)*
Tendido Cero *(SW5)**

North
Camino *(N1)*
Charles Lamb *(N1)*
Don Pepe *(NW8)*
The Islington Tapas Bar *(N1)*
El Parador *(NW1)**

South
Barcelona Tapas *(SE22)*
don Fernando's *(TW9)*
Lola Rojo *(SW11)**
La Mancha *(SW15)*
Meson don Felipe *(SE1)*
Rebato's *(SW8)*

Rick's Café *(SW17)*
El Rincón Latino *(SW4)*
La Rueda *(SW4)*
Tapas Brindisa *(SE1)**

East
Barcelona Tapas *(EC3, EC4)*
Eyre Brothers *(EC2)*
El Faro *(E14)**
Meson los Barilles *(E1)*
Moro *(EC1)**
Ortega *(EC1, EC3)*
La Tasca *(E14, EC2)*

STEAKS & GRILLS
Central
Black & Blue *(W1)*
Bodean's *(W1)*
Chez Gérard *(SW1,W1,WC2)*
Christopher's *(WC2)*
Gaucho Grill *(W1,WC2)*
The Guinea Grill *(W1)**
Quaglino's *(SW1)*
Rowley's *(SW1)*
Smollensky's *(WC2)*
Wolfe's *(WC2)*

West
Black & Blue *(SW7,W8)*
Bodean's *(SW6)*
Bowler Bar & Grill *(SW3)*
El Gaucho *(SW3, SW7)**
Gaucho Grill *(SW3)*
Notting Grill *(W11)*
Popeseye *(W14)*
Rôtisserie Jules *(SW7)*
Smollensky's *(W6)*
Sophie's Steakhouse *(SW10)*

North
Black & Blue *(NW3)*
Camden Brasserie *(NW1)*
Gaucho Grill *(NW3)*
Haché *(NW1)**
Hoxton Square Bar & Kitchen *(N1)*
Rôtisserie *(HA5, N20, NW6, NW8)*

South
Barnes Grill *(SW13)*
Bermondsey Kitchen *(SE1)*
Black & Blue *(SE1)*
Bodean's *(SW4)*
Butcher & Grill *(SW11)*
Chez Gérard *(SE1)*
Gaucho Grill *(SE1,TW10)*
Kew Grill *(TW9)*
La Pampa *(SW11)**
Le Pont de la Tour Bar & Grill *(SE1)*
Popeseye *(SW15)*

East
Arkansas Café *(E1)**
The Bar & Grill *(EC1)*
Chez Gérard *(EC2, EC3, EC4)*
Smiths (Dining Rm) *(EC1)*
Epicurean Lounge *(EC1)*

255

Gaucho Grill *(E14, EC2, EC3)*
Hawksmoor *(E1)**
Lilly's *(E1)*
Missouri Grill *(EC3)*
Prima *(EC3)*
Santa Maria del Buen Ayre *(E8)**
Simpson's Tavern *(EC3)*
Smiths (Top Floor) *(EC1)*
Smiths (Ground Floor) *(EC1)*
Smollensky's *(E1, E14)*

SWISS
Central
St Moritz *(W1)*

VEGETARIAN
Central
Food for Thought *(WC2)**
India Club *(WC2)*
The Lanesborough
  (Conservatory) *(SW1)*
Malabar Junction *(WC1)*
Masala Zone *(W1)*
Mildred's *(W1)**
Rasa Samudra *(W1)**
Woodlands *(SW1, W1)**

West
Blah! Blah! Blah! *(W12)*
Blue Elephant *(SW6)*
Blue Lagoon *(W14)*
The Gate *(W6)**
Masala Zone *(SW5)*
Woodlands *(W4)**

North
Chutneys *(NW1)*
Diwana B-P House *(NW1)*
Geeta *(NW6)*
Jashan *(HA0, N8)**
Manna *(NW3)*
Masala Zone *(N1)*
Rani *(N3)*
Rasa *(N16)**
Sakonis *(HA0)**
Vijay *(NW6)**
Woodlands *(NW3)**

South
Kastoori *(SW17)**
Le Pont de la Tour *(SE1)*
Sree Krishna *(SW17)**

East
Carnevale *(EC1)*
The Place Below *(EC2)**

AFTERNOON TEA
Central
Brasserie Roux *(SW1)*
The Fifth Floor Café *(SW1)*
Fortnum's, The Fountain *(W1)*
Ladurée *(SW1, W1)*
The Lanesborough
  (Conservatory) *(SW1)*
Pâtisserie Valerie *(SW1, W1)*
Richoux *(W1)*
The Ritz *(W1)*

Royal Academy *(W1)*
Sketch (Parlour) *(W1)*
Villandry *(W1)*
The Wolseley *(W1)*
Yauatcha *(W1)**

West
Daquise *(SW7)*
Napket *(SW3)*
Pâtisserie Valerie *(SW3, W8)*
Richoux *(SW3)*

North
Richoux *(NW8)*

BURGERS, ETC
Central
Black & Blue *(W1)*
Diner *(W1)**
Eagle Bar Diner *(W1)*
Ed's Easy Diner *(W1, WC2)*
Fine Burger Company *(W1)*
Gourmet Burger Kitchen *(W1, WC2)**
Hamburger Union *(W1, WC2)*
Hard Rock Café *(W1)*
Joe Allen *(WC2)*
Kettners *(W1)*
Maxwell's *(WC2)*
Planet Hollywood *(W1)*
Rainforest Café *(W1)*
Tootsies *(W1)*
The Ultimate Burger *(W1, WC1)*
Wolfe's *(WC2)*

West
Babes 'n' Burgers *(W11)*
Big Easy *(SW3)*
Black & Blue *(SW7, W8)*
Electric Brasserie *(W11)*
Gourmet Burger Kitchen *(SW5, SW6, SW7, W11, W2, W4)**
Ground *(W4)**
Henry J Beans *(SW3)*
Joe's Café *(SW3)*
Lucky Seven *(W2)**
Notting Grill *(W11)*
Pacific Bar and Grill *(W6)*
PJ's *(SW3)*
Sticky Fingers *(W8)*
Tootsies *(SW6, SW7, W11, W4)*

North
Black & Blue *(NW3)*
Fine Burger Company *(N1, N10, NW3)*
Gourmet Burger Kitchen *(NW3)**
Haché *(NW1)**
Hamburger Union *(N1, NW3)*
Hoxton Square Bar &
  Kitchen *(N1)*
Natural Burger Co & Grill *(NW8)*
No 77 Wine Bar *(NW6)*
Tootsies *(NW3)*

South
Black & Blue *(SE1)*
Dexter's Grill *(SW17)*

Fine Burger Company (SW12)
Gourmet Burger Kitchen (SW11,
SW15, SW4)*
Tootsies (SW11, SW15, SW19, SW4)

East
Arkansas Café (E1)*
The Bar & Grill (EC1)
The Diner (EC2)*
Smiths (Dining Rm) (EC1)
$ (EC1)
Gourmet Burger Kitchen (EC4)*

CRÊPES
West
Bluebird Café (SW3)

South
Chez Lindsay (TW10)

FISH & CHIPS
Central
Fryer's Delight (WC1)
Golden Hind (W1)*
North Sea Fish (WC1)*
Rock & Sole Plaice (WC2)
Seafresh (SW1)

West
Costa's Fish (W8)*
Geale's (W8)
Tom's Place (SW3)

North
Nautilus (NW6)*
The Sea Cow (N16)
Seashell (NW1)*
Toff's (N10)*
Two Brothers (N3)*

South
Brady's (SW18)*
Fish Club (SW11)*
Olley's (SE24)*
The Sea Cow (SE22, SW4)

East
Ark Fish (E18)*
Faulkner's (E8)*

ICE CREAM
North
Marine Ices (NW3)

PIZZA
Central
Delfino (W1)*
Fire & Stone (WC2)
Gourmet Pizza Co. (W1)
Kettners (W1)
Oliveto (SW1)*
Paradiso Olivelli (W1,WC1)
Piccolino (W1)
Pizza on the Park (SW1)
La Porchetta Pizzeria (WC1)
Rocket (W1)
Sapori (WC2)
La Spiga (W1)

West
Basilico (SW6)*
Buona Sera (SW3)
Cochonnet (W9)
Da Mario (SW7)
La Delizia (SW3)
Firezza (W11,W4)*
Frankie's Italian Bar & Grill (SW3)
Frankie's Italian Bar & Grill (W4)
Friends (SW10)
Made in Italy (SW3)
Mulberry Street (W2)
The Oak (W2)*
Osteria Basilico (W11)*
(Ciro's) Pizza Pomodoro (SW3)
Spago (SW7)

North
Il Bacio (N16, N5)
Basilico (N1, NW3)*
Cantina Italia (N1)*
Firezza (N1)*
Furnace (N1)
Marine Ices (NW3)
Pizzeria Oregano (N1)*
La Porchetta Pizzeria (N1, N4, NW1)

South
Al Forno (SW15, SW19)
Amano Café (SE1)
Basilico (SW11, SW14)*
Buona Sera (SW11)
Castello (SE16)*
Eco (SW4)
Eco Brixton (SW9)
Firezza (SW11, SW18)*
Frankie's Italian Bar &
Grill (SW15)
Fuego Pizzeria (SW8)
Gourmet Pizza Co. (SE1)
The Gowlett (SE15)
La Lanterna (SE1)
Paradiso Olivelli (SE1)
Piccolino (SW17, SW19)
Pizza Metro (SW11)*
Rocket Riverside (SW15)
Zero Degrees (SE3)

East
Bar Capitale (EC2, EC4)
Il Bordello (E1)*
Epicurean Lounge (EC1)
Gourmet Pizza Co. (E14)
(Ciro's) Pizza Pomodoro (EC2)
La Porchetta Pizzeria (EC1)
Rocket (EC2)
Story Deli (E1)*

SANDWICHES, CAKES, ETC
Central
Amato (W1)
Apostrophe (SW1,W1,WC2)
Aubaine (W1)
Baker & Spice (SW1)*
Bar Italia (W1)
Benugo (W1)*
Crussh (W1)*
Flat White (W1)*

La Fromagerie Café *(W1)**
Fuzzy's Grub *(SW1)**
Just Falafs *(W1,WC2)**
Konditor & Cook *(W1,WC1)**
Ladurée *(SW1,W1)*
Maison Bertaux *(W1)*
Monmouth Coffee
    Company *(WC2)**
Le Pain Quotidien *(W1)*
Pâtisserie Valerie *(SW1,W1)*
Paul *(W1,WC2)*
Richoux *(W1)*
Royal Academy *(W1)*
Salade *(W1)*
Sketch (Parlour) *(W1)*

West
Aubaine *(SW3)*
Baker & Spice *(SW3)**
Benugo *(SW7)**
Bluebird Café *(SW3)*
Crussh *(W12,W8)**
Gail's Bread *(W11)**
Hugo's *(SW7)*
Joe's Café *(SW3)*
Lisboa Pâtisserie *(W10)**
Napket *(SW3)**
Le Pain Quotidien *(SW3,W8)*
Pâtisserie Valerie *(SW3,W8)*
Paul *(SW7)*
Richoux *(SW3)*
Tom's *(W11)*
Troubadour *(SW5)*

North
Baker & Spice *(NW6,W9)**
Chamomile *(NW3)*
Gail's Bread *(NW3)**
Hugo's *(NW6)*
Kenwood (Brew House) *(NW3)*
Paul *(NW3)*
Richoux *(NW8)*

South
Boiled Egg *(SW11)*
Caffè Vergnano *(SE1)*
Konditor & Cook *(SE1)**
Monmouth Coffee
    Company *(SE1)*
Le Pain Quotidien *(SE1)*
Trinity Stores *(SW12)*

East
Apostrophe *(EC2, EC4)*
Benugo *(EC1)**
Brick Lane Beigel Bake *(E1)**
Crussh *(E14, EC3, EC4)**
Fuzzy's Grub *(EC2, EC3, EC4)**
Grazing *(EC3)**
Pâtisserie Valerie *(E1)*
Paul *(EC4)*
Salade *(EC4)*
Spianata *(E1, EC1, EC4)**

ARGENTINIAN
Central
Gaucho Grill *(W1,WC2)*

West
El Gaucho *(SW3, SW7)**
Gaucho Grill *(SW3)*

North
Gaucho Grill *(NW3)*

South
Gaucho Grill *(SE1,TW10)*
La Pampa *(SW11)**
Santa Maria del Sur *(SW8)**

East
Gaucho Grill *(E14, EC2, EC3)*
Santa Maria del Buen Ayre *(E8)**

BRAZILIAN
Central
Mocotó *(SW1)*

West
Rodizio Rico *(W2)*

North
Rodizio Rico *(N1)*

CUBAN
Central
Floridita *(W1)*

West
La Bodeguita del Medio *(W8)*

MEXICAN/TEXMEX
Central
Café Pacifico *(WC2)*
La Perla *(W1,WC2)*
Texas Embassy Cantina *(SW1)*
Wahaca *(WC2)*

West
Cactus Blue *(SW3)*
Crazy Homies *(W2)**
Taqueria *(W11)**

North
Mestizo *(NW1)*

East
Green & Red Bar & Cantina *(E1)**

SOUTH AMERICAN
North
La Piragua *(N1)**
Sabor *(N1)*

South
Las Iguanas *(SE1)*
El Vergel *(SE1)**

AFRO-CARIBBEAN
Central
Jerk City *(W1)*
The Terrace *(WC2)*

North
Cottons *(NW1)*
Mango Room *(NW1)*

South
Jerk City *(SW18)*

East
Cottons *(EC1)*

MOROCCAN
Central
Mamounia *(W1)*
Momo *(W1)*
Original Tajines *(W1)*
Souk Medina *(WC2)*
Zaytouna *(W1)*

West
Adams Café *(W12)*
Aziz *(SW6)**
Moroccan Tagine *(W10)*
Pasha *(SW7)*

NORTH AFRICAN
Central
Mamounia *(W1)*
Souk *(WC2)*
Souk Medina *(WC2)*

West
Azou *(W6)*

East
Kenza *(EC2)*

SOUTH AFRICAN
South
Chakalaka *(SW15)*

TUNISIAN
West
Adams Café *(W12)*

EGYPTIAN
North
Ali Baba *(NW1)**

ISRAELI
Central
Gaby's *(WC2)*

North
Harry Morgan's *(NW8)*
Solly's Exclusive *(NW11)*

KOSHER
Central
Reubens *(W1)*

North
Kaifeng *(NW4)*
Solly's Exclusive *(NW11)*

East
Bevis Marks *(EC3)*

LEBANESE
Central
Al Hamra *(W1)*
Al Sultan *(W1)**
Beiteddine *(SW1)*

Fairuz *(W1)**
Fakhreldine *(W1)*
Ishbilia *(SW1)**
Levant *(W1)*
Mamounia *(W1)*
Maroush *(W1)*
Noura *(SW1,W1)*
Ranoush *(SW1)*

West
Al-Waha *(W2)*
Beirut Express *(SW7,W2)*
Chez Marcelle *(W14)**
Fresco *(W2)**
Levantine *(W2)*
Maroush *(W2)*
Maroush *(SW3)*
Randa *(W8)*
Ranoush *(SW3,W2,W8)*
Simply Lebanese *(SW7)*

East
Kenza *(EC2)*

PERSIAN
West
Alounak *(W14,W2)*
Dish Dash *(SW10)*
Kandoo *(W2)*
Mohsen *(W14)**
Yas *(W14)*

South
Dish Dash *(SW12)*

SYRIAN
West
Abu Zaad *(W12)**

TURKISH
Central
Cyprus Mangal *(SW1)**
Efes Restaurant *(W1)*
Ishtar *(W1)**
Kazan *(SW1)**
Ozer *(W1)*
Sofra *(W1,WC2)*
Tas *(WC1)*

West
Best Mangal *(W14)**
Shish *(W2)*

North
Beyoglu *(NW3)*
Gallipoli *(N1)*
Gem *(N1)**
Izgara *(N3)**
Petek *(N4)**
Shish *(NW2)*
Sofra *(NW8)*

South
Ev Restaurant, Bar & Deli *(SE1)*
Tas Pide *(SE1)*

East
Haz *(E1,EC3)*

Mangal Ocakbasi *(E8)**
Shish *(EC1)*
Sofra *(EC1)*
Tas *(EC1)*

AFGHANI
North
Afghan Kitchen *(N1)**

BURMESE
West
Mandalay *(W2)*

CHINESE
Central
Bar Shu *(W1)**
China Tang *(W1)*
The Chinese Experience *(W1)*
Chuen Cheng Ku *(W1)*
Fung Shing *(WC2)**
Golden Dragon *(W1)*
Hakkasan *(W1)*
Harbour City *(W1)*
Hunan *(SW1)**
Imperial China *(WC2)**
Jade Garden *(W1)*
Jenny Lo's *(SW1)**
Joy King Lau *(WC2)**
Kai Mayfair *(W1)**
Ken Lo's Memories *(SW1)*
Mekong *(SW1)*
Mr Chow *(SW1)*
Mr Kong *(WC2)*
New Mayflower *(W1)**
New World *(W1)*
Princess Garden *(W1)**
Royal China *(W1)**
Royal China Club *(W1)*
Shanghai Blues *(WC1)**
Taman Gang *(W1)*
Wong Kei *(W1)*
Yauatcha *(W1)**
Yming *(W1)**
Zen Central *(W1)**

West
Choys *(SW3)*
The Four Seasons *(W2)**
Good Earth *(SW3)**
Ken Lo's Memories *(W8)**
Made in China *(SW10)**
Magic Wok *(W2)*
Mandarin Kitchen *(W2)**
Mr Wing *(SW5)*
New Culture Rev'n *(SW3,W11)*
North China *(W3)**
Pearl Liang *(W2)**
Royal China *(W2)**
Royal China Fulham *(SW6)**
Stick & Bowl *(W8)*
Taiwan Village *(SW6)**
Yi-Ban *(SW6)**

North
Alisan *(HA9)**
Goldfish *(NW3)**
Good Earth *(NW7)**
Gung-Ho *(NW6)*

Kaifeng *(NW4)*
New Culture Rev'n *(N1, NW1)*
Phoenix Palace *(NW1)**
Royal China *(NW8)**
Sakonis *(HA0)**
Singapore Garden *(NW6)**
Snazz Sichuan *(NW1)**
Weng Wah House *(NW3)*
ZeNW3 *(NW3)*

South
Bayee Village *(SW19)*
Dalchini *(SW19)*
Dragon Castle *(SE17)**
Four Regions *(TW9)*
O'Zon *(TW1)*
Peninsular *(SE10)**
Royal China *(SW15)**

East
The Drunken Monkey *(E1)*
Imperial City *(EC3)*
Lotus *(E14)*
Royal China *(E14)**
Shanghai *(E8)**
Yi-Ban *(E16)**

CHINESE, DIM SUM
Central
The Chinese Experience *(W1)*
Chuen Cheng Ku *(W1)*
dim T *(W1)*
Golden Dragon *(W1)*
Hakkasan *(W1)*
Harbour City *(W1)*
Jade Garden *(W1)*
Joy King Lau *(WC2)**
New World *(W1)*
ping pong *(W1)*
Royal China *(W1)**
Royal China Club *(W1)*
Shanghai Blues *(WC1)**
Yauatcha *(W1)**

West
ping pong *(W2)*
Royal China *(W2)**
Royal China Fulham *(SW6)**

North
dim T *(N6)*
dim T *(NW3)*
Phoenix Palace *(NW1)**
Royal China *(NW8)**

South
dim T *(SE1)*
ping pong *(SE1)*
Royal China *(SW15)**

East
The Drunken Monkey *(E1)*
Lotus *(E14)*
Royal China *(E14)**
Shanghai *(E8)**

INDIAN

Central

Amaya *(SW1)**
Benares *(W1)**
Café Lazeez *(W1)*
Chor Bizarre *(W1)**
Chowki *(W1)*
The Cinnamon Club *(SW1)**
Gopal's of Soho *(W1)*
Imli *(W1)*
India Club *(WC2)*
Malabar Junction *(WC1)*
Masala Zone *(W1)*
Mela *(WC2)*
Mint Leaf *(SW1)*
Moti Mahal *(WC2)*
Nutmeg *(SW1)**
La Porte des Indes *(W1)*
Rasa Samudra *(W1)**
Red Fort *(W1)**
Salaam Namaste *(WC1)**
Sitaaray *(WC2)**
Soho Spice *(W1)*
Tamarind *(W1)**
Veeraswamy *(W1)**
Woodlands *(SW1,W1)**

West

Agni *(W6)**
Anarkali *(W6)*
Bombay Bicycle Club *(W11)**
Bombay Brasserie *(SW7)**
Bombay Palace *(W2)**
Brilliant *(UB2)**
Chutney Mary *(SW10)**
Durbar *(W2)**
Five Hot Chillies *(HA0)**
Green Chilli *(W6)**
Haandi *(SW7)**
Indian Zing *(W6)**
kare kare *(SW5)**
Karma *(W14)**
Khan's *(W2)*
Khan's of Kensington *(SW7)*
Khyber Pass *(SW7)*
Love India *(SW3)**
Ma Goa *(SW6)**
Madhu's *(UB1)**
Malabar *(W8)**
Masala Zone *(SW5)*
Memories of India *(SW7)*
Mirch Masala *(UB1)**
Monty's *(W5)*
Noor Jahan *(SW5,W2)**
The Painted Heron *(SW10)**
Rasoi Vineet Bhatia *(SW3)**
Shikara *(SW3)**
Standard *(W2)*
Star of India *(SW5)**
Tandoori Lane *(SW6)**
Vama *(SW10)**
Woodlands *(W4)**
Zaika *(W8)**

North

Anglo Asian Tandoori *(N16)*
Atma *(NW3)**
Bombay Bicycle Club *(NW3)*

Chutneys *(NW1)*
Diwana B-P House *(NW1)*
Emni *(N1)*
Eriki *(NW3)**
Eriki 2 *(NW8)**
Geeta *(NW6)*
Great Nepalese *(NW1)**
Jashan *(HA0, N8)**
Kovalam *(NW6)**
Masala Zone *(N1)*
The Parsee *(N19)*
Rani *(N3)*
Rasa *(N16)**
Rooburoo *(N1)**
Sakonis *(HA0)**
Vijay *(NW6)**
Woodlands *(NW3)**
Zaffrani *(N1)**
Zamzama *(NW1)*

South

Babur Brasserie *(SE23)**
Bengal Clipper *(SE1)**
Bombay Bicycle Club *(SW12)*
Chutney *(SW18)**
Dalchini *(SW19)*
Ekachai *(SW18)**
Everest Inn *(SE3)*
Ganapati *(SE15)**
Hara The Circle Bar *(SE1)**
Hot Stuff *(SW8)**
Indian Ocean *(SW17)**
Kastoori *(SW17)**
Kennington Tandoori *(SE11)*
Ma Goa *(SW15)**
Mirch Masala *(SW16, SW17)**
Nanglo *(SW12)**
Nazmins Balti House *(SW18)*
Origin Asia *(TW9)**
Sagar *(TW1)**
Sree Krishna *(SW17)**
Tabaq *(SW12)*
Tandoori Nights *(SE22)**
Tangawizi *(TW1)*
3 Monkeys *(SE24)*

East

Café Spice Namaste *(E1)**
Clifton *(E1)*
The Gaylord *(E14)**
Kasturi *(EC3)**
Lime *(E14)*
Memsaheb on Thames *(E14)**
Mirch Masala *(E1)**
New Tayyabs *(E1)**
Rajasthan III *(EC3)*
Scarlet Dot *(E1)*
Tiffinbites *(E14, EC2)*

INDIAN, SOUTHERN

Central

India Club *(WC2)*
Malabar Junction *(WC1)*
Quilon *(SW1)**
Ragam *(W1)**
Rasa *(W1)**
Rasa Maricham *(WC1)**
Woodlands *(SW1,W1)**

West
Sagar (W6)*
Woodlands (W4)*

North
Chutneys (NW1)
Geeta (NW6)
Kovalam (NW6)*
Rani (N3)
Rasa (N16)*
Rasa Travancore (N16)*
Vijay (NW6)*
Woodlands (NW3)*

South
Kastoori (SW17)*
Sree Krishna (SW17)*
Vijaya Krishna (SW17)*

INDONESIAN
Central
Melati, Gt Windmill St (W1)
Trader Vics (W1)

West
Kiasu (W2)*

South
Nancy Lam's Enak Enak (SW11)

JAPANESE
Central
Abeno (WC1)
Abeno Too (WC2)*
Atami (SW1)
Benihana (W1)
Centrepoint Sushi (WC2)
Chisou (W1)*
Defune (W1)*
Dinings (W1)*
Edokko (WC1)*
Feng Sushi (SW1)
Gili Gulu (WC2)
Hazuki (WC2)
Ikeda (W1)*
Ikkyu (W1)
Itsu (W1)*
Kiku (W1)*
Kobe Jones (WC1)
Kulu Kulu (W1,WC2)*
Matsuri (SW1,WC1)*
Misato (W1)*
Mitsukoshi (SW1)
Miyama (W1)*
Nagomi (W1)
Nobu (W1)*
Nobu Berkeley (W1)*
Roka (W1)*
Sake No Hana (SW1)
Sakura (W1)*
Satsuma (W1)*
Shogun (W1)*
So (W1)
Soho Japan (W1)*
Sumosan (W1)
Sushi Hiroba (WC2)*
Taman Gang (W1)
Taro (W1)

Ten Ten Tei (W1)*
Toku (W1)*
Tokyo Diner (WC2)
Umu (W1)*
Wagamama (SW1,W1,WC1,WC2)
Yoshino (W1)*

West
Benihana (SW3)
L'Etranger (SW7)
Feng Sushi (SW10,W11,W8)
Inaho (W2)*
Itsu (SW3)*
Kulu Kulu (SW7)*
Nozomi (SW3)
Okawari (W5)
Sushi-Hiro (W5)*
Tosa (W6)*
Wagamama (W8)
Yakitoria (W2)
Yumenoki (SW10)
Zuma (SW7)*

North
Benihana (NW3)
Café Japan (NW11)*
Feng Sushi (NW3)
Jin Kichi (NW3)*
Sushi-Say (NW2)*
Wagamama (N1, NW1)
Wakaba (NW3)
Yuzu (NW6)
ZeNW3 (NW3)

South
Bincho Yakitori (SE1)*
Feng Sushi (SE1)
Fujiyama (SW9)*
Inshoku (SE1)
Matsuba (TW9)*
Slurp (SW19)*
Tsunami (SW4)*
Wagamama (SE1, SW15, SW19)

East
City Miyama (EC4)*
Itsu (E14)*
K10 (EC2)*
Kurumaya (EC4)*
Miyabi (EC2)
Moshi Moshi (E14, EC2)
Mugen (EC4)
Pham Sushie (EC1)*
Saki Bar & Food Emporium (EC1)*
Shimo (EC4)
Tajima Tei (EC1)*
Tatsuso (EC2)
Tokyo City (EC2)
Ubon (E14)
Wagamama (E14, EC2, EC3, EC4)

KOREAN
Central
Asadal (WC1)
Koba (W1)*
Ran (W1)

MALAYSIAN
Central
Melati, Gt Windmill St *(W1)*
Suka *(W1)*

West
Awana *(SW3)**
Kiasu *(W2)**
Nyonya *(W11)**
Satay House *(W2)*

North
Singapore Garden *(NW6)**

South
Champor-Champor *(SE1)**

East
Ekachai *(EC2)**
Singapura *(EC3, EC4)*

PAKISTANI
Central
Salloos *(SW1)**

West
Mirch Masala *(UB1)**

South
Mirch Masala *(SW16, SW17)**
Tabaq *(SW12)*

East
Lahore Kebab House *(E1)**
Mirch Masala *(E1)**
New Tayyabs *(E1)**

PAN-ASIAN
Central
Cocoon *(W1)*
dim T *(W1)*
Haiku *(W1)*
Hare & Tortoise *(WC1)*
Just Oriental *(SW1)*
Katana *(WC2)*
Noodle Noodle *(SW1)*
Pan-Asian Canteen *(SW1)**
Tamarai *(WC2)*

West
E&O *(W11)**
Eight Over Eight *(SW3)**
Hare & Tortoise *(W14, W5)*
Mao Tai *(SW6)**
Tampopo *(SW10)*
Uli *(W11)**

North
dim T *(N6)*
dim T *(NW3)*
Gilgamesh *(NW1)*
Oriental City *(NW9)**
XO *(NW3)*

South
The Banana Leaf Canteen *(SW11)*
dim T *(SE1)*
Hare & Tortoise *(SW15)*

Nancy Lam's Enak Enak *(SW11)*
O'Zon *(TW1)*

East
Chi Noodle & Wine Bar *(EC4)*
Cicada *(EC1)**
Gt Eastern Dining Rm *(EC2)**
Pacific Oriental *(EC2)*

THAI
Central
Benja *(W1)**
Blue Jade *(SW1)*
Blue Lagoon *(SW1)*
Busaba Eathai *(W1, WC1)**
C&R Cafe *(W1)**
Chiang Mai *(W1)**
Crazy Bear *(W1)**
Mango Tree *(SW1)*
Mekong *(SW1)*
Nahm *(SW1)*
Page in Pimlico *(SW1)*
Patara *(W1)**
Suzie Wong *(W1)*
Thai Café *(SW1)*
Thai Pot *(WC2)*
Thai Square *(SW1, W1, WC2)*

West
Addie's Thai Café *(SW5)**
Bangkok *(SW7)*
Bedlington Café *(W4)*
Blue Elephant *(SW6)*
Blue Lagoon *(W14)*
Café 209 *(SW6)*
Churchill Arms *(W8)**
Esarn Kheaw *(W12)**
Fat Boy's *(W5)*
Hammersmith Café *(W6)*
Latymers *(W6)*
Old Parr's Head *(W14)*
Patara *(SW3)**
Saran Rom *(SW6)*
Silks & Spice *(W4)*
Sugar Hut *(SW6)*
Sukho Thai Cuisine *(SW6)**
Tawana *(W2)**
Thai Bistro *(W4)*
Thai Square *(SW7)*
The Walmer Castle *(W11)*
Yelo Thai Canteen *(W11)*

North
Isarn *(N1)**
Silks & Spice *(NW1)*
Thai Square *(N1)*
Yelo *(N1)*
Yum Yum *(N16)**

South
Amaranth *(SW18)**
Fat Boy's *(TW1, TW8, W4)*
Kwan Thai *(SE1)*
The Pepper Tree *(SW4)*
Ratchada *(SE3)*
Talad Thai *(SW15)**
Thai Corner Café *(SE22)*
Thai Elephant *(TW10)*

Thai Garden *(SW11)*
Thai on the River *(SW11)*
Thai Square *(SW15)*
Thailand *(SE14)**

East
Ekachai *(EC2)**
Elephant Royale *(E14)*
Gt Eastern Dining Rm *(EC2)**
Hokkien Chan *(EC2)*
Silks & Spice *(EC4)*
Sri Nam *(E14)*
Thai Square *(EC4)*
Thai Square City *(EC3)*

VIETNAMESE
Central
Bam-Bou *(W1)*
Mekong *(SW1)*
Viet *(W1)**

West
Kiasu *(W2)**
Nam Long *(SW5)*
Saigon Saigon *(W6)*

North
Huong-Viet *(N1)**
Khoai *(N8)*
Viet Garden *(N1)*
Viet-Anh *(NW1)*

East
Cây Tre *(EC1)*
Namo *(E9)**
Pho *(EC1)*
Sông Quê *(E2)**
Viet Hoa *(E2)*

AREA OVERVIEWS

CENTRAL

Soho, Covent Garden & Bloomsbury
(Parts of W1, all WC2 and WC1)

Price	Restaurant	Cuisine	Ratings
£80+	Savoy Grill	*British, Traditional*	– – –
£70+	Lindsay House	*British, Modern*	3 3 2
	L'Atelier de Joel Robuchon	*French*	1 2 2
	Pearl	*"*	3 3 3
£60+	Adam Street	*British, Modern*	3 3 2
	Axis	*"*	4 3 4
	L'Escargot (Picasso Room)	*French*	2 1 2
	Asia de Cuba	*Fusion*	3 4 2
	Red Fort	*Indian*	2 3 3
	Matsuri	*Japanese*	2 2 4
£50+	Christopher's	*American*	4 4 4
	Alastair Little	*British, Modern*	3 2 5
	Homage	*"*	4 4 2
	Indigo	*"*	3 2 2
	The Ivy	*"*	3 2 2
	The Portrait	*"*	4 4 2
	Refuel	*"*	4 4 3
	Rules	*British, Traditional*	3 3 1
	Simpsons-in-the-Strand	*"*	4 4 2
	J Sheekey	*Fish & seafood*	1 2 2
	Zilli Fish	*"*	2 3 3
	Clos Maggiore	*French*	3 2 1
	Incognico	*"*	3 3 3
	Jaan	*Fusion*	2 3 4
	Quo Vadis	*Italian*	4 4 4
	Floridita	*Cuban*	5 5 3
	Yauatcha	*Chinese*	1 3 2
	Moti Mahal	*Indian*	3 4 4
	Asadal	*Korean*	3 4 5
£40+	Joe Allen	*American*	4 3 1
	Acorn House	*British, Modern*	3 3 3
	Café du Jardin	*"*	4 4 4
	The Club Bar & Dining	*"*	4 4 4
	Le Deuxième	*"*	3 2 4
	French House	*"*	4 3 3
	Stanza	*"*	4 4 4
	The Terrace	*"*	4 3 3
	Tuttons	*"*	4 4 4
	The National Dining Rooms	*British, Traditional*	4 4 4
	Cape Town Fish Market	*Fish & seafood*	– – –
	Livebait	*"*	4 4 4
	The Admiralty	*French*	5 4 5
	Arbutus	*"*	2 2 3
	Beotys	*"*	4 3 4
	Café des Amis du Vin	*"*	4 3 3
	Chez Gérard	*"*	5 4 4
	L'Escargot	*"*	2 2 2
	Mon Plaisir	*"*	4 3 2
	Le Palais du Jardin	*"*	3 4 3
	La Trouvaille	*"*	3 2 2
	The Forge	*International*	4 1 3

Ronnie Scott's	"	⑤④❶
Little Italy	Italian	④④❸
Orso	"	④②④
Signor Zilli	"	❸②❸
Vasco & Piero's Pavilion	"	❸②④
Albannach	Scottish	⑤④④
Barrafina	Spanish	❶❶❶
Cigala	"	④❸❸
Gaucho Grill	Steaks & grills	❸④④
St Moritz	Swiss	❸❸❸
Planet Hollywood	Burgers, etc	⑤⑤⑤
La Spiga	Pizza	❸④❸
Shanghai Blues	Chinese	❷❸❷
Malabar Junction	Indian	❸②❷
Kobe Jones	Japanese	④④④
Tamarai	Pan-Asian	④④❸
Patara	Thai	❷❷❸

£35+	Smollensky's	American	⑤⑤④
	TGI Friday's	"	⑤④⑤
	Belgo Centraal	Belgian	④④④
	Aurora	British, Modern	❸②❶
	Boulevard Bar & Dng Rm	"	❸④❸
	Konstam	"	❸❶❸
	Shampers	"	❸②❷
	Great Queen Street	British, Traditional	❷❸④
	Loch Fyne	Fish & seafood	④❸④
	Café Bohème	French	④④❷
	Randall & Aubin	"	❸❸❷
	So	Fusion	❸②❸
	Gay Hussar	Hungarian	④❸❷
	Bedford & Strand	International	⑤❷❸
	Bohème Kitchen	"	④④❸
	Boulevard	"	④④❸
	Browns	"	⑤⑤④
	National Gallery Café	"	④⑤❸
	Papageno	"	⑤④❷
	Sarastro	"	⑤⑤❸
	06 St Chad's Place	"	❸❸❸
	Bertorelli's	Italian	⑤⑤④
	Pasta Brown	"	④④⑤
	Rainforest Café	Burgers, etc	⑤④❷
	Wolfe's	"	④⑤⑤
	Kettners	Pizza	④❸❷
	Café Pacifico	Mexican/TexMex	④④❸
	Bar Shu	Chinese	❷④❸
	Fung Shing	"	❷❸⑤
	Imperial China	"	❷❸❸
	Rasa Maricham	Indian, Southern	❶❷④
	Edokko	Japanese	❶❶❸
	Ten Ten Tei	"	❷❷⑤
	Ran	Korean	❸❷❸
	Benja	Thai	❷❷❸

£30+	All Star Lanes	American	④④❷
	Bodean's	"	④④❸
	Maxwell's	"	④④❸
	Andrew Edmunds	British, Modern	❸❶❶
	Porters	British, Traditional	⑤⑤⑤
	Balans	International	⑤④❸

267

Cork & Bottle	"	⑤④❶
Sugar Reef	"	⑤⑤④
Aperitivo	Italian	❸❷❷
Ciao Bella	"	❸❶❶
Sapori	"	④❸❸
Meza	Spanish	⑤④❸
Mildred's	Vegetarian	❷❸❷
Fire & Stone	Pizza	④④❸
La Perla	Mexican/TexMex	④④❸
Souk Medina	Moroccan	④❷❶
Zaytouna	"	④④❸
Souk	North African	④④❷
Sofra	Turkish	④④④
The Chinese Experience	Chinese	❸❷④
Yming	"	❷❶❸
Café Lazeez	Indian	❸④❸
Mela	"	❸④④
Sitaaray	"	❷❷❷
Soho Spice	"	④❸④
Abeno	Japanese	❸❸④
Abeno Too	"	❷❷❸
Hazuki	"	❸❷④
Katana	Pan-Asian	④④❸
Chiang Mai	Thai	❷④④
Suzie Wong	"	❸❸❸
Thai Pot	"	④④⑤

£25+	The Easton	British, Modern	❷❷❷
	Real Greek Souvlaki & Bar	Greek	⑤⑤④
	Seven Stars	International	❸④❷
	Star Café	"	❸❷❸
	Amato	Italian	❸❷❸
	Spacca Napoli	"	❷④❸
	The Norfolk Arms	Mediterranean	❸❸❷
	Café España	Spanish	❸❷❷
	La Tasca	"	⑤④❸
	North Sea Fish	Fish & chips	❷❷④
	Paradiso Olivelli	Pizza	④④④
	Pâtisserie Valerie	Sandwiches, cakes, etc	④④❸
	Paul	"	❸④④
	Wahaca	Mexican/TexMex	❸❷❷
	Gaby's	Israeli	❸❸⑤
	Tas	Turkish	④❸❸
	Chuen Cheng Ku	Chinese	❸④④
	Golden Dragon	"	④⑤④
	Harbour City	"	❸❸④
	Jade Garden	"	❸④❸
	Mr Kong	"	– – –
	New Mayflower	"	❷④④
	New World	"	❸❸❸
	ping pong	Chinese, Dim sum	④④❷
	Chowki	Indian	❸④④
	Gopal's of Soho	"	❸❷④
	Imli	"	❸❸④
	Masala Zone	"	❸❸❸
	Salaam Namaste	"	❷❸④
	Itsu	Japanese	❷❸❸
	Kulu Kulu	"	❷④⑤
	Satsuma	"	❸④❸
	Sushi Hiroba	"	❷❷❸

	Melati, Gt Windmill St	*Malaysian*	④③④
	Busaba Eathai	*Thai*	②③②
	C&R Cafe	*"*	②④④
	Thai Square	*"*	④③③
£20+	Café Emm	*British, Modern*	④②②
	Café in the Crypt	*International*	– – –
	Gordon's Wine Bar	*"*	⑤③❶
	La Porchetta Pizzeria	*Italian*	❸④❸
	Bistro 1	*Mediterranean*	④②❸
	Leon	*"*	②❸❸
	Ed's Easy Diner	*Burgers, etc*	④❸②
	Gourmet Burger Kitchen	*"*	②④④
	Hamburger Union	*"*	❸④④
	The Ultimate Burger	*"*	④④④
	Rock & Sole Plaice	*Fish & chips*	❸④④
	Le Pain Quotidien	*Sandwiches, cakes, etc*	❸④②
	Joy King Lau	*Chinese*	②❸④
	Wong Kei	*"*	❸⑤④
	India Club	*Indian*	④④④
	Centrepoint Sushi	*Japanese*	❸❸❸
	Gili Gulu	*"*	④⑤⑤
	Misato	*"*	②④④
	Taro	*"*	❸❸④
	Wagamama	*"*	④❸④
	Hare & Tortoise	*Pan-Asian*	④④④
£15+	Square Pie Company	*British, Traditional*	❸④④
	Stock Pot	*International*	④❸❸
	Paolina Café	*Italian*	②②④
	Food for Thought	*Vegetarian*	②④④
	Bar Italia	*Sandwiches, cakes, etc*	④②❶
	Just Falafs	*"*	②②④
	Konditor & Cook	*"*	❶❸④
	Jerk City	*Afro-Caribbean*	❸④⑤
	Tokyo Diner	*Japanese*	④❸❸
	Viet	*Vietnamese*	②⑤⑤
£10+	Hummus Bros	*Mediterranean*	❸②④
	Nordic Bakery	*Scandinavian*	②❷❸
	Apostrophe	*Sandwiches, cakes, etc*	❸❸②
	Monmouth Coffee Company	*"*	❶②②
£5+	Caffè Vergnano	*Italian*	❸②②
	Fryer's Delight	*Fish & chips*	④④⑤
	Flat White	*Sandwiches, cakes, etc*	②②❸
	Maison Bertaux	*"*	❸④❶

Mayfair & St James's (Parts of W1 and SW1)

£130+	Sketch (Lecture Rm)	*French*	④❸④
£120+	Le Gavroche	*French*	②❶②
	Umu	*Japanese*	②❸❸
£100+	Alain Ducasse	*French*	– – –
	The Square	*"*	②②❸
	Sake No Hana	*Japanese*	– – –

Price	Restaurant	Cuisine	Ratings
£90+	The Ritz	*French*	④❷❶
£80+	Wiltons	*British, Traditional*	❸❷❷
	G Ramsay at Claridges	*French*	④❸❷
	The Greenhouse	*"*	❸❸❸
	L'Oranger	*"*	❸❷❷
	Connaught	*Mediterranean*	– – –
	Nobu	*Japanese*	❷④④
	Nobu Berkeley	*"*	❷④❸
£70+	The Cuckoo Club	*British, Modern*	⑤⑤④
	Dorchester Grill	*"*	④❸④
	Cipriani	*Italian*	⑤⑤④
	China Tang	*Chinese*	⑤④④
	Hakkasan	*"*	❸④❷
	Taman Gang	*"*	⑤⑤❸
	Trader Vics	*Indonesian*	⑤⑤④
	Sumosan	*Japanese*	❸④④
£60+	Bellamy's	*British, Modern*	❸❸❷
	Brian Turner	*"*	⑤④⑤
	Brown's Grill	*"*	④❷④
	Mews of Mayfair	*"*	④④④
	Patterson's	*"*	❷❷④
	Galvin at Windows	*French*	❸❸❷
	Hibiscus	*"*	– – –
	Mirabelle	*"*	④❸❸
	La Petite Maison	*"*	❸❸❷
	Cecconi's	*Italian*	④④❷
	Theo Randall	*"*	❷❷④
	Benares	*Indian*	❷❸❸
	Ikeda	*Japanese*	❶❸⑤
	Matsuri	*"*	❷❷④
	Miyama	*"*	❷❷⑤
	Haiku	*Pan-Asian*	④⑤⑤
£50+	The Avenue	*British, Modern*	④④④
	Le Caprice	*"*	❷❶❶
	Hush	*"*	④④❸
	Nicole's	*"*	④④④
	Quaglino's	*"*	⑤⑤⑤
	Rhodes W1 Brasserie	*"*	⑤⑤⑤
	The Wolseley	*"*	❸❷❷
	Green's	*British, Traditional*	❸❷❷
	Greig's	*"*	④④⑤
	Bentley's	*Fish & seafood*	❸❸❸
	Scott's	*"*	❷❷❶
	Brasserie Roux	*French*	❸❸❸
	Criterion Grill	*"*	⑤⑤❷
	maze	*"*	❷❸❸
	Sketch (Gallery)	*"*	④④④
	Franco's	*Italian*	④④④
	Giardinetto	*"*	❸❸⑤
	Luciano	*"*	④④④
	Mosaico	*"*	❸❸❸
	Pappagallo	*"*	❸❷❸
	Sartoria	*"*	❸❸④
	St Alban	*Mediterranean*	❸❷④
	The Guinea Grill	*Steaks & grills*	❷❸❸
	Rowley's	*"*	④④④

	Ladurée	Afternoon tea	③	④	❸
	Mamounia	Moroccan	④	④	❸
	Momo	"	④	⑤	❸
	Kai Mayfair	Chinese	❷	❷	④
	Princess Garden	"	❷	❷	④
	Mint Leaf	Indian	❸	④	❸
	Tamarind	"	❷	❷	❸
	Veeraswamy	"	❷	❸	❷
	Benihana	Japanese	④	❸	④
	Kiku	"	❷	❸	④
	Mitsukoshi	"	❸	❷	⑤
	Shogun	"	❷	❷	④
	Cocoon	Pan-Asian	④	④	❸
£40+	Automat	American	❸	④	❸
	Inn the Park	British, Modern	④	⑤	④
	Just St James	"	④	⑤	④
	Langan's Brasserie	"	④	❸	❷
	The Little Square	"	④	④	❸
	The Only Running Footman	"	—	—	—
	Pigalle Club	"	⑤	❸	❷
	Sotheby's Café	"	❷	❶	❷
	Wild Honey	"	❸	❷	❷
	Fortnum's, The Fountain	British, Traditional	—	—	—
	Pescatori	Fish & seafood	④	④	④
	Boudin Blanc	French	❸	❸	❷
	Chez Gérard	"	⑤	④	④
	Dover Street	"	⑤	④	❸
	Al Duca	Italian	❸	❸	❸
	Alloro	"	❷	❷	❸
	Diverso	"	④	④	⑤
	Getti	"	④	④	❸
	Ristorante Semplice	"	❷	❸	④
	Serafino	"	④	❸	④
	Via Condotti	"	❸	❷	❸
	Il Vicolo	"	❸	❸	⑤
	Truc Vert	Mediterranean	④	④	❸
	Gaucho Grill	Steaks & grills	❸	④	④
	Aubaine	Sandwiches, cakes, etc	④	⑤	❸
	Al Hamra	Lebanese	④	④	④
	Fakhreldine	"	❸	❸	④
	Levant	"	④	④	❶
	Noura	"	④	④	④
	Zen Central	Chinese	❷	❸	④
	Chor Bizarre	Indian	❷	❸	❷
	Quilon	Indian, Southern	❷	❷	④
	Chisou	Japanese	❷	❷	❸
	Patara	Thai	❷	❷	❸
£35+	Browns	International	⑤	⑤	④
	Living Room	"	⑤	④	④
	Caricatura	Italian	❸	❸	❸
	Rocket	Mediterranean	④	④	❸
	Hard Rock Café	Burgers, etc	④	❸	❷
	Delfino	Pizza	❷	❸	④
	Richoux	Sandwiches, cakes, etc	⑤	⑤	④
	Al Sultan	Lebanese	❷	❷	⑤
	Rasa	Indian	❶	❷	④
	Yoshino	Japanese	❷	❷	④

Price	Name	Cuisine	Ratings
£30+	The Windmill	British, Traditional	③③③
	L'Artiste Musclé	French	④④❶
	Running Horse	International	❷③❷
	Tiger Tiger	"	⑤⑤③
	Piccolino	Italian	④④④
	El Pirata	Spanish	③❷❷
	Royal Academy	Sandwiches, cakes, etc	④④③
	Sketch (Parlour)	"	④③③
	Sofra	Turkish	④④④
	Nagomi	Japanese	③❷③
	Just Oriental	Pan-Asian	③③③
£25+	Diner	Burgers, etc	❷④❷
	Gourmet Pizza Co.	Pizza	③④③
	Pâtisserie Valerie	Sandwiches, cakes, etc	④④③
	Ishtar	Turkish	❷③③
	Woodlands	Indian	❷❷④
	Itsu	Japanese	❷③③
	Sakura	"	❷⑤⑤
	Toku	"	❷③⑤
	Busaba Eathai	Thai	❷③❷
	Thai Square	"	④③③
£20+	Wagamama	Japanese	④③④
	Noodle Noodle	Pan-Asian	④③④
£15+	Stock Pot	International	④③③
	Salade	Sandwiches, cakes, etc	③④④
£10+	Apostrophe	Sandwiches, cakes, etc	③③❷
	Benugo	"	❷③③
	Crussh	"	❷❷④
	Fuzzy's Grub	"	❶❶③

Fitzrovia & Marylebone (Part of W1)

Price	Name	Cuisine	Ratings
£80+	Pied à Terre	French	❷❷③
£70+	Rhodes W1 Restaurant	French	– – –
£60+	Orrery	French	③❷③
	Texture	"	– – –
	5 Cavendish Square	Italian	④③❷
	Defune	Japanese	❶③⑤
	Suka	Malaysian	⑤⑤⑤
£50+	Oscar	British, Modern	④④④
	Elena's L'Etoile	French	③❷❷
	The Providores	Fusion	❷③④
	Caffè Caldesi	Italian	③③③
	Caldesi	"	③④④
	Camerino	"	④④⑤
	Locanda Locatelli	"	❷❷❷
	Passione	"	③③④
	Fino	Spanish	❶❷③
	Royal China Club	Chinese	③③④
	La Porte des Indes	Indian	③③❶
	Roka	Japanese	❶③❷

Price	Restaurant	Cuisine	Ratings
£40+	Blandford Street	British, Modern	④④④
	The Union Café	"	④❸④
	Odin's	British, Traditional	❸❶❶
	Back to Basics	Fish & seafood	❶❸④
	Pescatori	"	④④④
	Annex 3	French	④④❸
	Galvin Bistrot de Luxe	"	❶❶❷
	Villandry	"	❸④❷
	The Wallace	"	❸④❶
	Archipelago	Fusion	❸❶❶
	Hardy's	International	❸❸❸
	Michael Moore	"	❸❸❸
	Getti	Italian	④④❸
	Latium	"	❶❶❷
	Sardo	"	❷❸④
	2 Veneti	"	❷❷❸
	Black & Blue	Steaks & grills	❸❸④
	Reubens	Kosher	❸④④
	Fairuz	Lebanese	❷❸④
	Maroush	"	❸④④
	Koba	Korean	❷❶❸
	Crazy Bear	Thai	❷❷❶
	Bam-Bou	Vietnamese	❸❸❶
£35+	Fishworks	Fish & seafood	❸④④
	Seaport	"	❸④⑤
	Providores (Tapa Room)	Fusion	❷④④
	Bertorelli's	Italian	⑤⑤④
	Salt Yard	Mediterranean	❶❷❸
	Garbo's	Scandinavian	④❸④
	Royal China	Chinese	❶❸④
	Rasa Samudra	Indian	❶❷④
£30+	RIBA Café	British, Modern	④④❶
	Langan's Bistro	French	④❷❷
	Le Relais de Venise	"	❸④❷
	Hellenik	Greek	❸❶❸
	Eat & Two Veg	International	⑤④④
	Giraffe	"	④❸④
	Ooze	"	④④⑤
	O'Conor Don	Irish	④④❸
	La Rueda	Spanish	④④❸
	Tootsies	Burgers, etc	④❸④
	La Perla	Mexican/TexMex	④④❸
	Original Tajines	Moroccan	❸❸❸
	Ozer	Turkish	④❸❸
	Sofra	"	④④④
	Ragam	Indian, Southern	❶❷⑤
	Dinings	Japanese	❶❷④
	Ikkyu	"	❸④❸
£25+	Real Greek Souvlaki & Bar	Greek	⑤⑤④
	Navarro's	Spanish	❸❸❷
	Eagle Bar Diner	Burgers, etc	❸④❷
	Fine Burger Company	"	❸④④
	Paradiso Olivelli	Pizza	④④④
	La Fromagerie Café	Sandwiches, cakes, etc	❶❷❷
	Pâtisserie Valerie	"	④④❸
	Paul	"	❸④④
	Efes Restaurant	Turkish	④❸④

	ping pong	*Chinese, Dim sum*	④④❷
	Woodlands	*Indian*	❷❷④
	Soho Japan	*Japanese*	❷❸④
	dim T	*Pan-Asian*	④④❸
£20+	Leon	*Mediterranean*	❷❸❸
	Hamburger Union	*Burgers, etc*	❸④④
	The Ultimate Burger	''	④④④
	Le Pain Quotidien	*Sandwiches, cakes, etc*	❸④❷
	Wagamama	*Japanese*	④❸④
£15+	Pure California	*American*	❸④④
	Golden Hind	*Fish & chips*	❶❶❸
£10+	Apostrophe	*Sandwiches, cakes, etc*	❸❸❷
	Benugo	''	❷❸❸

Belgravia, Pimlico, Victoria & Westminster (SW1, except St James's)

£80+	Rib Room	*British, Traditional*	❸④④
	Pétrus	*French*	❶❶❷
£70+	The Lanesborough	*British, Modern*	④❸❶
	One-O-One	*Fish & seafood*	– – –
	Foliage	*French*	❶❶❷
	La Noisette	''	⑤④⑤
	Tsar	*Russian*	– – –
	Nahm	*Thai*	④⑤⑤
£60+	The Goring Hotel	*British, Traditional*	❸❶❷
	Roussillon	*French*	❶❶❸
	Santini	*Italian*	⑤④④
	Toto's	''	❸❷❷
	Mr Chow	*Chinese*	❸❸④
£50+	The Fifth Floor Restaurant	*British, Modern*	④④④
	Thomas Cubitt	''	❸❸❷
	La Poule au Pot	*French*	❸❸❶
	Boxwood Café	*International*	④❸❸
	Motcombs	''	④④❸
	Pomegranates	''	④❷❷
	Brumus	*Italian*	④❷⑤
	L'Incontro	''	④④❸
	Mimmo d'Ischia	''	④❸❸
	Quirinale	''	❷❶④
	Zafferano	''	❷❷❸
	Boisdale	*Scottish*	④❸❶
	Ladurée	*Afternoon tea*	❸④❸
	Mocotó	*Brazilian*	④④❸
	Amaya	*Indian*	❶❸❷
	The Cinnamon Club	''	❷❸❷
	Atami	*Japanese*	❸❸④
	Mango Tree	*Thai*	❸❸④
£40+	Atrium	*British, Modern*	⑤⑤④
	Bank Westminster	''	④④④
	Ebury Wine Bar	''	④④❸
	Langtry's	''	④④❸

	Name	Cuisine	Ratings
	Tate Britain	"	④❸❷
	Shepherd's	British, Traditional	④❷❸
	Olivomare	Fish & seafood	❷⓪❸
	Le Cercle	French	⓪❷❷
	The Chelsea Brasserie	"	④④⑤
	Chez Gérard	"	⑤④④
	Drones	"	④❸④
	The Ebury	"	④④④
	Mju	Fusion	❸❸⑤
	Caraffini	Italian	❸⓪❷
	Il Convivio	"	❸⓪❸
	Gran Paradiso	"	❸❸❸
	Olivo	"	❷❷④
	Sale e Pepe	"	❸❸❷
	Signor Sassi	"	❸❷❸
	Vivezza	"	④❷④
	Volt	"	❸❸❸
	The Fifth Floor Café	Mediterranean	⑤④④
	Oliveto	Pizza	❷❸④
	Beiteddine	Lebanese	❸❷⑤
	Noura	"	④④④
	Hunan	Chinese	⓪⓪④
	Ken Lo's Memories	"	❸❷❸
	Salloos	Pakistani	❷❸④
£35+	The Contented Vine	British, Modern	④④④
	Footstool	"	⑤⑤④
	Grenadier	British, Traditional	④④⓪
	City Café	International	④❷❸
	Grumbles	"	④❷❸
	Como Lario	Italian	④❷❷
	Uno	"	❸④④
	About Thyme	Mediterranean	④❸④
	Daylesford Organics	Organic	④❸⓪
	Baker & Spice	Sandwiches, cakes, etc	❷④④
	Texas Embassy Cantina	Mexican/TexMex	⑤⑤⑤
	Ishbilia	Lebanese	❷❷④
£30+	The Phoenix	British, Modern	④④❸
	Oriel	International	⑤⑤❸
	Pizza on the Park	Italian	④④❷
	2 Amici	"	❸❸❸
	Goya	Spanish	④❸❸
	Ranoush	Lebanese	❸④④
	Kazan	Turkish	❷⓪⓪
	Pan-Asian Canteen	Pan-Asian	❷④④
	Blue Lagoon	Thai	④❸❸
£25+	Royal Court Bar	British, Modern	④❸❷
	Vincent Rooms	"	❸④❸
	Chimes	British, Traditional	④④④
	Caramel	International	④❷❸
	Seafresh	Fish & chips	❸❷④
	Pâtisserie Valerie	Sandwiches, cakes, etc	④④❸
	Jenny Lo's	Chinese	❷❷④
	Feng Sushi	Japanese	❸④❸
	Blue Jade	Thai	❸⓪❸
	Page in Pimlico	"	❸❸❸
	Thai Café	"	❸❸⑤

£20+	Cyprus Mangal	*Turkish*	❶❷④
	Nutmeg	*Indian*	❷❷❸
	Wagamama	*Japanese*	④❸④
	Mekong	*Vietnamese*	④④⑤
£10+	Apostrophe	*Sandwiches, cakes, etc*	❸❸❷

Chelsea, South Kensington, Kensington, Earl's Court & Fulham (SW3, SW5, SW6, SW7, SW10 & W8)

£100+			
Gordon Ramsay	French	④⑤❷
Blakes	International	④④❶

£80+			
Aubergine	French	❶❷❸
The Capital Restaurant	"	❷❷❸
Tom Aikens	"	❷❷❸

£70+			
The Bentley Hotel	French	④❸④
Brunello	Italian	④❸❸
Rasoi Vineet Bhatia	Indian	❶❷❸

£60+			
Babylon	British, Modern	④④❷
The Collection	"	⑤⑤④
The Tenth Restaurant & Bar	"	❸❸❷
Bibendum	French	④❸❷
Cheyne Walk Bras'	"	❸④❸
L'Etranger	"	❸❸❸
Nozomi	Japanese	④④❸
Zuma	"	❶❸❶

£50+			
Bluebird	British, Modern	④❸❷
Clarke's	"	❷❷❸
Joe's Café	"	④④❸
Kensington Place	"	④❸④
Tom's Kitchen	"	❸④④
Deep	Fish & seafood	❷❸❸
Poissonnerie de l'Av.	"	❷❷❸
Le Suquet	"	❷④❸
Belvedere	French	❸❶❶
Papillon	"	❸❷❷
Aquasia	Fusion	⑤⑤④
Carpaccio's	Italian	⑤④❷
Daphne's	"	❸❸❷
Montpeliano	"	⑤④④
Osteria dell'Arancio	"	❸❷❸
San Lorenzo	"	⑤④④
Scalini	"	❸❸❷
Timo	"	❸❷④
Locanda Ottomezzo	Mediterranean	❸❷❸
Bombay Brasserie	Indian	❷❷❷
Chutney Mary	"	❷❷❷
Zaika	"	❷❸❸
Benihana	Japanese	④❸④
Blue Elephant	Thai	❸❸❶

£40+			
Big Easy	American	④④❸
PJ's	"	⑤⑤④
The Abingdon	British, Modern	❸❷❷
Admiral Codrington	"	④④❸
Bistrot 190	"	④⑤④
Brinkley's	"	④④❷
Duke on the Green	"	❸❸❸
11 Abingdon Road	"	④④⑤
Launceston Place	"	④❸❸

277

Name	Cuisine	Ratings
Vingt-Quatre	"	④ ❸ ❸
Whits	"	❷ ⓪ ❸
Ffiona's	British, Traditional	❸ ⓪ ⓪
Kensington Square Kitchen	"	– – –
Maggie Jones's	"	④ ❸ ⓪
Lundum's	Danish	❷ ⓪ ⓪
Lou Pescadou	Fish & seafood	❸ ④ ④
Tom's Place	"	– – –
La Bouchée	French	❷ ❸ ⓪
La Brasserie	"	④ ④ ❸
Brasserie St Quentin	"	④ ❸ ❸
Le Colombier	"	❸ ❷ ❷
Langan's Coq d'Or	"	④ ❷ ④
Racine	"	❷ ⓪ ❸
Brompton Quarter Café	International	⑤ ⑤ ④
The Enterprise	"	❸ ❷ ❷
606 Club	"	④ ④ ⓪
The Swag & Tails	"	❸ ❷ ⓪
The Ark	Italian	④ ❸ ❷
C Garden	"	❸ ⓪ ❸
Elistano	"	④ ④ ④
La Famiglia	"	❸ ❷ ❷
Frantoio	"	❸ ⓪ ❷
Lucio	"	❸ ❸ ❸
Manicomio	"	④ ④ ❸
Pellicano	"	❷ ❷ ❸
Il Portico	"	❸ ⓪ ❷
Ziani	"	❸ ❷ ❷
Cross Keys	Mediterranean	④ ④ ❷
Kicca	"	④ ④ ❸
Wódka	Polish	❸ ❸ ❷
Cambio de Tercio	Spanish	❷ ❷ ❷
L-Restaurant & Bar	"	④ ④ ④
Black & Blue	Steaks & grills	❸ ❸ ④
Gaucho Grill	"	❸ ④ ④
Aubaine	Sandwiches, cakes, etc	④ ⑤ ❸
Bluebird Café	"	⑤ ⑤ ④
Pasha	Moroccan	④ ④ ⓪
Maroush	Lebanese	❸ ④ ④
Good Earth	Chinese	❷ ❷ ❸
Ken Lo's Memories	"	⓪ ❷ ❸
Mr Wing	"	❸ ❸ ⓪
The Painted Heron	Indian	⓪ ❷ ❸
Vama	"	❷ ❷ ❸
Yumenoki	Japanese	❸ ❷ ④
Awana	Malaysian	❷ ❷ ❸
Eight Over Eight	Pan-Asian	❷ ❸ ❷
Mao Tai	"	❷ ❸ ❸
Patara	Thai	❷ ❷ ❸
Saran Rom	"	④ ❸ ❸
Sugar Hut	"	④ ④ ⓪
£35+ Sticky Fingers	American	⑤ ④ ❸
TGI Friday's	"	⑤ ④ ⑤
Bibendum Oyster Bar	British, Modern	❸ ❸ ❸
Bowler Bar & Grill	"	❸ ❷ ❸
Britannia	"	④ ④ ❸
Butcher's Hook	"	❸ ❸ ❸
The Farm	"	❷ ❷ ❷
Lots Road	"	❸ ❸ ❸

The Phoenix	"	④	④	❸
The Salisbury Tavern	"	④	④	④
Fishworks	Fish & seafood	❸	④	④
Chez Patrick	French	④	❸	④
The Pig's Ear	"	❸	❸	❷
Randall & Aubin	"	❸	❸	❷
Tartine	"	❸	❸	❸
The Cabin	International	❸	❷	❷
Coopers Arms	"	❸	④	❸
Foxtrot Oscar	"	–	–	–
Wine Gallery	"	④	❸	❷
Da Mario	Italian	❸	❷	❸
De Cecco	"	④	④	④
Il Falconiere	"	❸	❷	④
Made in Italy	"	❸	④	④
Napulé	"	❷	④	④
Nuovi Sapori	"	❷	❷	④
Ottolenghi	"	❶	❸	❸
Riccardo's	"	❸	❸	❸
Santa Lucia	"	❸	❷	❷
Polish Club	Polish	④	❷	❶
Tendido Cero	Spanish	❷	❷	❸
El Gaucho	Steaks & grills	❷	❷	❸
Napket	Afternoon tea	❷	❷	❸
Geale's	Fish & chips	④	❸	❸
Friends	Pizza	❸	❷	④
Baker & Spice	Sandwiches, cakes, etc	❷	④	④
Hugo's	"	❸	❸	❸
Richoux	"	⑤	⑤	④
La Bodeguita del Medio	Cuban	④	④	❸
Cactus Blue	Mexican/TexMex	⑤	⑤	④
Randa	Lebanese	❸	❷	④
Simply Lebanese	"	❸	❸	④
Made in China	Chinese	❷	❷	⑤
Royal China Fulham	"	❶	❸	④
Haandi	Indian	❷	❷	❸
Love India	"	❷	❷	④
Star of India	"	❷	❷	❸
Sukho Thai Cuisine	Thai	❶	❶	❷
Nam Long	Vietnamese	⑤	④	④

£30+	Bodean's	American	④	④	❸
	The Anglesea Arms	British, Modern	④	④	❷
	The Builder's Arms	"	❸	④	❷
	Joe's Brasserie	"	❸	❷	❷
	Le Metro	"	–	–	–
	The Oratory	"	④	④	❷
	White Horse	"	❸	❸	❷
	Balans	International	⑤	④	❸
	Giraffe	"	④	❸	④
	Glaisters	"	❸	❸	❷
	The Scarsdale	"	④	④	❶
	Aglio e Olio	Italian	❷	❸	④
	Buona Sera	"	④	❸	❷
	Frankie's Italian Bar & Grill	"	⑤	⑤	❸
	Miraggio	"	④	❷	❸
	Il Pagliaccio	"	④	❷	❷
	The Atlas	Mediterranean	❷	④	❷
	La Rueda	Spanish	④	④	❸
	Sophie's Steakhouse	Steaks & grills	❸	❸	❶

	Restaurant	Cuisine			
	Henry J Beans	Burgers, etc	5	4	4
	Tootsies	"	4	3	4
	Basilico	Pizza	2	3	4
	(Ciro's) Pizza Pomodoro	"	4	4	2
	Troubadour	Sandwiches, cakes, etc	5	3	1
	Ranoush	Lebanese	3	4	4
	Dish Dash	Persian	3	4	2
	Choys	Chinese	4	2	4
	Yi-Ban	"	2	2	2
	kare kare	Indian	2	2	3
	Ma Goa	"	1	2	3
	Malabar	"	2	2	2
	Noor Jahan	"	2	2	3
	Bangkok	Thai	3	2	4
£25+	The Arbiter	British, Traditional	3	3	3
	The Windsor Castle	International	4	3	1
	Pappa Ciccia	Italian	2	2	2
	Picasso's	"	5	4	4
	Rossopomodoro	"	3	4	3
	Spago	"	4	3	3
	Little Bay	Mediterranean	3	2	2
	Daquise	Polish	4	4	3
	Rôtisserie Jules	Steaks & grills	3	4	5
	Pâtisserie Valerie	Sandwiches, cakes, etc	4	4	3
	Paul	"	3	4	4
	Aziz	Moroccan	2	3	3
	Taiwan Village	Chinese	2	2	3
	Khan's of Kensington	Indian	3	3	4
	Khyber Pass	"	3	2	4
	Masala Zone	"	3	3	3
	Memories of India	"	3	2	4
	Shikara	"	2	3	4
	Tandoori Lane	"	2	2	3
	Feng Sushi	Japanese	3	4	3
	Itsu	"	2	3	3
	Kulu Kulu	"	2	4	5
	Tampopo	Pan-Asian	3	3	3
	Addie's Thai Café	Thai	2	2	3
	Thai Square	"	4	3	3
£20+	Costa's Grill	Greek	4	3	3
	Chelsea Bun Diner	International	3	3	4
	Mona Lisa	"	3	2	4
	Leon	Mediterranean	2	3	3
	Gourmet Burger Kitchen	Burgers, etc	2	4	4
	Costa's Fish	Fish & chips	2	2	4
	La Delizia	Pizza	3	4	4
	Le Pain Quotidien	Sandwiches, cakes, etc	3	4	2
	Beirut Express	Lebanese	3	3	4
	New Culture Rev'n	Chinese	5	4	5
	Wagamama	Japanese	4	3	4
	Café 209	Thai	3	2	1
£15+	Stock Pot	International	4	3	3
	Stick & Bowl	Chinese	3	4	5
	Churchill Arms	Thai	2	4	2
£10+	Benugo	Sandwiches, cakes, etc	2	3	3
	Crussh	"	2	2	4

Notting Hill, Holland Park, Bayswater, North Kensington & Maida Vale (W2, W9, W10, W11)

£60+					
	Beach Blanket Babylon	*British, Modern*	⑤	⑤	**❶**
	The Ledbury	*French*	**❶**	**❶**	**❷**
	I Thai	*Fusion*	⑤	⑤	④

£50+					
	Notting Hill Brasserie	*British, Modern*	**❶**	**❶**	**❷**
	Assaggi	*Italian*	**❶**	**❶**	**❸**
	Notting Grill	*Steaks & grills*	④	⑤	④

£40+					
	Harlem	*American*	④	④	**❸**
	Crescent House	*British, Modern*	**❸**	④	**❸**
	Formosa Dining Room	*"*	④	**❸**	**❸**
	The Frontline Club	*"*	④	**❸**	**❷**
	Island	*"*	④	④	④
	Julie's	*"*	⑤	④	**❶**
	The Waterway	*"*	**❸**	④	**❷**
	Bumpkin	*British, Traditional*	④	④	**❸**
	Hereford Road	*"*	–	–	–
	The Cow	*Fish & seafood*	**❸**	④	**❷**
	Angelus	*French*	–	–	–
	Le Café Anglais	*"*	–	–	–
	Père Michel	*"*	**❷**	**❸**	④
	Electric Brasserie	*International*	④	④	**❷**
	Arturo	*Italian*	④	**❷**	④
	Edera	*"*	④	**❸**	⑤
	Esenza	*"*	**❸**	**❷**	④
	Mediterraneo	*"*	**❷**	**❸**	**❸**
	Osteria Basilico	*"*	**❷**	**❸**	**❷**
	Maroush Gardens	*Lebanese*	**❸**	④	④
	Yakitoria	*Japanese*	**❸**	**❷**	**❷**
	E&O	*Pan-Asian*	**❷**	**❷**	**❶**

£35+					
	TGI Friday's	*American*	⑤	④	⑤
	First Floor	*British, Modern*	⑤	**❸**	**❶**
	The Ladbroke Arms	*"*	**❷**	④	**❷**
	Paradise, Kensal Green	*"*	**❷**	**❷**	**❶**
	Raoul's Café	*"*	④	④	**❸**
	The Warrington	*"*	–	–	–
	The Westbourne	*"*	**❸**	④	**❶**
	The Fat Badger	*British, Traditional*	④	④	**❸**
	Fishworks	*Fish & seafood*	**❸**	④	④
	Halepi	*Greek*	④	**❷**	**❸**
	Café Laville	*International*	④	④	**❷**
	202	*"*	**❸**	**❷**	**❶**
	L'Accento Italiano	*Italian*	**❸**	④	④
	Cristini	*"*	**❸**	**❷**	**❸**
	The Green Olive	*"*	**❸**	**❷**	**❸**
	Luna Rossa	*"*	④	⑤	⑤
	The Oak	*"*	**❷**	**❷**	**❶**
	Ottolenghi	*"*	**❶**	**❸**	**❸**
	The Red Pepper	*"*	**❷**	**❸**	**❸**
	Trenta	*"*	④	**❸**	④
	Cochonnet	*Mediterranean*	**❸**	④	④
	Raoul's Café & Deli	*"*	④	④	**❸**
	Baker & Spice	*Sandwiches, cakes, etc*	**❷**	④	④
	Rodizio Rico	*Brazilian*	④	④	④
	Levantine	*Lebanese*	**❸**	**❷**	**❸**
	Pearl Liang	*Chinese*	**❷**	**❸**	**❸**

281

Royal China	"	❶ ❸ ④
Bombay Palace	Indian	❶ ② ④

£30+			
All Star Lanes	American	④ ④ ❷
Lucky Seven	"	❷ ❸ ❷
The Union	British, Modern	④ ④ ❸
Seabass	Fish & seafood	– – –
The Academy	International	❸ ④ ❷
Wine Factory	"	④ ❷ ❷
Galicia	Spanish	④ ④ ❷
Tootsies	Burgers, etc	④ ❸ ④
Mulberry Street	Pizza	❸ ④ ❸
Crazy Homies	Mexican/TexMex	❷ ❺ ❷
Al-Waha	Lebanese	❸ ❸ ④
Ranoush	"	❸ ④ ④
Mandarin Kitchen	Chinese	❶ ④ ④
Bombay Bicycle Club	Indian	❸ ❸ ❸
Noor Jahan	"	❷ ❷ ❸
Inaho	Japanese	❶ ❺ ❺
Satay House	Malaysian	❸ ❷ ④
Tawana	Thai	❷ ❷ ④
The Walmer Castle	"	❸ ④ ❷

£25+			
Rôtisserie Jules	French	❸ ④ ❺
Rossopomodoro	Italian	❸ ④ ❸
Firezza	Pizza	❷ ❸ ❺
Tom's	Sandwiches, cakes, etc	④ ④ ❷
Taqueria	Mexican/TexMex	❷ ❸ ④
Alounak	Persian	❸ ❺ ❸
Shish	Turkish	④ ④ ❸
The Four Seasons	Chinese	❷ ❺ ❺
Magic Wok	"	❸ ❸ ④
ping pong	Chinese, Dim sum	④ ④ ❷
Durbar	Indian	❷ ❸ ④
Kiasu	Indonesian	❷ ④ ④
Feng Sushi	Japanese	❸ ④ ❸
Nyonya	Malaysian	❷ ❸ ④
Uli	Pan-Asian	❷ ❶ ❸

£20+			
Babes 'n' Burgers	American	❸ ④ ❺
S & M Café	British, Traditional	④ ④ ❸
Gourmet Burger Kitchen	Burgers, etc	❷ ④ ④
Moroccan Tagine	Moroccan	❸ ❷ ❸
Beirut Express	Lebanese	❸ ❸ ④
Kandoo	Persian	❸ ❸ ④
Mandalay	Burmese	❸ ❷ ④
New Culture Rev'n	Chinese	❺ ④ ❺
Standard	Indian	❸ ❸ ④
Yelo Thai Canteen	Thai	❸ ❷ ④

£15+			
Fresco	Lebanese	❷ ❷ ④
Khan's	Indian	❸ ④ ④

£10+			
Gail's Bread	Sandwiches, cakes, etc	❷ ❷ ❸

£5+			
Lisboa Pâtisserie	Sandwiches, cakes, etc	❶ ❸ ❸

Hammersmith, Shepherd's Bush, Olympia, Chiswick & Ealing (W4, W5, W6, W12, W14)

£60+	The River Café	Italian	❷❸❸

£50+	La Trompette	French	❶❶❷

£40+	High Road Brasserie	British, Modern	❸❷❷
	Pissarro's	"	❸❸❶
	Sam's Brasserie	"	④❸❸
	Snows on the Green	"	❸❸❸
	Fish Hook	Fish & seafood	❷❸④
	Chez Kristof	French	❸❸❸
	Le Vacherin	"	❷❸❸
	Cibo	Italian	❷❷④
	Vino Rosso	"	❷❸④

£35+	Pacific Bar and Grill	American	④④❷
	Smollensky's	"	⑤⑤④
	The Anglesea Arms	British, Modern	❶④❷
	The Brackenbury	"	❸❸❸
	Bush Bar & Grill	"	⑤④④
	Devonshire House	"	– – –
	Ealing Park Tavern	"	❷❷❷
	The Havelock Tavern	"	❷⑤❸
	Hole in the Wall	"	❸❸❸
	Olive Tree	"	❸❷❸
	The Rocket	"	❸❸❷
	The Roebuck	"	④❸❷
	Fishworks	Fish & seafood	❸④④
	Charlotte's Place	French	④④④
	Annie's	International	④❷❶
	The Grove	Mediterranean	❸❷❸
	Popeseye	Steaks & grills	❸❸④
	The Gate	Vegetarian	❷❸④
	Sushi-Hiro	Japanese	❶❷⑤

£30+	The Crown & Sceptre	British, Modern	❸❸❷
	The Pilot	"	④❸❷
	Queen's Head	"	④❸❶
	The Queens Arms	"	❸❸❷
	Stone Mason's Arms	"	❸❷❷
	The Thatched House	"	❸④❸
	Balans	International	⑤④❸
	Giraffe	"	④❸④
	Frankie's Italian Bar & Grill	Italian	⑤⑤❸
	Cumberland Arms	Mediterranean	❸④④
	The Swan	"	❸❷❷
	Tootsies	Burgers, etc	④❸④
	Yas	Persian	④⑤⑤
	Brilliant	Indian	❷④④
	Madhu's	"	❶❶❷
	Blue Lagoon	Thai	④❸❸
	Saigon Saigon	Vietnamese	❸❸❸

£25+	Priory House	Mediterranean	❸❷❷
	Goodness	Organic	④④❸
	Lowiczanka	Polish	④④④
	Patio	"	④❷❷

	La Tasca	*Spanish*	⑤④❸
	Blah! Blah! Blah!	*Vegetarian*	❸❸❸
	Ground	*Burgers, etc*	❷❷❸
	Firezza	*Pizza*	❷❸⑤
	Adams Café	*Moroccan*	❸❶❷
	Azou	*North African*	❸❶❸
	Chez Marcelle	*Lebanese*	❶④④
	Alounak	*Persian*	❸⑤❸
	Mohsen	*"*	❷❷④
	North China	*Chinese*	❷❷❸
	Agni	*Indian*	❷❶④
	Anarkali	*"*	❸❷④
	Green Chilli	*"*	❷❸④
	Indian Zing	*"*	❷❶❸
	Karma	*"*	❷❷⑤
	Monty's	*"*	❸❸④
	Woodlands	*"*	❷❷④
	Sagar	*Indian, Southern*	❷❷④
	Tosa	*Japanese*	❷❸④
	Esarn Kheaw	*Thai*	❶❸④
	Fat Boy's	*"*	❸❸❸
	Silks & Spice	*"*	❸❸❸
	Thai Bistro	*"*	❸❷④
£20+	Gourmet Burger Kitchen	*Burgers, etc*	❷④④
	Best Mangal	*Turkish*	❷❷④
	Mirch Masala	*Indian*	❶❸④
	Okawari	*Japanese*	❸❸❸
	Hare & Tortoise	*Pan-Asian*	④④④
	Bedlington Café	*Thai*	❸❸④
	Latymers	*"*	❸⑤⑤
£15+	Abu Zaad	*Syrian*	❷❸❷
	Hammersmith Café	*Thai*	❸❸④
	Old Parr's Head	*"*	❸❸④
£10+	Bush Garden Café	*Organic*	❸④❷
	Crussh	*Sandwiches, cakes, etc*	❷❷④

Hampstead, West Hampstead, St John's Wood, Regent's Park, Kilburn & Camden Town (NW postcodes)

£60+	Odette's	British, Modern	③④③
	Landmark (Winter Gdn)	"	③③❶
£50+	L'Aventure	French	❷❶❶
	Villa Bianca	Italian	④③③
	Benihana	Japanese	④③④
	Gilgamesh	Pan-Asian	④⑤④
£40+	Bradley's	British, Modern	③❷④
	The Engineer	"	③④❷
	The Hill	"	③④③
	The Wells	"	③③❶
	Oslo Court	French	❷❶❷
	Artigiano	Italian	③❷③
	Rosmarino	"	⑤④④
	Sardo Canale	"	③③❷
	Black & Blue	Steaks & grills	③③④
	Gaucho Grill	"	③④④
	Good Earth	Chinese	❷❷③
	Kaifeng	"	④④④
	Wakaba	Japanese	③④⑤
	XO	Pan-Asian	④④③
£35+	TGI Friday's	American	⑤④⑤
	Belgo Noord	Belgian	④④④
	Café Med	British, Modern	④④④
	Freemasons Arms	"	④④❷
	The Island	"	③③③
	The Lansdowne	"	③④❷
	The Lord Palmerston	"	③⑤④
	The North London Tavern	"	③④③
	The Old Bull & Bush	"	④③❷
	Wet Fish Cafe	"	③④❷
	Holly Bush	British, Traditional	③④❶
	Fishworks	Fish & seafood	③④④
	Somerstown Coffee House	French	④③④
	Retsina	Greek	③❷④
	The Arches	International	④❷❷
	Fratelli la Bufala	Italian	④⑤⑤
	Philpotts Mezzaluna	"	③❷③
	Salt House	"	④④❷
	The Salusbury	"	③③③
	Sarracino	"	❷❷③
	Café RED	Mediterranean	④③③
	Camden Brasserie	"	④④⑤
	Queen's Head & Artichoke	"	③③③
	The Vine	"	③③③
	Rôtisserie	Steaks & grills	③③④
	Manna	Vegetarian	③③④
	Baker & Spice	Sandwiches, cakes, etc	❷④④
	Hugo's	"	③③③
	Richoux	"	⑤⑤④
	Cottons	Afro-Caribbean	④⑤③
	Mango Room	"	③③❷

			Rating
	Goldfish	Chinese	❷❸④
	Royal China	"	❶❸④
	Snazz Sichuan	"	❷❷❸
	ZeNW3	"	❸❸❸
	Eriki	Indian	❶❶❸
	Jin Kichi	Japanese	❶❷④
	Sushi-Say	"	❶❶④
	Singapore Garden	Malaysian	❷❷❷
£30+	The Chapel	British, Modern	④❸❸
	The Garden Café	"	④④❷
	The Greyhound	"	❸❸❸
	The Horseshoe	"	❷❸❷
	The Junction Tavern	"	❸❷❷
	No 77 Wine Bar	"	④❸❷
	Roundhouse Café	"	④❸❸
	Walnut	"	④④❸
	Camden Bar & Kitchen	British, Traditional	④❸❸
	La Cage Imaginaire	French	❸❷❶
	Lemonia	Greek	④❷❶
	Giraffe	International	④❸④
	La Brocca	Italian	④❸❷
	La Collina	"	❸❸❸
	Zuccato	"	④❸④
	Don Pepe	Spanish	❸❷❷
	Tootsies	Burgers, etc	④❸④
	Seashell	Fish & chips	❷④⑤
	Basilico	Pizza	❷❸④
	Harry Morgan's	Israeli	④④⑤
	Solly's Exclusive	"	❸④④
	Sofra	Turkish	④④④
	Gung-Ho	Chinese	❸❷❷
	Phoenix Palace	"	❷④④
	Weng Wah House	"	④④④
	Atma	Indian	❷❷❸
	Bombay Bicycle Club	"	❸❸❸
	Yuzu	Japanese	❸④❸
£25+	Daphne	Greek	❸❷❷
	Kaz Kreol	International	❸❷❸
	Spaniard's Inn	"	④④❷
	L'Artista	Italian	❸❸❸
	Marine Ices	"	④❷❸
	The Little Bay	Mediterranean	❸❷❷
	William IV	"	④❸❸
	Trojka	Russian	④④❷
	El Parador	Spanish	❷❷④
	Fine Burger Company	Burgers, etc	❸④④
	Natural Burger Co & Grill	"	❸❸⑤
	Nautilus	Fish & chips	❶❷④
	Paul	Sandwiches, cakes, etc	❸④④
	Mestizo	Mexican/TexMex	❸❸④
	Shish	Turkish	④④❸
	Alisan	Chinese	❶❷④
	Vijay	Indian	❷❷④
	Woodlands	"	❷❷④
	Zamzama	"	❸④❸
	Café Japan	Japanese	❶❷④
	Feng Sushi	"	❸④❸
	dim T	Pan-Asian	④④❸

	Silks & Spice	*Thai*	❸❸❸
£20+	The Czech Restaurant	*Czech*	❸❸④
	La Porchetta Pizzeria	*Italian*	❸④❸
	Haché	*Steaks & grills*	❷❸❷
	Gourmet Burger Kitchen	*Burgers, etc*	❷④④
	Hamburger Union	*"*	❸④④
	Chamomile	*Sandwiches, cakes, etc*	❸❷❸
	Kenwood (Brew House)	*"*	④④❶
	Ali Baba	*Egyptian*	❷❸⑤
	Beyoglu	*Turkish*	❸❷④
	New Culture Revolution	*Chinese*	⑤④⑤
	Chutneys	*Indian*	❸④④
	Diwana B-P House	*"*	❸⑤④
	Five Hot Chillies	*"*	❷❷④
	Great Nepalese	*"*	❷❸④
	Jashan	*"*	❶❷⑤
	Kovalam	*Indian, Southern*	❷❷④
	Wagamama	*Japanese*	④❸④
	Oriental City	*Pan-Asian*	❷⑤⑤
£15+	Geeta	*Indian*	❸❷⑤
	Sakonis	*"*	❷④⑤
	Viet-Anh	*Vietnamese*	❸❶④
£10+	Gail's Bread	*Sandwiches, cakes, etc*	❷❷❸

Hoxton, Islington, Highgate, Crouch End, Stoke Newington, Finsbury Park, Muswell Hill & Finchley (N postcodes)

£80+	Fifteen Restaurant	*Italian*	⑤⑤④
£60+	Bacchus	*British, Modern*	❸❸④
£50+	Morgan M	*French*	❶❷④
	Fifteen Trattoria	*Italian*	④④④
£40+	The Bull	*British, Modern*	④❸④
	Frederick's	*"*	❸❷❷
	The House	*"*	❸④❸
	The Lock Dining Bar	*"*	❷❷❸
	The Pumphouse	*"*	④❸❶
	Chez Liline	*Fish & seafood*	❶❸⑤
	Sargasso Sea	*"*	❷❸❸
	The Almeida	*French*	④④④
	Bistro Aix	*"*	❸❸❷
	Metrogusto	*Italian*	④❷❷
	Cru	*Mediterranean*	④④❷
	Camino	*Spanish*	④❸④
£35+	The Albion	*British, Modern*	❸⑤❸
	The Barnsbury	*"*	❸❸❸
	The Drapers Arms	*"*	❸❸❷
	The Duke of Cambridge	*"*	❸④❸
	The Elk in the Woods	*"*	④④❷
	The Haven	*"*	❸❷❷
	Mosaica	*"*	❷❷❸
	The Three Crowns	*"*	❸❸❸

			Rating
	The Marquess Tavern	British, Traditional	②②❸
	St Johns	"	②②⓪
	Fishworks	Fish & seafood	❸④④
	Fig	French	②⓪②
	The Real Greek	Greek	④④❸
	Browns	International	⑤⑤④
	Hoxton Apprentice	"	❸②❸
	The Living Room	"	⑤④④
	Orange Tree	"	④④②
	Casale Franco	Italian	❸②❸
	Florians	"	④❸④
	Ottolenghi	"	⓪❸❸
	San Carlo	"	⑤④④
	Upper Glas	Scandinavian	④❸④
	Rôtisserie	Steaks & grills	❸❸④
	Hoxton Square	Burgers, etc	④④②
	Rodizio Rico	Brazilian	④④④
	Rasa Travancore	Indian, Southern	⓪②④
£30+	Pick More Daisies	American	②②②
	The Northgate	British, Modern	④❸❸
	Les Associés	French	❸②❸
	Le Sacré-Coeur	"	❸❸②
	Banners	International	❸②⓪
	The Fox Reformed	"	④④❸
	Giraffe	"	④❸④
	Cantina Italia	Italian	②②②
	Pizzeria Oregano	"	②❸④
	San Daniele	"	❸②②
	The Sea Cow	Fish & chips	❸❸❸
	Basilico	Pizza	②❸④
	Furnace	"	❸❸❸
	Sabor	South American	❸②❸
	The Parsee	Indian	❸②⑤
	Zaffrani	"	②②②
	Isarn	Thai	②⓪②
£25+	The Flask	British, Traditional	④④⓪
	La Petite Auberge	French	④❸❸
	Vrisaki	Greek	②②❸
	Charles Lamb	Spanish	❸❸②
	The Islington Tapas Bar	"	⑤④❸
	Fine Burger Company	Burgers, etc	❸④④
	Toff's	Fish & chips	②②④
	Two Brothers	"	②②④
	Il Bacio	Pizza	❸❸❸
	Firezza	"	②❸⑤
	La Piragua	South American	②❸②
	Petek	Turkish	②②②
	Emni	Indian	❸❸④
	Masala Zone	"	❸❸❸
	Rani	"	❸②④
	Rooburoo	"	②②❸
	dim T	Pan-Asian	④④❸
	Thai Square	Thai	④❸❸
	Yum Yum	"	②②⓪
	Viet Garden	Vietnamese	❸❸④
£20+	S & M Café	British, Traditional	④④❸
	Le Mercury	French	④②②

	La Porchetta Pizzeria	*Italian*	❸④❸
	Hamburger Union	*Burgers, etc*	❸④④
	Gallipoli	*Turkish*	④❸❷
	Gem	*"*	❷❷❸
	Izgara	*"*	❷❷❸
	New Culture Rev'n	*Chinese*	⑤④⑤
	Anglo Asian Tandoori	*Indian*	❸0❸
	Jashan	*"*	0❷⑤
	Rasa	*"*	00❸
	Wagamama	*Japanese*	④❸④
	Yelo	*Thai*	❸❷④
	Huong-Viet	*Vietnamese*	❷⑤④
	Khoai	*"*	❸④④
£15+	Afghan Kitchen	*Afghani*	❷④④

SOUTH

South Bank (SE1)

£70+	Oxo Tower (Rest')	British, Modern	⑤⑤❸
£60+	Le Pont de la Tour	British, Modern	④④❸
	Oxo Tower (Brass')	Mediterranean	⑤⑤❸
£50+	Skylon	British, Modern	❸❸❷
	Butlers W'f Chop-house	British, Traditional	④④④
	Roast	"	④⑤❸
	Tentazioni	Italian	❷❷❸
	Le Pont de la Tour Bar & Grill	Steaks & grills	❸❷❷
£40+	Blueprint Café	British, Modern	④④❸
	Cantina Vinopolis	"	④④④
	Livebait	Fish & seafood	④④④
	Chez Gérard	French	⑤④④
	Magdalen	"	❶❶❷
	Old Vic Brasserie	"	– – –
	Champor-Champor	Fusion	❷❷❶
	Village East	"	❸❷❷
	Cantina del Ponte	Italian	⑤④④
	Baltic	Polish	❸❸❷
	Black & Blue	Steaks & grills	❸❸④
	Gaucho Grill	"	❸④④
	Hara The Circle Bar	Indian	❶❷⑤
£35+	Archduke Wine Bar	British, Modern	⑤❸④
	Garrison	"	❸❸❶
	The Hartley	"	❸❸❷
	Mezzanine	"	④④④
	RSJ	"	❸❷⑤
	The Swan	"	– – –
	tamesa@oxo	"	⑤⑤④
	The Anchor & Hope	British, Traditional	❶❷❷
	fish!	Fish & seafood	④④④
	Wright Brothers	"	❷❷❷
	Brew Wharf	French	❸④④
	Riviera	"	⑤④④
	Browns	International	⑤⑤④
	Delfina Studio Café	"	❶❶❸
	Laughing Gravy	"	④❸❷
	Tate Restaurant	"	⑤④❷
	Bermondsey Kitchen	Mediterranean	❸④❸
	Tapas Brindisa	Spanish	❷❸❸
	Las Iguanas	South American	④④④
	Kwan Thai	Thai	❸❸④
£30+	Bankside	British, Modern	⑤⑤④
	Canteen	"	④❸❸
	Menier Chocolate Factory	"	④❷❷
	The Table	"	④④❸
	Tate Café	International	④④❸
	Giraffe	"	④❸④
	La Lanterna	Italian	❸❶❷
	Tas Pide	Turkish	④❸❸
	Bengal Clipper	Indian	❷❷❷

	Bincho Yakitori	Japanese	❷❷❷
£25+	Real Greek Souvlaki & Bar	Greek	⑤⑤④
	Zakudia	Russian	④④❷
	Meson don Felipe	Spanish	❸❸❶
	Amano Café	Pizza	❸❸❸
	Gourmet Pizza Co.	"	❸④❸
	Paradiso Olivelli	"	④④④
	Tas	Turkish	④❸❸
	ping pong	Chinese, Dim sum	④④❷
	Feng Sushi	Japanese	❸④❸
	Inshoku	"	④④⑤
	dim T	Pan-Asian	④④❸
£20+	Le Pain Quotidien	Sandwiches, cakes, etc	❸④❷
	Wagamama	Japanese	④❸④
£15+	Konditor & Cook	Sandwiches, cakes, etc	❶❸④
	El Vergel	South American	❶❷❸
£10+	Benugo	British, Modern	❷❸❸
	Monmouth Coffee Company	Sandwiches, cakes, etc	❶❷❷
£5+	Caffé Vergnano	Sandwiches, cakes, etc	❸❷❷

Greenwich, Lewisham & Blackheath
(All SE postcodes, except SE1)

£40+	Chapter Two	British, Modern	❷❷❸
	The Rivington Grill	"	④⑤⑤
	The Rosendale	"	— — —
	Lobster Pot	Fish & seafood	❷❸❷
	The Spread Eagle	French	❸❸❸
	Beauberry House	Fusion	④④④
£35+	Franklins	British, Modern	❸④④
	The Herne Tavern	"	❸❸❸
	Inside	"	❶❸④
	The Palmerston	"	❷④④
	The Trafalgar Tavern	British, Traditional	⑤④❷
	Bar du Musée	French	④④❸
	Le Chardon	"	❸❸❸
£30+	The Dartmouth Arms	British, Modern	❸❸❷
	The Lavender	"	④❸❷
	Joanna's	International	❸❷❷
	The Mansion	"	❸❸❷
	Olley's	Fish & chips	❷❷④
	The Sea Cow	"	❸❸❸
	Peninsular	Chinese	❷④④
	Babur Brasserie	Indian	❶❶❷
	Tandoori Nights	"	❷❷❸
	3 Monkeys	"	④④④
£25+	The Sun & Doves	British, Modern	❸④❷
	Arancia	Italian	❷❷❷
	Le Querce	"	❶❷④
	Barcelona Tapas	Spanish	④⑤❸
	Castello	Pizza	❷❸④

291

			Rating
	The Gowlett	"	❸❷❸
	Zero Degrees	"	❸④❸
	Dragon Castle	Chinese	❷❸❸
	Everest Inn	Indian	❸❷④
	Ganapati	"	❷❷❸
	Kennington Tandoori	"	❸❹④
	Ratchada	Thai	❸④⑤
	Thailand	"	❷❶❷
£20+	Thai Corner Café	Thai	❸❸❸
£15+	Green & Blue	International	❸❸❷

Battersea, Brixton, Clapham, Wandsworth Barnes, Putney & Wimbledon (All SW postcodes south of the river)

			Rating
£50+	Chez Bruce	British, Modern	❶❶❷
£40+	Buchan's	British, Modern	❸❸❷
	The Depot	"	④④❸
	Four O Nine	"	❷❷❷
	Grafton House	"	❸❸❸
	The Greyhound at Battersea	"	❸❷❸
	Harrison's	"	— — —
	Lamberts	"	❶❶❷
	Phoenix	"	❷❷❷
	Ransome's Dock	"	❸❷❸
	Redmond's	"	❸❷❸
	Sonny's	"	④❸❸
	Trinity	"	❷❸④
	The Victoria	"	❸❸❸
	Le Bouchon Bordelais	French	④④❸
	Gastro	"	④⑤❷
	Morel	"	④❸⑤
	La Saveur	"	❷❸❸
	The Light House	International	❸❷❸
	Naked Turtle	"	④❸❷
	Donna Margherita	Italian	❸❸④
	Enoteca Turi	"	❷❶❸
	Riva	"	❷❷④
	San Lorenzo Fuoriporta	"	④④④
	San Remo	"	④④④
	Zero Quattro	"	❸❸❸
	La Pampa	Argentinian	❷❸❸
£35+	Alma	British, Modern	❸❸❷
	The Bridge	"	❸④④
	The Brown Dog	"	❸④❸
	Cinnamon Cay	"	④④④
	The East Hill	"	❸❸❷
	The Fire Stables	"	④⑤❸
	The Freemasons	"	❸❷❷
	The Mason's Arms	"	❷❷❸
	Scoffers	"	④❸❶
	The Spencer Arms	"	④❸❸
	Tree House	"	④❸❸
	Willie Gunn	"	④④④
	Fishworks	Fish & seafood	❸④④

	Name	Cuisine	Ratings
	The Food Room	French	1 2 4
	Upstairs Bar	"	1 1 2
	Rapscallion	Fusion	3 4 3
	Annie's	International	4 2 1
	Duke of Cambridge	"	4 4 2
	Metro	"	4 4 2
	Newton's	"	4 4 4
	Isola del Sole	Italian	2 2 3
	Mooli	"	4 2 2
	Ost. Antica Bologna	"	4 3 3
	Rocket Riverside	Mediterranean	4 4 3
	La Mancha	Spanish	4 4 3
	Barnes Grill	Steaks & grills	4 4 4
	Butcher & Grill	"	4 4 5
	Popeseye	"	3 3 4
	Chakalaka	South African	3 3 4
	Royal China	Chinese	2 3 4
	Nancy Lam's Enak Enak	Indonesian	3 2 4
	Tsunami	Japanese	1 3 2
	Thai on the River	Thai	3 3 3
£30+	Bodean's	American	4 4 3
	The Abbeville	British, Modern	4 3 2
	The Aviary	"	4 4 3
	The Blue Pumpkin	"	4 3 4
	The Duke's Head	"	2 3 2
	Earl Spencer	"	2 3 2
	Emile's	"	2 2 2
	The Fentiman Arms	"	4 4 2
	The Lavender	"	4 3 2
	Gazette	French	3 3 4
	Louvaine	"	3 2 2
	Mini Mundus	"	3 0 2
	Giraffe	International	4 3 4
	Hudson's	"	4 4 2
	Putney Station	"	4 3 3
	The Ship	"	3 4 2
	Amici	Italian	4 4 2
	Antipasto & Pasta	"	3 3 3
	Buona Sera	"	4 3 2
	Frankie's Italian Bar & Grill	"	5 5 3
	Grissini	"	3 4 3
	Numero Uno	"	3 0 0
	Piccolino	"	4 4 4
	Pizza Metro	"	1 2 2
	Rick's Café	"	3 3 2
	The Fox & Hounds	Mediterranean	2 2 2
	The Stonhouse	"	4 4 2
	Lola Rojo	Spanish	2 3 4
	Rebato's	"	3 0 0
	La Rueda	"	4 4 3
	Dexter's Grill	Burgers, etc	4 3 3
	Tootsies	"	4 3 4
	Sea Cow	Fish & chips	3 3 3
	Basilico	Pizza	2 3 4
	Santa Maria del Sur	Argentinian	2 3 4
	Dish Dash	Persian	3 4 2
	Bayee Village	Chinese	3 2 3
	Dalchini	"	3 4 3
	Bombay Bicycle Club	Indian	3 3 3

	Ma Goa	"	❶❷❸
	Tabaq	"	❸④④
£25+	The Castle	British, Modern	❸④❸
	The Clarence	"	❸❸❸
	Fish Club	Fish & seafood	❶❷④
	Real Greek Souvlaki & Bar	Greek	⑤⑤④
	Bread & Roses	International	④④❸
	Il Cantuccio di Pulcinella	Italian	④❶❸
	Ferrari's	"	④④④
	Pappa Ciccia	"	❷❷❷
	The Little Bay	Mediterranean	❸❷❷
	Raviolo	"	④④④
	Bar Estrela	Portuguese	❸❷❷
	El Rincón Latino	Spanish	❸❶❶
	Fine Burger Company	Burgers, etc	❸④④
	Brady's	Fish & chips	❷❸❸
	Al Forno	Pizza	④❷❷
	Eco	"	❸❸❸
	Firezza	"	❷❸⑤
	Chutney	Indian	❷❶❷
	Ekachai	"	❷④❸
	Indian Ocean	"	❷❶❸
	Nanglo	"	❷❶❸
	Nazmins Balti House	"	❸❸④
	The Banana Leaf Canteen	Pan-Asian	❸❷❸
	Talad Thai	Thai	❷❸⑤
	Thai Garden	"	❸❸④
	Thai Square	"	④❸❸
£20+	Fish in a Tie	Mediterranean	④❸❷
	Gourmet Burger Kitchen	Burgers, etc	❷④④
	Fuego Pizzeria	Pizza	❸❷⑤
	Boiled Egg & Soldiers	Sandwiches, cakes, etc	❸④④
	Hot Stuff	Indian	❶❶❸
	Kastoori	"	❶❷④
	Mirch Masala SW16	"	❶❸④
	Sree Krishna	"	❷❷❸
	Fujiyama	Japanese	❷④❸
	Wagamama		④❸④
	Hare & Tortoise	Pan-Asian	④④④
	Amaranth	Thai	❷❸④
	The Pepper Tree	"	❸❷❸
£15+	Trinity Stores	Sandwiches, cakes, etc	❸❷❸
	Jerk City	Afro-Caribbean	❸④⑤
	Vijaya Krishna	Indian, Southern	❷❷④
	Slurp	Japanese	❷❸④

Outer western suburbs
Kew, Richmond, Twickenham, Teddington

£50+	The Glasshouse	British, Modern	❶❶❸
	Petersham Nurseries	"	❸④❷
£40+	The Wharf	British, Modern	④④❶
	A Cena	Italian	❷❷❷
	Gaucho Grill	Steaks & grills	❸④④
	Kew Grill	"	❸④④

			Rating
	Matsuba	*Japanese*	❷❷④
£35+	Fishworks	*Fish & seafood*	❸④④
	Loch Fyne	*"*	④❸④
	Brula	*French*	❷⓿❷
	La Buvette	*"*	❸❸❷
	Chez Lindsay	*"*	❸❸❸
	Ma Cuisine	*"*	❷❷❸
	Nosh	*International*	④❸❸
	Four Regions	*Chinese*	❸❷❸
	Origin Asia	*Indian*	❷❷④
£30+	The Inn at Kew Gardens	*British, Modern*	❸④❷
	Scarpetta	*Italian*	❷❷❷
	don Fernando's	*Spanish*	❸❷❸
	Tangawizi	*Indian*	❸❷❷
	Thai Elephant	*Thai*	❸⓿❸
£25+	Sagar	*Indian*	❷❷④
	Fat Boy's	*Thai*	❸❸❸
£20+	Stein's	*German*	❸④❸
	O'Zon	*Chinese*	❸⓿④

EAST

Smithfield & Farringdon (EC1)

£70+	Club Gascon	French	❷❸❸

£50+	Smiths (Top Floor)	British, Modern	❸❸❷
	Portal	Mediterranean	❸❸❷

£40+	The Bar & Grill	British, Modern	❸❸❷
	The Hat & Feathers	"	④④④
	Malmaison Brasserie	"	❸❷❷
	The Peasant	"	❸❸❸
	Vic Naylors	"	④❸❸
	Medcalf	British, Traditional	④④❸
	St John	"	❷❷❸
	Fish Shop	Fish & seafood	❸❸④
	Rudland & Stubbs	"	④④⑤
	Bleeding Heart	French	❷❷❷
	Café du Marché	"	❷❷❶
	Dans le Noir	"	⑤❶❷
	Le Rendezvous du Café	"	❸❸❷
	Le Saint Julien	"	❸④④
	Alba	Italian	❸❷④
	The Clerkenwell Dining Rm	Mediterranean	❸❸④
	Flâneur	"	❸④❸
	The Zetter	"	④④❸
	Potemkin	Russian	④⑤⑤
	Moro	Spanish	❶❷❷
	Saki Bar & Food Emporium	Japanese	❷❸④

£35+	Ambassador	British, Modern	❸❷④
	Coach & Horses	"	❸❸④
	The Larder	"	❸④④
	The Well	"	❸④❸
	The Quality Chop House	British, Traditional	❸❸❸
	Cellar Gascon	French	❸❸❸
	Comptoir Gascon	"	❶❷❷
	Smiths (Dining Rm)	Steaks & grills	❸④④
	Cottons	Afro-Caribbean	④⑤❸
	Cicada	Pan-Asian	❷❷❸

£30+	St Germain	British, Modern	④❷❸
	Vinoteca	"	❸❷❶
	$	International	④④❸
	Ortega	Spanish	④⑤❸
	Carnevale	Vegetarian	❸❸❸
	Epicurean Lounge	Pizza	❸④④
	Sofra	Turkish	④④④

£25+	The Real Greek Souvlaki	Greek	⑤⑤④
	The Eagle	Mediterranean	❷④❷
	The Little Bay	"	❸❷❷
	Shish	Turkish	④④❸
	Tas	"	④❸❸
	Tajima Tei	Japanese	❷❸④
	Cây Tre	Vietnamese	❸④⑤

£20+	Smiths (Ground Floor)	British, Modern	④④❷
	Cock Tavern	British, Traditional	❸❷⑤

	Fish Central	*Fish & seafood*	❷❸④	
	Kolossi Grill	*Greek*	④❶❷	
	La Porchetta Pizzeria	*Italian*	❸④❸	
	Pham Sushie	*Japanese*	❶❷❸	
	Pho	*Vietnamese*	❸❷❸	
£10+	Benugo	*Sandwiches, cakes, etc*	❷❸❸	
	Spianata	*"*	❷④④	

The City (EC2, EC3, EC4)

£80+	Tatsuso	*Japanese*	❸❸⑤
£70+	1 Lombard Street	*British, Modern*	④④④
	Prism	*"*	④④⑤
£60+	Rhodes 24	*British, Modern*	❸❸❷
	Fishmarket	*Fish & seafood*	④④④
	Aurora	*French*	❸❸❷
£50+	Addendum	*British, Modern*	❸❷④
	Bar Bourse	*"*	④④④
	Molloy's	*"*	④❸④
	Searcy's Brasserie	*"*	④❸❸
	Paternoster Chop House	*British, Traditional*	④④④
	Chamberlain's	*Fish & seafood*	❸④④
	Vertigo	*"*	⑤④❷
	Coq d'Argent	*French*	④④❸
	Sauterelle	*"*	④❸❸
	Refettorio	*Italian*	❸❸④
	Bonds	*Mediterranean*	④❸❸
£40+	Missouri Grill	*American*	❸❸❸
	The Princess	*Australian*	❷❷❸
	The Chancery	*British, Modern*	❷❷❸
	The Don	*"*	❷❷❷
	Home	*"*	④④❸
	Northbank	*"*	– – –
	The Rivington Grill	*"*	❸④❸
	Terminus	*"*	⑤⑤⑤
	The White Swan	*"*	❸❸④
	Gow's	*Fish & seafood*	❸④④
	Sweetings	*"*	❷❷❶
	Brasserie Pierre	*French*	④❷❸
	Chez Gérard	*"*	⑤④④
	Luc's Brasserie	*"*	❸④④
	The Royal Exchange	*"*	④⑤❷
	Prima	*International*	❸❷❸
	Vivat Bacchus	*"*	❸❶❸
	Caravaggio	*Italian*	④⑤④
	Leadenhall Italian	*"*	❸❶❸
	Perc%nto	*"*	⑤④⑤
	Taberna Etrusca	*"*	④④❸
	Boisdale of Bishopsgate	*Scottish*	④④④
	Eyre Brothers	*Spanish*	❸❸❸
	Gaucho Grill	*Steaks & grills*	❸④④
	Bevis Marks	*Kosher*	❸❶❸
	Kenza	*Lebanese*	– – –
	Imperial City	*Chinese*	❸❸❷

	Restaurant	Cuisine	Rating
	City Miyama	Japanese	**2** **3** 5
	Shimo	"	4 **2** **3**
	Gt Eastern Dining Room	Pan-Asian	**2** **2** **2**
	Pacific Oriental	"	– – –
£35+	The Fox	British, Modern	**3** **3** **3**
	The Hoxton Grille	"	4 **2** **2**
	The Sterling	"	4 5 4
	Wood Street	"	4 5 5
	George & Vulture	British, Traditional	5 4 **1**
	Browns	International	5 5 4
	Bertorelli's	Italian	5 5 4
	Rocket	Mediterranean	4 4 3
	Miyabi	Japanese	**3** **2** **3**
	Mugen	"	**3** **3** **3**
	Tokyo City	"	**3** 4 4
	Hokkien Chan	Thai	4 4 4
£30+	Bankside	British, Modern	5 5 4
	Ye Olde Cheshire Cheese	British, Traditional	5 4 **1**
	Zuccato	Italian	4 **3** 4
	Ortega	Spanish	4 5 **3**
	Bar Capitale	Pizza	**3** 4 4
	(Ciro's) Pizza Pomodoro	"	4 4 **2**
	Haz	Turkish	**3** **2** **2**
	Kasturi	Indian	**2** **2** **3**
	K10	Japanese	**2** 4 **3**
	Kurumaya	"	**2** **3** **3**
	Singapura	Malaysian	**3** **3** 4
£25+	Simpson's Tavern	British, Traditional	4 4 **1**
	The Wine Library	"	5 **3** **2**
	Barcelona Tapas	Spanish	4 5 **3**
	La Tasca	"	5 4 **3**
	The Diner	Burgers, etc	**2** 4 **2**
	Paul	Sandwiches, cakes, etc	**3** 4 4
	Rajasthan III	Indian	**3** **2** **3**
	Tiffinbites	"	**3** 4 4
	Moshi Moshi	Japanese	**3** 4 **3**
	Ekachai	Thai	**2** 4 **3**
	Silks & Spice	"	**3** **3** **3**
	Thai Square	"	4 **3** **3**
£20+	Club Mangia	British, Modern	**2** **2** **2**
	Hilliard	"	**1** **1** **3**
	Leon	Mediterranean	**2** **3** **3**
	Gourmet Burger Kitchen	Burgers, etc	**2** 4 4
	Wagamama	Japanese	4 **3** 4
	Chi Noodle & Wine Bar	Pan-Asian	**3** **2** **2**
£15+	The Place Below	Vegetarian	**2** 4 **3**
	Grazing	Sandwiches, cakes, etc	**2** **3** 4
	Salade	"	**3** 4 4
£10+	Apostrophe	Sandwiches, cakes, etc	**3** **3** **2**
	Crussh	"	**2** **2** 4
	Fuzzy's Grub	"	**1** **1** **3**
	Spianata	"	**2** 4 4

East End & Docklands (All E postcodes)

Price	Name	Cuisine	Ratings
£90+	Ubon	*Japanese*	**3** 4 4
£70+	Les Trois Garçons	*French*	4 **3 1**
£60+	Beach Blanket Babylon	*British, Modern*	5 5 **1**
	Plateau	*French*	4 4 4
	Quadrato	*Italian*	**3 3 3**
£50+	Hawksmoor	*Steaks & grills*	**2 3 3**
£40+	The Empress of India	*British, Modern*	4 4 4
	The Gun	*"*	**2 3 2**
	Hadley House	*"*	**3 3** 4
	Lanes	*"*	4 4 5
	The Morgan Arms	*"*	**2 3 2**
	Wapping Food	*"*	**3 3 1**
	St John Bread & Wine	*British, Traditional*	**2 2** 4
	Curve	*Fish & seafood*	4 4 5
	The Grapes	*"*	**2 3 1**
	Bistrotheque	*French*	4 **2 2**
	Rosemary Lane	*"*	**2 2** 4
	Amerigo Vespucci	*Italian*	**3 3 3**
	1 Blossom Street	*"*	**2 3 3**
	Gaucho Grill	*Steaks & grills*	**3** 4 4
	Café Spice Namaste	*Indian*	**2 2 3**
£35+	Smollensky's	*American*	5 5 4
	Cat & Mutton	*British, Modern*	4 4 4
	Frocks	*"*	4 4 4
	Royal Oak	*"*	**3 2 1**
	The Narrow	*British, Traditional*	**2** 4 **3**
	Browns	*International*	5 5 4
	The Prince Arthur	*"*	– – –
	Il Bordello	*Italian*	**2 1 2**
	Lilly's	*Steaks & grills*	**3 3 2**
	Green & Red Bar & Cantina	*Mexican/TexMex*	**1 3 2**
	Royal China	*Chinese*	**1 3** 4
	Lime	*Indian*	**3 2 3**
	Scarlet Dot	*"*	4 4 4
	Elephant Royale	*Thai*	4 **3 2**
	Sri Nam	*"*	**3 3** 4
£30+	All Star Lanes	*American*	4 4 **2**
	Canteen	*British, Modern*	4 **3 3**
	King Eddie's	*"*	**3** 4 **3**
	Kruger	*International*	4 4 4
	La Figa	*Italian*	**3 2 2**
	El Faro	*Spanish*	**1 2 3**
	Ark Fish	*Fish & chips*	**2 3** 5
	Santa Maria del Buen Ayre	*Argentinian*	**2 3 1**
	Haz	*Turkish*	**3 2 2**
	Lotus	*Chinese*	4 4 **3**
	Yi-Ban	*"*	**2 2 2**
£25+	LMNT	*British, Modern*	4 **3 1**
	Meson los Barilles	*Spanish*	**3 3 3**
	La Tasca	*"*	5 4 **3**
	Arkansas Café	*Steaks & grills*	**2** 4 4

			Rating
	Faulkner's	*Fish & chips*	❷❸⑤
	Gourmet Pizza Co.	*Pizza*	❸④❸
	Pâtisserie Valerie	*Sandwiches, cakes, etc*	④④❸
	Shanghai	*Chinese*	❷❷❸
	Memsaheb on Thames	*Indian*	❷❷❸
	Tiffinbites	"	❸④④
	Itsu	*Japanese*	❷❸❸
	Moshi Moshi	"	❸④❸
	Namo	*Vietnamese*	❷❸❸
£20+	S & M Café	*British, Traditional*	④④❸
	Stringray Globe Café	*Italian*	❷④④
	Leon	*Mediterranean*	❷❸❸
	Story Deli	*Organic*	❶❸❷
	The Drunken Monkey	*Chinese*	④④④
	Clifton	*Indian*	❸❷④
	The Gaylord	"	❷④④
	Mirch Masala	"	❶❸④
	Wagamama	*Japanese*	④❸④
	Lahore Kebab House	*Pakistani*	❶④⑤
	New Tayyabs	"	❶④❸
	Sông Quê	*Vietnamese*	❷⑤⑤
	Viet Hoa	"	❸④④
£15+	Square Pie Company	*British, Traditional*	❸④④
	Mangal Ocakbasi	*Turkish*	❷④④
£10+	E Pellicci	*Italian*	❸❷❶
	Crussh	*Sandwiches, cakes, etc*	❷❷④
	Spianata	"	❷④④
£5+	Brick Lane Beigel Bake	*Sandwiches, cakes, etc*	❷④⑤

MAPS

MAP 1 – LONDON OVERVIEW

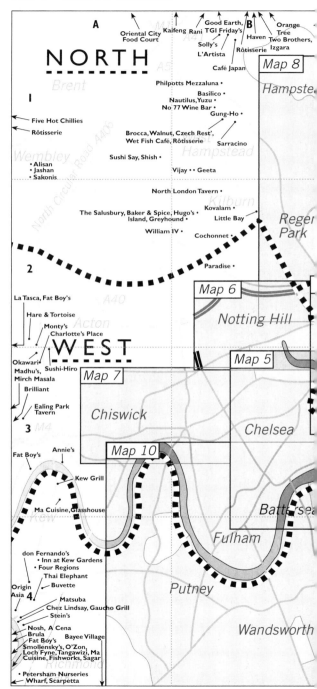

A

Oriental City Food Court

Kaifeng Rani

Good Earth, TGI Friday's

Solly's
L'Artista

Rôtisserie

Café Japan

B Haven

Orange Tree
Two Brothers, Izgara

Map 8

NORTH

Brent

Hampstea

I

Five Hot Chillies

Rôtisserie

Wembley *North Circular Road A406*

• Alisan
• Jashan
• Sakonis

Philpotts Mezzaluna •

Basilico •
Nautilus, Yuzu •
No 77 Wine Bar •

Gung-Ho •

Brocca, Walnut, Czech Rest',
Wet Fish Café, Rôtisserie

Sarracino

Hampstead

Sushi Say, Shish •

Vijay • • Geeta

Kilburn

North London Tavern •

The Salusbury, Baker & Spice, Hugo's,
Island, Greyhound •

Kovalam •

Little Bay

*Reger
Park*

William IV •

Cochonnet •

Paradise •

2

Map 6

La Tasca, Fat Boy's

A40

Notting Hill

Hare & Tortoise

Monty's
Charlotte's Place

Acton

W E S T

Map 5

Okawari
Madhu's, Sushi-Hiro
Mirch Masala

Map 7

Brilliant

Chiswick

Chelsea

Ealing Park
Tavern

3 *M4*

Fat Boy's

Annie's

Map 10

Kew Grill

Ma Cuisine, Glasshouse

Kew

don Fernando's
• Inn at Kew Gardens
• Four Regions
Thai Elephant
Buvette

Battersea

Fulham

Origin
Asia **4**

Matsuba

Chez Lindsay, Gaucho Grill

Stein's

Putney

Nosh, A Cena
Brula
Fat Boy's   Bayee Village
Smollensky's, O'Zon,
Loch Fyne, Tangawizi, Ma
Cuisine, Fishworks, Sagar

Richmond

Wandsworth

• Petersham Nurseries
Wharf, Scarpetta

MAP I – LONDON OVERVIEW

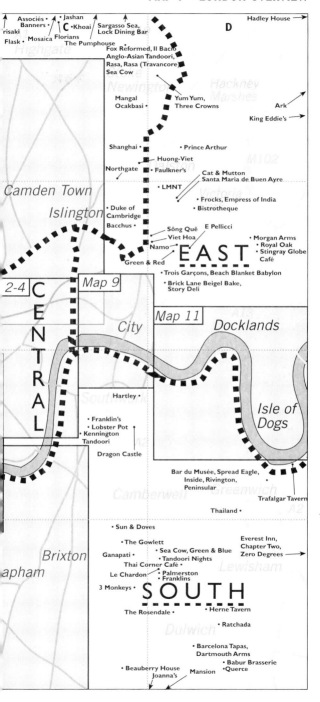

MAP 2 – WEST END OVERVIEW

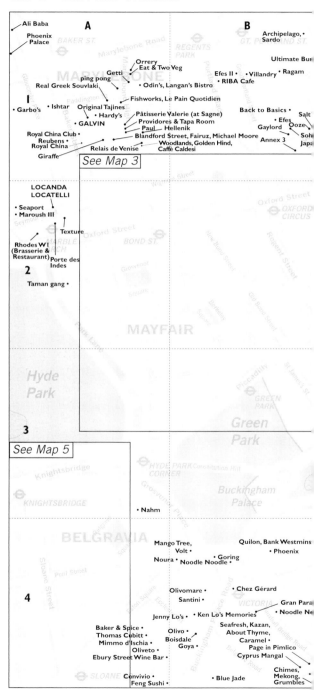

A

B

Ali Baba

Phoenix Palace

Archipelago, • Sardo

Ultimate Bur

Orrery
Eat & Two Veg
Getti
ping pong

Efes II • • Villandry • Ragam
• RIBA Cafe

Real Greek Souvlaki

• Odin's, Langan's Bistro

Fishworks, Le Pain Quotidien

• Garbo's   • Ishtar   Original Tajines
• Hardy's

Back to Basics •   Salt

• Efes
Gaylord   Ooze

Pâtisserie Valerie (at Sagne)

• GALVIN
Providores & Tapa Room
Paul — Hellenik

Annex 3   Soh
Japa

Royal China Club •
Reubens
Royal China

Blandford Street, Fairuz, Michael Moore
Woodlands, Golden Hind,
Relais de Venise   Caffe Caldesi

Giraffe

See Map 3

LOCANDA
LOCATELLI

• Seaport
• Maroush III

Texture

Rhodes W1
(Brasserie &
Restaurant) Porte des
Indes

OXFORD
CIRCUS

Taman gang •

MAYFAIR

Hyde
Park

Green
Park

3

See Map 5

• Nahm

BELGRAVIA

Mango Tree,
Volt •

Noura •   • Goring
Noodle Noodle •

Quilon, Bank Westmins
• Phoenix

Olivomare •
Santini •

• Chez Gérard

Gran Para
• Noodle Ne

Jenny Lo's •   • Ken Lo's Memories

Baker & Spice •
Thomas Cubitt •
Mimmo d'Ischia •
Oliveto •
Ebury Street Wine Bar •

Olivo •
Boisdale
Goya •

Seafresh, Kazan,
About Thyme,
Caramel •
Page in Pimlico
Cyprus Mangal

Chimes,
Mekong,
Grumbles

Convivio •
Feng Sushi •

• Blue Jade

MAP 2 – WEST END OVERVIEW

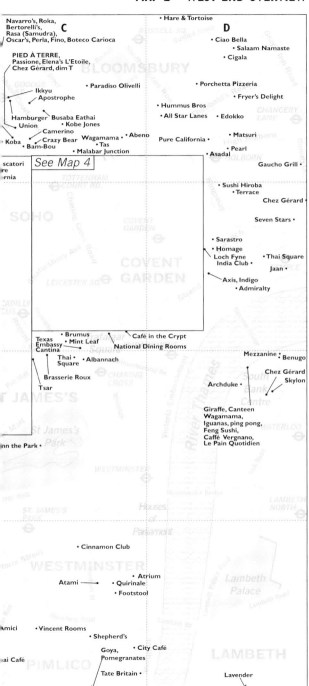

MAP 3 – MAYFAIR, ST JAMES'S & WEST SOHO

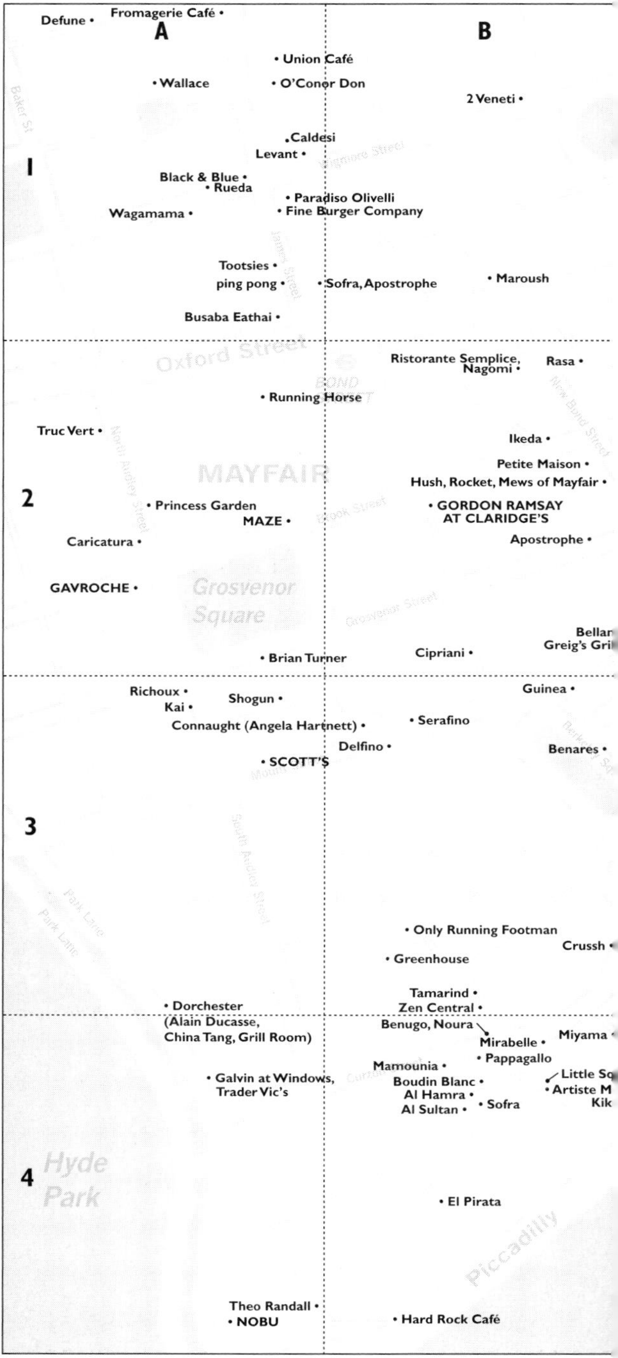

A

B

Defune •

Fromagerie Café •

• Union Café

• Wallace

• O'Conor Don

2 Veneti •

• Caldesi

Levant •

Black & Blue •

• Rueda

Wagamama •

• Paradiso Olivelli

• Fine Burger Company

I

Tootsies •

ping pong •

• Sofra, Apostrophe

• Maroush

Busaba Eathai •

Oxford Street

Ristorante Semplice,   Rasa •
Nagomi •

• Running Horse

Truc Vert •

Ikeda •

Petite Maison •

Hush, Rocket, Mews of Mayfair •

2

• Princess Garden

MAZE •

• GORDON RAMSAY
AT CLARIDGE'S

Caricatura •

Apostrophe •

GAVROCHE •

Grosvenor
Square

Bellar
Greig's Gril

• Brian Turner

Cipriani •

Richoux •

Kai •

Shogun •

Guinea •

Connaught (Angela Hartnett) •

• Serafino

Delfino •

Benares •

• SCOTT'S

3

• Only Running Footman

Crussh •

• Greenhouse

Tamarind •

Zen Central •

• Dorchester
(Alain Ducasse,
China Tang, Grill Room)

Benugo, Noura •

Mirabelle •   Miyama •

Mamounia •   • Pappagallo

• Galvin at Windows,
Trader Vic's

Boudin Blanc •

Little Sq

Al Hamra •

• Artiste M

Al Sultan •   • Sofra

Kik

4

Hyde
Park

• El Pirata

Piccadilly

Theo Randall •

• NOBU

• Hard Rock Café

MAP 3 – MAYFAIR, ST JAMES'S & WEST SOHO

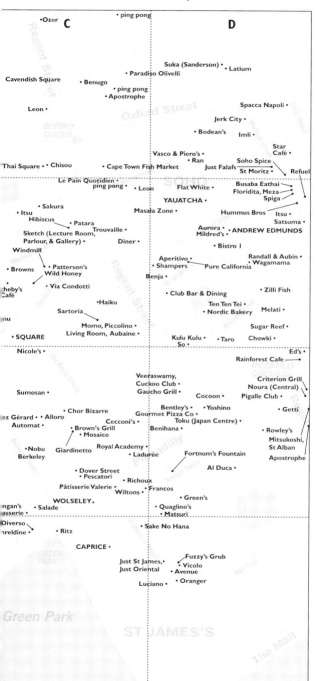

MAP 4 – EAST SOHO, CHINATOWN & COVENT GARDEN

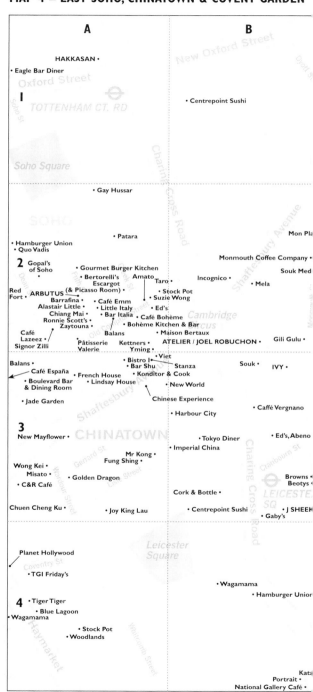

A

B

HAKKASAN •

• Eagle Bar Diner

Oxford Street

I

TOTTENHAM CT. RD

Soho Square

• Centrepoint Sushi

New Oxford Street

• Gay Hussar

SOHO

• Patara

Mon Pla

• Hamburger Union
• Quo Vadis

Monmouth Coffee Company •

2 Gopal's
of Soho
•

• Gourmet Burger Kitchen
• Bertorelli's
Escargot
(& Picasso Room) •

Amato

Taro •

Souk Med

Incognico •

• Mela

Red
Fort •

ARBUTUS

Barrafina •
Alastair Little •
Chiang Mai •
Ronnie Scott's •
Zaytouna •

• Café Emm
• Little Italy
• Bar Italia

Balans

• Stock Pot
• Suzie Wong

• Ed's

• Café Bohème
• Bohème Kitchen & Bar
• Maison Bertaux

Cambridge CIRCUS

Café
Lazeez •
Signor Zilli

Pâtisserie
Valerie

Kettners •
Yming •

ATELIER / JOEL ROBUCHON •

Gili Gulu •

Balans •

• Café España

• Boulevard Bar
& Dining Room

• Jade Garden

French House
• Lindsay House

• Bistro 1 •
• Bar Shu
• Konditor & Cook

Viet
Stanza

• New World

Souk •

IVY •

Chinese Experience

• Harbour City

• Caffé Vergnano

3

New Mayflower •

CHINATOWN

• Tokyo Diner

• Imperial China

• Ed's, Abeno

Wong Kei •
Misato •

• C&R Café

Mr Kong •
Fung Shing •

• Golden Dragon

Browns •
Beotys •

*LEICESTE.
SQ*

Chuen Cheng Ku •

Cork & Bottle •

• Joy King Lau

• Centrepoint Sushi
• Gaby's

• J SHEEK

*Leicester
Square*

Planet Hollywood

Coventry St

• TGI Friday's

• Wagamama

• Hamburger Union

4 • Tiger Tiger
• Blue Lagoon
• Wagamama

• Stock Pot
• Woodlands

Kata
Portrait •
National Gallery Café •

MAP 4 – EAST SOHO, CHINATOWN & COVENT GARDEN

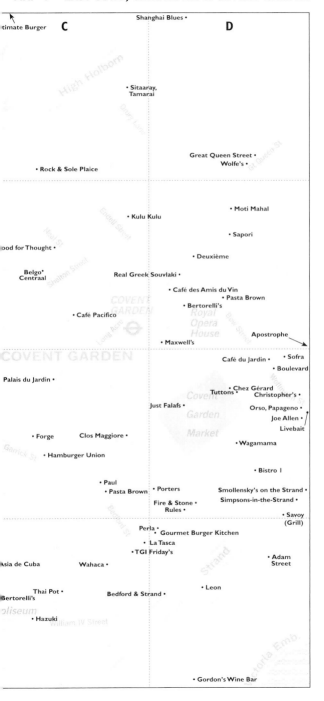

C

D

tltimate Burger

Shanghai Blues •

• Sitaaray, Tamarai

Great Queen Street •
Wolfe's •

• Rock & Sole Plaice

• Moti Mahal

• Kulu Kulu

• Sapori

ood for Thought •

• Deuxième

Belgo• Centraal

Real Greek Souvlaki •

• Café des Amis du Vin
• Pasta Brown
• Bertorelli's

• Café Pacifico

Apostrophe

• Maxwell's

Café du Jardin •   • Sofra
• Boulevard

Palais du Jardin •

• Chez Gérard
Tuttons •   Christopher's •

Just Falafs •   Orso, Papageno •
Joe Allen •
Livebait

• Forge   Clos Maggiore •

• Wagamama

• Hamburger Union

• Bistro 1

• Paul
• Pasta Brown   • Porters   Smollensky's on the Strand •

Fire & Stone •   Simpsons-in-the-Strand •
Rules •
• Savoy (Grill)

Perla •
• Gourmet Burger Kitchen
• La Tasca
•TGI Friday's

Asia de Cuba   Wahaca •   • Adam Street

Thai Pot •   • Leon
Bertorelli's   Bedford & Strand •

• Hazuki

• Gordon's Wine Bar

MAP 5 – KNIGHTSBRIDGE, CHELSEA & SOUTH KENSINGTON

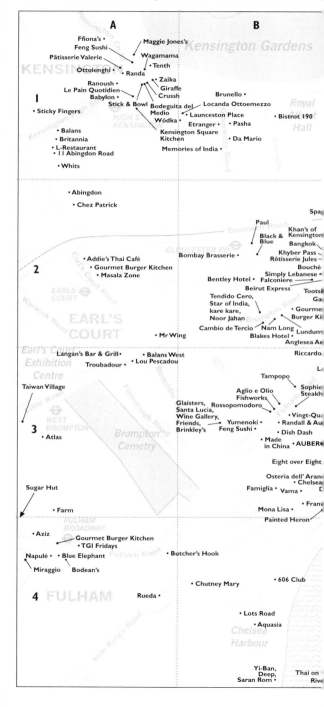

A

Ffiona's •
Feng Sushi •
Pâtisserie Valerie •
Ottolenghi •
• Randa

Kensington Gardens

Maggie Jones's •
Wagamama •
• Tenth

Ranoush •
Le Pain Quotidien •
Babylon •
Stick & Bowl •

• Zaika
Giraffe
Crussh

Bodeguita del
Medio
Wódka •

• Sticky Fingers

B

Brunello •
Locanda Ottoemezzo

• Launceston Place
Etranger •   • Pasha
Kensington Square
Kitchen

• Balans
• Britannia
• L-Restaurant
• 11 Abingdon Road

Memories of India •

• Da Mario

• Bistrot 190

Royal
Albert
Hall

• Whits

1

• Abingdon

• Chez Patrick

Spag

Paul
Black &   Khan's of
Blue   Kensington
          Bangkok

• Addie's Thai Café
• Gourmet Burger Kitchen
• Masala Zone

Bombay Brasserie •

Khyber Pass
Rôtisserie Jules ~
Bouché
Bentley Hotel •   Simply Lebanese •
                  Falconiere
          Beirut Express

Tendido Cero,   Tootsi
Star of India,   Ga
kare kare,   • Gourmet
Noor Jahan   Burger Ki

• Mr Wing

Cambio de Tercio • Nam Long   Lundum
                   Blakes Hotel •
                   Anglesea Ar

2

Langan's Bar & Grill •   • Balans West
Troubadour •   • Lou Pescadou

Taiwan Village

Riccardo

Le

Tampopo
              Sophie
Aglio e Olio   Steakh
Fishworks
Glaisters, Rossopomodoro
Santa Lucia,
Wine Gallery,   • Vingt-Qua
Friends,   Yumenoki • • Randall & Au
Brinkley's Feng Sushi • • Dish Dash
           • Made
           in China • AUBER

• Atlas

Eight over Eight

Osteria dell' Aran
         • Chelsea
Famiglia • Vama •   D

Sugar Hut

• Farm

Mona Lisa •   • Fran
Painted Heron •

3

• Aziz
        Gourmet Burger Kitchen
        • TGI Fridays
Napulé • • Blue Elephant
Miraggio   Bodean's

• Butcher's Hook

• Chutney Mary

• 606 Club

4 FULHAM   Rueda •

• Lots Road
  • Aquasia

Chelsea
Harbour

Yi-Ban,
Deep,
Saran Rom •

Thai on
Rive

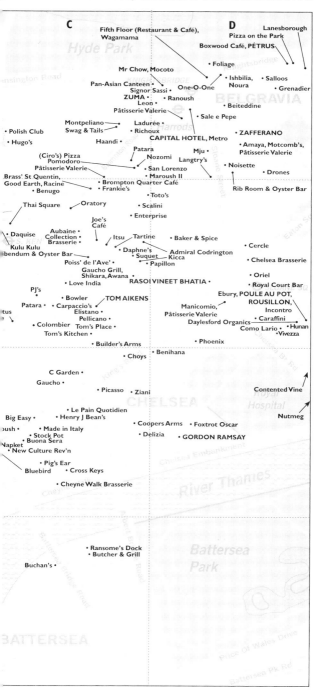

Hyde Park

BELGRAVIA

CHELSEA

Royal Hospital

River Thames

Battersea Park

BATTERSEA

Lanesborough
Pizza on the Park
Boxwood Café, PÉTRUS
• Foliage
Fifth Floor (Restaurant & Café), Wagamama
Mr Chow, Mocoto
Pan-Asian Canteen •
Signor Sassi •
ZUMA •
Leon •
Pâtisserie Valerie •
One-O-One
• Ranoush
• Ishbilia, Noura • Salloos • Grenadier
• Beiteddine
• Sale e Pepe
Montpeliano
Swag & Tails
Ladurée •
• Richoux
CAPITAL HOTEL, Metro
• ZAFFERANO
• Amaya, Motcomb's, Pâtisserie Valerie
• Polish Club
• Hugo's
Haandi •
Patara
Nozomi
Mju •
Langtry's
• Noisette • Drones
(Ciro's) Pizza
Pomodoro
Pâtisserie Valerie •
Brass' St Quentin,
Good Earth, Racine
• Benugo
• San Lorenzo
• Maroush II
• Brompton Quarter Café
• Frankie's
Rib Room & Oyster Bar
Thai Square
Oratory
• Toto's
• Scalini
• Enterprise
Joe's Café
• Daquise
Aubaine
Collection •
Brasserie
Kulu Kulu
bendum & Oyster Bar
Itsu
Tartine
Daphne's
Suquet
Kicca
• Papillon
• Baker & Spice
Admiral Codrington
• Cercle
• Chelsea Brasserie
Poiss' de l'Ave •
Gaucho Grill,
Shikara, Awana
• Love India
RASOI VINEET BHATIA •
• Oriel
• Royal Court Bar
Ebury, POULE AU POT,
ROUSILLON,
Incontro
PJ's
• Bowler
Patara •
• Carpaccio's
TOM AIKENS
Manicomio,
Pâtisserie Valerie
Daylesford Organics
• Caraffini
Como Lario • • Hunan
•Vivezza
tus
e
Elistano •
Pellicano •
• Colombier Tom's Place •
Tom's Kitchen •
• Builder's Arms
• Benihana
• Phoenix
• Choys
C Garden •
Gaucho •
• Picasso • Ziani
Contented Vine
Big Easy •
• Le Pain Quotidien
• Henry J Bean's
oush •
Napket
• Made in Italy
• Stock Pot
• Buona Sera
• New Culture Rev'n
• Coopers Arms • Foxtrot Oscar
• Delizia • GORDON RAMSAY
Nutmeg
• Pig's Ear
Bluebird • Cross Keys
• Cheyne Walk Brasserie
• Ransome's Dock
• Butcher & Grill
Buchan's •

MAP 6 – NOTTING HILL & BAYSWATER

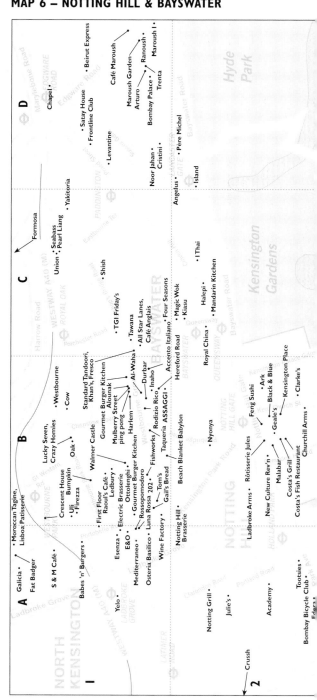

MAP 7 – HAMMERSMITH & CHISWICK

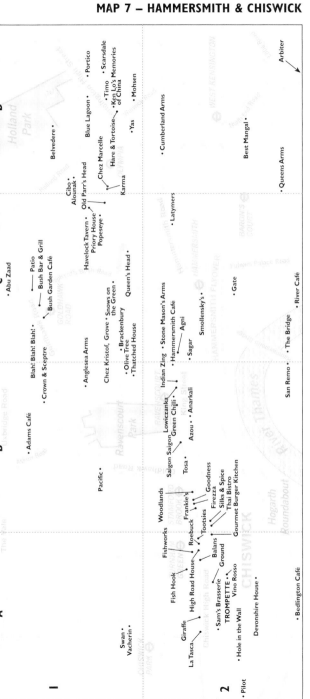

MAP 8 – HAMPSTEAD, CAMDEN TOWN & ISLINGTON

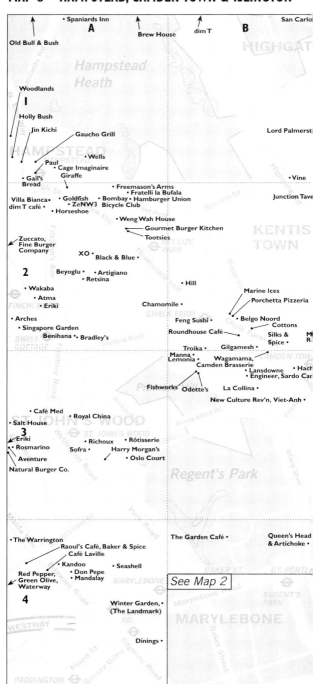

A **B**

HIGHGAT

- Spaniards Inn
Brew House
dim T
San Carlo

Old Bull & Bush

Hampstead Heath

Woodlands

1

Holly Bush

Jin Kichi

Gaucho Grill

Lord Palmerst

HAMPSTEAD

- Wells

Paul
- Cage Imaginaire
Giraffe

- Gail's Bread

- Vine

- Freemason's Arms
- Fratelli la Bufala
Villa Bianca
dim T café
- Goldfish
- ZeNW3
- Horseshoe
- Bombay
- Hamburger Union
Bicycle Club

Junction Tave

- Weng Wah House

Gourmet Burger Kitchen
Tootsies

KENTIS
TOWN

Zuccato,
Fine Burger
Company

XO
Black & Blue

BELSIZE
PARK

2

Beyoglu
- Artigiano
- Retsina

- Hill

- Wakaba
- Atma
- Eriki

FINCHLE

Chamomile

Marine Ices
Porchetta Pizzeria
Cottons

- Arches
- Singapore Garden
Benihana
- Bradley's

CHALK FARM

Feng Sushi
- Belgo Noord

SWISS
COTTAGE

Roundhouse Café

Silks &
Spice
M
R

Troika
Manna
Lemonia
Gilgamesh

CAMDEN TOW

Wagamama,
Camden Brasserie

3

Fishworks
Odette's

- Lansdowne
- Engineer, Sardo Car
- Hach

La Collina

New Culture Rev'n, Viet-Anh

- Café Med
- Royal China

ST. JOHN'S WOOD

- Salt House

Eriki
- Rosmarino
- Richoux
- Rôtisserie
Sofra
Harry Morgan's
Aventure
- Oslo Court

Natural Burger Co.

Regent's Park

The Garden Café

Queen's Head
& Artichoke

- The Warrington

Raoul's Café, Baker & Spice
Café Laville

- Kandoo
Red Pepper,
Green Olive,
Waterway
- Don Pepe
- Mandalay
- Seashell

MARYLEBONE

See Map 2

REGENT'S
PARK

GT. PORTLA

4

Winter Garden,
(The Landmark)

MARYLEBONE

WESTWAY

Dinings

PADDINGTON

MAP 8 – HAMPSTEAD, CAMDEN TOWN & ISLINGTON

Porchetta Pizzeria • • Petek
Chez Liline • **D**

FINSBURY
PARK

C
Pick More Daisies,
Bistro Aix
Fine Burger Company

FINSBURY
PARK

'HWY'

• St Johns

ARSENAL

Il Bacio •

TUFNELL
PARK

San Daniele del Friuli •

HOLLOWAY
RD.

afé RED

KENTISH
TOWN

CALEDONIAN RD •

HIGHBURY
AND

Morgan M •

Firezza •

House,
Marquess
Tavern

Cantina Italia

Viet Garden •
Barnsbury •

Piragua •

Gem
Petit Auberge •
Mercury, Porchetta Pizzeria •
Almeida •

Ottolenghi

Casale Franco, Fishworks • Sabor

Gallipoli
Zaffrani Isarn •

Drapers Arms

Gallipoli • Giraffe

Sacré-Coeur, Metrogusto Gallipoli

• Daphne

Fine Burger Company

• Kaz Kreol

Pizzeria Oregano •

Camden Bar & Kitchen

Fig •

Masala Zone •
Rodizio Rico •

Albion •

MORNINGTON
CRESCENT

Browns   S&M Café   Living
Afghan Kitchen   Room
Wagamama •   • Emni

Rooburoo •   Upper Glas •

• El Parador

Camino

Hamburger Union •   Charles
Thai Square   Lamb
Elk in

Basilico •   the Woods

• Somerstown Coffee House

New
Culture
Rev'n

Frederick's •

• Great Nepalese

Snazz Sichuan •   06 St. Chad's Place •

• Paolina Café
• Acorn House

• Fish Shop

• Konstam at the Prince Albert

• Rasa (Maricham)   • Peasant

Mestizo
• Diwana Bhel-Poori House, Chutneys,
Zamzama

See Map 9

• Norfolk Arms

Square Pie Co. • North
Sea Fish

EN ST.   EUSTON
SQ.

BLOOMSBURY

RUSSELL
SQ.

FARRINGDON

DGE ST.

CHANCERY
LANE

HOLBORN

TOTTENHAM
COURT ROAD

xford Street

OXFORD CIRCUS

MAP 9 – THE CITY

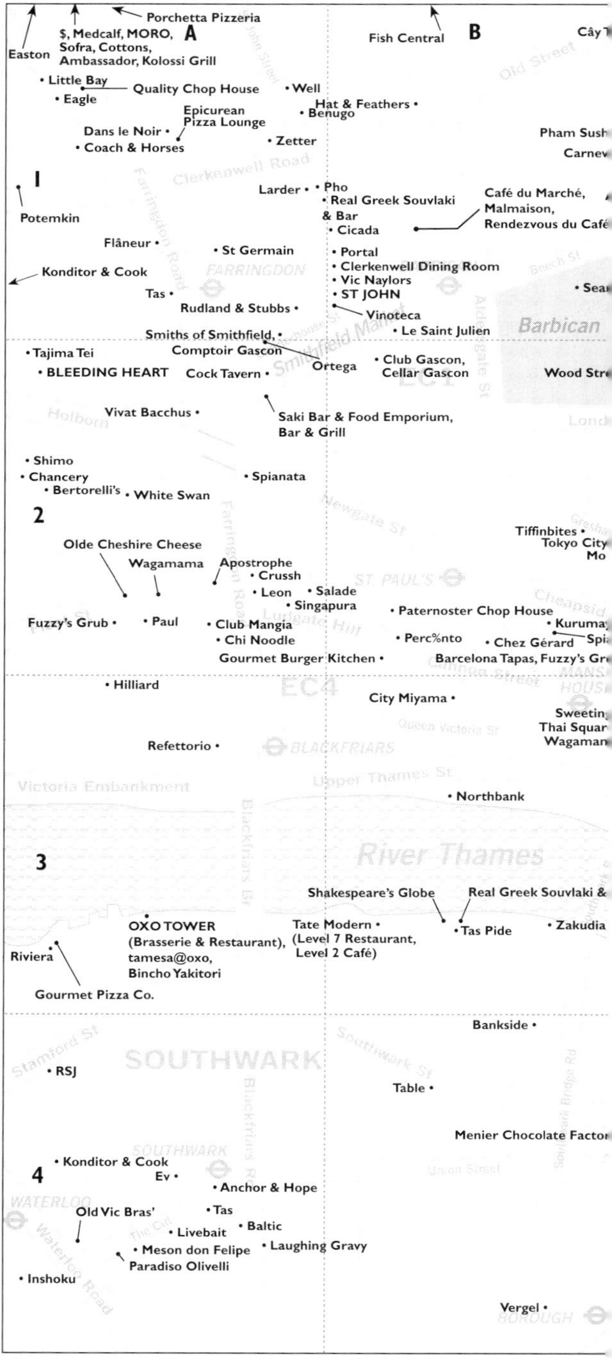

A
B

Porchetta Pizzeria

Fish Central

Câv T

Easton

$, Medcalf, MORO,
Sofra, Cottons,
Ambassador, Kolossi Grill

Old Street

• Little Bay
• Eagle

Quality Chop House

• Well
Hat & Feathers •
• Benugo

Epicurean
Pizza Lounge
Dans le Noir •
• Coach & Horses

• Zetter

Pham Sush

Carnev

Clerkenwell Road

I

Larder •
• Pho
• Real Greek Souvlaki
& Bar
• Cicada

Café du Marché,
Malmaison,
Rendezvous du Café

Potemkin

Flâneur •

• St Germain

FARRINGDON

• Portal
• Clerkenwell Dining Room
• Vic Naylors
• ST JOHN

Brock St

• Sear

— Konditor & Cook

Tas •

Rudland & Stubbs •

Vinoteca

Barbican

• Le Saint Julien

Smiths of Smithfield, •
Comptoir Gascon
• Tajima Tei
• BLEEDING HEART   Cock Tavern   Ortega

• Club Gascon,
Cellar Gascon

Wood Stre

Vivat Bacchus •

Saki Bar & Food Emporium,
Bar & Grill

Holborn

London

• Shimo
• Chancery
• Bertorelli's   • White Swan

• Spianata

2

Newgate St

Tiffinbites •
Tokyo City
Mo

Olde Cheshire Cheese
Wagamama   Apostrophe
• Crussh

ST PAUL'S

Cheapsid

Fuzzy's Grub •   • Paul

• Leon • Salade
• Singapura
• Club Mangia
• Chi Noodle
Gourmet Burger Kitchen •

• Paternoster Chop House

• Perc%nto

• Kuruma

• Chez Gérard Spi

Barcelona Tapas, Fuzzy's Gr

EC4

• Hilliard

City Miyama •

HOUS

Refettorio •

BLACKFRIARS

Queen Victoria St

Sweetin
Thai Squar
Wagaman

Victoria Embankment

Upper Thames St

• Northbank

Blackfriars Br

3

River Thames

Shakespeare's Globe   Real Greek Souvlaki &

OXO TOWER
(Brasserie & Restaurant),
tamesa@oxo,
Bincho Yakitori

Tate Modern •
(Level 7 Restaurant,
Level 2 Café)

• Tas Pide   • Zakudia

Riviera

Gourmet Pizza Co.

Bankside •

Stamford St

SOUTHWARK

Southwark St

• RSJ

Table •

Southwark Bridge Rd

Menier Chocolate Factor

4 • Konditor & Cook
Ev •
• Anchor & Hope

SOUTHWARK

Union Street

WATERLOO
Old Vic Bras'
• Tas
• Livebait • Baltic
• Meson don Felipe • Laughing Gravy
Paradiso Olivelli

• Inshoku

Waterloo Road

Vergel •

BOROUGH

MAP 9 – THE CITY

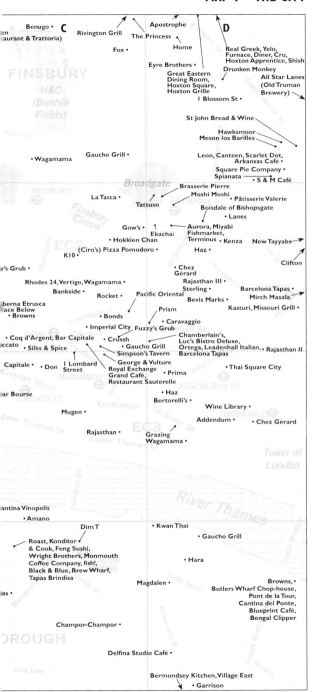

Benugo • **C**
Apostrophe
Rivington Grill
The Princess
D
en
aurant & Trattoria)
Fox •
Home
Real Greek, Yelo,
Furnace, Diner, Cru,
Hoxton Apprentice, Shish
Eyre Brothers •
Drunken Monkey
Great Eastern
Dining Room,
Hoxton Square,
Hoxton Grille
All Star Lanes
(Old Truman
Brewery)
I Blossom St •

FINSBURY
HAC
(Bunhill
Fields)

St John Bread & Wine

Hawksmoor
Meson los Barilles

•Wagamama
Gaucho Grill •
Leon, Canteen, Scarlet Dot,
Arkansas Café •
Square Pie Company •
Spianata • S & M Café
Broadgate
Brasserie Pierre
Moshi Moshi
La Tasca •
• Pâtisserie Valerie
MOORGATE
Tatsuso
Boisdale of Bishopsgate
• Lanes
Gow's •
Aurora, Miyabi
Fishmarket,
Terminus • Kenza
New Tayyabs
Ekachai
• Hokkien Chan
(Ciro's) Pizza Pomodoro •
Haz •
K10 •
Clifton
EC2
• Chez
y's Grub •
Gérard
Rajasthan III •
Rhodes 24, Vertigo, Wagamama •
Sterling •
Barcelona Tapas •
Bankside
Mirch Masala
Rocket •
Pacific Oriental
Bevis Marks •
berna Etrusca
Kasturi, Missouri Grill •
lace Below
Prism
• Browns
• Bonds
• Caravaggio
• Imperial City Fuzzy's Grub
Chamberlain's,
• Coq d'Argent, Bar Capitale
• Crussh
Luc's Bistro Deluxe,
ccato
• Silks & Spice
• Gaucho Grill
Ortega, Leadenhall Italian, • Rajasthan II
Simpson's Tavern
Barcelona Tapas
George & Vulture
Capitale •
• Don
I Lombard
Royal Exchange
Street
Grand Café,
• Prima
• Thai Square City
Restaurant Sauterelle
MONUMENT
FENCHURCH ST.
ar Bourse
• Haz
Bertorelli's •
Eastcheap
Wine Library
TOWER HILL
pper Thames St
Addendum •
• Chez Gérard
Mugen •
Rajasthan •
Grazing
Wagamama •
Lower Thames St
Tower of
London

River Thames

antina Vinopolis
• Amano
Dim T
• Kwan Thai
Roast, Konditor
• Gaucho Grill
& Cook, Feng Sushi,
Wright Brothers, Monmouth
Coffee Company, fish!,
• Hara
Black & Blue, Brew Wharf,
Tapas Brindisa
Magdalen •
Browns, •
as •
Butlers Wharf Chop-house,
Pont de la Tour,
Cantina del Ponte,
Blueprint Café,
Bengal Clipper
Champor-Champor •
OROUGH
Delfina Studio Café •
Long Lane
Bermondsey Kitchen, Village East
• Garrison

MAP 10 – SOUTH LONDON (& FULHAM)

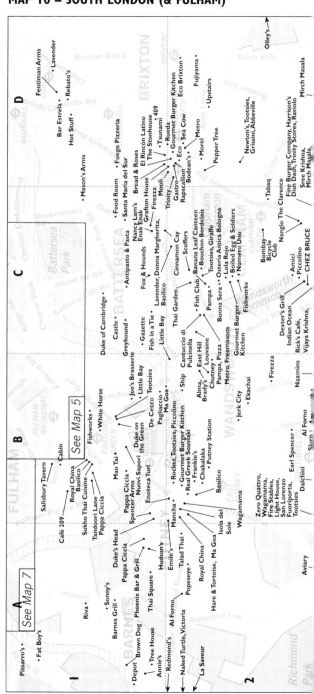

MAP 11 – EAST END & DOCKLANDS

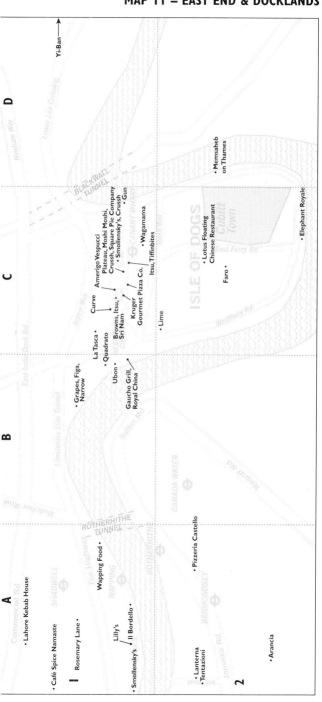